WORRY AND ITS PSYCHOLOGICAL DISORDERS

The Wiley Series in

CLINICAL PSYCHOLOGY

Adrian Wells (Series Advisor)	**School of Psychological Sciences, University of Manchester, UK**
Graham C.L. Davey and Adrian Wells (Editors)	Worry and Its Psychological Disorders: Theory, Assessment and Treatment

Titles published under the series editorship of:

J. Mark G. Williams (Series Editor)	**School of Psychology, University of Wales, Bangor, UK**
Richard G. Moore and Anne Garland	Cognitive Therapy for Chronic and Persistent Depression
Ross G. Menzies and Padmal de Silva (Editors)	Obsessive-Compulsive Disorder: Theory, Research and Treatment
David Kingdon and Douglas Turkington (Editors)	The Case Study Guide to Cognitive Behaviour Therapy of Psychosis
Hermine L. Graham, Alex Copello, Max J. Birchwood and Kim T. Mueser (Editors)	Substance Misuse in Psychosis: Approaches to Treatment and Service Delivery
Jenny A. Petrak and Barbara Hedge (Editors)	The Trauma of Sexual Assault: Treatment, Prevention and Practice
Gordon J.G. Asmundson, Steven Taylor and Brian J. Cox (Editors)	Health Anxiety: Clinical and Research Perspectives on Hypochondriasis and Related Conditions
Kees van Heeringen (Editor)	Understanding Suicidal Behaviour: The Suicidal Process Approach to Research, Treatment and Prevention
Craig A. White	Cognitive Behaviour Therapy for Chronic Medical Problems: A Guide to Assessment and Treatment in Practice
Steven Taylor	Understanding and Treating Panic Disorder: Cognitive-Behavioural Approaches
Alan Carr	Family Therapy: Concepts, Process and Practice
Max Birchwood, David Fowler and Chris Jackson (Editors)	Early Intervention in Psychosis: A Guide to Concepts, Evidence and Interventions
Dominic H. Lam, Steven H. Jones, Peter Hayward and Jenifer A. Bright	Cognitive Therapy for Bipolar Disorder: A Therapist's Guide to Concepts, Methods and Practice

A list of earlier titles in the series follows the index.

WORRY AND ITS PSYCHOLOGICAL DISORDERS

Theory, Assessment and Treatment

Edited by

Graham C.L. Davey
University of Sussex, UK

and

Adrian Wells
University of Manchester, UK

WILEY

Other Wiley Editorial Offices

John Wiley & Sons Inc., 111 River Street, Hoboken, NJ 07030, USA

Jossey-Bass, 989 Market Street, San Francisco, CA 94103-1741, USA

Wiley-VCH Verlag GmbH, Boschstr. 12, D-69469 Weinheim, Germany

John Wiley & Sons Australia Ltd, 42 McDougall Street, Milton, Queensland 4064, Australia

John Wiley & Sons (Asia) Pte Ltd, 2 Clementi Loop #02-01, Jin Xing Distripark, Singapore
129809

John Wiley & Sons Canada Ltd, 22 Worcester Road, Etobicoke, Ontario, Canada M9W 1L1

Wiley also publishes its books in a variety of electronic formats. Some content that appears
in print may not be available in electronic books.

Library of Congress Cataloging-in-Publication Data
Worry and its psychological disorders : theory, assessment, and treatment / edited by
    Graham C. L. Davey and Adrian Wells.
        p.   cm. — (The Wiley series in clinical psychology)
    Includes bibliographical references and indexes.
    ISBN-13: 978-0-470-01278-9 (cloth : alk. paper),   ISBN-10: 0-470-01278-1 (cloth : alk. paper)
    ISBN-13: 978-0-470-01279-6 (pbk. : alk. paper),   ISBN-10: 0-470-01279-X (pbk. : alk. paper)
    1. Worry—Treatment.   2. Anxiety—Treatment.   3. Clinical psychology.
    I. Davey,   Graham.   II. Wells,   Adrian.   III. Series.
    [DNLM: 1. Anxiety Disorders—diagnosis.   2. Anxiety Disorders—therapy.
    3. Psychological Theory.   WM 172 W9285 2006]
RC531.W67   2006
616.85'22306—dc22   2005028318

British Library Cataloguing in Publication Data
A catalogue record for this book is available from the British Library

ISBN-13 978-0-470-01278-9 (HB) 978-0-470-01279-6 (PB)

Typeset in 10/12pt Palatino by TechBooks, New Delhi, India
Printed and bound in Great Britain by TJ International, Padstow, Cornwall
This book is printed on acid-free paper responsibly manufactured from sustainable forestry
in which at least two trees are planted for each one used for paper production.

CONTENTS

Part III   Theories of Chronic and Pathological Worry

Part IV   Treatment Methods

ABOUT THE EDITORS

Graham Davey is Professor of Psychology at the University of Sussex in Brighton, UK. He has been an active researcher in areas associated with anxiety and its disorders, especially pathological worrying, phobias, and perseverative psychopathologies generally. He has published his research in many high-impact international journals including *Journal of Abnormal Psychology, Behavioral & Brain Sciences, Journal of Experimental Psychology*, and *Behaviour Research & Therapy*. He has authored or edited a total of 11 books, including Davey, G.C.L. (1997) (Ed) *Phobias: A handbook of theory, research and treatment*, Chichester: Wiley, and Davey, G.C.L. & Tallis, F. (1994) (Eds) *Worrying: Perspectives on theory, assessment and treatment*, Chichester: Wiley. He was elected President of the British Psychological Society from 2002–2003.

Adrian Wells is Professor of Clinical & Experimental Psychopathology at the University of Manchester, and Professor II in Clinical Psychology at the Norwegian University of Science and Technology, Trondheim. He is Honorary Consultant Clinical Psychologist in Manchester Mental Health Trust. He has published over 100 scientific papers and book chapters in the area of cognitive theory and therapy of emotional disorders. His books include Wells, A. (1997) *Cognitive Therapy of Anxiety Disorders: A Practice Manual and Conceptual Guide*, Chichester, UK: Wiley, and Wells, A. (2000) *Emotional Disorders and Metacognition: Innovative Cognitive Therapy*, Chichester, UK: Wiley. He is the originator of metacognitive therapy and has also contributed to the development of cognitive therapy for anxiety disorders. He is a founding fellow of the Academy of Cognitive Therapy, USA.

LIST OF CONTRIBUTORS

Ian M. Anderson — *Neuroscience and Psychiatry Unit, University of Manchester, Room G809 Stopford Building, Oxford Road, Manchester M13 9PT, UK*

T.D. Borkovec — *Department of Psychology, 544 Moore Bldg., Penn State University, University Park, PA 16802, USA*

Sam Cartwright-Hatton — *The University of Manchester Department of Child Psychiatry, Royal Manchester Children's Hospital, Pendlebury, Manchester M27 4HA, UK*

Graham C.L. Davey — *Department of Psychology, University of Sussex, Brighton BN1 9QH, UK*

Michel J. Dugas — *Department of Psychology (PY-170), Concordia University, 7141 Sherbrooke Street West, Montreal, Quebec H4B 1R6, Canada*

Robert C. Durham — *Department of Psychiatry, University of Dundee, Ninewells Hospital & Medical School, Dundee DD1 9SY, UK*

Thane M. Erickson — *Department of Psychology, 544 Moore Bldg., Penn State University, University Park, PA 16802, USA*

Peter L. Fisher — *The University of Manchester, Department of Clinical Psychology, Rawnsley Building, Manchester Royal Infirmary, Oxford Road, Manchester M13 9WL, UK*

Gregory J. Funke — *Department of Psychology, University of Cincinnati, Cincinnati, OH 45221, USA*

Jennifer Harrington — *Department of Psychology, University of Waterloo, Waterloo, ON N2L 3G1, Canada*

Richard G. Heimberg — *Adult Anxiety Clinic, Department of Psychology, Temple University, 1701 North 13th Street, Philadelphia, PA 19122-6085, USA*

Robert M. Holaway   *Adult Anxiety Clinic, Department of Psychology, Temple University, 1701 North 13th Street, Philadelphia, PA 19122-6085, USA*

Paul King   *North Manchester General Hospital, Department of Clinical Psychology, Delauneys Road, Crumpsall, Manchester M8 5RB, UK*

Naomi Koerner   *Department of Psychology (PY-170), Concordia University, 7141 Sherbrooke Street West, Montreal, Quebec H4B 1R6, Canada*

Gerald Matthews   *Department of Psychology, University of Cincinnati, Cincinnati, OH 45221-0376, USA*

Marisha E. Palm   *Neuroscience and Psychiatry Unit, University of Manchester, Room G807 Stopford Building, Oxford Road, Manchester M13 9PT, UK*

Costas Papageorgiou   *Senior Lecturer/Consultant Clinical Psychologist, Doctoral Programme in Clinical Psychology, Institute for Health Research, Lancaster University, Lancaster LA1 4YT, UK*

Christine Purdon   *Department of Psychology, University of Waterloo, Waterloo, ON N2L 3G1, Canada*

Melisa Robichaud   *Department of Psychology (PY-170), Concordia University, 7141 Sherbrooke Street West, Montreal, Quebec H4B 1R6, Canada*

Thomas L. Rodebaugh   *Adult Anxiety Clinic, Department of Psychology, Temple University, 1701 North 13th Street, Philadelphia, PA 19122-6085, USA*

Nicholas J. Sibrava   *Department of Psychology, 544 Moore Bldg., Penn State University, University Park, PA 16802, USA*

Helen M. Startup   *Department of Psychology, PO Box 77, Institute of Psychiatry, Denmark Hill, London SE5 8AF, UK*

Cynthia L. Turk   *Department of Psychology, Washburn University, 1700 College Avenue, Topeka, KS 66621, USA*

Adrian Wells   *The University of Manchester, Department of Clinical Psychology, Rawnsley Building, Manchester Royal Infirmary, Oxford Road, Manchester M13 9WL, UK*

Julie L. Wetherell   *Assistant Professor in Residence, Department of Psychiatry, University of California, San Diego, VA San Diego Healthcare System, 3350 La Jolla Village Drive (116B), San Diego, CA 92161, USA*

Andrew T. Wolanin   *Department of Psychology, La Salle University, 1900 W. Olney Ave., Philadelphia, PA 19141, USA*

PREFACE

We all worry about things to some degree—and, indeed, many people find it beneficial to think about how they might deal with challenging future events. Of course thinking about future events need not take the form of worry, and important distinctions have been made between worry and other types of thinking. Despite the normality of worry it can become a pervasive daily activity and develop a number of features that make it disabling and a source of extreme emotional discomfort. For example, (1) worrying becomes a chronic and pathological activity that is not only directed at major life issues (e.g. health, finances, relationships, work-related matters), but also to many minor day-to-day issues and hassles that others would not perceive as threatening, (2) worrying is perceived as uncontrollable—the individual experiencing pathological worry usually feels they cannot control either the onset or termination of a worry bout, and (3) worrying is closely associated with catastrophising leading to increasing levels of anxiety and distress, which can seem to make the problem *worse* rather than better. Worry is the cardinal diagnostic feature of generalised anxiety disorder (GAD), but is also a prominent feature of most other anxiety disorders, including specific phobias, obsessive-compulsive disorder, panic disorder, and PTSD.

This volume covers the nature, theory, assessment, and treatment of worry and illustrates the role of worry and its treatment across a range of disorders. The audience for whom this book is intended is clinical psychologists, clinical researchers, students studying clinical or abnormal psychology at advanced level, postgraduate research students involved in clinical research and experimental psychopathology, and those employed in disciplines closely related to clinical psychology (e.g. psychiatry, psychiatric nursing, counselling). The book is divided into four parts designed to give an up-to-date and inclusive overview of all important aspects of worrying, including the nature of worry across a range of disorders, the assessment of worry, contemporary theories of worry, and methods of treatment for worrying. Chapters are written by international experts in each of these areas, and we believe the book will provide an invaluable resource for both researchers and practitioners.

In Part I, The Nature of Worry, there are chapters covering the epidemiology of worry and generalised anxiety disorder (Holaway, Rodebaugh &

Heimberg), the role of worry and rumination in depression (Papageorgiou), and in anxious psychopathology generally (Purdon & Harrington). This section also covers the role that information processing biases play in pathological worrying (Matthews & Funke), and describes the nature of worry in older adults (Wetherell) and in children and adolescents (Cartwright-Hatton).

Part II looks in some detail at the assessment of worry, including the uses and psychometric properties of the Penn State Worry Questionnaire (Startup & Erickson), the Anxious Thoughts Inventory and closely related concepts (Wells). It also includes a thorough discussion of assessment in generalised anxiety disorder (Turk & Wolanin), as well as some potential clinical and research uses of the catastrophising interview procedure (Davey).

Part III deals with recent theories accounting for the development and maintenance of pathological worry and generalized anxiety disorder. Chapters in this section focus on concepts that include the role of meta-cognition (Wells), and intolerance of uncertainty (Koerner & Dugas) in maintaining chronic and pathological worrying. Chapters also address the causes of the perseverative nature of pathological worrying (Davey), and the view that worry serves an anxiety-maintaining avoidant function (Sibrava & Borkovec).

The final part deals with the treatment of pathological worrying, and the approaches described include Metacognitive Therapy (Wells), Applied Relaxation and Cognitive Therapy (Borkovec), Cognitive-Behavioral treatments targeting intolerance of uncertainty (Robichaud & Dugas), and Pharmacological treatments (Anderson & Palm). Because pathological worrying is a characteristic of a range of psychological disorders, the treatment of worry across disorders using a case-formulation approach is presented (King). Finally, the effectiveness of worry treatments is reviewed in chapters discussing the efficacy of psychological treatments for generalised anxiety disorder (Fisher) and the predictors of treatment outcome (Durham).

As an edited volume, we hope this book provides an integrated set of contributions reflecting conceptual and practical methods for understanding, assessing and working with worry and its associated dysfunctions.

Graham Davey
Adrian Wells
July 2005

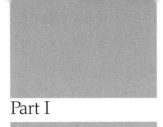

Part I

THE NATURE OF WORRY

Chapter 1

THE EPIDEMIOLOGY OF WORRY AND GENERALIZED ANXIETY DISORDER

Robert M. Holaway, Thomas L. Rodebaugh and Richard G. Heimberg

THE EPIDEMIOLOGY OF WORRY AND GENERALIZED ANXIETY DISORDER

Once considered synonymous with the cognitive components of anxiety (Mathews, 1990; O'Neill, 1985), worry has emerged as a more specific construct that can not only be distinguished from a larger subset of cognitive aspects of anxiety, but also studied in its own right (Davey, 1993; Davey, Hampton, Farrell & Davidson, 1992; Zebb & Beck, 1998). One of the first attempts to define worry was provided by Borkovec, Robinson, Pruzinsky, and DePree (1983, p. 10):

Worry is a chain of thoughts and images, negatively affect-laden and relatively uncontrollable; it represents an attempt to engage in mental problem-solving on an issue whose outcome is uncertain but contains the possibility of one or more negative outcomes; consequently, worry relates closely to the fear process.

More recent formulations have extended this definition of worry, describing it as an anxious apprehension for future, negative events (Barlow, 2002) that involves "a predominance of negatively valenced verbal thought activity" and minimal levels of imagery (Borkovec, Ray & Stober, 1998, p. 562). These definitions have been largely derived from participants' reports regarding what they do when they worry.

Research on the epidemiology of worry has largely evolved over the past 20 years. Much research appears to have been spurred by the adoption of worry as the essential feature of generalized anxiety disorder (GAD) in the revised, third edition of the *Diagnostic and Statistical Manual of Mental*

Worry and Its Psychological Disorders: Theory, Assessment and Treatment. Edited by G. C. L. Davey and A. Wells. © 2006 John Wiley & Sons, Ltd.

Disorders (DSM-III-R; American Psychiatric Association [APA], 1987). These studies have provided valuable data regarding the prevalence, content, and functions of worry and GAD. In this chapter, we review the existing research on the prevalence and phenomenology of worry (both normal and pathological) and GAD and available data on gender, age, ethnic, and cultural differences in the manifestation and occurrence of both phenomena.

The Phenomenology of Normal and Pathological Worry

Few empirical studies have actually examined the occurrence and phenomenology of worry independent of GAD (Tallis, Davey & Capuzzo, 1994). As a result, much of our empirical understanding regarding what actually occurs when people worry, what they most often worry about, and how frequently they worry has been derived from examinations of nonanxious control groups. As noted by Ruscio (2002), these studies may not provide an accurate representation of the frequency and manifestation of normal worry because participants in these groups have been selected based on low worry scores and an absence of anxiety. In much of the empirical literature, normal worry has been regarded as "mild, transient, generally limited in scope, and experienced by the majority of individuals" (Ruscio, 2002, p. 378). However, without adequate studies of worry in normal individuals (i.e., not simply low-anxiety individuals), it is difficult to determine how much the above perception is based on specific characteristics of the available samples.

Tallis and colleagues (1994) conducted one of the few direct examinations of the phenomenology of non-pathological worry. In a mixed sample of 128 university students and working adults (aged 18–59), 38% reported worrying at least once per day; 19.4% indicated they worried once every 2–3 days; and 15.3% reported they worried about once a month. It is unclear how frequently the remaining 27.3% experienced worry. Participants were also asked how long their worry episodes typically lasted. About 24% reported that their worries were fleeting or lasted less than 1 minute, and 38% endorsed a typical duration of 1–10 minutes. The remainder endorsed longer durations of their typical worry (18%, 10–60 minutes; 11%, 1–2 hours; 9%, two hours or more). In addition, participants reported that they most often worried during the late evening or early morning hours and that their worries frequently occurred in response to impending matters, such as upcoming events or interpersonal interactions (Tallis et al., 1994). Participants' mean score on a measure of pathological worry fell in the moderate range and was significantly lower than scores typically associated with a diagnosis of GAD (see Fresco, Mennin, Heimberg & Turk,

2003; Molina & Borkovec, 1994). In terms of worry content, 17% of respondents reported they worried most often about their competence at work, followed by academic performance (11%), health issues (10%), financial circumstances (10%), and intimate relationships (9%). Finally, 83% of respondents reported that they believed worry helped them to find solutions to problems in their environment (Tallis et al., 1994). This finding is, to some extent, consistent with recent research by Szabó and Lovibond (2002), in which 48% of naturally occurring worry episodes primarily reflected a problem-solving process (i.e., using worry to generate solutions to problematic situations), whereas 17% were characterized as primarily involving the anticipation of negative outcomes. Further examination revealed that more severe levels of worry were associated with reduced problem-solving success, although the causal direction of this relationship is unclear.

Studies have consistently, and perhaps not surprisingly, found that people who experience pathological worry as a part of GAD rate their worry as more pervasive and less controllable than people without pathological worry. Craske, Rapee, Jackel and Barlow (1989) examined several dimensions of worry by comparing individuals with DSM-III-R GAD to a nonanxious control group consisting of friends of clients receiving treatment for anxiety. Both groups reported similar ratings of worry duration, worry aversiveness, attempts to resist worry, anxiety associated with resisting worry, and perceived likelihood of the occurrence of worrisome outcomes. However, individuals in the nonanxious control group reported that they worried, on average, 18.2% of the day during the past month compared to 60.7% reported by the GAD group. In addition, nonanxious individuals rated their worries as more controllable, reported greater success in resisting or reducing their worries, indicated that their worries were more often associated with a specific and discernable precipitant, and perceived their worries to be more realistic than those reported by individuals with GAD. Other studies have also found differences with respect to the pervasiveness of worry, as nonanxious controls have consistently reported fewer worrisome topics than individuals with GAD (Borkovec, Shadick & Hopkins, 1991; Dugas et al., 1998; Hoyer, Becker & Roth, 2001; Roemer, Molina & Borkovec, 1997).

Studies comparing the content of worry among individuals with GAD and nonanxious controls have typically reported on the frequency of specific worry domains: 1) work and school, 2) family and interpersonal relationships, 3) financial issues, 4) illness, health, and injury, and 5) miscellaneous topics (e.g., minor matters, punctuality, home repairs). Across several investigations, roughly one-third of participants' worries, regardless of GAD status, have pertained to family and interpersonal issues (Borkovec et al., 1991; Craske et al., 1989; Roemer et al., 1997). Relationships thus seem to be a common source of worry, a conclusion further bolstered by two studies finding that over 70% of people with GAD endorsed frequent worry about either family or relationships (Dugas et al., 1998; Sanderson & Barlow, 1990). Contrary to this conclusion, Craske and colleagues (1989) found health and injury to be the most frequently reported topic of worry among individuals with GAD (30.6% of reported worries). However, most studies report health and injury worries to be rather infrequent in both GAD (Borkovec et al., 1991; Dugas et al., 1998; Roemer et al., 1997; Sanderson & Barlow, 1990) and nonanxious control groups (Craske et al., 1989; Roemer et al., 1997).

The most consistent finding regarding differences in worry content between nonanxious controls and GAD samples has pertained to worry regarding miscellaneous topics, such as car troubles or being late for appointments. Across three studies, miscellaneous worry topics reported by nonanxious control groups comprised 0%–19.7% of all reported worries, whereas miscellaneous worries among individuals with GAD comprised between 25.2%–31.3% of reported worries (Borkovec et al., 1991; Craske et al., 1989; Roemer et al., 1997). Other content differences between individuals with and without GAD have been observed with regard to worry about work and school. Two studies found nonanxious controls to report a greater proportion of worries related to work and school (30.4%–36.6%) than individuals with GAD (13.9%–22%) (Craske et al., 1989; Roemer et al., 1997), although Borkovec and colleagues (1991) found the opposite. The conclusion that people in nonanxious control groups worry more about work and school is fairly consistent with Tallis and colleagues' (1994) assessment of non-pathological worry, in which the most frequent topics of concern reported by participants pertained to academic performance and competence at work. Similar to concerns regarding work and school, worries about financial circumstances have generally been more frequently reported by individuals without GAD, as two studies have reported the proportion of total worries pertaining to finances to range from 12.5%–26.1% among nonanxious control groups and 2.8%–8.9% among GAD samples (Borkovec et al., 1991; Craske et al., 1989). However, in contrast, Roemer and colleagues (1997) found individuals with GAD to report a greater proportion of worries related to financial circumstances (10.8%) than nonanxious controls (5.6%).

The studies reviewed above have revealed several similarities and differences in the phenomenology of worry among individuals with and without GAD. Most notably, individuals with GAD spend significantly more time worrying, report more worry topics, and perceive themselves as having considerably less control over their worry than nonanxious controls. In addition, miscellaneous worry topics appear to be more prevalent among individuals with GAD than nonanxious controls. Most similarities observed between the two groups have regarded the frequency of worries pertaining to family and interpersonal relationships, with roughly a third of all reported worries relating to this topic.

Despite these general patterns, there have been many inconsistencies across studies. Several factors may account for these differences. First, with the exception of Roemer et al. (1997), sample sizes for both GAD and nonanxious control groups have been relatively small (e.g., $n = 13–31$), which may limit external validity. Second, the manner in which the frequency and content of worry was assessed varied by study. For example, whereas participants in the Craske et al. (1989) study monitored and recorded the nature of their worry each day for three weeks, other studies have assessed worry phenomenology using diagnostic interviews (e.g., Roemer et al., 1997). Finally, demographic differences across study samples, especially with respect to age, gender, and employment, may have influenced the frequency of specific worry topics, as these concerns seem likely to shift according to the nature of one's daily life.

Differentiating Pathological Worry from GAD

Recent research by Ruscio, Borkovec, and Ruscio (2001) has provided empirical support for a dimensional structure of worry, suggesting that normal and pathological worry represent opposite ends of a continuum, not discrete constructs. However, in most cases, investigations of normal and pathological worry have typically examined individuals with a diagnosis of GAD and have rarely examined pathological worry independent of GAD, leaving pathological worry outside the context of GAD poorly understood (Ruscio, 2002; Ruscio & Borkovec, 2004).

In an attempt to identify delimiting characteristics of pathological worry and GAD, Ruscio (2002) recently compared high worriers with and without a diagnosis of GAD. Surprisingly, only 20% of individuals who reported experiencing extreme levels of pathological worry (worry scores above the threshold commonly associated with GAD) actually met diagnostic criteria for the disorder. Follow-up analyses indicated that, across two samples, 68%–78% of people who reported high levels of worry but not GAD met only 0–1 of the four required DSM-IV criteria, with chronic/excessive worry and associated distress and impairment best differentiating individuals with GAD from high worriers without GAD (Ruscio, 2002, Study 1). Individuals with GAD also reported greater levels of depression, more frequent worry, and less control over their worry. In a follow-up study, individuals with high levels of worry but without GAD experienced all symptoms of GAD less severely than individuals with GAD, even though they reported their worry to be excessive and uncontrollable (Ruscio, 2002, Study 2).

Ruscio's (2002) findings underscore the need for future studies to distinguish GAD from pathological worry. Specifically, they suggest that examining differences between worry in normal participants and participants with GAD may not actually provide information about the differences between nonpathological and pathological worry. In a recent comparison of people with high worry who either did or did not have GAD, Ruscio and Borkovec (2004) found that negative beliefs about worry (e.g., "worry is harmful") were specific to participants with GAD. In line with Roemer and colleagues' (1997) position that worry may function as a strategy for avoidance of more emotional topics among persons with GAD, Holaway, Hambrick and Heimberg (2003) found that people with GAD reported experiencing their emotions as more intense and more confusing than people without GAD who experienced high levels of worry. Such results, although preliminary, suggest that pathological worry within the context of GAD may be subject to additional factors (e.g., different beliefs about worry, increased emotion dysregulation) that may render it significantly different from pathological worry without GAD. This caveat should be kept in mind when large-scale epidemiological studies, which concern GAD rather than worry *per se*, are reviewed below.

The Epidemiology of Generalized Anxiety Disorder

Since their first iteration in DSM-III (APA, 1980) to their current version in DSM-IV (APA, 1994), the diagnostic criteria for GAD have been revised repeatedly, with revisions resulting in a greater focus on the presence of excessive and uncontrollable worry, an increase in the required duration of symptoms, fewer required physical symptoms, and the added requirement that worry and associated symptoms be accompanied by significant distress or impairment. In later editions, GAD was no longer considered a residual category that could only be diagnosed in the absence of other anxiety disorders. These significant changes to the structure of GAD have hampered long-term investigations of the course of the disorder and resulted in considerable heterogeneity in studies examining prevalence rates (Kessler, Walters & Wittchen, 2004; Wittchen, Zhao, Kessler & Eaton, 1994). Nevertheless, several epidemiological surveys provide valuable information regarding the prevalence, course, and associated features of GAD.

Prevalence

Table 1.1 shows the current, 12-month, and lifetime prevalence rates for GAD in population-based surveys of adults conducted in several countries

Table 1.1 Prevalence of generalized anxiety disorder in the community

Source	Country	Diagnostic Criteria	Assessment Instrument	Sample Size	Age of Participants	Current Prevalence	12-Month Prevalence	Lifetime Prevalence
Blazer et al., 1991								
ECA, Durham, NC	United States	DSM-III	DIS	3,422	18–65+	1.2%	3.6%	6.6%
ECA, Los Angeles, CA	United States	DSM-III	DIS	2,432	18–65+	1.4%	2.0%	4.1%
ECA, Saint Louis, MO	United States	DSM-III	DIS	2,683	18–65+	1.3%	2.9%	6.6%
Chen et al., 1993	China	DSM-III	DIS	7,229	18–64	—	—	7.8% males / 11.1% females
Hwu et al., 1989	Taiwan	DSM-III	DIS	5,005	18–64+	—	3.4%	3.7%
Bijl et al., 1998	Netherlands	DSM-III-R	CIDI	7,076	18–64	0.8%	1.2%	2.3%
Faravelli et al., 1989	Italy	DSM-III-R	SADS-L	1,110	15–61+	2.0%	—	3.9%
Kawakami et al., 2004	Japan	DSM-III-R	CIDI	1,029	20–65+	0.8%	1.1%	1.4%
Offord et al., 1996	Canada	DSM-III-R	CIDI	8,116	15–64	—	1.1%	—
Wang et al., 2000	United States	DSM-III-R	CIDI-SF	3,032	25–74	—	3.3%	—
Wittchen et al., 1994	United States	DSM-III-R ICD-10	CIDI	8,098	15–54	1.6%	3.1% 5.0%	5.1% 8.9%
Jenkins et al., 1997	Great Britain	ICD-10	CIS-R	10,108	16–64	3.1%	—	—
Bhagwanjee et al., 1998	South Africa	DSM-IV	Clinical Interview	354	18–50+	3.7%	—	—
Carter et al., 2001	Germany	DSM-IV	CIDI	4,181	18–65	—	1.5%	—
Hunt et al., 2002	Australia	DSM-IV ICD-10	CIDI	10,641	18–65+	2.8% 3.6%	3.6% 5.1%	—

Note: ECA = Epidemiologic Catchment Area Study; DS = Diagnostic Interview Schedule; CIDI = Composite International Diagnostic Interview; CIDI-SF = Composite International Diagnostic Interview—Short Form; SADS-L = Schedule for Affective Disorders and Schizophrenia—Lifetime Version; CIS-R = Revised Clinical Interview Schedule around the world. Most likely because the diagnostic criteria for GAD in DSM-III-R are more stringent than the criteria in DSM-III, prevalence rates appear to have dropped from studies employing DSM-III to those using DSM-III-R. Though lifetime prevalence rates of DSM-IV GAD among adults in the general population have yet to be reported, existing studies have found the current and 12-month prevalence rates for the disorder to be equivalent to, or perhaps slightly higher than the rates found using the DSM-III-R.

Fewer prevalence data for GAD are available from epidemiological surveys using the *International Classification of Diseases and Related Health Problems, 10th revision* (ICD-10; World Health Organization, 1990). Surveys employing ICD-10 criteria have generally found current and 12-month prevalence rates of GAD to be relatively comparable to those for DSM-III-R and DSM-IV (Hunt et al., 2002; Wittchen et al., 1994) (see Table 1.1). However, larger differences have been observed in lifetime prevalence rates, which have been attributed to the less stringent criteria of ICD-10 (Wittchen et al., 1994). Interestingly, Slade and Andrews (2001) reported that, though ICD-10 and DSM-IV yield similar 12-month prevalence rates for GAD (3.0% and 2.6%, respectively), less than 50% of those diagnosed by one system were also diagnosed by the other, suggesting that the two systems diagnose overlapping, but largely different, groups of people.

The prevalence of GAD has also been assessed in primary care settings. Findings from large scale investigations in several countries indicate that GAD is one of the most frequently diagnosed mental disorders in primary care, with a current prevalence rate between 3.7% and 8% (Maier et al., 2000; Olfson et al., 1997; Ormel et al., 1994; Üstün & Sartorius, 1995) and a 12-month prevalence rate of 10.3% (Ansseau et al., 2004). Among high utilizers of medical care, 21.8% of those who reported significant emotional distress met criteria for a current diagnosis of GAD, whereas 40.3% met criteria for GAD at some point in their lives (Katon et al., 1990). As noted by Wittchen (2002), the higher prevalence of GAD in primary care settings compared to the general population differs from patterns observed in most other anxiety disorders, suggesting that individuals with GAD are likely to be frequent utilizers of health care services.

Age of Onset and Clinical Course

Few population-based surveys have reported the average age of onset of GAD. Based on findings of the Epidemiologic Catchment Area (ECA) study, Blazer and colleagues (1991) reported that age of onset for individuals with GAD was distributed rather evenly across the lifespan. However, investigations of clinical populations have found the typical age of onset of GAD to occur between the late teens and late 20s, with later onset occurring when GAD develops after another anxiety disorder (Barlow, Blanchard, Vermilyea, Vermilyea & DiNardo, 1986; Brawman-Mintzer et al., 1993; Hoehn-Saric, Hazlett & McLeod 1993; Massion, Warshaw & Keller, 1993; Woodman, Noyes, Black, Schlosser & Yagla, 1999; Yonkers, Massion, Warsaw & Keller, 1996).

Epidemiological surveys and long-term investigations of clinical course have often found GAD to be chronic and unremitting. In the ECA study, 40% of respondents with GAD reported a duration of longer than five years (Blazer et al., 1991), and participants in clinical samples have often reported a duration of more than 20 (Barlow et al., 1986; Woodman et al., 1999; Yonkers et al., 1996). Yonkers and colleagues (1996) found only 40% of individuals with GAD had a full remission of symptoms after two years; the same study later showed a partial remission rate of less than 50% and a full remission rate of 38% after five years (Yonkers, Dyck, Warshaw & Keller, 2000). Among individuals who achieved partial or full remission, 39% and 27% were found to have a full relapse during the five-year follow-up period. Similarly, in a study by Woodman and colleagues (1999), 45% of individuals with GAD were found to reach full remission during a five-year follow-up period; however, only 18% of the sample was in full remission at the five-year assessment point, indicating significant relapse. Factors most predictive of chronicity and relapse in GAD over the long-term have been found to be early age of onset and the presence of comorbid diagnoses, particularly Axis II disorders (Mancuso, Townsend & Mercante, 1993; Massion et al., 2002; Woodman et al., 1999; Yonkers et al., 2000).

Comorbidity and Associated Impairment

Early findings from the ECA study indicated a lifetime diagnosis of DSM-III GAD was associated with at least one additional Axis I disorder in 58% to 65% of respondents, with panic disorder and major depression the most frequent comorbid diagnoses (Blazer et al., 1991). As noted by Kessler and colleagues (2004), high rates of comorbidity for DSM-III GAD observed in early studies resulted in significant modifications to the disorder's diagnostic criteria, particularly the increase in required duration.

Despite these changes, high rates of comorbidity continue to be found. In the National Comorbidity Study (NCS), 66.3% of respondents currently meeting criteria for DSM-III-R GAD and 90.4% of individuals with a lifetime diagnosis were found to meet criteria for at least one additional Axis I diagnosis, with major depression being the most frequent co-occurring disorder (Wittchen et al., 1994). Findings from epidemiological surveys of the 12-month prevalence of DSM-IV GAD show 93.1% of respondents in one study meeting criteria for an additional Axis I disorder (Carter et al., 2001) and 60.6% of respondents in a separate study meeting criteria for an Axis II disorder (Grant et al., 2005). Though GAD appears to be a highly comorbid disorder in general population studies, Wittchen and colleagues (1994) showed that the frequency of individuals with GAD reporting one or more comorbid diagnoses is not much higher than rates observed in other anxiety or mood disorders.

In clinical studies of individuals with GAD, rates of comorbid Axis I disorders have ranged from 45% to 98% (Barlow et al., 1986; Brawman-Mintzer et al., 1993; DiNardo & Barlow, 1990; Goisman, Goldenberg, Vasile & Keller, 1995; Sanderson, DiNardo, Rapee & Barlow, 1990; Yonkers et al., 1996). Similar to findings in the general population, major depressive disorder has frequently been the most commonly diagnosed comorbid disorder among individuals with GAD, followed by social phobia, specific phobia, and panic disorder (e.g., Brawman-Mintzer et al., 1993; Goisman et al., 1995; Massion et al., 1993). Recent research also found personality disorders to be fairly common among individuals with GAD. For example, 37.7% of individuals with GAD participating in the Harvard/Brown Anxiety Research Program study met criteria for one or more Axis II disorders, with avoidant personality disorder being the most frequent (Dyck et al., 2001).

In addition to high rates of comorbidity, GAD has also been found to be associated with significant impairment in social and occupational functioning (Kessler, DuPont, Berglund & Wittchen, 1999; Maier et al., 2000), as well as reduced quality of life (Massion et al., 1993). In a sample of primary care patients, Olfson and colleagues (1997) found individuals with GAD to report greater disability and more absences from work than individuals without a mental disorder. Similarly, Ormel and colleagues (1994) found individuals with pure GAD to report significantly greater occupational impairment and work absences than individuals without a mental disorder, even after controlling for the presence of co-occurring medical illnesses.

Ethnic and Cross-Cultural Differences

Based on findings from available epidemiological surveys, most countries around the world appear to have a fairly similar prevalence of GAD (see Table 1.1). Genuine cross-cultural differences are difficult to determine given differences in methodology, particularly in diagnostic and assessment methods. However, an examination of ICD-10 GAD across several primary care centers revealed significant differences in prevalence rates between countries, with current GAD prevalence rates highest in Rio de Janeiro, Brazil (22.6%) and lowest in Ankara, Turkey (1.0%; Maier et al., 2000).

Though several studies have examined differences in the occurrence of anxiety among various ethnic groups within a specific country, few have reported specifically on differences in the prevalence of GAD (e.g., Jenkins et al., 1997). Overall, findings from three epidemiological surveys conducted in the US have revealed few differences in the prevalence of GAD among representative ethnic groups (Blazer et al., 1991; Wang et al., 2000; Wittchen et al., 1994).

In an examination of ethnic differences in worry in a nonclinical population, Scott, Eng, and Heimberg (2002) compared Caucasian, African-American, and Asian/Asian-American students on measures of pathological worry, worry domains, and generalized anxiety. No differences were observed among the three groups with respect to pathological worry or generalized anxiety; however, African-American participants reported significantly less worry regarding relationship stability, self-confidence, future aims, and work incompetence than the other two groups. In addition, Asian/Asian-American participants endorsed significantly more worry regarding future goals than the other groups. Further, whereas Caucasian and Asian/Asian-American students reported a similar amount of worry across domains, African-American participants reported worrying most frequently about financial issues (Scott et al., 2002).

Gender and Lifespan Differences

Several studies have found GAD to be roughly twice as prevalent among women as men (e.g., Bijl et al., 1998; Blazer et al., 1991; Carter et al., 2001; Hunt et al., 1997; Wittchen et al., 1994). However, though Maier and colleagues (2000) found GAD to be more prevalent among female primary care patients in most countries, there were contrary findings in some locations (e.g., Nagasaki, Japan).

The few studies of gender differences in worry have found women to worry more than men (e.g., Lewinsohn, Gotlib, Lewinsohn, Seeley & Allen, 1998; Stavosky & Borkovec, 1988). Robichaud, Dugas and Conway (2003) found women to score higher than men on two widely-used worry measures. Few differences in worry content were observed; however, women were found to worry significantly more about self-confidence than men.

Available data on the community prevalence of GAD across the lifespan are shown in Table 1.2. Based on these findings, GAD appears to be most prevalent between the ages of 25 and 54, with lower rates of occurrence above and below that range. However, investigations of GAD among individuals younger than 18 (overanxious disorder [OAD] in DSM-III and DSM-III-R) and older than 65, have also found the disorder to be fairly prevalent. For

Table 1.2 Twelve-month prevalence of generalized anxiety disorder by age

Source	Country	Diagnostic Criteria	Age Group					
			18–24	25–34	35–44	45–54	55–64	65+
Wang et al., 2000	United States	DSM-III-R	—	3.2%	5.0%	3.8%	1.4%	0.8%
Wittchen et al., 1994	United States	DSM-III-R	1.4%[a]	4.1%	3.4%	3.5%[b]		—
Carter et al., 2001	Germany	DSM-IV	1.0%	0.7%	1.5%	2.0%	2.2%[c]	—
Hunt et al., 2002	Australia	DSM-IV	3.0%	3.9%	4.5%	4.9%	3.0%	1.6%

Note: [a] 15–24 age range; [b] ≥45 age range; [c] ≥55 age range.

example, the prevalence rate of OAD in children ages 7–11 at a primary care center was 4.6% (Costello et al., 1988), whereas the occurrence of OAD in a sample of 11 year-old children was 2.9% (Anderson, Williams, McGee & Silva, 1987).

Several studies have found GAD to be the most prevalent anxiety disorder among elderly individuals (e.g., Beekman et al., 1998; Flint, 1994). As shown in Table 1.2, the 12-month prevalence of GAD in people 65 years of age and older appears to fall between 0.8% and 1.6%. However, a recent epidemiological survey of 4,051 individuals between the ages of 65 and 86 yielded higher rates, with 3.2% of participants meeting criteria for current GAD (Schovers, Beekman, Deeg, Jonker & van Tilburg, 2003).

Conclusion

Normal worry appears to be a fairly common phenomenon, and recent research suggests that pathological worry independent of GAD may be more prevalent that previously thought. Though some similarities have emerged between normal worry and worry associated with GAD, most investigations have found that individuals with GAD worry more frequently, worry more about miscellaneous topics, and find their worry more difficult to control than their nonanxious counterparts. However, as noted by Ruscio (2002), most comparisons of normal and pathological worry to date have involved individuals with GAD and those not meeting criteria for an anxiety disorder. Thus, given that most individuals who report pathological worry do not actually meet criteria for GAD, observed differences between GAD and nonanxious control samples may not be representative of true differences between normal and pathological worry. Future research would greatly benefit from more focused examinations of what actually constitutes normal worry, as well as examinations of differences in properly operationalized normal and pathological worry.

Since becoming an official diagnostic category in 1980, GAD has been a frequent topic of study, and valuable information regarding its prevalence, course, and associated characteristics have accrued. Epidemiological surveys and clinical investigations conducted around the world suggest that GAD is a highly prevalent disorder in both the general population and primary care settings and typically has a chronic and unremitting course. In addition, GAD is commonly associated with high rates of comorbidity and impairment, and revisions to the diagnostic criteria have had only a modest effect on prevalence and comorbidity rates. However, in contrast to what has commonly been argued, Wittchen and colleagues (1994) have shown GAD to have comorbidity rates not much higher than that associated with other anxiety and mood disorders.

Though GAD appears to be equally prevalent across the lifespan, most investigations have found a gender ratio of 2:1, with the disorder being more common in women. Interestingly, though this same pattern has been observed in several countries around the world, a few cultures have reported contrary findings. Further investigation of cross-cultural differences, especially in non-industrialized countries, would be of value. Ethnic differences in the prevalence of GAD have been less commonly reported, although most investigations conducted in the United States have revealed few differences. It is important to note, however, that attempts to assess differences across ethnic groups within a specific country have often been hampered by small sample sizes. Focused investigations of the prevalence, phenomenology, and course of GAD across a wide range of cultures and ethnic groups is an important research agenda.

REFERENCES

American Psychiatric Association (1980). *Diagnostic and statistical manual of mental disorders* (3rd ed.). Washington, DC: Author.

American Psychiatric Association (1987). *Diagnostic and statistical manual of mental disorders* (Rev. 3rd ed.). Washington, DC: Author.

American Psychiatric Association (1994). *Diagnostic and statistical manual of mental disorders* (4th ed.). Washington, DC: Author.

Anderson, J., Williams, S., McGee, R. & Silva, P. (1987). DSM-III disorders in preadolescent children. *Archives of General Psychiatry, 44*, 69–76.

Ansseau, M., Dierick, M., Buntinkx, , F., Cnockaert, P., De Smedt, J., Van Den Haute, M. & Vander Mijnsbrugge, D. (2004). High prevalence of mental disorders in primary care. *Journal of Affective Disorders, 78*, 49–55.

Barlow, D. (2002). *Anxiety and its disorders: The nature and treatment of anxiety and panic* (2nd Ed.). New York: Guilford Press.

Barlow, D., Blanchard, E., Vermilyea, J., Vermilyea, B. & DiNardo, P. (1986). Generalized anxiety and generalized anxiety disorder: Description and reconceptualization. *American Journal of Psychiatry, 143*, 40–44.

Beekman, A., Bremmer, M., Deeg, D., van Balkom, A., Snut, J., de Beurs, E., van Dyck, R. & van Tilburg, W. (1998). Anxiety disorders in later life: A report from the longitudinal aging study Amsterdam. *International Journal of Geriatric Psychiatry, 13*, 717–726.

Bhagwanjee, A., Parekh, A., Paruk, Z., Petersen, I. & Subedar, H. (1998). Prevalence of minor psychiatric disorders in an adult African rural community in South Africa. *Psychological Medicine, 28*, 1137–1147.

Bijl, R., Ravelli, A. & van Zessen, G. (1998). Prevalence of psychiatric disorder in the general population: Results of the Netherlands Mental Health Survey and Incidence Study (NEMESIS). *Social Psychiatry and Psychiatric Epidemiology, 33*, 587–595.

Blazer, D., Hughes, D., George, L., Swartz, M. & Boyer, R. (1991). Generalized anxiety disorder. In L.N. Robins & D.A. Regier (Eds) *Psychiatric disorders in America* (pp. 180–203). New York: Free Press.

Borkovec, T., Ray, W. & Stöber, J. (1998). Worry: A cognitive phenomenon intimately linked to affective, physiological, and interpersonal behavioral processes. *Cognitive Therapy and Research*, **22**, 561–576.

Borkovec, T., Robinson, E., Pruzinsky, T. & DePree, J. (1983). Preliminary exploration of worry: Some characteristics and processes. *Behaviour Research and Therapy*, **21**, 9–16.

Borkovec, T., Shadick, R. & Hopkins, M. (1991). The nature of normal and pathological worry. In R. Rapee & D. Barlow (Eds), *Chronic anxiety: Generalized anxiety disorder and mixed anxiety-depression* (pp. 29–51). New York: Guilford Press.

Brawman-Mintzer, O., Lydiard, B., Emmanuel, N., Payeur, R., Johnson, M., Roberts, J., Jarrell, M. & Ballenger, J. (1993). Psychiatric comorbidity in patients with generalized anxiety disorder. *American Journal of Psychiatry*, **150**, 1216–1218.

Carter, R., Wittchen, H.-U., Pfister, H. & Kessler, R. (2001). One-year prevalence of subthreshold and threshold DSM-IV generalized anxiety disorder in a nationally representative sample. *Depression and Anxiety*, **13**, 78–88.

Chen, C., Wong, J., Lee, N., Chan-Ho, M., Lau, J. & Fung, M. (1993). The Shatin Community Mental Health Survey in Hong Kong: Major findings. *Archives of General Psychiatry*, **50**, 125–133.

Costello, E., Costello, A., Edelbrock, C., Burns, B., Dulcan, M., Brent, D. & Janiszewski, S. (1988). Psychiatric disorders in pediatric primary care: Prevalence and risk factors. *Archives of General Psychiatry*, **45**, 1107–1116.

Craske, M., Rapee, R., Jackel, L. & Barlow, D. (1989). Qualitative dimensions of worry in DSM-III-R generalized anxiety disorder subjects and nonanxious controls. *Behaviour Research and Therapy*, **27**, 397–402.

Davey, G. (1993). A comparison of three worry questionnaires. *Behaviour Research and Therapy*, **31**, 51–56.

Davey, G., Hampton, J., Farrell, J. & Davidson, S. (1992). Some characteristics of worrying: Evidence for worrying and anxiety as separate constructs. *Personality and Individual Differences*, **13**, 133–147.

Dugas, M., Freeston, M., Ladouceur, R., Rhéaume, J., Provencher, M. & Boisvert, J.-M. (1998). Worry themes in primary GAD, secondary GAD, and other anxiety disorders. *Journal of Anxiety Disorders*, **12**, 253–261.

Dyck, I., Phillips, K., Warshaw, M., Dolan, R., Shea, M.T., Stout, R., Massion, A., Zlotnick, C. & Keller, M. (2001). Patterns of personality pathology in patients with generalized anxiety disorder, panic disorder with and without agoraphobia, and social phobia. *Journal of Personality Disorders*, **15**, 60–71.

Faravelli, C., Guerrini Degl'Innoceni, B. & Giardinelli, L. (1989). Epidemiology of anxiety disorders in Florence. *Acta Psychiatrica Scandinavica*, **79**, 308–312.

Flint, A. (1994). Epidemiology and comorbidity of anxiety disorders in the elderly. *American Journal of Psychiatry*, **151**, 640–649.

Fresco, D., Mennin, D., Heimberg, R. & Turk, C. (2003). Using the Penn State Worry Questionnaire to identify individuals with generalized anxiety disorder: A receiver operating characteristic analysis. *Journal of Behavior Therapy and Experimental Psychiatry*, **34**, 283–291.

Goisman, R., Goldenberg, I., Vasile, R. & Keller, M. (1995). Comorbidity of anxiety disorders in a multicenter anxiety study. *Comprehensive Psychiatry*, **36**, 303–311.

Grant, B., Hasin, D., Stinson, F., Dawson, D., Chou, S., Ruan, W. & Huang, B. (2005). Co-occurrence of 12-month mood and anxiety disorders and personality disorders in the US: Results from the national epidemiologic survey on alcohol and related conditions. *Journal of Psychiatric Research*, **39**, 1–9.

Hoehn-Saric, R., Hazlett, R. & McLeod, D. (1993). Generalized anxiety disorder with early and late onset of anxiety symptoms. *Comprehensive Psychiatry*, **34**, 291–298.

Holaway, R., Hambrick, J. & Heimberg, R. (November, 2003). *Emotion dysregulation in pathological worry and generalized anxiety disorder: A potential distinguishing factor*. Poster presented at the annual meeting of the Association for the Advancement of Behavior Therapy, Boston, MA.

Hoyer, J., Becker, E. & Roth, W. (2001). Characteristics of worry in GAD patients, social phobics, and controls. *Depression and Anxiety*, **13**, 89–96.

Hunt, C., Issakidis, C. & Andrews, G. (2002). DSM-IV generalized anxiety disorder in the Australian National Survey of Mental Health and Well-Being. *Psychological Medicine*, **32**, 649–659.

Hwu, H.-G., Yeh, E.-K. & Chang, L.-Y. (1989). Prevalence of psychiatric disorders in Taiwan defined by the Chinese Diagnostic Interview Schedule. *Acta Psychiatrica Scandinavica*, **79**, 136–147.

Jenkins, R., Lewis, G., Bebbington, P., Brugha, T., Farrell, M., Gill, B. & Meltzer, H. (1997). The National Psychiatric Morbidity Surveys of Great Britain—initial findings from the Household Survey. *Psychological Medicine*, **27**, 775–789.

Katon, W., Von Korff, M., Lin, E., Lipscomb, P., Russo, J., Wagner, E. & Polk, E. (1990). Distressed high utilizers of medical care: DSM-III-R diagnoses and treatment needs. *General Hospital Psychiatry*, **12**, 355–362.

Kawakami, N., Shimizu, H., Haratani, T., Iwata, N. & Kitamura, T. (2004). Lifetime and 6-month prevalence of DSM-III-R psychiatric disorders in an urban community in Japan. *Psychiatry Research*, **121**, 293–301.

Kessler, R., Walters, E. & Wittchen, H.-U. (2004). Epidemiology. In R. Heimberg, C. Turk & D. Mennin (Eds), *Generalized anxiety disorder: Advances in research and practice* (pp. 29–50). New York: Guilford Press.

Lewinsohn, P., Gotlib, I., Lewinsohn, M., Seely, J. & Allen, N. (1998). Gender differences in anxiety disorders and anxiety symptoms in adolescents. *Journal of Abnormal Psychology*, **107**, 109–117.

Maier, W., Gänsicke, M., Freyberger, J., Linz, M., Heun, R. & Lecrubier, Y. (2000). Generalized anxiety disorder (ICD-10) in primary care from a cross-cultural perspective: A valid diagnostic entity? *Acta Psychiatrica Scandinavica*, **101**, 29–36.

Mancuso, D., Townsend, M. & Mercante, D. (1993). Long-term follow-up of generalized anxiety disorder. *Comprehensive Psychiatry*, **34**, 441–446.

Massion, A., Dyck, I., Shea, T., Phillips, K., Warshaw, M. & Keller, M. (2002). Personality disorders and time to remission in generalized anxiety disorder, social phobia, and panic disorder. *Archives of General Psychiatry*, **59**, 434–440.

Massion, A., Warshaw, M. & Keller, M. (1993). Quality of life and psychiatric morbidity in panic disorder and generalized anxiety disorder. *American Journal of Psychiatry*, **150**, 600–607.

Mathews, A. (1990). Why worry? The cognitive function of anxiety. *Behaviour Research and Therapy*, **28**, 455–468.

Molina, S. & Borkovec, T. (1994). The Penn State Worry Questionnaire: Psychometric properties and associated characteristics. In G. Davey & F. Tallis (Eds) *Worrying: Perspectives on theory, assessment and treatment* (pp. 265–283). Chichester, England: John Wiley & Sons, Ltd.

Offord, D., Boyle, M., Campbell, D., Goering, P., Lin, E., Wong, M. & Racine, Y. (1996). One-year prevalence of psychiatric disorder in Ontarians 15 to 64 years of age. *Canadian Journal of Psychiatry*, **41**, 559–563.

Olfson, M., Fireman, B., Weissman, M., Leon, A., Sheehan, D., Kathol, R., Hoven, C. & Farber, L. (1997). Mental disorders and disability among patients in a primary care group practice. *American Journal of Psychiatry*, **154**, 1734–1740.

O'Neill, G. (1985). Is worry a valuable concept? *Behaviour Research and Therapy*, **23**, 479–480.

Ormel, J., VonKorff, M., Üstün, T., Pini, S., Korten, A. & Oldehinkel, T. (1994). Common mental disorders and disability across cultures: Results from the WHO Collaborative Study on Psychological Problems in General Health Care. *Journal of the American Medical Association*, **272**, 1741–1748.

Robichaud, M., Dugas, M. & Conway, M. (2003). Gender differences in worry and associated cognitive-behavioral variables. *Journal of Anxiety Disorders*, **17**, 501–516.

Roemer, L., Molina, S. & Borkovec, T. (1997). An investigation of worry content among generally anxious individuals. *Journal of Nervous and Mental Disease*, **185**, 314–319.

Ruscio, A. (2002). Delimiting the boundaries of generalized anxiety disorder: Differentiating high worriers with and without GAD. *Journal of Anxiety Disorders*, **16**, 377–400.

Ruscio, A. & Borkovec, T. (2004). Experience and appraisal of worry among high worriers with and without generalized anxiety disorder. *Behaviour Research and Therapy*, **42**, 1469–1482.

Ruscio, A., Borkovec, T. & Ruscio, J. (2001). A taxometric investigation of the latent structure of worry. *Journal of Abnormal Psychology*, **110**, 413–422.

Sanderson, W. & Barlow, D. (1990). A description of patients diagnosed with DSM-III revised generalized anxiety disorder. *Journal of Nervous and Mental Disease*, **178**, 588–591.

Sanderson, W., DiNardo, P., Rapee, R. & Barlow, D. (1990). Syndrome comorbidity in patients diagnosed with a DSM-III-R anxiety disorder. *Journal of Abnormal Psychology*, **99**, 308–312.

Schoevers, R., Beekman, A., Deeg, D., Jonker, C. & van Tilburg, W. (2003). Comorbidity and risk-patterns of depression, generalized anxiety disorder and anxiety-depression in later life: Results from the AMSTEL study. *International Journal of Geriatric Psychiatry*, **18**, 994–1001.

Scott, E., Eng, W. & Heimberg, R. (2002). Ethnic differences in worry in a nonclinical population. *Depression and Anxiety*, **15**, 79–82.

Slade, T. & Andrews, G. (2001). DSM-IV and ICD-10 generalized anxiety disorder: Discrepant diagnoses and associated disability. *Social Psychiatry and Psychiatric Epidemiology*, **36**, 45–51.

Stavosky, J. & Borkovec, T. (1988). The phenomenon of worry: Theory, research, treatment and its implications for women. *Women and Therapy*, **6**, 77–95.

Szabó, M. & Lovibond, P. (2002). The cognitive content of naturally occurring worry episodes. *Cognitive Therapy and Research*, **26**, 167–177.

Tallis, F., Davey, G. & Capuzzo, N. (1994). The phenomenology of non-pathological worry: A preliminary investigation. In G. Davey & F. Tallis (Eds), *Worrying: Perspectives on theory, assessment and treatment* (pp. 61–89). Chichester, England: John Wiley & Sons, Ltd.

Üstün, T. & Sartorius, N. (Eds). (1995). *Mental illness in general health care: An international study*. Chichester, England: John Wiley.

Wang, P., Berglund, P. & Kessler, R. (2000). Recent care of common mental disorders in the United States. *Journal of General Internal Medicine*, **15**, 284–292.

Wittchen, H.-U. (2002). Generalized anxiety disorder: Prevalence, burden, and cost to society. *Depression and Anxiety*, **16**, 162–171.

Wittchen, H.-U., Zhao, S., Kessler, R. & Eaton, W. (1994). DSM-III-R generalized anxiety disorder in the National Comorbidity Survey. *Archives of General Psychiatry*, **51**, 355–364.

Woodman, C., Noyes, R., Black, D., Schlosser, S. & Yagla, S. (1999). A 5-year follow-up of generalized anxiety disorder and panic disorder. *Journal of Nervous and Mental Disease*, **187**, 3–9.

World Health Organization (1990). *International classification of diseases and related health problems (10th rev.): Classification of mental and behavioral disorders. Diagnostic criteria for research*. Geneva: Author.

Yonkers, K., Dyck, I., Warshaw, M. & Keller, M. (2000). Factors predicting the clinical course of generalized anxiety disorder. *British Journal of Psychiatry*, **176**, 544–549.

Yonkers, K., Massion, A., Warshaw, M. & Keller, M. (1996). Phenomenology and course of generalised anxiety disorder. *British Journal of Psychiatry*, **168**, 308–313.

Zebb, B. & Beck, J. (1998). Worry versus anxiety: Is there really a difference? *Behavior Modification*, **22**, 45–61.

Chapter 2

WORRY AND RUMINATION: STYLES OF PERSISTENT NEGATIVE THINKING IN ANXIETY AND DEPRESSION

Costas Papageorgiou

Although the tendency to engage in recurrent negative thinking about past stressful events, current difficulties, and anticipated future problems is a common psychological feature of a range of disorders, worry and rumination are considered to be core cognitive processes in generalised anxiety disorder and major depressive disorder, respectively. This chapter begins by examining definitions and characteristics of worry and rumination. The second section discusses processes implicated in maladaptive worry and rumination. The affective, behavioural and cognitive consequences of worry and rumination are considered in the third section of this chapter. In the fourth section, both conceptual and empirical comparisons are made between worry and rumination. The final section considers factors that may predispose certain individuals to engage in worry and rumination

THE CONCEPT OF WORRY AND RUMINATION

Definitions and Characteristics of Worry

Worry is a common mental activity in both clinical and non-clinical populations. According to Borkovec and colleagues, worry is 'a chain of thoughts and images, negatively affect-laden and relatively uncontrollable' (Borkovec, Robinson, Pruzinsky & Depree, 1983, p. 10). Worry is a cardinal diagnostic feature of DSM-IV (American Psychiatric Association, 1994)

Worry and Its Psychological Disorders: Theory, Assessment and Treatment. Edited by G. C. L. Davey and A. Wells. © 2006 John Wiley & Sons, Ltd.

generalised anxiety disorder (GAD) and it is predominantly experienced in verbal rather than imaginal form (Borkovec & Inz, 1990). Research has shown that normal and GAD worries differ little in their content, but individuals with GAD perceive them as subjectively less controllable and less successfully reduced by corrective attempts compared to normal worries (Craske, Rapee, Jackel & Barlow, 1989). The content of worrisome thinking is associated with a number of themes including health, social and intimate relationships, finances and work/academic performance. Certain individuals, particularly those with GAD, worry about worry itself (called meta-worry), which is a feature at the heart of Wells' (1995, 1997) cognitive model of GAD (see Chapter 11).

Chronic worrying may be initiated by an involuntary intrusive thought. However, it can also be triggered and maintained in a volitional way on the basis of its perceived functions (Wells, 1995). Once triggered, chains of worrisome thinking involve 'What if . . . ?' type questions about anticipated threat or danger to oneself or others. For example, 'What if I fail my test?', 'What if I do not get a promotion?', and 'What if I become ill?'. Although chronic worry is a clinical feature that characterises GAD, it is also a common cognitive process in other psychological disorders. For instance, individuals with panic disorder worry about the physical or mental catastrophic consequences of having a panic attack; those with social phobia worry about embarrassing or humiliating themselves in public; individuals with obsessive-compulsive disorder may worry about being contaminated by germs; those with post-traumatic stress disorder worry about re-experiencing the trauma; and individuals with anorexia nervosa worry about gaining weight. Therefore, chronic worry, although central to GAD, is also prevalent in other disorders as well as non-clinical populations.

Definitions and Characteristics of Rumination

Rumination is a relatively common response to negative moods (Rippere, 1977) and a salient cognitive feature of dysphoria and DSM-IV (American Psychiatric Association, 1994) major depressive disorder. Although rumination may be symptomatic of dysphoria or clinical depression, it may also be perceived as serving a function. Research has demonstrated that the content of rumination is experienced in both verbal and imaginal form and it is similar in depressed and non-depressed individuals (Papageorgiou & Wells, 1999a, 1999b, 2004). The content of ruminative thinking involves themes about past personal loss and failure. Like worry, rumination may also be activated initially as a response to an intrusive thought, and it can be perpetuated depending on its perceived functions (Papageorgiou & Wells,

2001a, 2004; Wells & Matthews, 1994). Chains of ruminative thought are characterised by 'Why' type questions. For example, 'Why did it happen to me?', 'Why do I feel so depressed?', and 'Why don't I feel like doing anything?'. Martin and Tesser (1989, 1996) view rumination as a generic term that refers to several types of recurrent thinking or the entire class of thought that has a tendency to recur. Clearly, this view of rumination is also intimately linked to worry but it could form the basis for a non-specific framework for understanding different varieties of perseverative thinking, albeit negative or positive in content.

A more specific and frequently cited definition of depressive rumination was that proposed by Nolen-Hoeksema. The response styles theory of depression (Nolen-Hoeksema, 1991) views rumination as repetitive and passive thinking about symptoms of depression and the possible causes and consequences of these symptoms. According to this theory, rumination consists of 'repetitively focusing on the fact that one is depressed; on one's symptoms of depression; and on the causes, meanings, and consequences of depressive symptoms' (Nolen-Hoeksema, 1991, p. 569).

Alloy and colleagues (Alloy et al., 2000; Robinson & Alloy, 2003) proposed a conceptual extension of the response styles theory of depression. The concept of stress-reactive rumination was developed in order to refer to the tendency to ruminate on negative inferences following stressful life events. Stress-reactive rumination is thought to occur prior to the onset of depressed mood, whereas emotion-focused rumination, as suggested by Nolen-Hoeksema's (1991) response styles theory, is thought to occur in response to depressed mood. Stress-reactive rumination has been shown to play a key role in depression. Alloy et al. (2000) found that the inter-action between negative cognitive styles (e.g., negative attributional style, dysfunctional attitudes) and stress-reactive rumination predicted the retro-spective lifetime rate of major depressive episodes as well as hopelessness depressive episodes. In a subsequent study, Robinson and Alloy (2003) showed that the same interaction predicted the prospective onset, num-ber and duration of both major depressive and hopelessness depressive episodes.

Other recent definitions of depressive rumination have been proposed by examining rumination on current feelings of sadness or 'rumination on sadness' (Conway, Csank, Holm & Blake, 2000). In Conway et al.'s (2000) definition, rumination 'consists of repetitive thoughts concerning one's present distress and the circumstances surrounding the sadness' (p. 404). According to this definition, the ruminative thoughts (1) relate to the an-tecedents or nature of negative mood, (2) are not goal-directed and do not motivate individuals to make plans for remedial action, and (3) are not socially shared while individuals are engaged in rumination.

Finally, Treynor, Gonzalez and Nolen-Hoeksema (2003) revised the Ruminative Responses Scale (RRS; Nolen-Hoeksema & Morrow, 1991) and produced a new measure of rumination, which was unconfounded with depression content. Factor analysis yielded a two-factor solution with one factor labelled 'reflection' and the other 'brooding'. Reflection was concerned with efforts to overcome problems and difficulties whereas brooding was related to thinking anxiously and/or gloomily about events. Although both factors were significantly correlated with indices of depression, reflection was linked to less depression over time whilst brooding was associated with more depression, suggesting that only the brooding factor may be related to the style of persistent negative thinking characterised by rumination. Future research could further explore the relationships between brooding, reflection and depression.

Although there is little debate as to the concept of worry, it appears that different theorists define rumination somewhat differently despite the obvious similarities between the various definitions proposed. It has been noted that this problem is particularly reflected in the existing measures of rumination (Siegle, Moore & Thase, 2004). In a factor analytic study of different measures of rumination, Siegle et al. (2004) showed that there were several separate constructs represented in the measures. Thus, there appears to be a range of constructs of rumination, and it is conceivable that their contribution to dysphoria/depression may differ. Moreover, psychometric tools assessing worry and rumination have been found to be highly correlated with each other, and with other measures of perseverative thinking, anxiety and depression (Fresco, Frankel, Mennin, Turk & Heimberg, 2002, Harrington & Blankenship 2002, Segerstrom, Tsao, Alden & Craske, 2000). Future research may assist in operationalising the type and component of rumination being examined and reduce content overlap between measures of worry and rumination.

MALADAPTIVE WORRY AND RUMINATION

As we have seen so far, both worry and rumination are normal as well as pathological cognitive processes. So, what factors determine when these processes become maladaptive and unhelpful activities? Are worry and rumination failures of emotional self-regulation such as failed problem-solving and ineffective coping strategies? As will be discussed later, there are important sources of individual differences that may increase proneness to worry and rumination. However, there are other central factors that contribute to pathological varieties of worry and rumination. Although the content of worry and rumination is not likely to influence whether these processes are normal or abnormal, their frequency and duration is certainly likely to contribute to psychopathology. Moreover, in the Self-Regulatory Executive Function (S-REF) model of emotional disorders, Wells and Matthews (1994, 1996) suggest that there are at least three factors that contribute to worry and rumination becoming pathological. For purposes of assessment, it may be useful to view these factors as the 3-Ws: (1) When worry or rumination is used (e.g., in response to negative mood, before, during and/or after threatening situations), (2) What worry or rumination may be used for (e.g., predominant problem-solving and coping strategies), and (3) Whether worry or rumination is negatively appraised (e.g., 'I have no control over my worry/rumination'). The contribution of these factors to pathological varieties of worry and rumination is clearly supported by empirical evidence (for reviews, see Papageorgiou & Wells, 2004; Wells, 2000). The following examples will serve to illustrate these factors in maladaptive worry and rumination. An initial thought of an anticipated test is likely to become maladaptive (i.e., perseverative and disruptive) if the individual begins to contemplate the catastrophic consequences of not revising enough or failing the test, if worry is perceived as a useful strategy for coping with the resulting anxiety and preparing the individual to face the test, and if worry is viewed as uncontrollable and dangerous. In terms of rumination, if the individual had failed the test or not achieved an adequate grade, thinking is likely to become maladaptive if it is in response to depressed mood, if it is focused on repeatedly understanding or gaining insight into something that has happened in the past, and if it is appraised as harmful and difficult to control. These examples of maladaptive worry and rumination are based on the 3-Ws factors from the S-REF model, but are clearly represented in idiosyncratic metacognitive models of worry and GAD (Wells, 1995, 1997) and rumination and depression (Papageorgiou & Wells, 2003, 2004), which are described in the final section of this chapter.

CONSEQUENCES OF WORRY AND RUMINATION

Consequences of Worry

Worry has been linked to several negative consequences. Experimental inductions of worry have been shown to produce short-term increments in negative intrusive thoughts (e.g., York, Borkovec, Vasey & Stern, 1987). Furthermore, worrying briefly about a self-selected concern leads to increases in both anxiety and depression in non-clinical samples (Andrews & Borkovec, 1988). Wells and Papageorgiou (1995) examined the effects of worry on negative intrusive images following exposure to laboratory-induced stress (i.e., a brief film of an industrial accident). Following this film, participants were assigned randomly to one of five experimental conditions: (1) worry about the film and its implications in verbal form, (2) image about the film and its implications, (3) engage in a distraction task consisting of letter cancellation, (4) worry about the things they usually worry about, and (5) settle down. At the end of the experimental manipulation, participants were asked to record the occurrence of negative intrusive images about the film over the next three days. Wells and Papageorgiou (1995) demonstrated that worrying about the stressor led to significantly greater negative intrusive thoughts over the next three days than the other conditions, suggesting that worry affects the process of recovery from stressful and anxiety-provoking events. In addition to these effects, worry has been found to predict both anxious and depressive symptomatology in individuals with post-traumatic stress disorder (e.g., Ehlers, Mayou & Bryant, 1998; Holeva, Tarrier & Wells, 2001; Mayou, Ehlers & Bryant, 2002; Murray, Ehlers & Mayou, 2002).

Consequences of Rumination

The negative consequences of dysphoric or depressive rumination have been studied extensively and this has led to a large volume of research. It is beyond the scope of this chapter to review in depth these consequences. Readers may wish to refer to Lyubomirsky and Tkach's (2004) comprehensive review of the consequences of dysphoric rumination. Empirical support for the adverse effects of rumination comes from both experimental and questionnaire-based studies. The most powerful evidence for these effects comes from the experimental literature that reports inductions of rumination in naturally dysphoric individuals followed by measurements of affect, behaviour and cognition (e.g., Lyubomirsky, Caldwell & Nolen-Hoeksema, 1998; Lyubomirsky & Nolen-Hoeksema, 1993, 1995). In questionnaire-based studies, investigators have assessed individual differences in rumination using measures of rumination such as the Ruminative Responses Scale and then have related scores to other variables of interest in prospective and cross-sectional designs. In their review, Lyubomirsky and Tkach (2004) list the following key consequences associated with rumination: (1) negative affect and depressive symptoms, (2) negatively biased thinking, (3) poor problem-solving, (4) impaired motivation and inhibition of instrumental behaviour, (5) impaired concentration and cognition, and (6) increased stress and specific problems (e.g., threats to physical health, impaired social relationships, stress and emotional adjustment). Finally, from an applied perspective, rumination has been shown to delay recovery from depression during cognitive-behavioural treatment (Siegle, Sagrati & Crawford, 1999). In summary, existing literature documents the deleterious consequences associated with worry and rumination, thus supporting the need to enhance our knowledge of these processes and develop effective interventions to address these phenomena in treatment.

COMPARISONS BETWEEN WORRY AND RUMINATION

The nature of worry and rumination suggests that these processes should overlap with and differ from each other. It is evident that worry and rumination can exist dynamically within the same individual. However, the study of similarities and differences between worry and rumination may offer a number of important opportunities. First, it may allow us to construct systematically a profile of the constituents of persistent negative thinking processes that contribute to specific and/or general manifestations of psychological disturbance. In this way, an examination of the similarities and differences between worry and rumination may also assist in refining the proposed concepts. Whether the similarities or differences are key contributors to psychopathology is not yet clear. Second, this research may also facilitate the development and validation of idiosyncratic models for understanding perseverative negative thinking in anxiety and depression. Third, knowledge of similarities and differences between worry and rumination may facilitate development of effective psychological interventions by targeting core manifestations of psychopathology. Thus, this section discusses comparisons between worry and rumination.

Worry appears to be intimately related to rumination. Worry has been reported to be elevated in individuals with depression (Starcevic, 1995). Previous research examining the nature of anxious and depressive thinking demonstrated that these types of cognitions were clearly distinct phenomena (Clark & de Silva, 1985; Clark & Hemsley, 1985). The content of chains of anxious (worrisome) thoughts is likely to differ from depressive (ruminative) thoughts in that the former may be particularly characterised by themes of anticipated threat or danger in the future (Beck, 1967, 1976; Borkovec et al., 1983), while rumination may involve themes of past personal loss or failure (Beck, 1967, 1976). Szabo and Lovibond (2002) content analysed naturally occurring worrisome thoughts and found that 48% of them could be characterised as reflecting a problem solving process, 17% as anticipation of future negative outcomes, 11% 'rumination', and 5% as reflecting 'palliative' thoughts and 'self-blame'. Worrisome thinking has also been characterised by more statements implying catastrophic interpretations of future events than dysphoric ruminative thinking (Molina, Borkovec, Peasley & Person, 1998). Therefore, to date, research shows that there are content differences between worry and rumination.

More recently, theoretical and empirical evidence suggests that other dimensions of thinking, apart from the thematic content of thought, are involved in vulnerability to, and maintenance of, psychopathology. Indeed, Wells and Matthews (1994, 1996) argue that it is not only the content of perseverative negative thinking that may be relevant to understanding psychopathology, but also the nature, flexibility and beliefs about thinking that have consequences for information processing and self-regulation.

According to Wells and Matthews (1994, 1996), two components of thinking styles should be considered in this context: (1) process dimensions (e.g., attentional involvement, dismissability, distraction, etc.) and (2) metacognitive dimensions (e.g., beliefs or appraisals about thinking and ability to monitor, objectify and regulate thinking). Recent empirical work has focused on exploring such process and metacognitive dimensions of worry and rumination.

In an initial study, Papageorgiou and Wells (1999a) compared the process and metacognitive dimensions of naturally occurring depressive (ruminative) thoughts and anxious (worrisome) thoughts in a non-clinical sample. Participants were provided with a diary for recording and rating the content of the first and second depressive and anxious thoughts occurring during a two-week period. The results showed that although ruminative and worrisome thinking shared a number of similarities, they also differed on several dimensions. In comparison with rumination, worry was found to be significantly greater in verbal content, associated with more compulsion to act, and with more effort and confidence in problem solving. Rumination was significantly more past-oriented than worry. The only remaining significant differences after adjustments for multiple comparisons were those concerned with dimensions of effort to problem-solve and past orientation. Relationships between dimensions of thinking and affective responses for each style of thinking were also explored in this study. The results showed that greater depression was correlated significantly with lower confidence in problem-solving ability and greater past orientation of the ruminative thoughts. In relation to the worrisome thoughts, greater anxiety was correlated significantly with less dismissability of worry, greater distraction by worry, meta-worry, compulsion to act on worry, and more attentional focus on worries. Therefore, these preliminary data appear to be consistent with the notion that different components of thinking style are associated with emotional experience (Wells & Matthews, 1994, 1996). In a recent study, Watkins, Moulds and Mackintosh (in press) attempted to replicate the study by Papageorgiou and Wells (1999a). Although some of their findings were consistent with this earlier study, in particular those concerned with the temporal content and orientation of worry and rumination, the Watkins et al. study had several methodological differences such as use of a cross-sectional rather than naturalistic repeated measures design, reliance on a different measurement approach (i.e., use of a questionnaire without formal psychometric properties being established instead of a naturalistic diary of thoughts), and the potential of Type II error due to the number of adjustments based on 53 multiple comparisons. This renders direct comparisons of findings across studies problematic.

In a subsequent study, Papageorgiou and Wells (1999b, 2004) extended the earlier findings in clinical samples. Individuals whose predominant style of

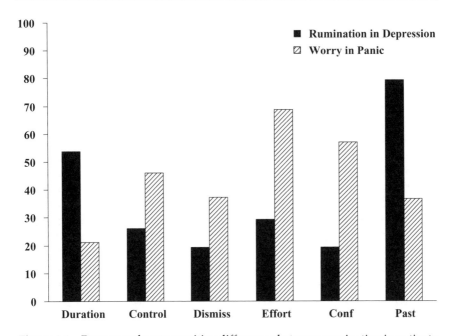

Figure 2.1   Process and metacognitive differences between rumination in patients with depression and worry in patients with panic disorder
Source: Papageorgiou, C. & Wells, A. (1999, November) *Dimensions of depressive rumination and anxious worry: A comparative study.* Paper presented at the 33rd Annual Convention of the Association for Advancement of Behavior Therapy, Toronto, Canada; (2004) Nature, functions, and beliefs about depressive rumination. In C. Papageorgiou & A. Wells, (Eds), *Depressive Rumination: Nature, Theory and Treatment.* Chichester, UK; John Wiley & Sons, Ltd.

thinking was characterised by anxious worry (e.g., individuals with panic disorder) and depressive rumination (e.g., individuals with major depressive disorder) were recruited into this study. To reduce the overlap between worry and rumination, it was ensured that there was no diagnostic overlap between the two clinical samples. This study can address the question: Are there any similarities or differences between the predominant styles of pathological thinking in each disorder (i.e., worry in panic disorder versus rumination in major depressive disorder)? In comparison with the worry of the panic disorder group, the rumination of the depressed group was rated as significantly longer in duration, less controllable, less dismissable, and associated with lower effort to problem-solve, lower confidence in problem solving, and a greater past orientation. These data are illustrated in Figure 2.1. After adjustments for multiple comparisons, the only remaining significant differences were those concerned with dimensions of effort to problem-solve, confidence in problem solving and past orientation. In future replication studies, these comparisons need to be made between individuals with GAD and major depressive disorder.

Therefore, initial empirical evidence suggests that although worry and rumination share a large number of similarities, they also differ on some dimensions (Papageorgiou & Wells, 1999a, 1999b, 2004). The overlap between worry and rumination may help to explain the high levels of comorbidity often detected between anxiety and depressive disorders. Again, whether the similarities and / or differences between worry and rumination are important contributors to psychopathology remains to be addressed in future research. However, these studies indicate that the most reliable differences found between these two styles of thinking are effort and confidence in problem solving and past orientation. It appears that pathological worry and rumination differ in terms of their motivational characteristics and metacognitive judgements of problem solving confidence. This may be important since both worry and rumination have been conceptualised as coping strategies (Wells & Matthews, 1994, 1996) and yet the characteristics of rumination seem ill suited to problem solving or coping when compared with worry.

Other studies investigating the relationships between worry, rumination, anxiety and depression have relied on self-report measures of worry and rumination to further explore the overlap and differences between these constructs (e.g., Fresco et al., 2002; Segerstrom et al., 2000). In these studies, worry has been measured using the Penn State Worry Questionnaire (PSWQ; Meyer et al. 1990) and rumination has been assessed using the Ruminative Responses Scale (RRS; Nolen-Hoeksema & Morrow, 1991). Segerstrom et al. (2000) found strong correlations between worry and rumination in both non-clinical and clinical samples. In addition, using structural equation modelling, they reported that a latent variable ('repetitive thought') involving manifest variables of worry and rumination was significantly correlated with anxiety and depression. These data led the authors to conclude that goal interruption, failures of emotional processing, and information processing may result in repetitive thought that increases negative mood states, such as anxiety and depression. Fresco et al. (2002) subjected the items from the PSWQ and RRS to factor analyses. This revealed a four-factor solution consisting of two worry factors labelled 'worry engagement' (e.g., 'I worry all the time') and 'absence of worry' (e.g., 'I find it easy to dismiss worrisome thoughts') and two rumination factors labelled 'dwelling on the negative' (e.g., 'Think about how passive and unmotivated you feel') and 'active cognitive appraisal' (e.g., 'Isolate yourself and think about the reasons why you feel sad'). The worry engagement and dwelling on the negative factors emerge as distilled measures of worry and rumination, respectively. Fresco et al. (2002) also reported that scores on these factors were highly correlated with each other and demonstrated equally strong relationships to anxiety and depression.

WHY DO PEOPLE WORRY AND RUMINATE?

In an earlier section of this chapter, the numerous negative consequences associated with worry and rumination were reviewed. Despite these consequences, it is puzzling to understand why people choose to engage in worry and rumination when stressors are encountered. Knowledge of the factors implicated in proneness to worry and rumination may contribute to our understanding of the mechanisms underlying the frequency and severity of worry and anxiety symptoms as well as rumination and depressive symptoms. Moreover, the modification of these factors may assist in reducing vulnerability to worry and rumination and maximising the efficacy of psychological interventions for anxiety and depression. A number of hypotheses have been advanced to account for the role of worry in anxiety and rumination in depression. Worry has been viewed as a form of avoidance (Borkovec & Inz, 1991; see Chapter 14), problem solving (Davey, 1994), coping strategy (Wells, 1994, 1997), and intolerance of uncertainty (Dugas, Gagnon, Ladouceur & Freeston, 1998; see Chapter 12). Similarly, rumination has been conceptualised as resulting from a failure to achieve higher order goals (Martin & Tesser, 1989, 1996), as a way of helping individuals to focus inwardly and evaluate their feelings and their problematic situation in order to gain insight (Nolen-Hoeksema, 1991) and as a primary coping activity (Papageorgiou & Wells, 2003, 2004). In particular, rumination can be viewed as a strategy used to understand one's problems, emotions and circumstances, and as a means of finding solutions to the problems precipitating depression (Papageorgiou & Wells, 2001a; Wells & Matthews, 1994, 1996).

A systematic account of worry and rumination should specify the mechanisms responsible for initiating and maintaining these activities and the factors contributing to the development of their pathological forms. The identification of the idiosyncratic nature and functions of worry and rumination within the context of information processing models may enhance our knowledge of the worrisome and ruminative processes involved in the onset, perpetuation and recurrence of anxiety and depression, respectively. Wells and Matthews' (1994, 1996) S-REF model of emotional disorders accounts for the information processing mechanisms that initiate and maintain worry and rumination and the pathological consequences of these styles of thinking. In the S-REF model, a particular cognitive attentional 'syndrome' consisting of heightened self-focus, repetitive negative thinking, maladaptive coping behaviours and threat monitoring contributes to emotional disturbance. An important component of this syndrome is perseverative negative thinking in the form of worry or rumination. The S-REF model views these processes as coping strategies that have counterproductive effects of perpetuating emotional disorders. Selection and execution of worry or rumination is linked to particular metacognitive beliefs and processes. Metacognition refers to the aspect of the information processing system that monitors, interprets, evaluates, and regulates the contents and processes of its organisation (Flavell, 1979; Wells 2000). According to the S-REF model, perseverative negative thinking is problematic for emotional self-regulation because of multiple effects on low level and strategic cognitive operations required for restructuring self-knowledge and developing effective coping strategies. For example, worrying may focus appraisals on negative outcomes, hence preventing the processing of positive information that can change negative beliefs. Furthermore, the use of strategies such as thought suppression may activate low level automatic processing that increases the probability of intrusion of unwanted material into consciousness. Building on the generic S-REF model, two specific metacognitive models of worry in anxiety (Wells, 1995, 1997) and rumination in depression (Papageorgiou & Wells, 2003, 2004) have been developed and evaluated, and suggest specific ways in which both worry and rumination are initiated, maintained and become pathological. Descriptions of these models will now be considered.

Wells (1995, 1997) proposed a metacognitive model of worry in GAD. This model is illustrated in Figure 2.2 (see Chapter 11). In this model, in response to a trigger (e.g., bad news, a negative intrusive thought or image, etc.), individuals with GAD select worry as a coping strategy. This selection is driven by the activation of positive beliefs about the benefits of worry (e.g., 'If I worry I can always be prepared'). Once Type I worries are set in motion, which are concerned with external daily events and non-cognitive internal events, negative appraisals about the process of worrying and accompanying emotion are activated. Negative appraisals of worry involve themes of uncontrollability and danger associated with this process (e.g., 'My worries are uncontrollable', 'Worrying is dangerous'). Table 2.1 lists additional examples of positive and negative appraisals of worry. According to Wells' (1995, 1997) model, it is Type II worry or meta-worry (i.e., worry about worry) that is associated with psychopathology. Indeed, in this model, pathological varieties of worry such as those found in GAD are linked to a high incidence of Type II worries. Once worry about worry has been established, three additional factors are then involved in the escalation and maintenance of the problem. These factors include behavioural responses, such as avoidance and reassurance seeking, thought control strategies, such as suppression and distraction, and emotional symptoms such as anxiety, tension, dissociation and even panic attacks and depression. Extensive

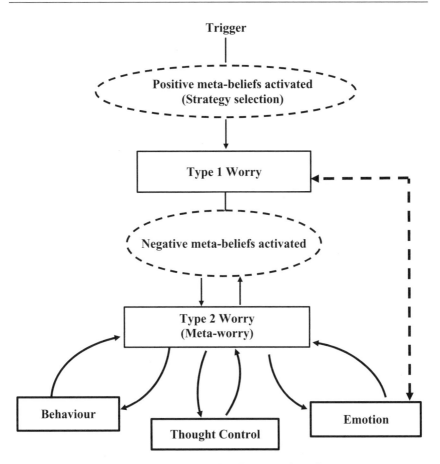

Figure 2.2   A cognitive model of generalised anxiety disorder
Source: Papageorgiou, C. & Wells, A. (1995, 1997) An empirical test of a clinical metacognitive model of rumination and depression. *Cognitive Therapy and Research*, **27**, 261–273; (2004) Nature, functions, and beliefs about depressive rumination. In C. Papageorgiou & A. Wells, (Eds), *Depressive Rumination: Nature, Theory and Treatment*. Chichester, UK; John Wiley & Sons, Ltd.

empirical evidence supports the metacognitive model of worry and GAD (see Chapter 11).

Figure 2.3 shows the basic components and structure of a clinical metacognitive model of rumination and depression (Papageorgiou & Wells, 2003, 2004). According to this model, following a specific trigger (e.g., a negative intrusive thought or image, a memory of loss or failure, or an external non-cognitive event), positive metacognitive beliefs about the benefits and advantages of rumination motivate individuals with depression to

Table 2.1 Examples of positive and negative metacognitive beliefs about worry

Positive Beliefs about Worry	Negative Beliefs about Worry
Worrying helps me to avoid problems in the future	My worrying is dangerous for me
I need to worry in order to remain organised	I could make myself sick with worrying
Worrying helps me to get things sorted out in my mind	If I let my worrying thoughts get out of control, they will end up controlling me
Worrying helps me to avoid disastrous situations	My worrying thoughts persist, no matter how I try to stop them
People who do not worry, have no depth	I cannot ignore my worrying thoughts
Worrying helps me cope	My worrying could make me go mad
If I did not worry, I would make more mistakes	Worry can stop me from seeing a situation clearly

Source: Cartwright-Hatton, S. & Wells, A. (1997). Beliefs about worry and intrusions: The Metacognitions Questionnaire and its correlates. *Journal of Anxiety Disorders*, **11**, 279–296.

engage in sustained ruminative thinking. Depressed individuals may believe that 'ruminating about my depression helps me to understand past mistakes and failures'. Once rumination is activated, and because of the numerous negative consequences associated with this process, individuals then appraise rumination as both uncontrollable and harmful (i.e., negative

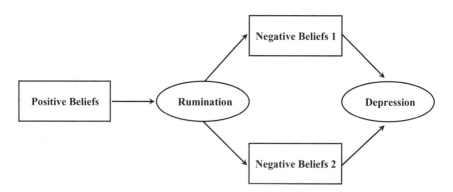

Figure 2.3 Basic components and structure of a clinical metacognitive model of rumination and depression
Source: Papageorgiou, C. & Wells, A. (2003). An empirical test of a clinical metacognitive model of rumination and depression. *Cognitive Therapy and Research*, **27**, 261–273; (2004) Nature, functions, and beliefs about depressive rumination. In C. Papageorgiou & A. Wells, (Eds), *Depressive Rumination: Nature, Theory and Treatment*. Chichester, UK; John Wiley & Sons, Ltd.

Table 2.2 Examples of positive and negative metacognitive beliefs about rumination

Positive Beliefs about Rumination	Negative Beliefs about Rumination
In order to understand my feelings of depression, I need to ruminate about my problems	Ruminating makes me physically ill
I need to ruminate about the bad things that have happened in the past to make sense of them	When I ruminate, I can't do anything else
I need to ruminate about my problems to find the causes of my depression	Ruminating means I'm out of control
Ruminating about my problems helps me to focus on the most important things	Ruminating will turn me into a failure
Ruminating about the past helps me to prevent future mistakes and failures	Ruminating means I'm a bad person
Ruminating about my feelings helps me to recognise the triggers for my depression	It is impossible not to ruminate about the bad things that have happened in the past
Ruminating about the past helps me to work out how things could have been done better	Only weak people ruminate

Source: Papageorgiou, C. & Wells, A. (2001) Metacognitive beliefs about rumination in recurrent major depression. *Cognitive and Behavioral Practice*, **8**, 160–164; (2001) Positive beliefs about depressive rumination: Development and preliminary validation of a self-report scale. *Behavior Therapy*, **32**, 13–26.

beliefs 1, e.g., 'It is impossible not to ruminate about the bad things that have happened in the past') and likely to produce detrimental interpersonal and social consequences (i.e., negative beliefs 2, e.g., 'Everyone would desert me if they knew how much I ruminate about myself'). Additional examples of positive and negative metacognitive beliefs about rumination are presented in Table 2.2. This model asserts that the activation of negative beliefs about rumination contributes to depression. Therefore, a number of vicious cycles of rumination and metacognition are hypothesised to be responsible for the perpetuation of depression. Evidence supporting some of the hypotheses postulated by this model is reviewed next.

Several cross-sectional, prospective and experimental studies provide initial support for the clinical metacognitive model of rumination and depression (Papageorgiou & Wells, 2003, 2004). In a preliminary study, Papageorgiou and Wells (2001a) conducted a number of semi-structured qualitative interviews with patients with DSM-IV recurrent major depression and found that they all reported positive and negative metacognitive beliefs about rumination. Some examples of these beliefs are shown in Table 2.2. Using these beliefs, the Positive Beliefs about Rumination

Scale (PBRS; Papageorgiou & Wells, 2001b) and the Negative Beliefs about Rumination Scale (NBRS; Papageorgiou, Wells & Meina, in preparation) were developed. Both the PBRS and NBRS have been shown to have good psychometric properties of reliability and validity (for a review, see Luminet, 2004). Studies have shown that the PBRS is significantly and positively associated with rumination and depression in both non-clinical samples (Papageorgiou & Wells, 2001a, Study 4; 2001c; 2003, Study 2) and patients with depression (Papageorgiou & Wells, 2003, Study 1; Papageorgiou et al., in preparation). In addition, both subtypes of negative metacognitive beliefs about rumination (i.e., beliefs concerning uncontrollability and harm, and the interpersonal and social consequences of rumination), as measured by NBRS1 and NBRS2 respectively, have been shown to be significantly and positively correlated with rumination and depression in non-clinical samples (Papageorgiou & Wells, 2001c; 2003, Study 2) and patients with depression (Papageorgiou & Wells, 2003, Study 1; Papageorgiou et al., in preparation). Studies have also shown that both positive and negative metacognitive beliefs about rumination significantly distinguish patients with recurrent major depression from patients with panic disorder and agoraphobia, and patients with social phobia (Papageorgiou & Wells, 2001a, Study 5; Papageorgiou et al., in preparation), suggesting specificity associated with such metacognitive beliefs. In another study, Sanderson and Papageorgiou (in preparation) found that positive and negative beliefs about rumination did not discriminate between currently and previously recurrently depressed individuals, suggesting that these beliefs may act or persist as a vulnerability factor. Indeed, Papageorgiou and Wells (2001c) conducted a prospective study to examine the causal status of the relationships between rumination, negative metacognitive beliefs about rumination and depression in a non-clinical sample. The results showed that negative metacognitive beliefs about the uncontrollability and harm associated with rumination predicted depression prospectively even after controlling statistically for initial levels of depression and rumination. Finally, using structural equation modelling, a good statistical model fit has been found for the clinical metacognitive model of rumination and depression in a depressed sample (Papageorgiou & Wells, 2003, Study 1).

SUMMARY AND CONCLUSION

The phenomenology of both worry and rumination was reviewed at the beginning of this chapter. It is evident that worry and rumination are common cognitive processes in non-clinical and clinical samples, particularly GAD and depression, respectively. Several factors contribute to these processes becoming maladaptive and unhelpful activities. These factors are represented in idiosyncratic metacognitive models of worry and GAD as well as rumination and depression. Understanding these factors may facilitate identification, differentiation and treatment of these phenomena in clinical practice. Worry and rumination are associated with a number of negative affective, behavioural and cognitive consequences, which highlights the need to advance our understanding of these core processes and develop effective interventions to target them in therapy. An important way of enhancing our knowledge of these processes is to study the similarities and differences between worry and rumination. Although there is little disagreement regarding the content differences between worry and rumination, there is no conclusive evidence concerning process and metacognitive differences. Moreover, whether the process and metacognitive similarities or differences are key contributors to psychopathology also remains to be addressed in the future. Finally, we have seen that several hypotheses have been proposed to account for the role of worry in anxiety and rumination in depression. Recent metacognitive approaches, which systematically specify the mechanisms implicated in the initiation and maintenance of worry and rumination, appear to be particularly promising.

ACKNOWLEDGEMENTS

I am grateful to Sue Thorgaard for her assistance in the preparation of the manuscript.

REFERENCES

Alloy, L.B., Abramson, L.Y., Hogan, M.E., Whitehouse, W.G., Rose, D.T., Robinson, M.S., Kim, R.S. & Lapkin, J.B. (2000). The Temple-Wisconsin Cognitive Vulnerability to Depression (CVD) Project: Lifetime history of Axis I psychopathology in individuals at high and low cognitive vulnerability to depression. *Journal of Abnormal Psychology*, **109**, 403–418.
American Psychiatric Association. (1994). *Diagnostic and statistical manual of mental disorders* (4th ed.). Washington, DC: Author.
Andrews, V.H. & Borkovec, T.D. (1988). The differential effects of inductions of worry, somatic anxiety, and depression on emotional experience. *Journal of Behavior Therapy and Experimental Psychiatry*, **19**, 21–26.
Beck, A.T. (1967). *Depression: Clinical, experimental, and theoretical aspects*. New York: Harper & Row.
Beck, A.T. (1976). *Cognitive therapy and the emotional disorders*. New York: International Universities Press.
Borkovec, T.D. & Inz, J. (1990). The nature of worry in Generalized Anxiety Disorder: A predominance of thought activity. *Behaviour Research and Therapy*, **28**, 153–158.
Borkovec, T.D., Robinson, E., Pruzinsky, T. & DePree, J.A. (1983). Preliminary exploration of worry: Some characteristics and processes. *Behaviour Research and Therapy*, **21**, 9–16.

Cartwright-Hatton, S. & Wells, A. (1997). Beliefs about worry and intrusions: The Metacognitions Questionnaire and its correlates. *Journal of Anxiety Disorders*, **11**, 279–296.

Clark, D.A. & de Silva, P. (1985). The nature of depressive and anxious, intrusive thoughts: Distinct or uniform phenomena? *Behaviour Research and Therapy*, **23**, 383–393.

Clark, D.A. & Hemsley, D.R. (1985). Individual differences in the experience of depressive and anxious, intrusive thoughts. *Behaviour Research and Therapy*, **23**, 625–633.

Conway, M., Csank, P.A.R., Holm, S.L. & Blake, C.K. (2000). On assessing individual differences in rumination on sadness. *Journal of Personality Assessment*, **75**, 404–425.

Craske, M.G., Rapee, R.M., Jackel, L. & Barlow, D.H. (1989). Qualitative dimensions of worry in DSM-III-R: Generalized Anxiety Disorder subjects and non-anxious controls. *Behaviour Research and Therapy*, **27**, 397–402.

Davey, G.C.L. (1994). Pathological worry as exacerbated problem solving. In: G.C.L. Davey & F. Tallis (Eds), *Worrying: Perspectives on Theory, Assessment, and Treatment* (pp. 35–60). Chichester, UK: John Wiley & Sons, Ltd.

Dugas, M.J., Gagnon, F., Ladouceur, R. & Freeston, M.H. (1998). Generalized anxiety disorder: A preliminary test of a conceptual model. *Behaviour Research and Therapy*, **36**, 215–226.

Ehlers, A., Mayou, R.A. & Bryant, B. (1998). Psychological predictors of chronic posttraumatic stress disorder after motor vehicle accidents. *Journal of Abnormal Psychology*, **107**, 508–519.

Flavell, J.H. (1979). Metacognition and metacognitive monitoring: A new area of cognitive-developmental inquiry. *American Psychologist*, **34**, 906-911.

Fresco, D.M., Frankel, A.N., Mennin, D.S., Turk, C.L. & Heimberg, R.G. (2002). Distinct and overlapping features of rumination and worry: The relationship of cognitive production to negative affective states. *Cognitive Therapy and Research*, **26**, 179–188.

Harrington, J. & Blankenship, V. (2002). Ruminative thoughts and their relation to depression and anxiety. *Journal of Applied Social Psychology*, **32**, 465–485.

Holeva, V., Tarrier, N. & Wells, A. (2001). Prevalence and predictors of acute PTSD following road traffic accidents: Thought control strategies and social support. *Behavior Therapy*, **32**, 65–84.

Luminet, O. (2004). Measurement of depressive rumination and associated constructs. In C. Papageorgiou & A. Wells (Eds), *Depressive Rumination: Nature, Theory and Treatment* (pp. 187–215). Chichester, UK: John Wiley & Sons, Ltd.

Lyubomirsky, S., Caldwell, N.D. & Nolen-Hoeksema, S. (1998). Effects of ruminative and distracting responses to depressed mood on retrieval of autobiographical memories. *Journal of Personality and Social Psychology*, **75**, 166–177.

Lyubomirsky, S. & Nolen-Hoeksema, S. (1993). Self-perpetuating properties of dysphoric rumination. *Journal of Personality and Social Psychology*, **65**, 339–349.

Lyubomirsky, S. & Nolen-Hoeksema, S. (1995). Effects of self-focused rumination on negative thinking and interpersonal problem solving. *Journal of Personality and Social Psychology*, **69**, 176–190.

Lyubomirsky, S. & Tkach, C. (2004). The consequences of dysphoric rumination. In C. Papageorgiou & A. Wells (Eds), *Depressive rumination: nature, theory and treatment* (pp. 21–41). Chichester, UK: Wiley & Sons Ltd.

Martin, L.L. & Tesser, A. (1989). Toward a motivational and structural theory of ruminative thought. In J.S. Uleman & J.A. Bargh, (Eds), *Unintended thought* (pp. 306–326). New York: Guilford Press.

Martin, L.L. & Tesser, A. (1996). Some ruminative thoughts. In R.S. Wyer (Ed.), *Advances in social cognition* (Vol. 9, pp. 1–47). Mahwah: Lawrence Erlbaum Associates.

Mayou, R.A., Ehlers, A. & Bryant, B. (2002). Posttraumatic stress disorder after motor vehicle accidents: 3-year follow-up of a prospective longitudinal study. *Behaviour Research and Therapy*, **40**, 665–675.

Meyer, T.J., Miller, M.L., Metzger, R.L. & Borkovec, T.D. (1990). Development and validation of the Penn State Worry Questionnaire. *Behaviour Research and Therapy*, **28**, 487–495.

Molina, S., Borkovec, T.D., Peasley, C. & Person, D. (1998). Content analysis of worrisome streams of consciousness in anxious and dysphoric participants. *Cognitive Therapy and Research*, **22**, 109–123.

Murray, J., Ehlers, A. & Mayou, R.A. (2002). Dissociation and posttraumatic stress disorder: Two prospective studies of road traffic accident survivors. *British Journal of Psychiatry*, **180**, 363–368.

Nolen-Hoeksema, S. (1991). Responses to depression and their effects on the duration of depressive episodes. *Journal of Abnormal Psychology*, **100**, 569–582.

Nolen-Hoeksema, S. & Morrow, J. (1991). A prospective study of depression and posttraumatic stress symptoms after a natural disaster: The 1989 Loma Prieta earthquake. *Journal of Personality and Social Psychology*, **61**, 115–121.

Papageorgiou, C. & Wells, A. (1999a). Process and metacognitive dimensions of depressive and anxious thoughts and relationships with emotional intensity. *Clinical Psychology and Psychotherapy*, **6**, 156–162.

Papageorgiou, C. & Wells, A. (1999b, November). *Dimensions of depressive rumination and anxious worry: A comparative study*. Paper presented at the 33rd Annual Convention of the Association for Advancement of Behavior Therapy, Toronto, Canada.

Papageorgiou, C. & Wells, A. (2001a). Metacognitive beliefs about rumination in recurrent major depression. *Cognitive and Behavioral Practice*, **8**, 160–164.

Papageorgiou, C. & Wells, A. (2001b). Positive beliefs about depressive rumination: Development and preliminary validation of a self-report scale. *Behavior Therapy*, **32**, 13–26.

Papageorgiou, C. & Wells, A. (2001c, November). *Metacognitive vulnerability to depression: A prospective study*. Paper presented at the 35th Annual Convention of the Association for Advancement of Behavior Therapy, Philadelphia, USA.

Papageorgiou, C. & Wells, A. (2003). An empirical test of a clinical metacognitive model of rumination and depression. *Cognitive Therapy and Research*, **27**, 261–273.

Papageorgiou, C. & Wells, A. (2004). Nature, functions, and beliefs about depressive rumination. In C. Papageorgiou & A. Wells (Eds), *Depressive Rumination: Nature, Theory and Treatment* (pp. 3–20). Chichester, UK: John Wiley & Sons, Ltd.

Papageorgiou, C., Wells, A. & Meina, L.J. *Development and Preliminary Validation of the Negative Beliefs about Rumination Scale*. Manuscript in preparation.

Rippere, V. (1977). 'What's the thing to do when you're feeling depressed?': A pilot study. *Behaviour Research and Therapy*, **15**, 185–191.

Robinson, S.M. & Alloy, L.B. (2003). Negative cognitive styles and stress-reactive rumination interact to predict depression: A prospective study. *Cognitive Therapy and Research*, **27**, 275–291.

Sanderson, J. & Papageorgiou, C. *Metacognitive beliefs about depressive rumination: Maintenance or vulnerability?* Manuscript in preparation.

Segerstrom, S.C., Tsao, J.C.I., Alden, L.E. & Craske, M.G. (2000). Worry and rumination: Repetitive thought as a concomitant and predictor of negative mood. *Cognitive Therapy and Research*, **24**, 671–688.

Siegle, G.J., Moore, P.M. & Thase, M.E. (2004). Rumination: One construct, many features in healthy individuals, depressed individuals, and individuals with lupus. *Cognitive Therapy and Research*, **28**, 645–668.

Siegle, G.J., Sagratti, S. & Crawford, C.E. (1999, November). *Effects of rumination and initial severity on response to cognitive therapy for depression.* Paper presented at the 33rd Annual Convention of the Association for the Advancement of Behavior Therapy. Toronto, Canada.

Starcevic, V. (1995). Pathological worry in major depression: A preliminary report. *Behaviour Research and Therapy*, **33**, 55–56.

Szabo, M. & Lovibond, P.F. (2002). The cognitive content of naturally occurring worry episodes. *Cognitive Therapy and Research*, **26**, 167–177.

Treynor, W., Gonzalez, R. & Nolen-Hoeksema, S. (2003). Rumination reconsidered: A psychometric analysis. *Cognitive Therapy and Research*, **27**, 247–259.

Watkins, E., Moulds, M. & Mackintosh, B. (in press). Comparisons between rumination and worry in a non-clinical sample. *Behaviour Research and Therapy*.

Wells, A. (1994). Attention and the control of worry. In G.C.L. Davey & F. Tallis (Eds), *Worrying: Perspectives on theory, assessment, and treatment.* Chichester, UK: John Wiley & Sons, Ltd.

Wells, A. (1995). Metacognition and worry: A cognitive model of generalized anxiety disorder. *Behavioural and Cognitive Psychotherapy*, **23**, 301–320.

Wells, A. (1997). *Cognitive therapy of anxiety disorders: A practice manual and Conceptual Guide.* Chichester, UK: John Wiley & Sons, Ltd.

Wells, A. (2000). *Emotional disorders and metacognition: Innovative cognitive therapy.* Chichester, UK: John Wiley & Sons, Ltd.

Wells, A. & Matthews, G. (1994). *Attention and emotion: A clinical perspective.* Hove, UK: Lawrence Erlbaum Associates.

Wells, A. & Matthews, G. (1996). Modelling cognition in emotional disorders: The S-REF model. *Behaviour Research and Therapy*, **34**, 881–888.

Wells, A. & Papageorgiou, C. (1995). Worry and the incubation of intrusive images following stress. *Behaviour Research and Therapy*, **33**, 579–583.

York, D., Borkovec, T.D., Vasey, M. & Stern, R. (1987). Effects of worry and somatic anxiety inductions on thoughts, emotion, and physiological activity. *Behaviour Research and Therapy*, **25**, 523–526.

Chapter 3

WORRY IN PSYCHOPATHOLOGY

Christine Purdon and Jennifer Harrington

WORRY IN PSYCHOPATHOLOGY

Historically, worry has been viewed as simply a symptom, or side-effect of anxiety and not an especially interesting topic for study on its own. For example, O'Neill (1985) argued that worry will extinguish through the same mechanisms as anxiety (e.g., flooding), and so does not need to be identified or treated as a separate construct. Borkovec (1985) disagreed, arguing that worry is the cognitive component of anxiety and its relationship to the physiological and behavioral components of anxiety needs to be understood. Furthermore, early research suggested that worry may serve to actually elicit and maintain anxiety. Thus, worry might be a causal factor in anxiety, as opposed to solely being part of its phenomenology.

This latter view now prevails (e.g., Barlow, 2002; Craske, 1999), and since those early debates, worry has been accepted as a topic of legitimate study. With respect to content, worry typically concerns negative future events and is an attempt to avoid negative outcomes or prepare for the worst (e.g., Borkovec, Ray & Stöber, 1998; Molina, Borkovec, Peasley & Person, 1998). In terms of process, worry is generally described as ruminative, consisting mainly of thought rather than image, as involving vague, as opposed to concrete ideas about threat and as involving problem elaboration as opposed to problem solution (Borkovec et al., 1998; Molina et al., 1998). In terms of its relation to anxiety, Barlow (2002) argues that worry is "...a closely associated consequence of anxious apprehension[1] that may be an attempt at coping with this process for many individuals" (p. 102). As anxiety increases, so does the process of worry.

For the past decade, research on worry has grown exponentially, in part because worry is now considered the cardinal feature of generalized anxiety

---

[1] "Anxious apprehension" is "...a future-oriented mood state in which one is ready or prepared to attempt to cope with upcoming negative events" (Barlow, 2002, p. 64).

Worry and Its Psychological Disorders: Theory, Assessment and Treatment. Edited by G. C. L. Davey and A. Wells. © 2006 John Wiley & Sons, Ltd.

disorder (GAD; APA, 2000). Detailed models for the development and persistence of GAD and comprehensive protocols for helping individuals overcome worry as it occurs within the context of GAD are now emerging (e.g., Borkovec & Ruscio, 2001; Brown, O'Leary & Barlow, 2001; Dugas & Ladouceur, 1998; Roemer & Orsillo, 2002; Rygh & Sanderson, 2004; Wells, 1997). To date, clinical interventions include the use of mindfulness meditation, cognitive restructuring of erroneous and maladaptive appraisal of worry (e.g., positive beliefs about the utility and function of worry, negative beliefs about not worrying, intolerance of uncertainty), relaxation training, and attention control training.

GAD is one of the more prevalent disorders, with a lifetime prevalence rate of 4–6% (Kessler et al., 1995). It also has very high rates of co-morbidity with other anxiety and mood disorders. For example, GAD without co-morbid psychiatric disorders accounts for only one-third of its total prevalence (Bruce, Machan, Dyck & Keller, 2001; Wittchen, Zhao, Kessler, et al., 1994). Indeed, clinical research indicates that the majority of patients (80–90%) with current GAD have an additional psychiatric diagnosis (Roy-Byrne & Katton, 1997). GAD has particularly high rates of co-morbidity with panic disorder, social phobia, specific phobias, major depressive episode/dysthymia, and substance abuse (e.g., Brown & Barlow, 1992; Bruce et al., 2001; Stein, 2002; Wittchen et al., 1994).

In their examination of the co-occurrence of current mood and anxiety disorders in a large clinical sample ($N = 1127$), Brown et al. (2001) found that the percentage of people with an anxiety disorder who also had GAD ranged from 20% (specific phobia, obsessive-compulsive disorder, post-traumatic stress disorder, panic disorder with agoraphobia) to 33% (panic disorder). The percentage of people diagnosed with a mood disorder and co-morbid GAD ranged from 14% (dysthymia) to 25% (major depressive disorder). However, it is important to bear in mind that a diagnosis of GAD is *not* given if the excessive worry occurs only in the context of mood disturbance. When all cases were examined, including those in which GAD co-occurred with a mood disorder, the above numbers increased considerably from 33% (panic disorder with agoraphobia) to 57% (major depressive episode). Thus, a significant proportion of individuals with an anxiety disorder or mood disorder are likely to experience problems with persistent, uncontrollable worry and its physiological sequelae.

GAD is also often co-morbid with alcohol dependence. The odds of having alcohol dependence are four times as high for men and three times as high for women who have GAD as opposed to those who do not have GAD (as reviewed in Kushner, Abrams & Borchardt, 2000). Individuals with GAD often experience insomnia; in one study, 75% of people reported difficulties falling or staying asleep (Bélanger, Morin, Langlois & Ladouceur, 2004). Indeed, 10–13% of individuals with severe sleep disturbances have co-morbid GAD (Brown et al., 2001; Mellinger, Balter & Uhlenhuth, 1985; Schneider et al., 2001). People with GAD are also more likely to have so-matoform disorders (e.g., health anxiety) than are individuals with other anxiety disorders (Brown et al., 2001). Additionally, there is a high preva-lence of GAD in individuals with unexplained somatic complaints (Stein, 2002).

These high rates of co-morbidity have implications for the course of GAD. Bruce et al. (2001) found that co-morbidity was associated with a lower rate of GAD remission, particularly when it is co-morbid with panic disorder or major depressive disorder. By the same token, co-morbid GAD often remits with psychosocial treatment of another anxiety disorder (Brown, Antony & Barlow, 1995). Similarly, anxiety appears to contribute to the maintenance of alcohol dependence and predicts relapse to problematic use of alcohol (Kushner et al., 2000). Taken together, these data suggest that frequent, uncontrollable worry is a common problem in those seeking treatment for various conditions.

Even if an individual does not have co-morbid GAD, worry may be an im-portant feature of the symptom presentation. First, assuming that Barlow's view of worry as resulting from anxious apprehension is correct, any dis-order characterized by anxiety will also be characterized by worry. Second, worry is common in many other disorders. For example, in the DSM-IVTR, criterion 2b for Panic Disorder is "worry about the implications of the [panic] attack or its consequences ... " (APA, 2000, p. 441). We also know that individuals with panic disorder experience considerable distress over when their next attack will occur and whether or not they will be able to cope with it. They spend much time planning ways to avoid the worst imagined outcomes of an attack, such as not driving alone, always having a cell phone on and charged, always carrying Ativan, and planning excuses for a speedy departure (e.g., Barlow, 2001; Rapee, 1993; Wells, 1997). As in worry, the distress focuses on future negative outcomes that are vague in nature and results in problem generation as opposed to problem resolu-tion (i.e., packing Ativan and a cell phone does not allay the anticipatory anxiety because there remains the possibility that something could hap-pen to overwhelm coping resources or thwart the safety plan). Thus, this preoccupation has much in common with worry.

Social anxiety is characterized by a "fear of one or more social or perfor-mance situations in which the person is exposed to unfamiliar people or to possible scrutiny by others" (APA, 2000, p. 456). Anticipatory anxiety is a hallmark feature of social anxiety, as these individuals "ruminate" about

upcoming social and performance situations, anticipating different problems that could arise and planning and rehearsing against them. However,
these efforts are futile because the anxiety persists (Wells, 1997, p. 170).

Worry is also a feature of health anxiety. Warwick and Salkovskis (1990)
describe individuals with health anxiety as being preoccupied with concerns about health and as ruminating about what the symptoms mean.
For example, a key feature of health anxiety is "Intrusive thoughts of the
possible negative consequences of not taking further action . . . in terms of
future handicap, inconvenience and physical discomfort . . . and in terms of
painful or noxious medical procedures" (p. 113). Papageorgiou and Wells
(1998) refer to this generation of negative, future-oriented outcomes as
"perseverative self-focused processing" (p. 194), which shares important
characteristics with the worry process (e.g., Wells, 1994).

Obsessive-compulsive disorder (OCD) and GAD have enough similarities
that there is a sizeable literature comparing the two disorders. The general conclusion is that worry and obsessions are distinct (e.g., Langlois,
Freeston & Ladouceur, 2000; Turner, Beidel & Stanley, 1992). However, it
appears that worry is both part of the phenomenology of OCD and a potential factor in its persistence. Wells and Papageorgiou (1998) note that self-
report symptom measures of OCD such as the Padua Inventory (Sanavio,
1988) actually include the word "worry" in items assessing the content of
obsessions (e.g., "I think or worry at length about having hurt someone
without knowing it"). In an empirical study, use of worry as a strategy
for managing obsessions was associated with greater symptom severity
(Amir, Cashman & Foa, 1997). Tallis and DeSilva (1992) found that worry in
OCD was more strongly associated with checking and doubting sub-types
than washing or slowness sub-types, and concluded that worry may actually evoke checking behaviour. Freeston, Ladouceur, Rhéaume, Letarte,
Gagnon and Thibodeau (1994) suggest that rather than being functionally
related, worry and checking may be concomitants of perceived loss of control over unwanted, distressing thoughts; that is, both may be strategies
used to manage the anxiety over feeling out of control of thoughts.

Worry-like processes are a feature of posttraumatic stress disorder (PTSD)
and have been conceptualized as a factor in the escalation and persistence of this condition (Wells & Matthews, 1994). Ehlers and Steil (1995)
proposed that negative interpretations of the meaning of persistent recollections about the past trauma (e.g., as an indication that the individual
may have been irreparably damaged by the trauma) result in "anticipation
of future negative events" (p. 229), as well as rumination about the past
traumatic event. In a prospective longitudinal study of children who had
experienced trauma, Ehlers, Mayou and Bryant (2003) found that rumination about the event was, among other factors, a predictor of later symptom

severity. Both anticipation of negative future events and rumination about past events have characteristics in common with worry (Papageorgiou & Wells, 2004).

In an analogue study, Wells and Papageorgiou (1995) found that individuals exposed to a gruesome film of an accident who were then instructed to worry about everyday matters had more thoughts about the film than those given a distracting task to complete and those instructed to imagine the film. In studies with clinical samples of individuals who had experienced trauma, use of worry as a thought control strategy has been found to distinguish those with Acute Stress Disorder (ASD) from those without, (Warda & Bryant, 1998), and those with ASD who went on to develop PTSD from those who did not (Holeva, Tarrier & Wells, 2001). Finally, in a clinical sample of individuals treated for PTSD, the reduced use of worry as a response to traumatic recollections was associated with decreases in PTSD symptoms (Bryant, Moulds & Guthrie, 2001).

Insomnia is also associated with worry. Harvey (2000) compared the pre-sleep cognitions of good sleepers to those diagnosed with sleep-onset insomnia. She found that the pre-sleep cognitions of individuals with insomnia were more focused on worries and problems than those without insomnia. In a further examination of pre-sleep cognitions, Harvey and Greenall (2003) found that individuals with primary insomnia catastrophized, or, worried, about the consequences of not sleeping to a much greater degree than did good sleepers, and that this worry was associated with higher anxiety.

Semler and Harvey (2004) found that monitoring for sleep-related threat (looking at the clock and calculating how much time is left for sleeping) triggers worries about the consequences of *not* sleeping, leading to the use of safety behaviors (planning to nap the next day), which in turn perpetuates the insomnia cycle. The researchers concluded that worry is a key factor in the maintenance of sleep disturbance. Consistent with these findings, Fichten et al. (2001) found that individuals with insomnia experienced greater distress about not sleeping than did good sleepers and that negative thoughts (i.e., worries about family and work) were an important predictor of distress over not sleeping. Interestingly, the research of Bastien, Vallières and Morin (2004) indicates that the onset of insomnia coincides with the occurrence of negative events (e.g., with family, health, work/school).

Depression and GAD are highly co-morbid, but there may be an actual interplay between rumination about past events (a hallmark of depression) and worry. Rumination and worry are both verbal/linguistic activities that feature negative views and are often viewed as difficult to control. The primary differences appear to be that worry is directed towards the future, whereas rumination is past-oriented. Additionally, compared to worry rumination is associated with less focus on problem-solving and poorer confidence in problem-solving ability (Papageorgiou & Wells, 2004). However, rumination and worry are not unrelated activities. For instance, Lavender and Watkins (2002) found that rumination about past events actually increased negative thinking about the future (i.e., worry). This may help explain why in correlational studies, rumination is consistently associated with anxiety (e.g., Fresco, Fankel, Mennin, Turk & Heimberg, 2002; Harrington & Blankenship, 2002; Muris, Roelofs, Meesters & Boomsma, 2004; Nolen-Hoeksema, 2000; Starcevic, 1995).

Finally, worry may also play a role in the persistence of psychotic disorders. Morrison (2001) has proposed a model of auditory hallucinations in which he suggests that hallucinations become problematic when they are interpreted as threatening the physical or psychological integrity of the individual, as opposed to being perceived as a benign occurrence (e.g., "that was a strange sensation, I must be tired"). When hallucinations are interpreted as threatening (e.g "The Devil is talking to me"), the individual worries about their meaning, implications, and consequences. This process increases anxiety, which in turn triggers more hallucinations. Baker and Morrison (1998) found that schizophrenics with hallucinations endorsed more positive beliefs about the utility of worry than did schizophrenics without hallucinations. Similarly, Morrison and Wells (2003) found that psychotic patients reported higher beliefs about the utility of worry compared to individuals with panic disorder and controls.

Taken together, these findings indicate that GAD, whose central feature is uncontrollable worry, is highly co-morbid with many disorders. Furthermore, worry is a common feature of psychopathology in general, even if GAD is not present, this being especially true for the mood and anxiety disorders. Given this information, there are several treatment implications that should be considered. First, when treating an individual for a disorder co-morbid with GAD, it may be quite helpful to keep in mind that they will be susceptible to the attentional biases and cognitive style that characterize GAD. Specifically, they may display elevated evidence requirements (i.e., the individual requires much more evidence on which to base a decision than others would; Tallis, Eysenck & Mathews, 1991), low problem-solving confidence (Davey, 1994) and a perseverative iterative style (i.e., can readily and rapidly generate outcomes of outcomes; Davey & Levy, 1998). GAD is also associated with higher anxiety sensitivity (e.g., Floyd, Garfield & LaSota, 2005). Thus, the individual may find interoceptive or in vivo exposure exercises more difficult to tolerate.

Finally, it is important to remember that even in the absence of GAD there may still be considerable worry. To date, little research has examined the phenomenology of worry that occurs within the context of other disorders.

However, it is likely that worry shares the same characteristics of being un-controllable, as generating more problems than solutions and as increasing, rather than decreasing, anxiety. As such, strategies that are effective in managing worry in the context of GAD may be useful in treatment of other disorders in which worry is a feature. There is some empirical support for this. For example, Papageorgiou and Wells (1998) used attention training, which is a key strategy for helping individuals disengage from, or disattend to, worry, in the successful treatment of hypochondriasis. Wells and Sembi (2004a) developed a treatment protocol for PTSD whose core treatment involves identification of rumination and worry as a central problem, and which directly focuses on reducing worry through "detached mindfulness", worry postponement, and examining positive beliefs about the utility of worry. Wells and Sembi (2004b) report significant reduction of PTSD symptoms in six individuals at post-treatment, three-month, six-month, and 18-month follow-up.

In sum, at this time worry appears to be a feature of many disorders, especially the mood and anxiety disorders. Considerable research is required to directly identify the extent to which individuals without GAD worry within the context of another Axis I disorder, and to examine the similarities and differences between this worry and that which occurs in the context of GAD. Clinicians are well-advised to consider the role of pathological worry in the primary problem they are treating, and be prepared to intervene to reduce worry as a means of ameliorating the target symptoms.

REFERENCES

American Psychiatric Association (2000). *Diagnostic and Statistical Manual of Mental Disorders (Text Revision)*. New York.

Amir, N., Cashman, L. & Foa, E.B. (1997). Strategies of thought control in obsessive compulsive disorder. *Behaviour Research and Therapy*, **35**, 775–777.

Baker, C.A. & Morrison, A.P. (1998). Cognitive processes in auditory hallucinations: attributional biases and metacognition. *Psychological Medicine*, **28**, 1199–1208.

Barlow, D.H. (2002). *Anxiety and its disorders* (2nd Ed). New York: Guilford Press.

Bastien, C.H., Vallières, A. & Morin, C.M. (2004). Precipitating factors of insomnia. *Behavioral Sleep Medicine*, **2**, 50–62.

Bélanger, L., Morin, C.M., Langlois, F. & Ladouceur, R. (2004). Insomnia and generalized anxiety disorder: Effects of cognitive behavior therapy for GAD on insomnia symptoms. *Anxiety Disorders*, **18**, 561–571.

Borkovec, T.D. (1985). Worry: A potentially valuable concept. *Behaviour Research and Therapy*, **23**, 481–482.

Borkovec, T.D., Ray, W.J. & Stöber, J. (1998). Worry: A cognitive phenomenon linked to affective, physiological and interpersonal behavioral processes. *Cognitive Therapy and Research*, **22**, 561–576.

Borkovec, T.D. & Ruscio, A.M. (2001). Psychotherapy for generalized anxiety disorder. *Journal of Clinical Psychiatry*, **62**, 37–42.

Brown, T.A., Antony, M.M. & Barlow, D.H. (1995). Diagnostic comorbidity in panic disorder: effect on treatment outcome and course of comorbid diagnoses following treatment. *Journal of Consulting and Clinical Psychology*, **63**, 408–418.

Brown, T.A. & Barlow, D.H. (1992). Comorbidity among anxiety disorders: Implications for treatment and DSM-IV. *Journal of Consulting and Clinical Psychology*, **60**, 835–844.

Brown, T.A., Campbell, L.A., Lehman, C.L., Grisham, J.R. & Mancill, R.B. (2001). Current and lifetime comorbidity of the DSM-IV anxiety and mood disorders in a large clinical sample. *Journal of Abnormal Psychology*, **110**, 585–599.

Brown, T.A., O'Leary, T.A. & Barlow, D.H. (2001). Generalized anxiety disorder. In D. H. Barlow (Ed.), *Clinical handbook of psychological disorders* (3rd ed.). New York: Guilford press.

Bruce, S.E., Machan, J.T., Dyck, I. & Keller, M. (2001). Infrequency of "pure" GAD: Impact of psychiatric co-morbidity on clinical course. *Depression and Anxiety*, **14**, 219–225.

Bryant, R.A., Moulds, M. & Guthrie, R.M. (2001). Cognitive strategies and the resolution of acute stress disorder. *Journal of Traumatic Stress*, **14**, 213–219.

Craske, M.G. (1999). *Anxiety disorders: Psychological approaches to theory and treatment*. Colorado: Westview.

Davey, G.C.L. (1994). Pathological worrying as exacerbated problem-solving. In G.C.L. Davey and F. Tallis (Eds), *Worrying: Perspectives on theory, assessment and treatment* (pp. 35–60). Chichester: John Wiley & Sons, Ltd.

Davey, G.C.L. & Levy, S. (1998). Catastrophic worrying: personal inadequacy and a perseverative iterative style as features of the catastrophizing process. *Journal of Abnormal Psychology*, **107**, 576–586.

Dugas, M.J., Gosselin, P. & Ladouceur, R. (2001). Intolerance of uncertainty and worry: investigating specificity in a nonclinical sample. *Cognitive Therapy and Research*, **25**, 551–558.

Dugas, M.J. & Ladouceur, R. (1998). Analysis and treatment of generalized anxiety disorder. In V.E. Caballo (Ed), *International handbook of cognitive and behavioural treatments for psychological disorders* (pp. 197–225). Oxford: Pergamon/Elsevier.

Ehlers, A., Mayou, R.A. & Bryant, B. (2003). Cognitive predictors of posttraumatic stress disorder in children: a prospective longitudinal study. *Behaviour Research and Therapy*, **41**, 1–10.

Ehlers, A. & Steil, R. (1995). Maintenance of intrusive memories in posttraumatic stress disorder: A cognitive approach. *Behavioural and Cognitive Psychotherapy*, **23**, 217–249.

Fichten, C., Libman, E., Creti, L., Amsel, R., Sabourin, S., Brender, W. & Bailes, S. (2001). Role of thoughts during nocturnal awake times in the insomnia experience of older adults. *Cognitive Therapy and Research*, **25**, 665–692.

Floyd, M., Garfield, A. & LaSota, M.T. (2005). Anxiety sensitivity and worry. *Personality and Individual Differences*, **38**, 1223–1229.

Freeston, M.H., Ladouceur, R., Rhéaume, J., Letarte, H., Gagnon, F. and Thibodeau, N. (1994). Self-report of obsessions and worry. *Behaviour Research and Therapy*, **32**, 29–36.

Fresco, D.M., Frankel, A.N., Mennin, D.S., Turk, C.L. & Heimberg, R.G. (2002). Distinct and overlapping features of rumination and worry: the relationship of cognitive production to negative affective states. *Cognitive Therapy and Research*, **26**, 179–188.

Harrington, J.A. & Blankenship, V. (2002). Ruminative thoughts and their relationship to depression and anxiety. *Journal of Applied Social Psychology*, **32**, 465–485.

Harvey, A.G. (2000). Pre-sleep cognitive activity: A comparison of sleep-onset in insomniacs and good sleepers. *British Journal of Clinical Psychology*, **39**, 275–286.

Harvey, A.G. & Greenall, E. (2003). Catastrophic worry in primary insomnia. *Journal of Behavior Therapy*, **32**, 11–23.

Holeva, V., Tarrier, N. & Wells, A. (2001). Prevalence and predictors of acute stress disorder and PTSD following road traffic accidents: Thought control strategies and social support. *Behavior Therapy*, **32**, 65–83.

Kessler, R.C., McGonagle, K.A., Zhao, S., Nelson, C.B., Hughes, M., Eshleman, S., Wittchen, H.U. & Kendler, K.S. (1995). Lifetime and 12-month prevalence of DSM-III-R psychiatric disorders in the United States. *Archives of General Psychiatry*, **51**, 8–19.

Kushner, M.G., Abrams, K. & Borchardt, C. (2000). The relationship between anxiety disorders and alcohol use disorders: a review of major perspectives and findings. *Clinical Psychology Review*, **20**, 149–171.

Langlois, F., Freeston, M.H. & Ladouceur, R. (2000). Differences and similarities between obsessive intrusive thoughts and worry in a non-clinical population: study I. *Behaviour Research and Therapy*, **38**, 157–173.

Lavender, A. & Watkins, E. (2004). Rumination and future thinking in depression. *British Journal of Clinical Psychology*, **43**, 129–142.

Mellinger, G.D., Balter, M.B. & Uhlenhuth, E.H. (1985). Insomnia and its treatment: prevalence and correlates. *Archives of General Psychiatry*, **42**, 225–232.

Molina, S., Borkovec, T.D., Peasley, C. & Person, D. (1998). Content analysis of worrisome streams of consciousness in anxious and dysphoric participants. *Cognitive Therapy and Research*, **22**, 109–123.

Morrison, A.P. (2001). The interpretation of intrusions in psychosis: an integrative cognitive approach to hallucinations and delusions. *Behavioural and Cognitive Psychotherapy*, **29**, 257–276.

Morrison, A.P. & Wells, A. (2003). A comparison of metacognitions in patients with hallucinations, delusions, panic disorder and non-patient controls. *Behaviour Research and Therapy*, **41**, 251–256.

Muris, P., Roelofs, J., Meesters, C. & Boomsma, P. (2004). Rumination and worry in nonclinical adolescents. *Cognitive Therapy and Research*, **28**, 539–554.

Nolen-Hoeksema, S. (2000). The role of rumination in depressive disorders and mixed anxiety/depressive symptoms. *Journal of Abnormal Psychology*, **109**, 504–511.

Obsessive Compulsive Cognitions Working Group (OCCWG). (2001). Development and initial validation of the Obsessive Beliefs Questionnaire and the Interpretation of Intrusions Inventory. *Behaviour Research and Therapy*, **39**, 987–1006.

O'Neill, G.W. (1985). Is worry a valuable concept? *Behaviour Research and Therapy*, **23**, 479–480.

Papageorgiou, C. & Wells, A. (1998). Effects of attention training on hypochondriasis: A brief case analysis. *Psychological Medicine*, **28**, 193–200.

Papageorgiou, C. & Wells, A. (2004). Nature, functions and beliefs about depressive rumination. In C. Papageorgiou and A. Wells (Eds), *Depressive Rumination: Nature, theory and treatment* (pp. 3–20). Chichester: John Wiley & Sons, Ltd.

Rapee, R.R.M. (1993). Psychological factors in panic disorder. Special Issue: panic, cognitions and sensations. *Advances in Behavior Research and Therapy*, **15**, 85–102.

Roemer, L. & Orsillo, S.M. (2002). Expanding our conceptualization of and treatment for generalized anxiety disorder: Integrating mindfulness/acceptance-based approaches with existing cognitive-behavioral models. *Clinical Psychology: Science and Practice*, **9**, 54–68.

Roy-Byrne, P.P. & Katton, W. Generalized anxiety disorder in primary care: The precursor/modifier pathway to increased health care utilization. *Journal of Clinical Psychiatry*, **58 (suppl 3)**, 34–38.

Rygh, J.L. & Sanderson, W.C. (2004). *Treating generalized anxiety disorder.* New York: Guilford.

Sanavio, P. (1988). Obsessions and compulsions: the Padua Inventory. *Behaviour Research and Therapy*, **23**, 169–177.

Semler, C.N. & Harvey, A.G. (2004). An investigation of monitoring for sleep-related threat in primary insomnia. *Behaviour Research and Therapy*, **42**, 1403–1420.

Starcevic, V. (1995). Pathological worry in major depression: a preliminary report. *Behaviour Research and Therapy*, **33**, 55–56.

Stein, D.J. (2002). Comorbidity in generalized anxiety disorder: Impact and implications. *Journal of Clinical Psychiatry*, **62 (suppl 11)**, 29–34.

Tallis, F. & DeSilva, P. (1992). Worry and obsessional symptoms: A correlational analysis. *Behaviour Research and Therapy*, **30**, 103–105.

Tallis, F., Eysenck, M. & Mathews, A. (1991). Elevated evidence requirements and worry. *Behaviour Research and Therapy*, **12**, 21–27.

Turner, S.M., Beidel, D.C. & Stanley, M.A. (1992). Are obsessional thoughts and worry different cognitive phenomena? *Clinical Psychology Review*, **12**, 257–270.

Warda, G. & Bryant, R.A. (1998). Thought control strategies in acute stress disorder. *Behaviour Research and Therapy*, **36**, 1171–1175.

Warwick, H.M.C. & Salkovskis, P.M. (1990). Hypochondriasis. *Behaviour Research and Therapy*, **28**, 105–117.

Wells, A. (1994). Attention and the control of worry. In G. Davey and F. Tallis (Eds), *Worrying: Perspectives on theory, assessment and treatment* (pp. 91–114). Chichester, UK: John Wiley & Sons, Ltd.

Wells, A. (1997). *Cognitive therapy of anxiety disorders: A practice manual and conceptual guide.* Chichester, UK: John Wiley & Sons, Ltd.

Wells, A. & Matthews, G. (1994). *Attention and emotion: A clinical perspective.* Hove, UK: Erlbaum.

Wells, A. & Papageorgiou, C. (1998). Relationships between worry, obsessive compulsive symptoms and meta-cognitive beliefs. *Behaviour Research and Therapy*, **36**, 899–913.

Wells, A. & Papageorgiou, C. (1995). Worry and the incubation of intrusive images following stress. *Behaviour Research and Therapy*, **33**, 579–583.

Wells, A. & Sembi, S. (2004a). Metacognitive therapy for PTSD: a core treatment manual. *Cognitive and Behavioral Practice*, **11**, 365–377.

Wells, A. & Sembi, S. (2004b). Metacognitive therapy for PTSD: a preliminary investigation of a new brief treatment. *Journal of Behavior Therapy and Experimental Psychiatry*, **35**, 307–318.

Whittchen, H.U., Zhao, S., Kessler, R.C., et al. (1994). DSM-IIIR generalized anxiety disorder in the National Comorbidity Survey. *Archives of General Psychiatry*, **51**, 355–364.

Chapter 4

WORRY AND INFORMATION-PROCESSING

Gerald Matthews and Gregory J. Funke

INTRODUCTION

From concerns about job performance, to anxiety before a test, to apprehension before a presentation, people commonly worry about the outcomes of future events (Tallis, Davey & Capuzzo, 1994). Worry has been previously defined as an anticipatory cognitive process involving thoughts and images that contain fear-producing content related to possible traumatic events and their potentially catastrophic implications, which are rehearsed repeatedly without being resolved (e.g., Borkovec, Ray & Stöber, 1978). Of key importance is that worry is primarily anticipatory in nature, relating mainly to future possibilities and the threats they pose.

According to Eysenck (1992), worry has three major functions: alarm, prompt, and preparation. Within his model, upon detection of an internal or external threat, the alarm function introduces information about the threat into conscious awareness. The prompt function then activates threat-related thoughts and images in long-term memory, and the preparation function supports the person's efforts to devise a solution to the problem (task-focused coping) or emotionally prepare for the expected negative consequences (emotion-focused coping). However, despite these adaptive functions, worry frequently appears to have maladaptive consequences. Worry is known to interfere with various cognitive processes that contribute to effective task performance (Zeidner, 1998). Excessive worry is also a common feature of various anxiety disorders, especially Generalized Anxiety Disorder (GAD: Wells, 2000).

This chapter reviews information-processing approaches to understanding worry and its behavioral consequences. We will develop three central themes. First, it is essential to distinguish *trait worry* from *state worry*. Trait worry refers to the person's general disposition to become worried,

Worry and Its Psychological Disorders: Theory, Assessment and Treatment. Edited by G. C. L. Davey and A. Wells. © 2006 John Wiley & Sons, Ltd.

especially in threatening situations. Cognitive theory (e.g., Beck & Clark, 1997; Matthews & Wells, 2004) supposes that traits of this kind reflect the content and accessibility of knowledge structures in long-term memory (LTM). Thus, to understand why some people are more worry-prone than others (and vulnerable to clinical pathology), it is necessary to investigate the nature of stable self-referent knowledge representations. State worry refers to the immediate experience of threat-related cognitions intruding into conscious awareness. In many contexts, including task performance, we may expect that state worry will be a more proximal influence than trait worry on information-processing and behavior (Zeidner, 1998). Traits and states may be interrelated within an interactional or transactional approach that sees the state as generated by the interaction of the trait with situational stressors (Matthews, Deary & Whiteman, 2003).

Our second theme is the interrelationship between worry and stress processes. Transactional theory (Lazarus, 1999) identifies appraisal, choice, and regulation of coping strategy as cognitive processes that shape the person's response to external demands, and concomitant emotional change. We also highlight the importance of *metacognitive* processes (Wells, 2000), referring to the person's appraisals and regulation of their own thoughts. Application of the transactional perspective to worry may afford greater understanding of how situational appraisals and stable self-knowledge interact to produce worry states. A focus on stress processes may also contribute to investigating how worry states may influence concurrent information-processing through mechanisms such as "cognitive interference" (Sarason, Sarason & Pierce, 1996) and refocusing of attention.

The third theme is the three-way dynamic interplay between external demands, worry-related cognitions, and the person's efforts at behavioral control of the situation. As elaborated in the Wells and Matthews (1994) theory of emotional disturbance, worry is often associated with dysfunctional patterns of person-situation interaction that serve to perpetuate the worry state and block adaptive coping. Such cyclic interactions are especially characteristic of pathological conditions.

The chapter is structured as follows. We first differentiate trait and state worry constructs, and then review the key processes that mediate the trait-state association, including appraisal, coping, and metacognition. Next, we review the consequences of worry for information-processing and performance. Finally, we outline the Self-Regulatory Executive Function (S-REF: Wells & Matthews, 1994) model that integrates various cognitive features of worry.

TRAITS AND STATE CONSTRUCTS

Worry may be conceptualized as both a stable trait and as a transient mental state. By contrast with research on trait and state anxiety (e.g., Eysenck, 1992), worry research has focused primarily on trait assessments, such as the Penn State Worry Questionnaire (PSWQ: Meyer et al., 1990). State worry has been investigated through thought sampling (Smallwood et al., 2004), measures of allied constructs, such as cognitive interference (Sarason et al., 1996), ad hoc indices, and multidimensional state assessment (Matthews, Campbell et al., 2002). We note briefly that there is considerable conceptual and empirical overlap between worry and rumination (e.g., Papageorgiou & Wells, 1999, Watkins, 2004; see Matthews & Wells, 2004, for a review of cognitive process models of rumination).

Trait worry represents an outgrowth of the more broadly-defined construct of trait anxiety, which is seen as a facet of the personality superfactor of neuroticism (Matthews et al., 2003). Thus, at least in part, trait worry is an aspect of these broader traits. Laboratory studies (Eysenck, 1992) and clinical investigations (e.g., Beck & Clark, 1997) indicate that anxiety traits may be conceptualized in primarily cognitive terms. Matthews (2004; Matthews et al., 2000) relates N and trait anxiety to multiple cognitive biases, including negative self-evaluations, elevated threat monitoring, attentional narrowing, predicting threat likelihood, and coping through emotion-focus and rumination on threat. Anxiety traits are given a functional unity by the adaptive goals linked to the trait (Matthews & Zeidner, 2004), i.e., elevated concerns about personal security, especially in regard to threats to self-esteem and social status. We may expect that individuals high in trait worry will share this adaptation. However, there may also be stable qualities of cognition that are unique to worry, such as its verbal content and its function of cognitive avoidance of threat (Borkovec et al., 1998).

Matthews et al. (2002) propose a broadly-based psychometric definition of worry. Factor analysis of various states of affect, motivation, and cognition identified a "state worry" factor defined by cognitive interference scales, but also by high private self-focus of attention and low self-esteem. This approach highlights internal focusing of attention and awareness of potentially negative evaluations by others as key elements of worry states. The factor analysis differentiated worry, as a purely cognitive state dimension, from further dimensions of task engagement and distress, that integrate elements of affect and cognition. Matthews and Zeidner (2004) propose that worry states indicate a "transactional theme", as defined by Lazarus (1999). In the case of worry, the state signals that the priority is to pull back mentally from the immediate task at hand to reevaluate its personal relevance and significance.

ETIOLOGY OF WORRY STATES: A COGNITIVE PERSPECTIVE

Next, we consider how the self-referent knowledge that supports dispositional worry traits is translated into states of worry. Interactionist theories of personality (see Matthews et al., 2003) imply that worry traits relate to various biases in the content and organization of self-knowledge, as represented in LTM. These memory structures remain latent until activated, for example, by an external threat stimulus (e.g., Moretti & Higgins, 1999). The worry state ensues when the activation of self-knowledge generates a high frequency of self-referent, predominantly negative thoughts related to themes of threat and personal insecurity.

There are multiple sources of cognitive bias that may elevate state worry in persons high in trait worry. Some biases are associated with neuroticism and trait anxiety, including negative self-beliefs, evidenced by their correlations with measures of self-concept, self-efficacy, self-esteem, and allied constructs (Matthews, et al., 2000, 2003). Following Beck and Clark (1997), these biases have been conceptualized in terms of individual differences in the self-schema, the structured set of propositions held in LTM, although implicit, procedural self-knowledge may be equally important (Wells & Matthews, 1994).

Worry has been related specifically to the content and accessibility of threat schemas stored by the individual in long-term memory. Worry related schemas may be organized around two types of themes: internal threats (e.g., negative self-evaluation) and external threats (e.g., criticism from others: Vasey, 1993). In turn, once activated, these schemas may cause a heightened vigilance for threats. More specifically, worries predominantly reflect themes of personal inadequacies and insecurities in regards to social evaluations (Kendall & Ingram, 1987; Davey & Levy, 1998).

Self-regulative theories (e.g., Carver & Scheier, 2000; Wells & Matthews, 1994) propose that discrepancies between ideal and actual status will initiate attempts to minimize the self-discrepancy. The various threat-related beliefs of the dispositional worrier are prone to instigate periods of self-regulation aimed at increasing personal security. Such self-regulation is supported by the appraisal and coping processes described by the transactional theory of stress and emotion (e.g., Lazarus, 1999), as well as metacognitive processes (Wells, 2000). Next, we survey how dispositional worry generates immediate situational worry via three key classes of mediating process: (1) encoding and appraisal, (2) coping, and (3) metacognition and mood-regulation.

Encoding and Appraisal

The worry process begins with the detection of a potential threat. Threat detection may be triggered by external stimuli (being reminded of an upcoming worrisome event) or generated internally (remembering the date of the event). The early stages of processing threat stimuli are influenced by attentional processes, in that selection and prioritization of threat stimuli is likely to increase worry. It is well-established that general anxiety is associated with a selective attention bias towards detection of threat related information (MacLeod & Rutherford, 2004). The source of bias is often seen as pre-attentive and "automatic," although Matthews & Wells (2000) review evidence suggesting a role for voluntary search for threat. Indeed, prioritization of threat processing may be supported by multiple component processes such as voluntary search for threat (Matthews & Harley, 1996), delayed disengagement from threat (Derryberry & Reed, 2002), and automatic threat encoding (Mathews & Mackintosh, 1998).

Another feature of selective attentional bias is that it may have *causal* effects on the etiology of anxiety and worry. MacLeod and Rutherford (2004) review several studies suggesting that inducing attentional and interpretative biases elevates vulnerability to anxiety. For example, subjects within the normal range of trait anxiety may be trained to complete ambiguous sentences consistent with either a threatening or non-threatening interpretation of the sentence. Subjects trained to interpret ambiguous material as threatening also experienced higher levels of state anxiety. Other studies (MacLeod & Rutherford, 2004) have induced biases in selective attention by consistently presenting attentional probe stimuli in close proximity to threatening words. Subjects trained in this way showed a more intense anxiety response to performing a subsequent, stressful task than subjects in whom an attentional bias away from threat was induced. A limitation of these studies is that they did not differentiate worry from emotional components of the anxiety response. It is generally unclear whether worry plays any role distinct from general anxiety in cognitive bias.

Following detection is appraisal, which refers to encoding the personal significance of a stimulus. In the case of threat, the person may make both a "primary" appraisal of threat, together with a "secondary" appraisal of personal capability to cope with the threat (Lazarus, 1999). Because appraisal is guided by the schemas representing self-knowledge, the threat schemas associated with dispositional worry are liable to amplify appraisal of threat, and appraisal of personal ineffectiveness in the face of danger. When a worrier considers a possible threat-related scenario, they tend to exaggerate the likelihood and magnitude of that scenario's negative implications (Vasey & Borkovec, 1992).

Worry may also be driven by an interpretive bias in which ambiguous cues are more likely to be construed as threatening. Rather than showing a detection bias, worriers may tend to select more threatening interpretations of cues relating to possible aversive events, an effect demonstrated in anxiety research (Calvo & Castillo, 2001). Related to this bias is the personality trait *intolerance of uncertainty*, which is defined as the excessive tendency of an individual to consider it unacceptable that a negative event may occur, however small the probability of its occurrence (Dugas, Schwartz & Francis, 2004). Intolerance of uncertainty predicts worry above positive beliefs about worry, negative problem orientation, and cognitive avoidance (Dugas et al., 2004). Thus, one source of elevated state worry in the dispositional trait worrier is the perception of uncertain events as more threatening and less manageable, leading to a greater need for further cognition and problem-solving. In support of this hypothesis, Tallis, Eysenck and Mathews (1991) report that worriers require more information before arriving at a decision, which suggests that they have elevated evidence requirements. Worriers also display more difficulties completing tasks that are ambiguous in nature compared to non-worriers (Metzger et al., 1993). Finally, studies have shown that targeting intolerance of uncertainty in the treatment of excessive worry leads to changes in level of worry, and that changes in intolerance of uncertainty generally precede changes in worry over the course of treatment (Dugas & Ladouceur, 2000).

So far as secondary appraisal is concerned, various studies (e.g., Craske, 2003; Kendall & Ingram, 1987) have shown that chronic worry relates to perceptions of personal incompetence and lack of confidence in problem-solving abilities. Worriers tend to have low confidence in their problem-solving abilities: studies indicate that poor problem-solving confidence is highly correlated with frequency measures of trait worrying (Davey, 1994). This problem may be further compounded by studies which report that worriers score significantly higher on measures of self-consciousness than do non-worriers (Meyer et al., 1990; Pruzinsky & Borkovec, 1990). In other words, worriers are overly-concerned about negative evaluation in social circumstances elicited by their (perceived) personal failings, and they are constantly on guard for even the most ambiguous validation of those feelings.

Dynamic factors extend awareness of worrisome outcomes following the occurrence of an anticipated threatening possibility. The generation of progressively more negative chains of outcomes as a result of a threat-related scenario has been termed *catastrophizing* (Vasey & Borkovec, 1992). Worriers differ from non-worriers in that they may be prone to generate longer sequences of worrisome outcomes following the occurrence of a threat (Vasey & Borkovec, 1992). Worriers may have tightly organized clusters of information related to their concerns and threat schemas stored in long-term memory (Provencher, Freeston, Dugas & Ladouceur, 2000). Thus, the strong links between cluster elements will result in low activation thresholds for cluster elements, and spreading activation will tend to activate other nodes within the cluster following activation of the first. Spreading activation throughout cluster elements would enable worriers to generate longer chains of negative outcomes. Negative mood state may tend to maintain this catastrophizing process (Johnston & Davey, 1997).

Coping

Dispositional worry also biases the form of coping adopted in the face of threat. In part, such bias follows from bias in secondary appraisal; threats appraised as beyond personal control are likely to attract emotion—rather than task-focused coping (Lazarus, 1999). In other words, the person is liable to engage in strategies such as self-criticism, for failing to anticipate the threat, and wishful thinking, rather than taking direct problem-focused action. This style of coping is typical of trait anxiety and neuroticism (Matthews et al., 2000). Further characteristics of dispositional worry may dispose the person towards avoidant coping. First, verbal processing of worrisome thought may inhibit the negative emotional experiences that accompany those thoughts, so that worry may be employed as an avoidance coping strategy (Borkovec et al., 1998). Such strategies may prevent current emotional processing without altering the negative emotional meaning of the source worries, thereby creating maintaining conditions for emotional disturbance.

Secondly, due to the verbal nature of worry, the content of worries may be expressed in abstractions that involve less concrete detail than that provided by imagery. Stöber (1997) has demonstrated that worrisome thought is indeed less concrete. Participants were asked to elaborate on various topics; results showed that elaborations on worry topics were of lower concreteness and lessened imagery quality as compared to non-worry topics. Stöber (1997) argued that, in response to initial aversive images, worry mitigates the vividness of further negative images and thereby mutes physiological reaction to their occurrence.

Metacognition

Thus far, we have conceptualized the biasing effects of dispositional worry largely in terms of the linear sequence of processing described by transactional theory (Lazarus, 1999), in which a stage (or stages) of stimulus evaluation (appraisal) are followed by stages of choosing and executing a coping strategy. However, there are also important metacognitive processes that modulate the sequence of processing, via internal feedback loops. Analogous to the distinction between appraisal and coping, metacognition may be decomposed into monitoring (of thoughts) and control activities intended to influence thinking (Mazzoni & Nelson, 1998), processes that are linked reciprocally. Dispositional worry may relate to biases in both types of metacognitive process that enhance the tendency to direct cognitive effort towards solving the problems posed by appraisals of threat.

An important clinical feature of worry is that its content often refers to worry itself; experiencing intrusive thoughts may itself be a focus for worry (Wells, 2000). Such metacognitions may be negative ("worrying could make me go crazy") or positive ("if I worry I'll be prepared"). Wells and colleagues have developed several scales for metacognitive traits, including "metaworry" (worry about worry: Wells, 1994), positive and negative beliefs about worry (Wells & Cartwright-Hatton, 2004), and typical strategies used for thought control (Wells & Davies, 2004). Evidence reviewed by Wells (2000) links each type of trait to dispositional worry. For example, in a study of thought control the PSWQ related to thought control strategies of deliberate worrying and punishment (for thinking unacceptable thoughts) (Wells & Davies, 1994). Metaworry has been found to predict trait worry, even with trait anxiety and level of worry about external threats controlled (Nuevo, Montorio & Borkovec, 2004; Wells & Carter, 1999). Positive beliefs are uniquely related to worry, beyond symptoms of negative affect (Francis & Dugas, 2004).

The metacognitive beliefs related to importance of monitoring thoughts associated with dispositional worry serve to focus attention on threat-related cognitions. Positive beliefs about the utility of worry, a feature of various anxiety traits (Wells, 2000), may motivate continued worrying. Regarding control, metacognitive traits take the form of preferred strategies for regulating thoughts and moods, as well as explicit beliefs. Watkins (2004) found that worry relates to increased effort used in dismissing intrusive thoughts, which may be an instance of avoidance coping. Dispositional worry and neuroticism are also linked to preferences for using worry and self-punishment as thought control strategies (Wells, 2000). Similar to holding positive beliefs about worry, voluntary choice of worrying will directly increase frequency of worry. The role of self-punishment in amplifying worry is less clear but it may integrate additional negative self-referent beliefs into the threat schemas.

Recent Evidence From Studies of the DSSQ

A limitation of some of the empirical studies we have cited is that they have not included a standardized worry state measure. Work from our laboratory, using the Dundee Stress State Questionnaire (DSSQ: Matthews et al., 2002), is exploring how dispositional worry constructs generate state worry. Matthews, Hillyard and Campbell (1999), in a study of test anxiety in students, showed that, at the trait level, there were two distinct cognitive factors that correlated with dispositional evaluation-worry. One factor represented a general dimension of heightened metacognition, defined by perceived uncontrollability of thoughts, positive and negative beliefs about thoughts, and meta-worry. A second factor of adaptive coping was defined most strongly by higher use of task-focused coping and reduced use of avoidance. Interestingly, emotion-focused coping, in the sense of self-criticism and wishful thinking, loaded primarily on metacognition, but also negatively on adaptive coping. A regression analysis showed that both factors independently contributed to the prediction of dispositional worry. Data were also collected on state worry responses to a significant university examination, using the DSSQ. The general metacognition factor predicted task-related and task-irrelevant cognitive interference, two of the core dimensions defining state worry. Several of the metacognition scales, including both positive and negative beliefs, predicted state self-consciousness, another key state worry component.

Other recent studies have focused on the role of situational appraisal and coping factors as predictors of states of worry. These performance studies have shown some striking dissociations between distress and worry responses to task stressors (Matthews, Campbell et al., 2002). High workload tasks, such as highly time-pressured working memory tasks, produce elevated distress (anxious emotion and reduced confidence), but also suppress worry (decreased cognitive interference and self-consciousness, elevated self-esteem). In fact, state worry typically declines during performance of various tasks, in line with its supposed anticipatory function, but it remains relatively high in tasks that threaten the person's sense of competence (impossible anagrams: Matthews et al., submitted) and tasks characterized by tedium and monotony (Matthews et al., 2002).

These studies have also investigated the relationship between worry states and situational appraisal and coping. Table 4.1 summarizes results from three recent studies, that used the DSSQ to measure worry following simulated customer service work (Study 1: Matthews & Falconer, 2002), simulated vehicle driving (Study 2: Funke, 2004) and performance of laboratory tasks including vigilance and working memory (Study 3: Matthews et al., submitted). Despite the very different tasks employed in these studies, the correlations between post-task worry and the cognitive process variables were highly consistent. Worry related most strongly to threat appraisal, lack of controllability of the situation, and use of emotion-focused coping. Interestingly, task-focus was also modestly but consistently associated with worry. Although some analyses (e.g., Borkovec et al., 1998)

Table 4.1   Correlations between DSSQ post-task worry and measures of situational appraisal and coping in three experimental studies

	Study 1 ($N = 91$)	Study 2 ($N = 168$)	Study 3 ($N = 200$)
Appraisal			
Threat	.54**	.33**	.36**
Challenge	.30**	.25**	.04
Controllability	−.39**	−.49**	−.44**
Coping			
Task-Focus	.36**	.20**	.14*
Emotion-Focus	.62**	.58**	.62**
Avoidance	.15	.24**	.51**

Note: $*p < .05, **p < .01.$

have related worry to avoidance coping, the worry—avoidance correlation showed some variability across studies, an issue that may require further investigation. In general, though, these findings suggest that worry is sensitive to various situational cognitions, in line with Matthews et al.'s (2002) view that worry signals attempts to adapt to external demands by reevaluating the personal relevance of the task situation.

WORRY AND TASK PERFORMANCE

Wells and Matthews (1994) point out that anxiety may have both direct and indirect effects on information-processing, attention, and performance. "Direct" effects are those that reflect the person's motivated attempts to cope with perceived threats and pressures. The prime example is the bias in selective attention towards threat associated with general anxiety. Worry may generate a feedback process in which bias in selective attention elevates awareness of threat and worry, which in turn maintains the focus of attention on sources of threat (Matthews & Wells, 2000). However, Yovel and Mineka (2005) found that general anxiety predicted selective attention bias for subliminally presented emotional Stroop stimuli, but the PSWQ did not. Worry may tend to affect later processing stages such as stimulus interpretation, metacognition, and volitional appraisal and coping processes more strongly than these early encoding processes. A recent study (Reidy, 2004) also suggests that trait anxiety may bias memory, by enhancing recall for statements concerning worry. Reidy attributed the finding to bias in thought content—relatively more worry in high trait anxiety—that leads to effects of trait anxiety on the organization of memory.

Given that worry has a preparatory function (Eysenck, 1992), it might be expected that worry has some beneficial effects also. Indeed, Luu, Tucker and Derryberry (1998) assert that anxiety and worry about task performance may be linked to success in occupations requiring well planned and regulated behavior. This viewpoint has been generally supported in studies of financial service salesmen (Corr & Gray, 1995) and managers (Perkins & Corr, 2005), but only for professionals with a high degree of cognitive ability. For professionals with a low degree of cognitive ability, worry is negatively correlated with job performance, indicating that cognitive ability may act as a moderator in the relationship between worry and task performance (Corr & Gray, 1995; Perkins & Corr, 2005).

Indirect effects of worry relate to the unintended consequences of directing mental effort, attentional resources and/or working memory to processing personal concerns, rather than the task at hand. The deleterious effects of such cognitive interference are well-known (see, e.g., Zeidner, 1998; Zeidner & Matthews, 2005), and we will not elaborate on them here. However, we will briefly highlight recent research that presents a more nuanced picture of cognitive interference. In general, self-referent thinking may be especially detrimental to task-focused attention: Kurosawa and Harackiewicz (1995) found that cognitive interference impaired performance of test anxious students primarily when self-focused attention was induced through a videotaping manipulation. However, the content of interfering thoughts may also be important. Smallwood et al. (2004) examined both task-unrelated and task-related thoughts during performance of sustained attention tasks, using a thought-sampling methodology as well as questionnaires. Task-unrelated thoughts appeared to relate to momentary lapses in attention, whereas task-related thoughts seemed to accompany attempts at strategic control of attention, and were associated with false positive responses.

Research on evaluative anxiety (Zeidner & Matthews, 2005) shows that cognitive interference is not necessarily a direct causal influence on performance impairment. There are some test anxious individuals whose worries are realistic (Zeidner, 1998). They are aware that they are poorly prepared for the test, and their lack of subject knowledge concurrently influences both cognitive interference and test performance. In addition, studies of anxiety in athletes suggest a role for metacognition as a moderator factor. Some athletes appear to find anxiety symptoms motivating and may perform better as a consequence. Hatzigeorgiadis and Biddle (2001) found that performance worries related to increases in effort for athletes holding higher goal attainment expectancies, but decreases in effort for those with lower goal attainment expectancies. Thus, high levels of worry often lead to performance decrements, but the person's beliefs about worry, especially as a source of motivation, may have a moderating effect.

THE S-REF MODEL OF WORRY

We conclude with a brief overview of an integrated cognitive model of attention and emotional distress that accommodates many of the empirical findings previously discussed. The S-REF model (Matthews & Wells, 2000; Wells & Matthews, 1994) begins with a three-level cognitive architecture comprising (1) stable declarative and procedural self-knowledge, (2) an executive system implementing controlled processing of self-referent information, including appraisal and coping processes, and (3) a set of lower level networks supporting stimulus-driven, "automatic" processing. The executive is activated by self-discrepancies that elicit reappraisal of the stimulus and a search for viable coping options. The processing routines run by the executive are shaped by generic routines accessed from self-knowledge, including metacognitive self-knowledge that assigns meaning to the person's awareness of their own thoughts, and may initiate thought control strategies. The executive influences behavior by biasing ongoing lower-level processing. It continues to operate until the self-discrepancy is removed.

Within such a system, worry states represent prolonged activity of the self-referent executive system as it attempts to resolve self-discrepancy related to themes of threat and personal vulnerability. The S-REF model isolates several independent cognitive factors that may increase the likelihood and duration of state worry episodes:

(1) The accessibility and organization in memory of items of self-knowledge pertaining to threat that bias selective attention and appraisal, and heighten threat salience. These include self-knowledge that guides secondary appraisal of personal ineffectiveness (cf. Craske, 2003).
(2) Metacognitive beliefs that focus attention on internal thoughts and their apparent consequences (Wells, 2000).
(3) Dynamic factors that perpetuate awareness of self-discrepancy, including intolerance of uncertainty (Dugas et al., 2004), elevated evidence requirements (Tallis et al., 1991), and spreading activation processes that support catastrophizing (Provencher et al., 2000).
(4) Preferences for coping through such processes as active monitoring for threat (though cf., Yovel & Mineka, 2005), and emotion-focused strategies such as self-criticism and avoidance.

Stable biases of these various kinds cause individual differences in dispositional worry, overlapping somewhat with general trait anxiety and neuroticism (Matthews et al., 2000). Importantly, traits relate to packages of biases that may be located in multiple, independent components of the architecture, given unity by their common functional orientation towards, in the case of dispositional worry, anticipation and preparation for threat (Matthews et al., 2003; Matthews & Zeidner, 2004). Traits such as neuroticism and dispositional metacognitive beliefs influence state worry in interaction with situational factors that may facilitate or inhibit the various process factors just listed.

The role of worry processes in clinical anxiety pathology is largely beyond the scope of this chapter (see Matthews & Wells, 2000; Wells, 2000 for more detailed accounts), but we will indicate two differences between normal and pathological states of elevated worry. First, recent work using the DSSQ shows that worry and emotional distress are rather easily dissociated in experimental studies in nonclinical samples. The modest correlations (0.2–0.3) typically observed in these studies represent the influence on the two state dimensions of personality traits such as neuroticism on both dimensions, as well as the effects of emotion-focused coping. By contrast, worry and anxious emotion may be more strongly interrelated in clinical patients. Wells' (2000) model of GAD suggests that metaworry itself is a source of distress, and the person's awareness of their own emotional state may breed further worries.

Second, dynamic person-situation interaction that promotes perseverative worry may be a unique feature of clinical anxiety (Wells, 2000; Wells & Matthews, 1994). In particular, worry may substitute for other more effective forms of coping so that the person never engages with the outside world in order to address the problem directly, with several harmful consequences. The person foregoes the opportunity to acquire the skills needed for problem-solving—and the confidence to deploy those skills when threatened—maintaining beliefs in personal ineffectiveness. Continued worry, without any problem resolution, is also likely to strengthen and elaborate the threat schemas that initially contributed to vulnerability to worry, blocking adaptive restructuring of self-knowledge. By contrast, subclinical worriers retain more flexibility in the allocation of attention that interrupts the worry cycle.

Finally, the S-REF model accommodates the various consequences of worry for performance previously described. "Direct" consequences of worry stem from its functional role in supporting threat preparation, for example in focusing attention on perceived threats. Positive effects of worry may reflect somewhat idiosyncratic metacognitive beliefs about worry as a motivating force. "Indirect" consequences of worry are a consequence of the drain on available attentional resources and working memory resulting from self-referent executive processing.

CONCLUSION

Both trait and state worry relate to multiple biases in information-processing and cognition, including a general tendency towards various forms of negative self-referent thinking. Key attributes of worry include accessibility and content of threat schemas, intolerance of uncertainty, appraisals of personal incompetence in handling threats, catastrophizing, use of worry as an avoidance coping strategy, and distinctive metacognitions and thought control strategies. Worry relates to multiple biases that may have a functional unity through supporting an adaptation to perceived threat. Worry represents an orientation to the demands and challenges of life that prioritizes anticipation and preparation for threats. As functional analyses of worry have emphasized, anticipation may sometimes be adaptive. However, this adaptive strategy also carries various risks related to excessive attention to potential threats, interference with beneficial emotional processing, harmful metacognitions, and vulnerability to dysfunctional interactions with the outside world that promote cognitive distortions and prolong cycles of worry.

REFERENCES

Beck, A.T. & Clark, D.A. (1997). An information processing model of anxiety: Automatic and strategic processes. *Behaviour Research & Therapy*, **35**, 49–58.

Borkovec, T.D., Ray, W.J. & Stöber, J. (1998). Worry: A cognitive phenomenon intimately linked to affective, physiological, and interpersonal behavioral processes. *Cognitive Therapy and Research*, **22**, 561–576.

Calvo, M.G. & Castillo, M.D. (2001) Bias in predictive inferences during reading. *Discourse Processes*, **32**, 43–71.

Carver, C.S. & Scheier, M.F. (2000). Autonomy and self regulation. *Psychological Inquiry*, **11**, 284–291.

Craske, M.G. (2003). *Origins of phobias and anxiety disorders: Why more women than men?* Boston: Elsevier.

Corr, P.J. & Gray, J.A. (1995). Attributional style, socialization and cognitive ability as predictors of sales success: A predictive validity study. *Personality and Individual Differences*, **18**, 241–252.

Davey, G.C.L. (1994). Pathological worry as exacerbated problem solving. In G.C.L. Davey & F. Tallis (Eds), *Worrying: Perspectives on theory, assessment, and treatment*. Chichester, UK: John Wiley & Sons, Ltd.

Davey, G.C.L. & Levy, S. (1998). Catastrophic worrying: Personal inadequacy and a perseverative iterative style as features of the catastrophizing process. *Journal of Abnormal Psychology*, **107**, 576–586.

Derryberry, D. & Reed, M.A. (2002). Anxiety-related attentional biases and their regulation by attentional control. *Journal of Abnormal Psychology*, **111**, 225–236.

Dugas, M.J. & Ladouceur, R. (2000). Treatment of GAD: Targeting intolerance of uncertainty in two types of worry. *Behavior Modification*, **24**, 635–657.

Dugas, M.J., Schwartz, A. & Francis, K. (2004). Intolerance of uncertainty, worry, and depression. *Cognitive Therapy & Research*, **28**, 835–842.

Eysenck, M.W. (1992). *Anxiety: The cognitive perspective*, Hillsdale, NJ: Erlbaum.

Francis, K. & Dugas, M.J. (2004). Assessing positive beliefs about worry: Validation of a structured interview. *Personality & Individual Differences*, **37**, 405–415.

Hatzigeorgiadis, A. & Biddle, S.J.H. (2001). Athletes' perceptions of how cognitive interference during competition influences concentration and effort. *Anxiety, Stress & Coping: An International Journal*, **14**, 411–429.

Johnston, W.M. & Davey, G.C.L. (1997). The psychological impact of negative TV news bulletins: The catastrophizing of personal worries. *British Journal of Psychology*, **88**, 85–91.

Kendall, P.C. & Ingram, R.E. (1987). The future for cognitive assessment of anxiety: Let's get specific. In L. Michaelson & L.M. Ascher (Eds), *Anxiety and stress disorders: Cognitive-behavioural assessment and treatment*. New York: Guilford Press.

Kurosawa, K. & Harackiewicz, J.M. (1995). Test anxiety, self-awareness, and cognitive interference: A process analysis. *Journal of Personality*, **63**, 931–951.

Lazarus, R.S. (1999). *Stress and emotion: A new synthesis*. New York: Springer Verlag.

Luu, P., Tucker, D.M. & Derryberry, D. (1998). Anxiety and the motivational basis of working memory. *Cognitive Therapy & Research*, **22**, 577–594.

MacLeod, C. & Rutherford, E. (2004). Information-processing approaches: Assessing the selective functioning of attention, interpretation, and retrieval. In R.G. Heimberg, C.L. Turk & D.S. Mennin (Eds), *Generalized Anxiety Disorder: Advances in research and practice* (pp. 109–142). New York: Guilford Press.

Mathews, A. & Mackintosh, B. (1998). A cognitive model of selective processing in anxiety. *Cognitive Therapy & Research*, **22**, 539–560.

Mathews, A. & MacLeod, C. (2002). Induced processing biases have causal effects on anxiety. *Cognition & Emotion*, **16**, 331–354.

Matthews, G. (2004). Neuroticism from the top down: Psychophysiology and negative emotionality. In R. Stelmack (Ed.), *On the psychobiology of personality: Essays in honor of Marvin Zuckerman* (pp. 249–266). Amsterdam: Elsevier Science.

Matthews, G., Emo, A.K., Funke, G., Zeidner, M., Roberts, R.D. & Costa P.T., Jr. (submitted). *Emotional intelligence, personality, and task induced stress*.

Matthews, G., Campbell, S.E., Falconer, S., Joyner, L.A., Huggins, J., Gilliland, K., Grier, R. & Warm, J.S. (2002). Fundamental dimensions of subjective state in performance settings: Task engagement, distress, and worry. *Emotion*, **2**, 315–340.

Matthews, G., Deary, I.J. & Whiteman, M.C. (2003) *Personality traits* (2nd ed.). Cambridge: Cambridge University Press.

Matthews, G. & Harley, T.A. (1996). Connectionist models of emotional distress and attentional bias. *Cognition & Emotion*, **10**, 561–600.

Matthews, G., Hillyard, E.J. & Campbell, S.E. (1999) Metacognition and maladaptive coping as components of test anxiety. *Clinical Psychology and Psychotherapy*, **6**, 111–125.

Matthews, G., Schwean, V.L., Campbell, S.E., Saklofske, D.H. & Mohamed, A.A.R. (2000) Personality, self-regulation and adaptation: A cognitive-social framework. In M. Boekarts, P.R. Pintrich & M. Zeidner (Eds), *Handbook of self-regulation* (pp. 171–207). New York: Academic.

Matthews, G. & Wells, A. (2000). Attention, automaticity, and affective disorder. *Behavior Modification*, **24**, 69–93.

Matthews, G. & Wells, A. (2004) Rumination, depression, and metacognition: The S-REF model. In C. Papageorgiou & A. Wells (Eds), *Rumination: Nature, theory, and treatment* (pp. 125–151). Chichester, UK: John Wiley & Sons, Ltd.

Matthews, G. & Zeidner, M. (2004) Traits, states and the trilogy of mind: An adaptive perspective on intellectual functioning. In D. Dai & R.J. Sternberg (Eds), *Motivation, emotion, and cognition: Integrative perspectives on intellectual functioning and development* (pp. 143–174). Mahwah, NJ: Lawrence Erlbaum.

Metzger, R.L., Miller, M.L., Cohen, M., Sofka, M. & Borkovec, T.D. (1990). Worry changes decision making: The effect of negative thoughts on cognitive processing. *Journal of Clinical Psychology*, **46**, 78–88.

Meyer, T.J., Miller, M.L., Metzger, R.L., Borkovec, T.D., et al. (1990). Development and validation of the Penn State Worry Questionnaire. *Behaviour Research and Therapy*, **28**, 487–495.

Moretti, M.M. & Higgins, E. (1999). Own versus other standpoints in self-regulation: Developmental antecedents and functional consequences. *Review of General Psychology*, **3**, 188–223.

Mazzoni, G. & Nelson, T.O. (1998). *Metacognition and cognitive neuropsychology: Monitoring and control processes*. Mahwah, NJ: Erlbaum.

Nuevo, R., Montorio, I. & Borkovec, T.D. (2004). A test of the role of metaworry in the prediction of worry severity in an elderly sample. *Journal of Behavior Therapy & Experimental Psychiatry*, **35**, 209–218.

Papageorgiou, C. & Wells, A. (1999) Process and metacognitive dimensions of depressive and anxious thoughts and relationships with emotional intensity. *Clinical Psychology and Psychotherapy*, **6**, 156–162.

Perkins, A.M. & Corr, P.J. (2005). Can worriers be winners? The association between worrying and job performance. *Personality and Individual Differences*, **38**, 25–31.

Provencher, M.D., Freeston, M.H., Dugas, M.J. & Ladouceur, R. (2000). Catastrophizing assessment of worry and threat schemata among worriers. *Behavioural and Cognitive Psychotherapy*, **28**, 211–224.

Pruzinsky, T. & Borkovec, T.D. (1990). Cognitive and personality characteristics of worriers. *Behaviour Research and Therapy*, **28**, 507–512.

Reidy, J. (2004). Trait anxiety, trait depression, worry, and memory. *Behaviour Research & Therapy*, **42**, 937–948.

Russell, M. & Davey, G.C.L. (1993). The relationship between life events measures and anxiety and its cognitive correlates. *Personality and Individual Differences*, **14**, 317–322.

Sarason, I.G., Pierce, G.R. & Sarason, B.R. (1996). Domains of cognitive interference. In I.G. Sarason & G.R. Pierce (Eds), *Cognitive interference: Theories, methods, and findings* (pp. 139–152). Hillsdale, NJ: Erlbaum.

Smallwood, J., Davies, J.B., Heim, D., Finnigan, F., Sudberry, M., O'Connor, R. & Obonsawin, M. (2004). Subjective experience and the attentional lapse: Task engagement and disengagement during sustained attention. *Consciousness & Cognition: An International Journal*, **13**, 657–690.

Stöber, J. (1998). Worry, problem elaboration and suppression of imagery: The role of concreteness. *Behaviour Research & Therapy*, **36**, 751–756.

Tallis, F., Davey, G.C.L. & Capuzzo, N. (1994). The phenomenology of non-pathological worry: A preliminary investigation. In G.C.L. Davey & F. Tallis (Eds), *Worrying: Perspectives on theory, assessment and treatment* (pp. 61–89). New York: John Wiley & Sons, Inc.

Tallis, F., Eysenck, M. & Mathews, A. (1991). Elevated evidence requirements in worry. *Personality and Individual Differences*, **12**, 21–27.

Vasey, M.W. & Borkovec, T.D. (1992). A catastrophizing assessment of worrisome thoughts. *Cognitive Therapy and Research*, **16**, 1–16.

Watkins, E. (2004). Appraisals and strategies associated with rumination and worry. *Personality & Individual Differences*, **37**, 679–694.

Wells, A. (1994) A multidimensional measure of worry: Development and preliminary validation of the Anxious Thoughts Inventory. *Anxiety, Stress and Coping*, **6**, 289–299.

Wells, A. (2000). *Emotional disorders and metacognition: Innovative cognitive therapy*. Chichester, UK: John Wiley & Sons, Ltd.

Wells, A. & Carter, K. (1999). Preliminary tests of a cognitive model of generalized anxiety disorder. *Behaviour Research & Therapy*, **37**, 585–594.

Wells, A. & Cartwright-Hatton, S. (2004). A short form of the metacognitive questionnaire: Properties of the MCQ30. *Behavior, Research and Therapy*, **42**, 385–396.

Wells, A. & Davies, M.I. (1994). The Thought Control Questionnaire: A measure of individual differences in the control of unwanted thoughts. *Behaviour Research & Therapy*, **32**, 871–878.

Wells, A. & Matthews, G. (1994) *Attention and emotion: A clinical perspective*. Hove: Lawrence Erlbaum.

Yovel, I. & Mineka, S. (2005). Emotion-congruent attentional biases: The perspective of hierarchical models of emotional disorders. *Personality & Individual Differences*, **38**, 785–795.

Zeidner, M. (1998). *Test anxiety: The state of the art*. New York, NY: Plenum Press.

Zeidner, M. & Matthews, G. (2005) Evaluation anxiety. In A. Elliot & C. Dweck (Eds), *Handbook of competence and motivation* (pp. 141–163). New York: Guilford Press.

Chapter 5

WORRY IN OLDER ADULTS

Julie Loebach Wetherell

PREVALENCE

Approximately 15% of the elderly are self-described worriers (Wisocki, 1994). In spite of the fact that many serious life problems, such as medical illness, functional limitations, and cognitive impairment, are more common among older adults than among younger adults, research indicates that older adults worry less, on average, than younger adults do (Wisocki, 1994). For example, comparisons of undergraduates and older community volunteers typically find that older adults score lower on self-report measures of worry (Babcock, Laguna, Laguna & Urusky, 2000; Hunt, Wisocki & Yanko, 2003; Powers, Wisocki & Whitbourne, 1992). Older adults also appear to worry less than middle-aged adults do (Doucet, Ladouceur, Freeston & Dugas, 1998; Skarborn & Nicki, 2000), although worry may increase among the oldest old (Neikrug, 2003). Prevalence of worry is low even in samples of homebound older adults, although homebound elders and those who are ill worry more than older adults who are healthy and active (Skarborn & Nicki, 1996; Wisocki, 1994).

Furthermore, epidemiological research suggests that the prevalence of generalized anxiety disorder (GAD) is lower in those over 65 than in younger age groups (Blazer, George & Hughes, 1991). As is the case with most cross-sectional comparisons, it is impossible to determine the reason for these differences. It is possibly due to survival biases, in that people who have higher levels of worry are less likely to live to old age, or to cohort differences, given that people who are currently elderly survived World War II and the Great Depression and were typically raised with the values of self-reliance and minimizing or not discussing negative emotions. Older adults may not remember past episodes of worry. It is also possible that over the course of a lifetime, older adults develop wisdom (e.g. develop

This work is supported by NIMH Grant K23 MH067643.

effective coping strategies or a positive, and perhaps healthier, perspective on the world). As the "baby boom" generation, who were raised in an era more supportive of emotional expression and more willing to express discontent, moves into old age, it will be interesting to see whether age differences remain in levels of expressed worry.

ASSESSMENT

Several measures of worry content, frequency, and severity have been validated with older adult samples. One in particular, the Worry Scale (WS), was developed specifically for older adults (Wisocki, Handen & Morse, 1986). The initial version of the WS was a 35-item questionnaire assessing frequency of worry across three domains: finances, health, and social conditions. The scale has adequate internal consistency and convergent validity in normal older adults and in GAD patients.

A revised and expanded 88-item version of the WS has also been validated in the elderly (WSR; Wisocki, 1994; Hunt et al., 2003). This expanded version includes six dimensions: finances, health, social/interpersonal, personal concerns such as crime or psychological problems, family concerns, and world issues. Additional items assess the amount of time spent worrying, age of onset of worry, significant life events, feelings or physical conditions, methods of control, degree of interference and control, functions of worry, coping strategies, and information about social relationships. Cronbach's alpha for the WSR in older adults is .97 for the total scale and ranges from .88–.95 for subscales.

An 8-item brief form of the WS was used with a group of Alzheimer's disease patients and normal controls (LaBarge, 1993). Psychometric properties of the scale (internal consistency and unidimensional factor structure) were adequate in both groups. Worry correlated with state and trait anxiety and depression, but only modestly with measures of anger or self-esteem, and not with measures of cognitive or personality changes reported by a collateral source.

The Penn State Worry Questionnaire (PSWQ; Meyer, Miller, Metzger & Borkovec, 1990; see Chapter 7) has also been validated in older GAD patients and normal controls. One comparison found adequate internal consistency and a two-factor structure comprised of the negatively and positively worded items (Beck, Stanley & Zebb, 1995). Higher levels of worry were associated with more worry domains, more self-reported obsessive-compulsive symptoms, greater depression, and higher levels of state and trait anxiety. An 8-item version of the PSWQ appeared to have better psychometrics than the original with older GAD patients, in part because of the omission of the reverse-scored items, which many older people find difficult to interpret (Hopko et al., 2003). This brief form demonstrated a unifactorial structure and a remarkable degree of cross-cultural invariance in a comparison of older Americans and Spaniards (Nuevo, Mackintosh, Gatz, Montorio & Wetherell, submitted).

Stanley, Beck and Zebb (1996) evaluated the State-Trait Anxiety Inventory (STAI), WS, Fear Questionnaire (FQ), and Padua Inventory (PI) in an older sample with GAD and a comparison group of normal older controls. In the GAD sample, internal consistency was adequate (>.7) for the STAI, WS, PI, and their subscales, and for the total and Blood-Injury subscales of the FQ, but not for the Agoraphobia or Social Phobia subscales of the FQ. Adequate convergent validity was found for the STAI-Trait, WS, and PI, but not for the STAI-State or FQ. In the normal controls, internal consistency was adequate for all scales and subscales except the Social Phobia subscale of the FQ and the Behavior Control subscale of the PI. Test-retest reliability was adequate for the STAI-Trait, the WS except for the WS-Health subscale, and the PI, except for the Mental Control and Checking subscales. Test-retest reliability was lower for the STAI-State, as would be expected, and was also low for the FQ. Convergent validity was adequate for all measures in the normal control sample.

In a follow-up study, Stanley and colleagues (2001) evaluated the PSWQ, STAI, WS, and FQ in a sample of 57 older adults with GAD. Women reported greater social and agoraphobic fears than men. Lower education was associated with more worry, avoidance, and fear. Coefficient alphas were acceptable (.79–.94) except for the FQ blood injury and social phobia subscales. Test-retest reliability was acceptable (.70–.85), except for the PSWQ and STAI. There was no evidence for discriminant validity of the STAI with respect to depressive symptoms, but adequate discriminant validity for the PSWQ and FQ.

WORRY CONTENT

The content of worry appears different in later life than in early or midlife. Work-related concerns are less salient for older individuals, who are typically retired, and health issues and the maintenance of independence and functional impairment are more frequent topics of concern (Doucet et al., 1998; Montorio, Nuevo, Marquez, Izal & Losada, 2003). The most prevalent topic of worry in older adults appears to be health (Wisocki et al., 1986). Although family matters continue to be an important source of worry in later life, social and interpersonal worries are less common (Ladouceur, Freeston, Fournier, Dugas & Doucet, 2002). Older adults also worry about declines in vision, hearing, or cognition, falls, incontinence, poor health of loved ones, victimization, and being a burden (Kogan & Edelstein, 2002).

In a comparison of normal older adults, those with subsyndromal anxiety, and GAD patients, worries about family and personal health were the most common topics of concern in all groups, but GAD patients worried more about all topics than the other groups (Montorio et al., 2003). All older adults tended to worry more about present concerns rather than past or future concerns. Worry correlated with anxiety. Interference of worry with daily life and worry about minor matters were the best predictors of GAD in this sample.

Worry contents distinguishing older GAD patients from normal older controls in another study included minor matters, family, finances, social or interpersonal matters, personal health, and miscellaneous worries (all more common among GAD patients), but not work or current events (infrequent in both groups) or family health (equally common in both groups) (Wetherell, Le Roux & Gatz, 2003). In another sample, older adults with GAD reported worrying about a wider variety of topics than normal controls, but there were no significant differences in the content of worry (Diefenbach, Stanley & Beck, 2001). This latter finding is consistent with data from younger adults which suggest that it is the frequency and uncontrollability of worry, and not its content, that best distinguishes GAD patients from normals.

ASSOCIATED FACTORS, GENETICS, AND CONSEQUENCES

Worry in the elderly is associated with anxiety, distress, and negative affect (Skarborn & Nicki, 1996; Wisocki, 1994; Wisocki et al., 1986); poor self-perceived health, presence of medical conditions, or functional limitations (Hadjistavropoulos, Snider & Hadjistavropoulos, 2001; Skarborn & Nicki, 1996; Wisocki, 1988); approaching retirement (Skarborn & Nicki, 2000); and lower levels of knowledge about aging (Neikrug, 1998). In one recent study, older GAD patients reported impairment in quality of life comparable to that associated with major depression and more than that associated with Type II diabetes or recent acute myocardial infarct (Wetherell et al., 2004).

Older adult worries tend to be less future-oriented than those of younger adults (Montorio et al., 2003; Powers et al., 1992). For older adults, worry is associated with poorer satisfaction with social support and lower income (Babcock et al., 2000). As is the case with younger adults, worry is associated with external locus of control and negative affect (Powers et al., 1992). However, some evidence suggests that worry is not as closely associated with depression in the elderly as it is in younger persons (Wisocki, 1994).

Younger adults in one study used a significantly greater number of coping strategies (e.g., smoking, sleeping, talking to oneself, writing down the worry, laughing about it, and reasoning with oneself) than older adults (who were more likely to endorse maintaining a positive attitude and "thinking young;" Hunt et al., 2003). This finding may reflect the generally lower levels of worry in the elderly, who therefore do not need as wide a range of coping strategies. Conversely, it may be that older adults "specialize" in a few highly effective coping strategies which they use successfully to keep worry at a minimum.

Mackintosh and colleagues (in press) investigated genetic and environmental influences on self-reported worrying and the proportion of genetic and environmental variation in worrying behavior that is shared with neuroticism in older adult twins. Univariate biometric models indicated that 27% of the variance in worrying was related to genetic factors, whereas 73% reflected environmental factors unique to the individual. Bivariate analyses indicated that approximately one-third of the genetic influences on worry were in common with genetic influences on neuroticism, whereas only 1% of unique environmental influences were shared between worry and neuroticism. Results indicate that both worrying and neuroticism are moderately heritable in older adults.

Worry, along with other affect-related personality traits such as neuroticism and optimism, predicted perceived susceptibility to age-related diseases in a large sample of middle-aged and older women (Gerend, Aiken & West, 2004). Worry about falls was a significant predictor of subsequent falls in a sample of older adults admitted to the hospital after a fall who were reassessed two months later (McKee et al., 2002). Worry remained a significant predictor of falls even after controlling for prefall functional limitations and length of hospital stay (a proxy for severity of injury).

A study of older adults reporting sleep difficulties indicated that they reported higher levels of worry than either self-reported good sleepers or normal controls (Pallesen et al., 2002), suggesting that insomnia may be one consequence of worry in later life. This is consistent with data from Wetherell, Le Roux et al. (2003) indicating that sleep disturbance is one of the best discriminators among older adults with GAD, those with subsyndromal anxiety symptoms, and normal controls.

Worry also has a negative impact on recovery from depression in older adults. Excessive worry and subjective anxiety significantly predicted relapse in older adults with major depression who recovered after nortriptyline treatment (Meyers, Gabriele, Kakuma, Ippolito & Alexopoulos, 1996). In a sample of psychiatric inpatients with major depression, age and depression were associated with health worries, but medical illness burden was not (Lyness, King, Conwell, Cox & Caine, 1993).

THEORIES OF WORRY

Relatively few studies have attempted to apply theories about worry to older adults. Because older adults appear to experience lower levels of arousal due to physiological changes in the autonomic nervous system associated with aging, worry may form a more important component of anxiety in the elderly than in younger adults. One recent investigation tested Wells' cognitive model of pathological worry in a sample of older Spanish adults and found that metaworry (positive and negative beliefs about worry) was a significant predictor of severity of worry and interference of worry in daily life even after controlling for trait anxiety, worry content, and uncontrollability of worry (Nuevo, Montorio & Borkovec, 2004).

A follow-up to this study examined which types of beliefs about worry were predictive of GAD symptoms in a sample of senior center attendees (Montorio, Wetherell & Nuevo, submitted). Positive beliefs about worry, negative beliefs about worry, and beliefs about worry as a demonstration of personal responsibility all distinguished GAD patients from normals, and negative beliefs were a significant independent predictor of GAD severity, even after controlling for level of trait worry.

CULTURAL FACTORS

Little research to date has addressed cultural factors that may affect the expression of worry in older adults. Most extant research has been performed on Caucasian, North American samples. Even in studies in which research has been carried out in other locations (e.g., Spain), cross-cultural comparisons are lacking.

One exception to this trend is a report comparing worries, as assessed by the WSR and the PSWQ, in older Japanese Americans and European Americans (Watari & Brodbeck, 2000). In this study, worry was not related to internment status during World War II, but the interned Japanese group reported higher levels of defensiveness on a scale of social desirability. No reliable differences were found between ethnic groups. In both groups, higher levels of worry were associated with poorer self-rated health and poorer perceived financial status.

A comparison of Polish immigrants and indigenous British older adults found that immigrants reported more worry (Keith, 1995). Worry was related to lower levels of life satisfaction in both groups.

Nuevo and colleagues (submitted) used confirmatory factor analysis and Rasch modeling to examine cross-cultural invariance in an 8-item brief form of the PSWQ. Results supported the use of the PSWQ in American and

Spanish older adults, and more importantly, demonstrated the viability of these techniques for determining the suitability of translated scales.

GENERALIZED ANXIETY DISORDER

A number of investigations have focused on worry in the context of GAD, often using discriminant function analysis to distinguish older GAD patients from normal controls. In one such study, interference of worry in daily life, worry about minor matters, and worry about the future distinguished GAD from normal aging (Montorio et al., 2003). Similarly, frequency, excessiveness, number of topics of worry, perceived difficulty controlling worry, restlessness, fatigue, irritability, muscle tension, and sleep disturbance distinguished older GAD patients and normals (Wetherell, Le Roux et al., 2003). Older GAD patients reported higher levels of state and trait anxiety, worry, depression, and social fears than normal older adults (Beck et al., 1995). Subsyndromal GAD symptoms, or "minor GAD," can be differentiated from both syndromal GAD and normal controls by scores on measures of pathological worry (PSWQ) and trait anxiety in the elderly (Diefenbach et al., 2003). Difficulty controlling worry and distress or impairment were the most useful features distinguishing minor GAD from syndromal GAD in later life (Diefenbach et al., 2003; Wetherell, Le Roux et al., 2003). One study found that GAD could be distinguished from panic disorder in older adults by irritability and depression rather than by trait anxiety or worry (Mohlman et al., 2004).

A comparison of older adults with early vs. midlife onset of GAD found that early onset patients had higher levels of trait anxiety and depression (Beck, Stanley & Zebb, 1996). Another such study found evidence for more severe worry, more psychiatric comorbidity, and higher use of psychotropic medications among the early onset group (Le Roux, Gatz & Wetherell, 2005). Role disability appeared to be a risk factor for late-onset GAD in this investigation.

TREATMENT

Most research on the alleviation of worry in older adults has focused on treatment of GAD. An exception was an "open-label" trial of participation in a focus group about worry (Powers & Wisocki, 1997). Level of worry decreased following focus group participation in 21 older self-described worriers one year after participation in the group.

Several recent investigations have used cognitive-behavioral therapy (CBT) to treat older GAD patients (see also Chapter 16). CBT for late-life

GAD has typically included the elements of psychoeducation and recognition of anxiety symptoms, relaxation training, cognitive restructuring, and imaginal and *in vivo* exposure to worrisome thoughts and situations with prevention of overly cautious behaviors. Effect sizes (Cohen's d) immediately following treatment have typically been in the large range for those studies comparing CBT to wait list or usual care (Mohlman et al., 2003, .65; Stanley et al., 2003, .75; Stanley et al., 2003, 1.01; Wetherell, Gatz, & Craske, 2003, .85) and in the small to medium range for those studies comparing CBT to an alternative treatment or attention placebo (Gorenstein et al., 2005, .36; Stanley et al., 1996, .28; Wetherell, Gatz et al., 2003, .29). These results are generally less favorable than in comparable studies with younger adults.

In a pooled analysis of CBT trials for late-life GAD, amount of at-home practice was the most consistent predictor of improvement, both immediately after treatment and at 6-month follow-up (Wetherell, Hopko et al., 2005). One investigation compared response to CBT for GAD in older adults with intact executive function (EF), impaired EF, and those who initially showed impaired EF but demonstrated improvement in cognitive function along with anxiety symptoms (Mohlman & Gorman, 2005). CBT in this study included reminder telephone calls and enhanced feedback on at-home practice assignments. Results suggested that individuals with impaired EF did not respond to CBT (mean effect size .31 relative to WL; no patients classified as responders), whereas those with intact and improved EF were more likely to respond (mean effect sizes of .78 and 1.3 and response rates of 40% and 60% respectively, compared to WL).

The first randomized, controlled trial of an SSRI for late-life GAD found a medium effect for citalopram over pill placebo (Lenze et al., 2005, $d = .54$). A recent "open label" trial based on a conception of GAD as involving intolerance of uncertainty produced a much larger mean effect on anxiety symptoms, $d = 1.67$, in a sample of 8 older GAD patients (Ladouceur, Leger, Dugas, & Freeston, 2004) (see Chapter 17). Unlike the other studies, the treatment used in this trial involved cognitive techniques such as reevaluating beliefs about worry and problem-solving skills training rather than behavioral strategies such as relaxation training, suggesting that these types of interventions may be more helpful for older adults with pathological worry. Results from a randomized, controlled trial of this treatment protocol with older GAD patients are eagerly anticipated.

Other ongoing work in this area involves the translation of CBT for anxiety to the primary care setting (Stanley et al., 2003; Wetherell, Sorrell, Thorp, & Patterson, 2005). Innovations currently under investigation include the use of telephone contact to supplement in-person sessions and flexible, modular content to meet the needs of older adults with diverse symptoms (Wetherell, Sorrell et al., 2005). Other modifications to facilitate learning in anxious older adults with impaired executive functions, such as attention training and repeated practice on executive tasks, are also under investigation (Mohlman, 2005).

CONCLUSION

Although older adults worry less than younger adults do, and the content of worry shifts away from work and social concerns toward a focus on health and functional capacity in later life, research does not suggest major age differences in the construct of worry. Several measurement tools, particularly the Worry Scale and Penn State Worry Questionnaire, appear to have adequate psychometric properties in the elderly. Pathological worry and its related disorder, GAD, are associated with negative outcomes and impaired quality of life. Psychological treatment of late-life GAD appears to be less effective than it is with younger adults, although new approaches are currently being tested.

Future research should address the following questions: Why do older adults worry less than younger adults do? Longitudinal research, perhaps following a late-middle-aged cohort as they advance into old age, will be required to determine whether this is a developmental or cohort effect. Second, why do some older adults develop pathological worry or GAD for the first time in old age? Although most older adults with GAD report an onset in childhood or adolescence, as many as 40% report an onset in middle to late life (Blazer et al., 1991; Le Roux et al., 2005). Knowledge of risk and protective factors may help to prevent new cases in older people. Finally, why are psychosocial treatments for GAD less effective with older adults than with younger adults? Research on the theoretical underpinnings of worry in late life may ultimately help to create more effective interventions for pathological worry in older people.

REFERENCES

Babcock, R.L., Laguna, L.B., Laguna, K.D. & Urusky, D.A. (2000). Age differences in the experience of worry. *Journal of Mental Health and Aging*, **6**, 227–235.
Beck, J.G., Stanley, M.A. & Zebb, B.J. (1996). Characteristics of generalized anxiety disorder in older adults: A descriptive study. *Behaviour Research and Therapy*, **34**, 225–234.
Beck, J.G., Stanley, M.A. & Zebb, B.J. (1995). Psychometric properties of the Penn State Worry Questionnaire in older adults. *Journal of Clinical Geropsychology*, **1**, 33–42.

Blazer, D., George, L.K. & Hughes, D. (1991). The epidemiology of anxiety disorders: An age comparison. In C. Salzman & B.D. Lebowitz (Eds), *Anxiety in the elderly: Treatment and research*, (pp. 17–30). New York: Springer Publishing.

Diefenbach, G.J., Hopko, D.R., Feigon, S., Stanley, M.A., Novy, D.M., Beck, J.G. & Averill, P.M. (2003). 'Minor GAD': Characteristics of subsyndromal GAD in older adults. *Behaviour Research and Therapy*, **41**, 481–487.

Diefenbach, G.J., Stanley, M.A. & Beck, J.G. (2001). Worry content reported by older adults with and without generalized anxiety disorder. *Aging and Mental Health*, **5**, 269–274.

Doucet, C., Ladouceur, R., Freeston, M.H. & Dugas, M.J. (1998). Themes d'inquietudes et tendance a s'inquieter chez les aines. [Worry themes and the tendency to worry in older adults.] *Canadian Journal on Aging*, **17**, 361–371.

Gerend, M.A., Aiken, L.S. & West, S.G. (2004). Personality factors in older women's perceived susceptibility to diseases of aging. *Journal of Personality*, **72**, 243–270.

Gorenstein, E.E., Papp, L.A., Kleber, M.S., Mohlman, J., et al. (2005). Cognitive-behavioral therapy for management of anxiety and medication taper in older adults. *American Journal of Geriatric Psychiatry*.

Hadjistavropoulos, H.D., Snider, B.S. & Hadjistavropoulos, T. (2001). Anxiety in older persons waiting for cataract surgery: Investigating the contributing factors. *Canadian Journal on Aging*, **20**, 97–111.

Hopko, D.R., Stanley, M.A., Reas, D.L., Wetherell, J.L., Beck, J.G., Novy, D.M. & Averill, P.M. (2003). Assessing worry in older adults: Confirmatory factor analysis of the Penn State Worry Questionnaire and psychometric properties of an abbreviated model. *Psychological Assessment*, **15**, 173–183.

Hunt, S., Wisocki, P. & Yanko, J. (2003). Worry and use of coping strategies among older and younger adults. *Anxiety Disorders*, **17**, 547–560.

Keith, P.M. (1995). A comparison of the resources and concerns of the Polish and indigenous aged in Britain. *Journal of Cross-Cultural Gerontology*, **10**, 219–231.

Kogan, J.N. & Edelstein, B.A. (2002). Modification and psychometric examination of a self-report measure of fear in older adults. *Journal of Anxiety Disorders*, **18**, 397–409.

LaBarge, E. (1993). A preliminary scale to measure the degree of worry among mildly demented Alzheimer disease patients. *Physical and Occupational Therapy in Geriatrics*, **11**, 43–57.

Ladouceur, R., Freeston, M.H., Fournier, S., Dugas, M.J. & Doucet, C. (2002). The social basis of worry in three samples: High-school students, university students, and older adults. *Behavioural and Cognitive Psychotherapy*, **30**, 427–438.

Ladouceur, R., Leger, E., Dugas, M., & Freeston, M. H. (2004). Cognitive-behavioral treatment of generalized anxiety disorder (GAD) for older adults. *International Psychogeriatrics*, **16**, 195–207.

Le Roux, H., Gatz, M. & Wetherell, J.L. (2005). Age at onset of generalized anxiety disorder in older adults. *American Journal of Geriatric Psychiatry*, **13**, 23–30.

Lenze, E.J., Mulsant, B.H., Shear, M.K., Dew, M.A., Miller, M.D., Pollock, B.G., Houck, P., Tracey, B. & Reynolds, C.F. 3rd. Efficacy and tolerability of citalopram in the treatment of late-life anxiety disorders: Results from an 8-week randomized, placebo- controlled trial. *American Journal of Psychiatry*, **162**, 146–150.

Lyness, J.M., King, D.A., Conwell, Y., Cox, C. & Caine, E. D. (1993). "Somatic worry" and medical illness in depressed inpatients. *American Journal of Geriatric Psychiatry*, **4**, 288–295.

Mackintosh, M.-A., Gatz, M., Wetherell, J.L. & Pedersen, N.L. (2005, in press). *A twin study of worry in older adults: Shared genetic and environmental influences between neuroticism and self-reported worrying*.

McKee, K.J., Orbell, S., Austin, C.A., Bettridge, R., Liddle, B.J., Morgan, K. & Radley, K. (2002). Fear of falling, falls efficacy, and health outcomes in older people following hip fracture. *Disability and Rehabilitation*, **24**, 327–333.

Meyer, T.M., Miller, M.L., Metzger, R.L. & Borkovec, T.D. (1990). Development and validation of the Penn State Worry Questionnaire. *Behaviour Research and Therapy*, **28**, 487–495.

Meyers, B.S., Gabriele, M., Kakuma, T., Ippolito, L. & Alexopoulos, G. (1996). Anxiety and depression as predictors of recurrence in geriatric depression: A preliminary report. *American Journal of Geriatric Psychiatry*, **4**, 252–257.

Mohlman, J. (2005). Does executive dysfunction affect treatment outcome in late-life mood and anxiety disorders? *Journal of Geriatric Psychiatry & Neurology*, **18**, 97–108.

Mohlman, J., de Jesus, M., Gorenstein, E.E., Kleber, M., Gorman, J.M. & Papp, L.A. (2004). Distinguishing generalized anxiety disorder, panic disorder, and mixed anxiety states in older treatment-seeking adults. *Journal of Anxiety Disorders*, **18**, 275–290.

Mohlman, J., Gorenstein, E.E., Kleber, M., de Jesus, M., Gorman, J.M. & Papp, L.A. (2003). Standard and enhanced cognitive-behavior therapy for late-life generalized anxiety disorder: two pilot investigations. *American Journal of Geriatric Psychiatry*, **11**, 24–32.

Mohlman, J. & Gorman, J.M. (2005). The role of executive functioning in CBT: A pilot study with anxious older adults. *Behaviour Research and Therapy*, **43**, 447–465.

Montorio, I., Nuevo, R., Márquez, M., Izal, M. & Losada, A. (2003). Characterization of worry according to the severity of anxiety. *Aging and Mental Health*, **7**, 334–341.

Montorio, I., Wetherell, J.L. & Nuevo, R. (submitted). *Beliefs about worry in older adults.*

Neikrug, S.M. (1998). The value of gerontological knowledge for elders: A study of the relationship between knowledge on aging and worry about the future. *Educational Gerontology*, **24**, 287–296.

Neikrug, S.M. (2003). Worrying about a frightening old age. *Aging and Mental Health*, **7**, 326–333.

Nuevo, R., Mackintosh, M.-A., Gatz, M., Montorio, I. & Wetherell, J.L. (submitted). *Cross-cultural comparison of a brief version of the Penn State Worry Questionnaire in American and Spanish older adults.*

Nuevo, R., Montorio, I. & Borkovec, T.D. (2004). A test of the role of metaworry in the prediction of worry severity in an elderly sample. *Journal of Behavior Therapy and Experimental Psychiatry*, **35**, 209–218.

Pallesen, S., Nordhus, I.H., Kvale, G., Havik, O.D., Nielsen, G.H., Johnsen, B.H., Skjøtskift, S. & Hjeltnes, L. (2002). Psychological characteristics of elderly insomniacs. *Scandinavian Journal of Psychology*, **43**, 425–432.

Powers, C.B. & Wisocki, P. A. (1997). An examination of the therapeutic benefits of focus groups on elderly worriers. *International Journal of Aging and Human Development*, **45**, 159–167.

Powers, C.B., Wisocki, P.A. & Whitbourne, S.K. (1992). Age differences and correlates of worrying in young and elderly adults. *The Gerontologist*, **32**, 82–88.

Regier, D.A., Boyd, J.H., Burke, J.D., Rae, D.S., Myers, J.K., Kramer, M., Robins, L.N., George, L.K., Karno, M. & Locke, B.Z. (1988). One-month prevalence of mental disorders in the United States: Based on five Epidemiologic Catchment Area sites. *Archives of General Psychiatry*, **45**, 977–986.

Skarborn, M. & Nicki, R. (1996). Worry among Canadian seniors. *International Journal of Aging and Human Development*, **43**, 169–178.

Skarborn, M. & Nicki, R. (2000). Worry in pre- and post-retirement persons. *International Journal of Aging and Human Development*, **50**, 61–71.

Stanley, M.A., Beck, J.G. & Glassco, J.D. (1996). Treatment of generalized anxiety in older adults: A preliminary comparison of cognitive-behavioral and supportive approaches. *Behavior Therapy*, **27**, 565–581.

Stanley, M.A., Beck, J.G. & Zebb, B.J. (1996). Psychometric properties of four anxiety measures in older adults. *Behaviour Research and Therapy*, **34**, 827–838.

Stanley, M.A., Beck, J.G., Novy, D.M., Averill, P.M., Swann, A.C., Diefenbach, G.J. & Hopko, D.R. (2003). Cognitive-behavioral treatment of late-life generalized anxiety disorder. *Journal of Consulting and Clinical Psychology*, **71**, 309–319.

Stanley, M.A., Hopko, D.R., Diefenbach, G.J., Bourland, S.L., Rodriguez, H. & Wagener, P. (2003). Cognitive-behavior therapy for late-life generalized anxiety disorder in primary care: Preliminary findings. *American Journal of Geriatric Psychiatry*, **11**, 92–96.

Stanley, M.A., Novy, D.M., Bourland, S.L., Beck, J.G. & Averill, P.M. (2001). Assessing older adults with generalized anxiety: A replication and extension. *Behaviour Research and Therapy*, **39**, 221–235.

Watari, K.F. & Brodbeck, C. (2000). Culture, health, and financial appraisals: Comparison of worry in older Japanese Americans and European Americans. *Journal of Clinical Geropsychology*, **6**, 25–39.

Wetherell, J.L., Gatz, M. & Craske, M.G. (2003). Treatment of generalized anxiety disorder in older adults. *Journal of Consulting and Clinical Psychology*, **71**, 31–40.

Wetherell, J.L., Hopko, D.R., Diefenbach, G.J., Averill, P.M., Beck, J.G., Craske, M.G., Gatz, M., Novy, D.M. & Stanley, M.A. (2005). Cognitive-behavioral therapy for late-life generalized anxiety disorder: Who gets better? *Behavior Therapy*, **36**, 147–156.

Wetherell, J.L., Le Roux, H. & Gatz, M. (2003). DSM-IV criteria for generalized anxiety disorder in older adults: Distinguishing the worried from the well. *Psychology and Aging*, **18**, 622–627.

Wetherell, J.L., Sorrell, J.T., Thorp, S.R. & Patterson, T.L. (2005). Psychological interventions for late-life anxiety: A review and early lessons from the CALM Study. *Journal of Geriatric Psychiatry and Neurology*, **18**, 72–82.

Wetherell, J.L., Thorp, S.R., Patterson, T.L., Golshan, S., Jeste, D.V. & Gatz, M. (2004). Quality of life in geriatric generalized anxiety disorder: A preliminary investigation. *Journal of Psychiatric Research*, **38**, 305–312.

Wisocki, P.A. (1994). The experience of worry among the elderly. In G.C.L. Davey & F. Tallis (Eds), Worrying: *Perspectives on theory, assessment, and treatment*, (pp. 247–261). New York: John Wiley & Sons, Inc.

Wisocki, P.A. (1988). Worry as a phenomenon relevant to the elderly. *Behavior Therapy*, **19**, 369–379.

Wisocki, P.A., Handen, B. & Morse, C.K. (1986). The Worry Scale as a measure of anxiety among homebound and community active elderly. *The Behavior Therapist*, **5**, 91–95.

Chapter 6

WORRY IN CHILDHOOD AND ADOLESCENCE

Sam Cartwright-Hatton

Writing their review of worry in childhood, in 1994, Vasey and Daleiden stated that:

While the theoretical and empirical literature concerning worry has grown large . . . surprisingly little of it concerns worry among children and adolescents. p. 185.

Writing a decade on, it might have been predicted that this state of affairs would have changed. Unfortunately, this is not so, and although new work will be reported here, our understanding of childhood worry has advanced relatively little in recent years.

The chapter begins with an overview of the epidemiology of childhood worry, and will move on to what we know about the processes involved in its aetiology and maintenance. Some developments in our understanding of familial and parental roles in child worry will be discussed, as will potential treatments for conditions of worry in younger populations, and methods that may be used for evaluating these. It will conclude with an examination of some of the issues that need further research attention.

HOW COMMON IS WORRY IN CHILDHOOD AND ADOLESCENCE?

Perhaps the most well researched aspect of childhood worry is the prevalence and range of worries, together with the demographic factors associated with these. It has now become clear that worry is really very common in adolescence, and probably also in childhood. In their study of 193 Dutch children aged 8–13 years, Muris et al. (1998) found that 68.9% of participants reported worrying at least 'now and then'. Similarly, Orton (1982) studied children in early adolescence, and found that 70% of them

Worry and Its Psychological Disorders: Theory, Assessment and Treatment. Edited by G. C. L. Davey and A. Wells. © 2006 John Wiley & Sons, Ltd.

reported ten or more things about which they worried. Even in children and adolescents (5–18 years) who have never had a psychiatric diagnosis, approximately 15% reported symptoms of worry that could be described as excessive (Bell-Dolan, Last & Strauss, 1990). Similar studies of the prevalence of *fears* in childhood (on which there is considerably more research) add weight to this indication that worrying during childhood is, to some extent, normal.

Gender and Worry

A number of studies have examined the contribution of gender to the experience of worry. On balance, the consensus seems to be that girls worry more than boys. For instance, Bell-Dolan et al. (1990) found that almost 20% of never-psychiatrically ill 5–18 year old females reported 'excessive worry' in an interview, compared to 8% of boys.

Similarly, in their larger study (193 children, aged 8–13 years), Muris et al. (1998) found that girls worried significantly more than boys. Kaufman et al. (1993) studied adolescents attending hospital for minor physical concerns, and reported that females endorsed more worries on a checklist than males.

However, in a study measuring a number of aspects of worry, and including a number of domains of worries, Suarez and Bell-Dolan (2001) reported that the only realm in which early adolescent females were found to score higher than their male counterparts was in worry in response to threatening and everyday events.

Unfortunately, from most of the studies, it is not clear whether females worry more frequently than males, or have a wider range of concerns about which they worry, or simply worry more intensively about their concerns. However, Silverman et al. (1995) found that 7–12 year old females reported more worries than their male counterparts, but did not report that these worries were more frequent or more intense. In contrast, comparing a clinically anxious sample, and children with no diagnosis, Perrin and Last (1997) found no gender differences in either number or severity of worries.

Age and Worry

Children's age might also have a role to play in the frequency, number and type of worries that they report. However, there is little consensus in the literature pertaining to this aspect. Although some studies report that younger children worry more than older ones (e.g. Morris Finkelstein &

Fisher, 1976), a number of studies report that older children worry more than younger ones (e.g. Henker, Whalen & O'Neil, 1995; Vasey, Crnic & Carter, 1994). Henker et al. (1995) suggest that these different findings may have arisen from the different methods employed to measure worry. For instance, in their study, in which children were *interviewed* about their worries, they found more worries reported by children in the 8th grade, than by those in the 4th grade, but suggest that alternative techniques, using, for example, checklists, may have yielded different results.

Ethnicity and Worry

There are still very few studies that have examined racial or ethnic differences in childhood worry. In one that did (Silverman et al., 1995) more worries were reported by African American youth than by their White or Hispanic peers.

WHAT DO CHILDREN AND ADOLESCENTS WORRY ABOUT?

Perhaps the most important factor in dictating what a child is likely to worry about is their age. The research consistently shows that the content of worries develops from more concrete and physical concerns in younger children, through to increasingly psychological and abstract issues in adolescence. In addition, the variety of areas about which children report worry increases with age. For example, Muris et al. (1994) reported that the number of worries reported by a group of 8 year olds was almost double that reported by a group of 5 year olds.

Muris, Merckelbach and Luijten (2002) reported a similar change in content of worries with age, and suggested that this may have an evolutionary basis, preparing children for developmentally appropriate challenges in their environment. This study also showed that worries were more prevalent in normally developing children, as compared to their same-aged learning disabled peers, indicating a role for cognitive development in the presentation of worry.

The role of the developing self concept has also been explored in relation to worry. Vasey et al. (1994) showed that children with the least well-developed self concepts reported worrying about physical harm, compared to children with the most well-developed self concepts who worried more about potential harm to their psychological wellbeing and about social issues. Social issues (e.g. performance and appearance) were also reported more by older children compared to younger ones in a study of clinically referred anxious children (Weems, Silverman & La Greca, 2000). Similarly, Last, Strauss and Francis (1987) reported that children with a diagnosis of Overanxious Disorder/Generalised Anxiety Disorder, were more likely to have a comorbid diagnosis of Social Phobia than any other anxiety disorder, indicating that in excessive worriers, worries about one's social functioning are paramount.

Surprisingly, it appears that there are only minor differences in the content of worries reported by males and females (Silverman et al., 1995), although girls may report more worry about global and societal issues than boys (Henker et al., 1995). This study (Silverman et al., 1995) also appears to be the only one to examine ethnic differences in worries, finding that there were rather few differences in content of reported worries, when comparing African-American, White and Hispanic adolescents.

Both academic and popular speculation surrounds the changing nature of worry in children as societies alter over time. Clearly it is difficult to study worry over historical time periods, but in one study that attempted this, the worries of North American children in the 5th and 6th grade in 1977, were compared to those reported by a similar cohort in 1939. It was found that boys in the 1930s worried more about economic issues, and girls in the 1970s worried more about all areas except for personal health. In general, both girls and boys in the 1970s, for reasons that are unclear, reported more worry about issues that appear related to separation anxiety, e.g. kidnappers, strangers, and death of a family member (Orton, 1982).

SHOULD WE BE WORRIED ABOUT WORRY IN CHILDHOOD?

It is now widely recognised that generic child anxiety, when severe, is deleterious to functioning, and can have long-term negative outcomes. For example, anxious children often subsequently develop depression (Kovacs, Gatsonis, Paulauskas & Richards, 1989), and may be at increased risk of substance misuse. (Kushner, Sher & Beitman, 1990). Even less serious levels of anxiety have been shown to have an impact on children's academic and social functioning (Pine, 1997).

However, to the author's knowledge, no research has yet examined the impact of worrying (as distinct from generic anxiety symptoms) on children's functioning. However, if, as seems likely, excessive worry has the same impact on young sufferers as it does on adults, and if it has the same impact that we now know high levels of *generic* anxiety to have on children, then this is an area that should be of serious concern.

NORMAL AND CLINICAL WORRY

It is clear that children and adolescents do experience worry, but to what extent do they experience levels that would qualify them for a diagnosis of Generalised Anxiety Disorder (GAD)? Epidemiological studies vary substantially in the degree to which they report prevalences of GAD (or its earlier counterpart—overanxious disorder). In a large epidemiological study of British children (Ford, Goodman & Meltzer, 1999) GAD (using DSM-IV criteria) was found to be present in less than 1% of 5–10 olds. However, in a study employing slightly less conservative DSM-III-R criteria for 'overanxious disorder' Boyle, Offord, Racine, et al. (1993) reported overanxious disorder in over 11% of their US sample of 6–11 year olds. However, these rates must be interpreted in the context of the sample under investigation, and in light of the particular instruments, criteria and other methodology employed.

Few studies have examined differences in process or content of worry in clinical and non-clinical worriers. However, according to one study (Weems et al., 2000), which compared the content of worry in children with GAD and with simple phobias, the content was rather similar, except that those with GAD worried more about the future and about 'peer scapegoating' and those with simple phobia worried more about the health of others and of their family. There appeared to be no difference between these two groups in the frequency of worries, although the children with GAD reported their worries to be more intense.

Similarly, Perrin and Last (1997) examined worry in pre-adolescents, diagnosed with anxiety disorders, ADHD, or no diagnosis. They found that the groups did not differ significantly in the numbers of worries that they reported, but that the anxious children reported more 'intense worries'. Interestingly, however, only one-third of those with anxiety disorders reported that they had any 'intense worry'.

PROCESS AND MECHANISMS
IN WORRY IN CHILDHOOD

An examination of the extant research into childhood worry confirms that this field is still in its infancy. As such, research that has been carried out, has tended to focus on describing the phenomenon, and exploring its content and epidemiology. The process and mechanisms of worry, which are now so widely explored in the adult literature, are still very poorly understood in younger populations. This situation is exacerbated by a number of difficulties that are inherent in studying worry in children. In particular, there is a very limited selection of instruments available for assessing worry and associated factors in younger people. Development of further instruments is hampered by the developmental constraints on children's functioning. For instance, it is far from clear whether younger children even have a reliable concept of what worry is. Henker et al. (1995) reports that even teenagers may struggle to distinguish worry and fear, although they are generally able to report that fear is more intense.

However, there is now a small body of research examining psychological processes associated with worry. In most cases this research examines the applicability of models that are already well-developed in the adult literature:

Worry and Cognitive/Attentional Biases

There is now substantial evidence in the adult literature to suggest that anxious adults have cognitive biases towards threat information, and overestimate the likelihood of such threat. Evidence is now beginning to suggest that these biases are apparent early on in the development of anxiety disorders—i.e. in childhood and adolescence, (see Ehrenreick and Gross (2002) for a review).

The literature examining such biases in relation to worry, and in particular, to worry in childhood has lagged behind other developments, but a very small number of studies are able to elucidate the area. Using a non-clinical sample, Silverman et al. (1995) showed that children aged 7–12 years reported worry about both everyday and infrequent events (e.g. being kidnapped). This was despite the participants' clear recognition that some of the events were extremely improbable. This may be taken as evidence that children can have attentional biases that cause them to worry about improbable threats, when they perceive the threat as very dangerous. Similarly, in a study of 277 5th-6th graders, Suarez and Bell-Dolan (2001) showed that worry levels were correlated with threat interpretation biases in both threatening and ambiguous scenarios, as measured by an instrument designed by the authors.

Coping and Control

It is becoming clear that children and adolescents do worry. Moreover, young worriers are likely to detect potential threats easily, and sometimes inappropriately. What, then, do we know about children's responses to their worrying, once it has begun? There is now evidence that children find worry as difficult to manage as their adult counterparts. Muris et al. (1998) examined worry control strategies in 193 largely non-clinical participants aged 8–13 years, and found that on average, participants' worry was 'rather difficult to stop'. The worry control strategies employed by these participants would be familiar to adults, and included: engaging in another activity; thinking of something else; and 'talking about it'. The large non-clinical majority of this sample reported that their most frequently used technique was self-distraction, by engaging in another activity. However, the small number of children who were thought to be in the clinical range, reported that they were most likely to attempt to manage their worry by discussing it with another person.

In an earlier unpublished study, Vasey (cited in Vasey & Daleiden, 1994) showed that child worriers used more 'emotion focussed' strategies for coping with their worries, in comparison to controls, who employed more 'problem focussed' strategies. This was despite the fact that the two groups did not differ when asked how other children manage their worries.

Laugesen, Dugas and Bukowski (2003) examined worry, and a number of cognitive factors and processes in a large sample of 14–18 year olds. They found that worry, as measured by the Penn State Worry Questionnaire (PSWQ) was correlated with scores on the 'Intolerance of Uncertainty Scale', as well as a 'negative problem solving orientation', use of thought suppression to manage worry, and scores on the 'Why Worry II Scale'—an instrument designed to measure beliefs about the utility of worry. In a regression analysis, 'intolerance of uncertainty' explained most of the variance in worry, with the 'Why Worry II' scale and 'problem solving orientation' also explaining significant variance. Notably, however, thought suppression did not explain significant variance once the other factors were taken into account. However, with the exception of the worry measure, the instruments were not validated for use in an adolescent sample, and care must, therefore, be taken in the interpretation of the results.

Meta-cognition

The recent interest in meta-cognition and worry in the adult literature has been paralleled by a similar interest in the child literature. Studies investigating children's knowledge and beliefs about their own worry show that up to 30% of participants expressed an opinion about the origins of their worry, (Muris et al., 1998). In the same study (described in more detail above), 28% of children reported positive features of their worry, although notably, none of the children who scored in the putative clinical range were able to do so.

Research from our group supports relationships between beliefs about worry, and anxiety (Cartwright-Hatton, Mather, Illingworth et al., 2004;

Mather & Cartwright-Hatton, 2004). A large sample of adolescents was given an adolescent version of the Meta-Cognitions Questionnaire. The results indicated that children as young as 13 years reported the range of beliefs about their worry as reported by adults, and implicated in the meta-cognitive model (i.e. both positive and negative beliefs about worry, including some 'superstitious' type beliefs, and beliefs about the controllability of worry). They also engaged in examining their worry in the same way as adults. Moreover, the extent to which they endorsed these beliefs and processes was correlated with their anxiety levels in the same way as in adults. The meta-cognitive model of worry (Wells, 1995) is outlined in full in Chapter 11, but briefly, it was shown that adolescents who endorsed beliefs about the dangerousness of worry, and also, to some extent, the need to worry in order to stay safe and in control, were more likely to report excessive levels of anxiety.

Can We Extrapolate What We Know From the Adult Literature?

As the literature on childhood worry is so limited, clinicians and researchers have tended to extrapolate findings from the adult literature. But is this an appropriate action? What aspects of childhood worry can be assumed to be the same in children as in adults, and where must we draw comparisons with care?

As described above, theories that have developed to account for worry in adults have been shown to have substantial relevance for younger worriers. This suggests that at least some aspects of the worry process are similar in adults and children. However, most of this research has been conducted on adolescents, and it is not clear that the same processes are active in younger children. In their review of developmental factors in the worry process, Vasey and Daleiden (1994) give an eloquent description of the developmental factors that are likely to impact on the process of worry in the developing child. However, they also point out that prior to about 8 years of age, the cognitive processes that we currently describe as worry may be too visual to qualify as worry as an adult would recognise it. If this is the case, then different processes may be at work, and adult models must be extrapolated to this population with care.

Briefly, Vasey and Daleiden (1994) suggest that to engage in worry as an adult would understand it, a child needs the ability to anticipate threat, and to elaborate threatening possibilities from a situation. It is not clear at what age this ability develops.

Additionally, according to Vasey and Daleiden (1994), development of self concept seems likely to be important in worry, as worry, particularly in clinical samples, is very self-related. This seems to be true for adults and for children (see above). However, before the age of about 8 years, children tend not to compare their functioning to that of others, but to fixed indicators of achievement, so worry in younger children is likely to be different in this respect to that of adults. Finally, they consider the impact of a child's developing meta-cognitive knowledge upon their capacity to worry. Very little is known about this, but they suggest that a knowledge of which psychological phenomena are 'normal', and which represent a deviation from normality is likely to be limited in young children. This, and an understanding of what can be done to manage worry, is likely to impact on children's response to their worry.

In support of this proposition, Muris, Merckelbach, Meesters et al. (2002) studied 248 children aged 3–14 years. Children were given Piagetian tasks to assess their level of cognitive development. The authors reported that level of cognitive development was positively correlated with an ability to elaborate worries, and with the presence or absence of a personal worry. The authors concluded that cognitive development mediated the relationship between worry and age that has been described.

In summary, much of what is written in this book will apply to children at some stages of development. However, developmental issues must be taken into account, and theories will always warrant further exploration with young populations before conclusions can be drawn.

PARENTS AND FAMILIES

Parent-child Relationships and Worry

In considering a child presenting with excessive worry, no assessment would be complete without an examination of the role that the parents might have in the genesis and maintenance of the difficulties. Until recently, there has been little information on the role of parents. However, in recent years, a number of studies have cast some light on the issue.

It has now been demonstrated on a number of occasions, that childhood anxiety in general is associated with a pattern of parenting characterised by over-protection (see Wood, McLeod, Sigman et al. (2003) for a review). This finding has now been extended specifically to childhood worry, in a study by Muris (2002), which demonstrated that over-protective parenting (as reported by children) was associated with worry, in a large questionnaire study of 13–16 year olds.

Similarly, we know that impaired parent-child attachment is associated with increased anxiety in the child (e.g. Warren, Huston, Egeland & Sroufe, 1997), and it has now been demonstrated that impaired attachment is also associated with worry. Muris, Meesters, Merckelbach et al. (2000) showed that securely attached children had lower worry scores than ambivalently/avoidantly attached children, although some of the results were robust only for boys. Additionally, the results deserve replication with other instruments, as the measure of attachment employed here may have been confounded with worry, as one question asked children whether they were 'worried my best friend doesn't really like me'.

Additional aspects of parenting that have been associated with anxiety in general, are 'rejection', 'emotional warmth', 'anxious parenting' and 'controlling' parenting, (which is similar to the concept of 'over-protection' described above). These constructs too, have now been associated specifically with worry. The Muris study described above (Muris et al., 2000), found that rejecting parenting was positively correlated with worry in male and female adolescents. Anxious rearing by either parent was correlated with worry, as was overcontrol by the mother, but only for boys. Emotional warmth from mothers was negatively correlated with worry for both male and female adolescents.

In a study of young adults (aged 18–26 years) Cartwright-Hatton and McNicol (submitted) showed a correlation between meta-worry (worry about worry) as measured by the Anxious Thoughts Inventory (AnTI–Wells (1994)) and retrospective reports of having been subject to an over-reactive parenting style, as measured by a modified version of the Parenting Scale (Arnold, O'Leary, Wolff & Acker, 1993). Over-reactive parenting is characterised by harsh discipline and frequent displays of anger. Over-reactive parenting was also shown to correlate with current anxiety symptoms in general, but not, as had been predicted, with the subscales of the AnTI measuring social or health worry.

Interestingly, in the same study (Cartwright-Hatton & McNicol, submitted), over-reactive parenting was also correlated with positive and negative meta-cognitive beliefs about worry, as measured by an adolescent version of the meta-cognitions questionnaire (Cartwright-Hatton, Mather et al., 2004). These beliefs appeared to mediate the relationship between reported parenting received as a child, and current anxiety levels. It was tentatively suggested that the style of parenting received in childhood shapes individuals' beliefs about their thought processes, and that this, in turn, shapes their response to anxiety and worry, and, therefore, the extent to which these are experienced as problematic.

Parents and Coping with Worry

It seems likely, from the studies described above, that worried children employ different coping styles to their less worried peers. If this is the case, is it possible that they have learnt some of these coping styles from their families? In an unpublished study, (Vasey, Hilliker, Williams & Daleiden, 1993) cited in Vasey and Daleiden (1994), it is reported that parents of worried children differed from the parents of control children in the types of coping strategies that they thought children should use to control their worries. In particular, the parents of the worried children appeared to endorse avoidance and distraction strategies more strongly than the parents of the controls.

It is becoming clear that parents have an important role in teaching children to manage their emotions. For example, there is now a substantial literature outlining the role that parents have in helping their children to cope in difficult or stressful circumstances (in particular, stressful medical procedures e.g. Salmon and Pereira (2002)). This literature demonstrates that parents' responses and reactions explain a large proportion of the variance in their children's coping. It seems likely, therefore, that parents' reactions to their children's worry, and perhaps the responses that they model in reaction to their own worry, will have a role to play in teaching children their coping responses.

INTERVENTIONS FOR CHILDHOOD WORRY

Unfortunately, there are (to this author's knowledge) no interventions that have been directed specifically at childhood worry. There are now a number of Cognitive Behaviour Therapy (CBT) based treatments that appear to have efficacy in treating childhood and adolescent anxiety in general (e.g. see Cartwright-Hatton, Roberts, Chitasabesan et al. (2004) for a review). However, these interventions have largely been targeted at the emotional (e.g. fear) and physiological aspects of anxiety. Very few treatment protocols have modules specifically for dealing with worry. Indeed, because of the developmental limitations on children's ability to use the more cognitive elements of CBT, most interventions focus heavily on behavioural elements, such as exposure and relaxation. If evidence from the adult literature is indicative, it seems unlikely that these elements will have a substantial impact on worry. Where cognitive elements are incorporated into treatment, these are usually limited to some 'positive self talk', or basic 'talking back' to fears. The newer approaches to worry, as taken in the adult field, such as stimulus control of worry, and attentional training, have not yet been reported in the child literature. Given the evidence cited above, it seems likely that where such interventions are found to have utility with adults, there is merit in attempting these with children. Developmental considerations would clearly need to be taken into account, but the reduced load that these interventions place on cognitive, and in particular, linguistic manipulation of information, suggests that they might have particular applicability for young worriers.

ASSESSMENT

As will have become clear, there are very few instruments that are designed to measure worry in children and adolescents. Most of the studies described above have employed idiosyncratic checklists or interviews designed for the study in question, with varying levels of attention to the psychometric properties of these. In large part, this lack of high-quality measures is due to the difficulties in measuring a concept that is as slippery as worry. This difficulty is compounded by the developmental issues that children bring. For instance, it is far from clear that young children have access to a reliable definition of worry, and their ability to report on this, therefore, with any degree of reliability and validity is constrained. A number of instruments are now available for assessing fears and anxiety in general, and a number of these have scales, or at least a few items, that attempt to measure worry. For instance, the widely used 'Revised Manifest Anxiety Scale for Children' (Reynolds & Richmond, 1978), has a 'worry/oversensitivity scale'. However, the reliability and validity of these worry-related items and subscales is often unclear. Instruments for measuring childhood anxiety in general are thoroughly reviewed elsewhere, (e.g. Langley, Bergman & Piacentini, 2002; Myers & Winters, 2002) and this information, therefore, will not be repeated here.

To this author's knowledge, there are only three modern, published, self-report instruments that are intended specifically to measure worry in children or adolescents. Probably the most widely used is the 'Penn State Worry Questionnaire for Children' (Chorpita, Tracey, Brown, Collica & Barlow, 1997). The instrument is a downwards translation of the well known 'Penn State Worry Questionnaire' (Meyer, Miller, Metzger & Borkovec, 1990), which was designed for use with adults. Minor wording changes have been made to enable it to be completed by a child with an average second grade reading level, and the number of items was reduced from 16 to 14. Employing a sample of 2nd-12th grade participants (approximately 7–18 years), the instrument was shown to have a single factor solution, and good internal consistency (alpha = .89). This factor solution and reliability did not differ substantially when repeated for older and younger sections of the sample. A recent re-examination of the psychometric properties of a Dutch translation of the PSWQ-C with a large sample of 8–12 year olds, has suggested that an 11-item version, with reverse-scored items removed, would have stronger internal consistency and factor structure. (Muris, Meesters & Gobel, 2001).

The 'Things I Worry About Scale' (Miller & Gallagher, 1996) has been developed on 13–19 year olds. It comprises 138 items, which appear to fall into 13 categories. Internal reliability alphas for all categories exceeded 0.8. However, limited validity data is available.

'The Worry Scale' (reported in Perrin & Last, 1997) is a 31 item instrument measuring 'worrisome thoughts. In children aged 5–13 years, it has good evidence of reliability (alpha > .88) for non-clinically referred children, as well as children with anxiety disorders. It is reported to correlate highly with a number of widely used measures of child anxiety.

Finally, it is worth noting that each of these instruments, and those assessing anxiety more generally, are designed using 'adult' conceptions of anxiety and worry. As Henker et al. (1995) write, the information that is obtained via these is 'filtered through the cognitive schemas of the adults who construct the instruments . . .' (Henker et al., 1995 p. 688). This brings us back to the most critical difficulty that this field faces, which is an understanding of what constitutes worry for children and adolescents, and indeed the issue of whether worry as an adult would understand it actually exists at all.

QUESTIONS AND FUTURE RESEARCH

The lack of thoughtfully developed, reliable and valid instruments for assessing worry and associated psychological factors in children and adolescents has been perhaps the most serious constraint on our understanding of childhood worry. More instruments are urgently needed. However, this complex task will require the researcher to take into account not only the conceptual issues that are involved in measuring worry and associated factors, but the developmental issues brought by young participants. Separate instruments will probably be needed to assess younger and older children. In addition, the nature of the assessment will need to be taken into account, as it seems likely that the way in which children are asked about their worry has an impact on what is reported (Henker et al., 1995). With young children (probably younger than about 8 years) it may be necessary to have instruments that do not rely on the ability to read. Indeed, it may be preferable to have instruments that are rated by someone other than the child themselves—perhaps by employing some kind of observational coding system. Each of these solutions brings difficulties of its own.

The conceptual question of what constitutes worry in these younger age groups is deserving of serious consideration. Is worry present in younger children? If not, are there analogous processes, and do these predispose the child to becoming a worrier as an adult? Prospective and longitudinal studies are needed to answer these questions.

Much of the research described in this chapter has employed non-clinical populations. Although worry is thought to operate on a continuum, and analogue samples have been successfully used in the adult literature, we have little evidence that extrapolations of this nature can be made with children. More research on clinical worriers is urgently required.

Much of the fruitful research that has been described in this chapter has been downward extensions of theories that have been useful in understanding adult worry. This is probably a sensible strategy. However, in doing this, care must be taken not to neglect areas of special importance in the understanding of mental health in children. In particular, the role of families is critical. There is evidence that the most effective interventions with anxious children are those that include families in treatment (Cobham, Dadds & Spence, 1998). If families are to be included in the treatment of childhood disorders of worry, more must be known about their contribution to its aetiology and maintenance. In particular, we need to know more about how parents respond to worry in their children, at what point they should intervene, and how best they should do this. As anxiety often aggregates in families, more attention must be paid to the mechanisms by which worry can be transmitted between generations. In particular, it seems likely that beliefs about worry and employment of particular coping styles may be modelled from parent to child.

CONCLUSION

This evidence leaves us with the suggestion that the processes involved in worrying may begin at a rather young age. The implications for treatment research are clear—far more needs to be done to address worry in childhood. However, if treatments are to progress, we have a long way to go in our understanding of the basic processes that are operating in these early stages of worry.

REFERENCES

Arnold, D.S., O'Leary, S.G., Wolff, L.S. & Acker, M.M. (1993). The Parenting Scale: A Measure of Dysfunctional Parenting in Discipline Situations. *Psychological assessment*, **5(2)**, 137–144.

Bell-Dolan, D.J., Last, C.G. & Strauss, C.C. (1990). Symptoms of Anxiety Disorders in Normal Children. *Journal of the American Academy of Child and Adolescent Psychiatry*, **29(5)**, 759–765.

Boyle, M.H., Offord, D.R., Racine, Y., Sanford, M., Szatmari, P., Fleming, J.E., et al. (1993). Evaluation of the Diagnostic Interview for Children and Adolescents for use in general population samples. *Journal of Abnormal Child Psychology*, **21(6)**, 663–681.

Cartwright-Hatton, S., Mather, A., Illingworth, V., Brocki, J., Harrington, R. & Wells, A. (2004). Development and Preliminary Validation of the Meta-Cognitions

Questionnaire—Adolescent Version. *Journal of Anxiety Disorders*, **18(3)**, 411–422.

Cartwright-Hatton, S. & McNicol, K. (submitted). Early Parenting and Anxiety and Worry in a Sample of Young Adults: An Exploratory Study of the Relationship with Schemata and Meta-Cognitive Beliefs.

Cartwright-Hatton, S., Roberts, C., Chitsabesan, P., Fothergill, C. & Harrington, R. (2004). Systematic Review of the Efficacy of Cognitive Behaviour Therapies for Childhood and Adolescent Anxiety Disorders. *British Journal of Clinical Psychology*, **43**, 421–436.

Chorpita, B.F., Tracey, S.A., Brown, T.A., Collica, T.J. & Barlow, D.H. (1997). Assessment of worry in children and adolescents: An adaptation of the Penn State Worry Questionnaire. *Behaviour Research and Therapy*, **35(6)**, 569–581.

Cobham, V.E., Dadds, M.R. & Spence, S.H. (1998). The Role of Parental Anxiety in the Treatment of Childhood Anxiety. *Journal of Consulting and Clinical Psychology*, **66(6)**, 893–905.

Ehrenreich, J.T. & Gross, A.M. (2002). Biased attentional behavior in childhood anxiety. A review of theory and current empirical investigation. *Clinical Psychology Review*, **22**, 991–1008.

Ford, T., Goodman, R. & Meltzer, H. (1999). The British Child and Adolescent Mental Health Survey: The Prevalence of DSM-IV Disorders. *Journal of the American Academy of Child & Adolescent Psychiatry*, **42(10)**, 1203–1211.

Henker, B., Whalen, C.K. & O'Neil, R. (1995). Worldly and Workaday Worries: Contemporary Concerns of Children and Young Adolescents. *Journal of Abnormal Child Psychology*, **23(6)**, 685–702.

Kaufman, K.L., Brown, R.T., Graves, K., Henderson, P. & Revolinski, M. (1993). What, Me Worry? *Clinical Pediatrics*, 8–14.

Kovacs, M., Gatsonis, C., Paulauskas, S. & Richards, C. (1989). Depressive Disorders in Childhood. IV. A Longitudinal Study of Comorbidity with and Risk for Anxiety Disorders. *Archives of General Psychiatry*, **46**, 776–782.

Kushner, M., Sher, K. & Beitman, B. (1990). The Relation Between Alcohol Problems and Anxiety Disorders. *American Journal of Psychiatry*, **147(6)**, 685–695.

Langley, A.K., Bergman, R.L. & Piacentini, J. (2002). Assessment of Childhood Anxiety. *International Review of Psychiatry*, **14**, 102–113.

Last, C.G., Strauss, C.C. & Francis, G. (1987). Comorbidity among childhood anxiety disorders. *The Journal of Nervous and Mental Disease*, **175**, 726–730.

Laugesen, N., Dugas, M.J. & Bukowski, W.M. (2003). Understanding Adolescent Worry: The Application of a Cognitive Model. *Journal of Abnormal Child Psychology*, **31(1)**, 55–64.

Mather, A. & Cartwright-Hatton, S. (2004). Cognitive Predictors of Obsessive-Compulsive Symptoms in Adolescence: A Preliminary Investigation. *Journal of Clinical Child and Adolescent Psychology*.

Meyer, T.J., Miller, M.L., Metzger, R.L. & Borkovec, T.D. (1990). Development and validation of the Penn State Worry Questionnaire. *Behaviour Research and Therapy*, **28**, 487–495.

Miller, R. & Gallagher, M. (1996). The 'Things I Worry About' scale: Further developments in surveying the worries of postprimary school pupils. *Educational and Psychological Measurement*, **56(6)**, 972–994.

Morris, L.W., Finkelstein, C.S. & Fisher, W.R. (1976). Components of School Anxiety: Developmental Trends and Sex Differences. *Journal of Genetic Psychology*, **128**, 49–57.

Muris, P. (2002). Parental rearing behaviors and worry in adolescents. *Psychological Reports*, **91**, 428–430.

Muris, P., Meesters, C. & Gobel, M. (2001). Reliability, validity, and normative data of the Penn State Worry Questionnaire in 8–12-yr-old children. *Journal of Behavior Therapy & Experimental Psychiatry*, **32(2)**, 63–72.

Muris, P., Meesters, C., Merckelbach, H. & Hulsenbeck, P. (2000). Worry in Children is Related to Perceived Parental Rearing and Attachment. *Behaviour Research and Therapy*, **38(5)**, 487–497.

Muris, P., Meesters, C., Merckelbach, H., Sermon, A. & Zwakhalen, S. (1998). Worry in normal children. *Journal of the American Academy of Child & Adolescent Psychiatry*, **37(7)**, 703–710.

Muris, P., Merckelbach, H. & Luijten, M. (2002). The connection between cognitive development and specific fears and worries in normal children and children with below-average intellectual abilities: a preliminary study. *Behaviour Research and Therapy*, **40**, 37–56.

Muris, P., Merckelbach, H., Meesters, C. & van den Brand, K. (2002). Cognitive development and worry in normal children. *Cognitive Therapy and Research*, **26(6)**, 775–787.

Myers, K. & Winters, N. (2002). Ten-year review of rating scales. II: Scales for internalizing disorders. *Journal of the American Academy of Child and Adolescent Psychiatry*, **41(6)**, 634–659.

Orton, G.L. (1982). A comparative study of children's worries. *Journal of Psychology*, **110**, 153–162.

Perrin, S. & Last, C.G. (1997). Worrisome thoughts in children clinically referred for anxiety disorders. *Journal of Child Clinical Psychology*, **26**, 181–189.

Pine, D.S. (1997). Childhood Anxiety Disorders. *Current Opinion in Pediatrics*, **9**, 329–339.

Reynolds, C.R. & Richmond, B.O. (1978). What I Think and Feel: A Revised Version of the Children's Manifest Anxiety Scale. *Journal of Abnormal Child Psychology*, **5**, 237–249.

Salmon, K. & Pereira, J.K. (2002). Predicting Children's Response to an Invasive Medical Investigation: The Influence of Effortful Control and Parent Behavior. *Journal of Pediatric Psychology*, **27(3)**, 227–233.

Silverman, W.K., La Greca, A.M. & Wasserstein, S. (1995). What do children worry about? Worries and their relation to anxiety. *Child Development*, **66**, 671–686.

Suarez, L. & Bell-Dolan, D.J. (2001). The Relationship of Child Worry to Cognitive Biases: Threat Interpretation and Likelihood of Event Occurrence. *Behavior Therapy*, **32**, 425–442.

Vasey, M.W., Crnic, K.A. & Carter, W.G. (1994). Worry in Childhood: A Developmental Perspective. *Cognitive Therapy and Research*, **18(6)**, 529–549.

Vasey, M.W. & Daleiden, E.L. (1994). Worry in Children. In G. Davey & F. Tallis (Eds), *Worrying. Perspectives on Theory, Assessment and Treatment* (pp. 185–208). Chichester, UK: John Wiley & Sons, Ltd.

Vasey, M.W., Hilliker, D., Williams, L.L. & Daleiden, E.L. (1993). *The regulation of worrisome thoughts in anxiety-disordered and normal children: Parental perspectives.* Paper presented at the Biennial meeting of the Society for Research in Child Development, New Orleans.

Warren, S.L., Huston, L., Egeland, B. & Sroufe, L.A. (1997). Child and Adolescent Anxiety Disorders and Early Attachment. *Journal of the American Academy of Child and Adolescent Psychiatry*, **36(5)**, 637–644.

Weems, C.F., Silverman, W.K. & La Greca, A.M. (2000). What Do Youth Referred for Anxiety Problems Worry About? Worry and Its Relation to Anxiety and Anxiety Disorders in Children and Adolescents. *Journal of Abnormal Child Psychology*, **28(1)**, 63–72.

Wells, A. (1994). A multi-dimensional measure of worry: development and preliminary validation of the Anxious Thoughts Inventory. *Anxiety Stress and Coping*, **6**, 289–299.

Wells, A. (1995). Meta-cognition and worry: A cognitive model of generalized anxiety disorder. *Behavioural & Cognitive Psychotherapy*, **23(3)**, 301–320.

Wood, J., McLeod, B.D., Sigman, M., Hwang, W.-C. & Chu, B.C. (2003). Parenting and childhood anxiety: Theory, empirical findings and future directions. *Journal of Child Psychology & Psychiatry & Allied Disciplines*, **44(1)**, 134–151.

Part II

THE ASSESSMENT OF WORRY

Chapter 7

THE PENN STATE WORRY QUESTIONNAIRE (PSWQ)

Helen M. Startup and Thane M. Erickson

Since publication of an earlier review (cf. Molina & Borkovec, 1994), the quantity and quality of worry-related research has flourished. Research has sought to elucidate both content and process characteristics of the phenomenon, to consider the mechanisms that transform general worry into clinical worry, and to differentiate it from related constructs such as ruminative thought and obsessive thought (Davey, Tallis & Bond, 1994; Startup & Davey, 2001, 2003; Turner, Beidel & Stanley, 1992; Watkins, 2004). Furthering our conceptual understanding in this way has relied on the availability of reliable and valid assessment tools. Notably, the Penn State Worry Questionnaire (Meyer, Miller, Metzger & Borkovec, 1990) has been the most widely-used measure of the frequency, intensity, and uncontrollability of worry. It has been employed within both clinical and non-clinical populations and is routinely used by both practicing clinicians and those engaged in applied research (Molina & Borkovec, 1994).

The need for a psychometrically sound measure of worry was reinforced by the introduction of DSM-III-R (American Psychiatric Association, 1987). With its introduction, Generalized Anxiety Disorder ceased being a residual diagnostic category. Although exclusion criteria still existed, the key variable of "unrealistic or excessive anxiety and worry (apprehensive expectation)" assumed paramount definitional significance for the disorder (APA, 1987, p. 252). The fundamental significance of this feature was further buttressed in the fourth edition of DSM (DSM-IV, APA, 1994), which added the requirement that worry be perceived as "uncontrollable" (Brown, Barlow & Liebowitz, 1994). With this in mind and by drawing together the available research of the time, Silvia Molina and Tom Borkovec (1994) noted that in order to adequately tap this phenomenon, it followed that a trait measure of worry would need to evaluate the following: a) the *typical* tendency of the individual to worry, b) the *excessiveness* or intensity of the worry experience, and c) the tendency to worry in *general* without

Worry and Its Psychological Disorders: Theory, Assessment and Treatment. Edited by G. C. L. Davey and A. Wells. © 2006 John Wiley & Sons, Ltd.

restricting the topic to one or a small number of situations. Tom Meyer's (1988) master's thesis aimed to do just this and to provide a trait measure of worry, which focused on clinically significant and pathological aspects of the process.

The aim of this chapter is not to review all available research on worry and worry assessment to date, which would indeed constitute a rather unwieldy task given the quantity of relevant published work currently available. Rather, our aim is to provide a useful, selective, and sufficiently broad summary of published work relevant to the assessment of worry to be of use to both clinicians and researchers. This chapter will consider the psychometric properties and descriptive characteristics of the PSWQ, including relevant means and standard deviations across key criterion and demographic groups. Some recent modifications and novel uses of the PSWQ will also be reported. The relationship of the Penn State Worry Questionnaire to other relevant measurement tools, such as a key measure of the content of worry, will also be summarized, as will the relationship of worry to anxiety and depression. Finally, consideration will be given to what can be deduced about the similarities and differences between worry and other related cognitive phenomena, such as obsessive thought and ruminative thought (see also Chapter 2).

SCALE DEVELOPMENT

For a comprehensive description of the initial development of the PSWQ, the reader is referred to Meyer et al. (1990) and Molina and Borkovec (1994). To summarize Molina and Borkovec (1994), the PSWQ was derived from the factor analysis of 161 items thought to be related to worry. These items were drawn from clinical and research experience with GAD patients and worriers, daily diaries from GAD patients, a prior cognitive-somatic anxiety inventory, and theoretical views on worry. The resulting questionnaire, which asked participants to rate each item on a 5-point scale ("not at all typical" to "very typical"), was administered to 337 college students and submitted to factor analysis with oblique rotation. Seven factors emerged. However, because the goal was to create a trait measure of the general tendency to worry without regard to content-specific topics, subsequent attention was focused on the first factor, which reflected the frequency and intensity of worry in general (accounting for 22.6% of the variance). The final 16-item questionnaire reflected those items and sufficiently met the requirements sought by Molina and Borkovec (1994).

THE PSWQ AND SCORING PROTOCOL

The PSWQ (see Table 7.1) consists of 16 items, of which five items are negatively loaded and have to be reverse-scored (items 1, 3, 8, 10 and 11).

Table 7.1   The Penn State worry questionnaire

Enter the number that describes how typical or characteristic each item is of you, putting the number next to each item.

1	2	3	4	5
Not at all typical		somewhat typical		Very typical

1. If I don't have enough time to do everything, I don't worry about it. — (R)
2. My worries overwhelm me. —
3. I don't tend to worry about things. — (R)
4. Many situations make me worry. —
5. I know I shouldn't worry about things, but I just can't help it —
6. When I'm under pressure, I worry a lot. —
7. I am always worrying about something. —
8. I find it easy to dismiss worrisome thoughts. — (R)
9. As soon as I finish one task, I start to worry about everything else I have to do. —
10. I never worry about anything. — (R)
11. When there is nothing more I can do about a concern, I don't worry about it anymore. — (R)
12. I've been a worrier all my life. —
13. I notice that I have been worrying about things. —
14. Once I start worrying, I can't stop. —
15. I worry all the time. —
16. I worry about projects until they are all done. —

Participants are instructed to indicate how typical statements are of them. Responses to each statement are scored on a five-point scale varying from "not at all typical of me" to "very typical of me." A total score is calculated by summing the items (noting those that are reverse-scored). Scores range from 16–80 and a higher score represents a greater degree of pathological worry.

FACTOR STRUCTURE OF THE PSWQ

Principal components analyses of the PSWQ have tended to yield a uni-factorial solution (e.g., Brown et al., 1992; Meyer et al., 1990; van Rijsoort, Emmelkamp & Vervaeke, 1999), with some exceptions (e.g., Stöber, 1995). However, subsequent confirmatory factor analyses have suggested that the PSWQ contains a first factor comprised of the 11 items worded in the direction of worry endorsement, as well as a second factor consisting of the five reverse-scored items (Brown, 2003; Fresco, Heimberg, Mennin & Turk, 2002; Hazlett-Stevens, Ullman & Craske, 2004). Even so, the PSWQ is best conceptualized as representing a single underlying factor (i.e. excessive/uncontrollable worry), and the clustering of the reverse scored items results from method effects (as the "Absence of Worry"; Fresco et al., 2002) rather than holding any theoretical significance (Brown, 2003).

RELIABILITY OF THE PSWQ–INTERNAL CONSISTENCY AND STABILITY

The 16-item PSWQ has routinely demonstrated high internal consistency in the case of both clinical and non-clinical criterion groups (Molina & Borkovec, 1994). Cronbach's alpha coefficients have been shown to range between 0.88 and 0.95 for clinical samples (GAD patients and mixed anxiety disorder samples, as diagnosed by the Anxiety Disorders Interview Schedule-Revised; ADIS-R, Di Nardo & Barlow, 1988) and non-clinical college student and community derived samples (assessed by questionnaire; Borkovec, 1994; Brown et al., 1992; Davey, 1993; Molina & Stöber, 1998; van Rijsoort et al., 1999). The PSWQ also demonstrates good test-retest reliability amongst samples of college students (r = 0.74-0.92 over intervals of 2 to 10 weeks; Molina & Borkovec, 1994; Meyer et al., 1990; Stöber, 1998), as well as substantial inter-rater reliability amongst college students (when comparisons are made with peer ratings, intraclass correlation coefficient 0.42; Stöber, 1998) and between peer and self-ratings (interclass correlation 0.55; Stöber, 1998). The PSWQ has also demonstrated sensitivity to change across both 6-week and 12-week therapeutic interventions for GAD (Borkovec & Costello, 1993).

PSWQ DESCRIPTIVE STATISTICS

Because the PSWQ has been utilized in assessing various symptomatic and asymptomatic groups, we provide representative descriptive values, serving as a heuristic to aid clinicians and researchers in making judgments about particular cases or patient/participant selection. Table 7.2 contains the means, standard deviations, and sample sizes for PSWQ scores collated across criterion groups from a number of studies summarized below. The burgeoning quantity of recent research on pathological worry, as well as space constraints of this chapter, prohibits an exhaustive review of PSWQ descriptive values. However, the present section partially updates the review of Molina and Borkovec (1994), both drawing from and extending it.

General Samples

As might be expected, the lowest PSWQ scores tend to occur in *non-anxious selected groups* and *unselected groups* (i.e., persons not categorized according to any criteria). For instance, when individuals are categorized as

Table 7.2   PSWQ means and standard deviations for various criterion groups

	Mean	Standard deviation*	n	Number of data sets
General Samples				
Non-anxious selected groups				
GADQ	44.27	11.44	2056	6
GAD-Q-IV	37.50	11.50	1175	3
Diagnostic interview (ADIS-R; adults)	30.98	8.13	74	3
Diagnostic interview (SCID I/P; older adults)	39.7	12.52	10	1
Unselected groups				
Predominantly college students	47.42	13.40	2271	11
Community samples (adults)	42.67	11.71	405	2
Community samples (older adults)	38.94	10.98	156	2
Analogue GAD Samples				
GAD by questionnaire (GADQ)	63.24	9.33	324	7
GAD by questionnaire (GAD-Q-IV)	63.58	10.81	298	3
Analogue Clinical Non-GAD Samples				
PTSD by questionnaire	57.40	7.30	11	1
OCD by questionnaire	54.80	12.20	12	1
Panic disorder by questionnaire	50.68	16.84	68	1
Social phobia by questionnaire	50.28	14.15	154	1
Irritable Bowel Syndrome by questionnaire	53.83	13.58	77	1
Clinical Samples				
GAD (adults)	67.16	9.16	324	7
GAD (older adults)	63.23	9.66	274	3
Panic disorder with agoraphobia	58.30	13.65	64	1
Panic disorder	55.2	14.33	145	2
Social phobia	55.81	14.41	254	3
OCD	59.16	15.35	64	3
Specific phobia	50.89	16.01	45	2
PTSD	56.30	14.60	25	1
Major depressive disorder (no GAD)	61.77	13.98	355	2
Patients with persecutory delusions	52.27	18.44	40	2
Psychiatric controls	43.10	14.90	141	1
Primary insomnia (older adults)	44.80	10.90	60	1

*Note: Pooled standard deviation is reported for cells with combined data from multiple studies.

non-anxious according to diagnostic screen self-report questionnaires such as the original Generalized Anxiety Disorder Questionnaire (GADQ; Roemer, Borkovec, Posa & Borkovec, 1995) or a version revised to match *DSM-IV* criteria (GAD-Q-IV; Newman et al., 2000), they show average PSWQ scores near or below the scale's midpoint (Erickson, 2002; Molina &

Borkovec, 1994). Persons not meeting GAD criteria during structured diagnostic interviews (in this case, the Anxiety Disorders Interview Schedule-Revised, ADIS-R; DiNardo & Barlow, 1988) yield low scores as well (Molina & Borkovec, 1994). Unselected groups, whether in predominantly student samples (Erickson, 2004; Molina & Borkovec, 1994; Sibrava, 2005) or community samples (Gillis, Haaga & Ford, 1995; van Rijsoort et al., 1999) tend to exhibit slightly higher average scores, presumably reflecting the natural inclusion of a subset of high worriers in any general sample, raising the mean score.

Analogue Clinical GAD Samples

Whereas unselected and non-anxious selected individuals report relatively low levels of worry, analogue clinical (GAD) samples exhibit significantly higher PSWQ scores. Such samples are typically comprised of individuals "diagnosed" by a version of the GADQ. Remarkably similar mean levels have been reported for individuals identified as having analogue GAD via the GADQ (reported in Borkovec & Molina, 1994) or GAD-Q-IV (Erickson, 2002). Of course, analogue samples may differ appreciably from clinical samples, and thus must be regarded with caution; however, knowledge of these means is important given that many experimental studies recruit analogue GAD participants (e.g., East & Watts, 1994; Erickson & Pincus, in press), as do studies testing "interventions" with subclinical samples (e.g., Stoeber & Bittencourt, 1998). Nonetheless, analogue GAD samples demonstrate mean PSWQ levels near those of clinical GAD samples.

Clinical GAD Samples

Clinical samples, in which patients receive GAD diagnosis on the basis of a structured diagnostic interview, consistently manifest the highest PSWQ scores. This fact attests to the criterion validity of the PSWQ because individuals seeking treatment for excessive, uncontrollable, and pervasive worry ought to score most highly. Such a finding has been borne out in many studies (Borkovec & Costello, 1993; Borkovec et al., 2002; Brown, Antony & Barlow, 1992; Brown, Moras, Zinbarg & Barlow, 1993; Chelminski & Zimmerman, 2003; Fresco, Mennin, Heimberg & Turk, 2003; Starcevic, 1994).

Non-GAD Symptomatic Samples

Given the status of pathological worry as the cardinal symptom of GAD, one would expect higher PSWQ scores in GAD groups than in those within other diagnostic categories. Nevertheless, high PSWQ scores are often present in non-GAD analogue clinical samples, including those with symptoms of post-traumatic stress disorder (PTSD) and obsessive compulsive disorder (OCD; both in Molina & Borkovec, 1994), as well as panic disorder and social phobia (both from Erickson, 2002). Similarly, individuals diagnosed by questionnaire with analogue irritable bowel syndrome exhibit high levels of worry (Hazlett-Stevens, Craske, Mayer, Chang & Naliboff, 2003). Despite substantial worry elevation in these analogue non-GAD groups, analogue GAD groups manifest slightly higher average scores, as indicated in Table 7.2. However, because analogue studies have infrequently screened out other comorbid analogue conditions, such groups may well be symptomatically heterogeneous.

In samples with clinically diagnosed patients, a parallel picture has emerged; GAD patients tend to show higher PSWQ scores than other patients, though not in every case. For example, GAD patients have scored significantly higher than those with (excluding secondary GAD) simple phobia, panic disorder with and without agoraphobia, social phobia, or OCD (Brown et al., 1992, 1993). Likewise, in a large adult outpatient sample, GAD patients manifested significantly greater scores than those with "pure" forms of social phobia, specific phobia, PTSD, panic disorder, major depressive disorder, and OCD. However, these other diagnostic groups are characterized by heightened, but not extreme, worry, as are patients with persecutory delusions (predominantly inpatients with paranoid schizophrenia; Freeman & Garety, 1999; Startup, Freeman, & Garety, 2005). Patients without anxiety or mood disorders (i.e., psychiatric control sample; Chelminski & Zimmerman, 2003) exhibit lower PSWQ scores than patients with anxiety and mood disorders.

Although patients with other diagnoses may sometimes report PSWQ levels comparable to those with GAD (e.g., depression, in Starcevic, 1995), this may be a result of high levels of comorbid GAD in the comparison groups, or perhaps because *DSM-IV* hierarchy rules do not permit diagnosis of GAD if symptoms occur during episodes of other disorders (Chelminski & Zimmerman, 2003). Fresco et al. (2003) found essentially equivalent PSWQ levels for patients with GAD versus comorbid social phobia and GAD (~68), but pure social phobia scores were significantly lower (~56). Chelminski and Zimmerman (2003) also found no differences between pure GAD versus major MDD with GAD (both around 68), but pure MDD was significantly lower.

In summary, contrasting mean PSWQ scores across criterion groups indicates that worry is highest in GAD, though prevalent across a spectrum of psychological disorders, supporting the overall capacity of the PSWQ to discriminate GAD symptoms. However, determination of ideal score values that distinguish groups requires brief consideration of studies examining cut-scores.

PSWQ Cut-Points For Differentiating Various Groups

Recent studies have enhanced the utility of the PSWQ by testing for optimal cut-scores to screen for GAD "caseness." Several studies have applied receiver operating characteristic analysis to determine PSWQ scores that optimize sensitivity (likelihood of identifying "true positives" from all persons with positive diagnosis according to the questionnaire) and specificity (likelihood of identifying "true negatives" from all persons without diagnosis on the measure) vis-à-vis clinician diagnosis or questionnaire-selected analogue GAD. Behar, Alcaine, Zuellig and Borkovec (2003) found that a PSWQ score of 45 optimized sensitivity and specificity in discriminating treatment-seeking GAD clients from non-anxious controls; in contrast, in a large student sample, a score of 62 performed best. This latter, higher, score was required to differentiate analogue GAD individuals (categorized via GAD-Q-IV) from those with self-reported diagnoses of social anxiety disorder, moderate depression, and/or PTSD. This highlights the fact that the ability of the PSWQ to identify GAD depends on the sample composition in relation to other affective symptomatology.

Similarly, Fresco et al. (2003) found that optimal PSWQ scores for identifying clinician-diagnosed GAD caseness varied depending on the goal (i.e., sensitivity, specificity, or both) and the target group from which GAD was being differentiated. For discrimination of "pure" GAD from "pure" social anxiety disorder, scores that optimized sensitivity (57), specificity (69), and both (65) were reported. In comparison, discrimination of primary or secondary GAD from pure social phobia yielded scores of 57, 68, and 65, respectively. Chelminski and Zimmerman (2003) reported convergent results in regard to a score that provides the best balance of sensitivity and specificity in differentiating GAD patients from non-GAD patients, arriving at a score of 64 in a large outpatient sample. It is noteworthy that several of these optimized cut-scores fall in a comparable range with aforementioned means for GAD patients.

In sum, the PSWQ demonstrates the ability to discriminate GAD, but this capacity depends upon the context and purpose for utilizing the questionnaire; clinicians and researchers should choose cut-scores based upon consideration of their goals. If the aim is to avoid failing to detect individuals with GAD symptoms, lower scores may be used; to avoid false positives, higher scores are recommended. Furthermore, higher scores are required to discriminate GAD from other conditions prone to heightened worry, whereas lower scores suffice when the comparison group is a non-anxious sample.

PSWQ Scores in Relation to Demographic Variables

Gender. Consideration of various uses for the PSWQ additionally requires taking account of whether scores remain stable across demographic groups. With regard to gender, mixed results have surfaced; scores sometimes differ little between males and females, as shown in community samples varying in age (Gillis et al., 1995; van Rijsoort et al., 1999), mixed-age clinical samples (e.g., Brown et al., 1991), and in older adult GAD patient groups (e.g., Stanley, Novy, Bourland, Beck & Averill, 2001). When gender differences are present, females invariably score higher than males. For instance, females have scored higher in (a) child and adolescent general samples on the standard PSWQ or a modified version (Chorpita, Tracey, Brown, Collica & Barlow, 1997; Muris, Meesters & Gobel, 2001), (b) selected non-anxious college student samples (e.g., Erickson, 2002) and, (c) older adult community samples (Skarborn & Nicki, 2000). Most typically, gender differences occur largely in general or non-anxious groups, rather than clinical samples. The structure of the PSWQ demonstrated invariance across males and females in a large outpatient sample (Brown, 2003), consistent with the original conclusion of Molina and Borkovec (1994) that gender has little consistent effect on levels of worry endorsement in GAD patient samples.

Ethnicity. With rare exceptions (e.g., Min & Won, 1999), the PSWQ has not been assessed across particular ethnic, racial, or cultural designations. However, one non-clinical sample reported no PSWQ differences between Caucasian, African American, and Asian American college students (Scott, Eng & Heimberg, 2002). A community sample of older adults also found comparable PSWQ scores across Japanese Americans and European Americans (combined samples yielded $m = 33.94$, $sd = 13.10$, $n = 129$; Watari & Brodbeck, 2000). At present, there is no reason to assume ethnic or cultural differences in PSWQ scores exist, although the dearth of relevant research underscores the need for further investigation.

Age. In contrast to ethnicity, age is a demographic variable that exerts apparent influence on PSWQ scores. Older adults have reported significantly lower scores than younger adults in samples of both unselected community members (Gillis et al., 1995) and GAD patients (Hopko et al., 2003). Older age may also impact PSWQ psychometric properties; in studies employing clinical samples of older adults with GAD, the PSWQ has demonstrated reasonable internal consistency and validity (Beck, Stanley & Zebb, 1995; Stanley et al., 2001), but poor temporal stability (Stanley et al., 2001). Also, although two factors were obtained for the PSWQ in one study (Beck et al., 1995), existing one- and two-factor solutions (based on younger adults) proved unsatisfactory in another sample of older adults (Hopko et al., 2003). However, after the removal of eight items (retaining items 2, 4, 5, 6, 7, 9, 12, and 13), an abbreviated version of the PSWQ demonstrated good psychometric properties (Hopko et al., 2003).

Even though the PSWQ displays more consistent psychometric properties in younger than older adult samples, it has been utilized in several studies with the former. Table 7.2 reports descriptive data for samples that used the standard version in older samples with GAD (Hopko et al., 2003; Stanley et al., 2001; Wetherell, Gatz, & Craske, 2003), primary insomniacs (Pallesen et al., 2002), primary care patients without diagnosis (Stanley et al., 2003), and unselected community samples (Pallesen et al., 2002; Skarborn & Nicki, 2000). Means have also been obtained for the revised (8-item) PSWQ in a sample with older adult GAD patients ($m = 30.9$, $sd = 6.6$, $n = 160$; Hopko et al., 2003). (It should be noted that this measure has a range of 8–40 versus the standard 16–80.) In a sample of older primary care patients with GAD versus no diagnosis, Stanley et al. (2003) identified a cut-point of 50 for the standard version, and 22 for the modified PSWQ in optimizing prediction of group membership. However, further research must determine optimal cut-scores and psychometric adequacy, for both the standard and modified PSWQ in older populations (see Chapter 5).

The PSWQ can also be used to assess worry in children (see Chapter 6), but may perform better in a revised format. Chorpita et al. (1997) adapted the PSWQ for youth by rewording nine items to second grade level and changing the Likert response scale from five to four points (0–3). Examination of psychometric properties in a community school sample of youth in grades 1–12 led to the elimination of two items. The remaining 14 items had a range of 0–42, yielding the PSWQ for Children (PSWQ-C). This measure demonstrated a single-factor structure, as well as satisfactory psychometric properties in student and clinical samples (see Table 7.3 for descriptives). In the unselected community sample, adolescents (age 12–18) scored higher than younger (age 6-11) children. In a separate sub-study, youths with GAD scored significantly higher than those with other anxiety disorders, who in turn scored significantly higher than non-anxious youths. Muris et al. (2001) examined PSWQ-C scores in a student sample, finding that girls scored significantly higher than boys. Principal components analysis of the PSWQ-C in a student sample led Muris et al. (2001) to drop the three remaining negatively-worded items, giving a total score range of 0–27.

Overall, the PSWQ does not seem prone to marked bias across various demographic variables. However, several studies suggest that gender and

Table 7.3   PSWQ-C means and standard deviations

	Mean	Standard deviation*	n	Number of data sets
General Samples				
Unselected samples	15.24	14.18	679	2
Selected non-GAD	9.50	4.3	10	1
Clinical Samples				
GAD	27.07	5.43	14	1
Other anxiety disorders	20.80	8.97	10	1

*Note: Pooled standard deviation is reported for cells with combined data from multiple studies.

age may influence scores. If so, versions adapted for usage with children or older adults may be more appropriate to use with these respective groups.

THE PSWQ AND RELATED COGNITIVE PHENOMENA—SIMILARITY AND DIFFERENCE

Anxiety and Depression

As might be expected, within analogue samples the PSWQ correlates significantly with anxiety and depression as measured by the State Trait Anxiety Inventory (STAI; Spielberger, 1983) and the Beck Depression Inventory (BDI; Beck et al., 1961) respectively. Correlations with the STAI trait are found to be r = 0.64-0.79 (Meyer et al., 1990; Davey, 1993; van Rijsoort et al., 1999; Wells & Carter, 1999). A lower correlation is reported with the STAI state, r = 0.49 (Meyer et al., 1990), whereas correlations with the BDI are more variable, r = 0.36-0.62 (Meyer et al., 1990; Van Rijsoort et al., 1999). Both worry (as measured by the PSWQ) and depressive rumination (as measured by the Response Styles Questionnaire, RSQ; Nolen-Hoeksema & Morrow, 1991) are also highly correlated in a non-clinical population (r = 0.51; Watkins, 2004).

Within clinical populations, few studies have explored these relationships. In one small study (n = 14) of individuals meeting the criteria for GAD (via GADQ), PSWQ scores correlated with trait anxiety (STAI) but not with scores on the Beck Anxiety inventory (Beck et al., 1988) or Beck Depression inventory (Freeman & Garety, 1999).

Worry and Intrusive/Obsessive Thought

At present, GAD joins OCD in being the only anxiety disorders with a core cognitive component as its defining feature (GAD-worry,

OCD-obsessions). Moreover, it is perhaps the potential overlap between these two cognitive features that threatens the discriminability of the two disorders (Brown, Dowdall, Cote & Barlow, 1994).

Significant correlations between measures of obsessions and worry have been reported for non-clinical populations (Freeston et al., 1994; Tallis & de Silva, 1992; Wells & Papageorgiou, 1998; van Rijsoort et al., 2001; Wells & Papageorgiou, 1998) and clinical populations (Brown et al., 1993). Associations between worry and obsessions have mostly been investigated by correlating the PSWQ with the Maudsley Obsessive Compulsive Inventory (MOCI; Hodgson & Rachman, 1977) and the Padua Inventory (PI; Sanavio, 1988) or the PI-WSUR (Padua Inventory-Washington State University, PI-WSUR; Burns, Keortge, Formea & Sternberger, 1996). The PSWQ is found to correlate most highly with the cognitive subscales of both questionnaires (i.e. Doubting, r = 0.45; and Checking, r = 0.43 for the MOCI), and Mental Control for the PI (r = 0.66).

Worry and Ruminative Thought

Rumination is considered the cognitive component of depression and has been defined as "behaviors and thoughts that focus one's attention on one's depressive symptoms and the implications and consequences of these symptoms" (Nolen-Hoeksema & Morrow, 1993, pp. 561–562) (see Chapter 2). Within a non-clinical population, worry (as measured by the PSWQ), depressive rumination (as measured by the Response Style Questionnaire, RSQ; Nolen-Hoeksema & Morrow, 1991), anxiety and depression (as measured by the Hospital Anxiety and Depression Scale, HADS; Zigmond & Snaith, 1983) are all significantly positively correlated (smallest r = 0.43) (Watkins, 2004).

THE PSWQ AND OTHER MEASURES OF WORRY

Numerous additional measures assessing the content and process features of worry have emerged over recent years. A selection of these will be summarized here, although a key measure for assessing worry content (the Worry Domains Questionnaire, WDQ) will be considered in more detail. The WDQ was chosen for more detailed review in order to provide an example of a *content*-based worry measure. It is beyond the scope of this chapter to provide a detailed review of all available worry assessment tools. However, a useful summary of key available measures will follow; interested readers are encouraged to consult references for further description.

The Content of Worry—The Worry Domains Questionnaire (Tallis, Davey & Bond, 1992)

Within the literature, attention has been given to the content features of worry. The rationale for considering clusters of worry content types was driven by the theoretical view that there exist semantically cohesive domains of worry-related material stored in memory (Eysenck, 1984). This culminated in production of the WDQ (Tallis, Eysenck & Mathews, 1992), the most widely used content-based measure of worry. There is also a shortened version of the WDQ, which has 10 rather than 25 items and high internal consistency (WDQ-SF; Stöber & Joorman, 2001).

The Worry Domains Questionnaire was developed as an instrument to measure non-pathological worry. By means of a cluster analytic method, six domains of worry were highlighted: (1) Relationships, (2) Lack of Confidence, (3) Aimless Future, (4) Work Incompetence, (5) Financial and (6) Socio-Political (for a full description of scale development, see Tallis et al., 1994). The scale is comprised of 30 items. The prefix "I worry ..." is followed by a list of 30 worries (e.g., "that I will lose close friends") that cover the six worry domains, however, the sixth cluster (socio-political) may be dropped. For each item, participants indicate how much they worry on a five-point scale from "not at all" (0) to "extremely" (4). The WDQ can distinguish between high and low worriers drawn from a non-clinical population. The total WDQ score gives an indication of worry frequency, and the subscales provide information with respect to worry content. The resultant scale has shown internal consistency (Cronbach's alpha) of at least .89 (Davey, 1993; Joormann & Stöber, 1997; Stöber, 1998) and test-retest reliability coefficients of 0.79–0.85 over a period of four weeks (Davey, 1993; Stöber, 1998). Furthermore, the scale demonstrates substantial convergent validity with measures of anxiety. Average agreement amongst peers has produced intraclass correlations of 0.47 and an aggregated self-peer agreement of 0.42 (Stöber, 1998).

The WDQ correlates highly with measures of trait anxiety and depression (Davey, 1993; Van Rijsoort et al., 1999) and with other associated measures such as the MOCI (see Tallis et al., 1994 for more detail). Van Rijsoort and colleagues (1999) argued for the inclusion of an additional health worry domain and created a revised version of the WDQ on this basis (WDQ-R). The PSWQ and WDQ are significantly intercorrelated, with r = 0.63 (Davey, 1993; Joorman & Stöber, 1997; Stöber, 1995) or higher (r = 0.68; Stöber, 1998). The magnitudes of these correlations are to be expected given that the measures are tapping highly related, though conceptually distinct facets of the same phenomena.

Meta-worry

A further endeavor has been to assess *process* characteristics of worry. Perhaps most noteworthy have been attempts to elucidate meta-level beliefs about worry. In his meta-cognitive model of worry in GAD, Wells (1995, 1997) suggests that positive and negative beliefs about worry give rise to "Type 1" worry (worry about external events and non-cognitive internal events) and also to the more pathological "Type 2" worry (or worry about worry) (see Chapter 11). Assessing such dimensions is of interest to clinicians because such beliefs, particularly beliefs about the negative consequences of worry, may actually be central to the transformation of everyday worry into clinical GAD worry (Wells 1994; Cartwright-Hatton & Wells, 1997).

Wells (1994) developed the Anxious Thoughts Inventory (AnTI) to measure individual differences in proneness to multiple dimensions of worry, including both content and process dimensions (see Chapter 9). This is a 22-item self-report scale assessing three dimensions of worry, two related to content and one to process characteristics: health worry (e.g. "I worry about having a heart attack or cancer"), social worry (e.g. "I worry about making a fool of myself"), and meta-worry (e.g. "I worry that I cannot control my thoughts as well as I would like to"). All three of the individual subscales and the scale total score correlate with the PSWQ (social worry, $r = 0.58$, health worry, $r = 0.39$, meta-worry, $r = 0.50$, total score, $r = 0.61$) (Wells, 1997). A related measure of meta-level cognitions about worry is the Meta-Cognitions Questionnaire (MCQ; Cartwright-Hatton & Wells, 1997), a 65-item self-report measure that assesses positive and negative beliefs about worry, various intrusive thoughts, perceived cognitive functioning, and individual differences in the tendency to monitor thought processes. Both measures have good psychometric properties (cf. Wells & Papageorgiou, 1998).

The Why Worry? questionnaire (WW) comprises another measure tapping perceived "positive" aspects of worry. This scale consists of 20 items offering reasons why people say they worry. It correlates with the PSWQ ($r = 0.58$) and demonstrates good psychometric properties (Freeston et al., 1994). The questionnaire measures two constructs concerned with: a) worry as a means of preventing undesirable outcomes, diminishing possible guilt, and distracting from worse thoughts, and b) worry as a means of problem-solving, which putatively helps individuals increase control and find solutions. Such beliefs about worry distinguish between participants who meet both cognitive and somatic criteria for GAD, those meeting somatic criteria only, and those meeting neither somatic nor cognitive criteria (Freeston et al., 1994). Also, compared with non-clinical moderate worriers, GAD patients believe that worrying is more useful in helping to find solutions and preventing negative outcomes (Ladouceur et al., 1998).

The Consequences of Worrying Scale (Davey, Tallis, & Capuzzo, 1996) assesses the perceived positive and negative consequences of worrying and can be used with non-clinical samples. The scale assesses three dimensions representing the negative consequences of worrying: (1) worrying disrupts effective performance, (2) worrying exaggerates the problem, and (3) worrying causes emotional discomfort. There are two factors representing the positive consequences of worrying: (1) worry motivates and (2) worry helps analytic thinking. From the limited data available, the scale demonstrates good psychometric properties (Davey et al. 1996). The sub-scales correlate with other measures of worry, such as the PSWQ and WDQ and with relevant measures of psychopathology such as trait anxiety (BAI) and depression (BDI) (Davey et al. 1996). Interestingly, one study found that participants who held *both* negative and positive beliefs about the consequences of worrying scored significantly higher on various indices of psychopathology than those who held primarily negative beliefs about the consequences of worrying (Davey et al., 1996).

CONCLUSION

In conclusion, the PSWQ provides a psychometrically sound means of assessing pathological worry, demonstrating utility across a wide variety of diagnostic and criterion groups. While worry is a feature of psychopathology across the continuum of affective and anxiety disorders, the PSWQ possesses sufficient specificity to discriminate GAD from other disorders. Because of this utility, recent modifications for youth and older adults have been adopted, and these also exhibit desirable psychometric properties. PSWQ scores relate meaningfully to parallel cognitive processes such as rumination and obsessions. However, further research is necessary (a) to clarify how pathological worry and these other cognitive processes overlap, and (b) to define the mechanisms whereby normal worry becomes rigid and dysfunctional. Most likely, the PSWQ will figure prominently as an assessment tool in the clinical and research endeavors that seek to achieve these goals.

REFERENCES

Abel, J.L. & Borkovec, T.D. (1995). Generalizability of DSM-III-R generalized anxiety disorders to proposed DSM-IV criteria and cross-validation of proposed changes. *Journal of Anxiety Disorders*, **9(4)**, 303–315.

Beck, A.T., Epstein, N., Brown, G. & Steer, R.A. (1988). An inventory for measuring depression. *Archives of General Psychiatry*, **4**, 561–571.

Behar, E., Alcaine, O., Zuellig, A.R. & Borkovec, T.D. (2003). Screening for generalized anxiety disorder using the Penn State Worry Questionnaire: A receiver operating characteristic analysis. *Journal of Behavior Therapy and Experimental Psychiatry*, **34**, 25–43.

Borkovec, T.D. & Costello, E. (1993). Efficacy of applied relaxation and cognitive-behavioral therapy in the treatment of generalized anxiety disorder. *Journal of Consulting and Clinical Psychology*, **61**, 611–619.

Borkovec, T.D., Newman, M.G., Pincus, A.L. & Lytle, R. (2002). A component analysis of cognitive behavioral therapy for generalized anxiety disorder and the role of interpersonal problems. *Journal of Consulting and Clinical Psychology*, **70**, 288–298.

Borkovec, T.D., Ray, W.J. & Stöber, J. (1998). Worry: a cognitive phenomenon intimately linked to affective, physiological, and interpersonal behavioral processes. *Cognitive Therapy and Research*, **22**, 561–576.

Borkovec, T.D., Robinson, E., Pruzinsky, T. & DePree, J.A. (1983). Preliminary exploration of worry: Some characteristics and processes. *Behaviour Research and Therapy*, **21**, 9–16.

Brown T.A., Antony M.M. & Barlow D.H. (1992). Psychometric properties of the Penn State Worry Questionnaire in a clinical anxiety disorders sample. *Behaviour Research & Therapy*, **30**, 33–37.

Brown, T.A., Barlow, D.H. & Liebowitz, M.R. (1994). The empirical basis of Generalized Anxiety Disorder. *American Journal of Psychiatry*, **151** 1272–1280.

Brown T.A., Dowdall D.J., Cote G. & Barlow D.H. (1994). Worry and obsessions: The distinction between generalized anxiety disorder and obsessive-compulsive disorder. In G.C.L. Davey & F. Tallis (Eds) *Worrying: Perspectives on Theory, Assessment and Treatment*. Chichester, UK: John Wiley & Sons, Ltd.

Brown, T.A., Moras, K., Zinbarg, R.E. & Barlow, D.H. (1993). Diagnostic and symptom distinguishability of generalized anxiety disorder and obsessive-compulsive disorder. *Behaviour Therapy*, **24**, 227–240.

Burns, G.L., Keortge, S.G., Formea, G.M. & Sternberger, L.G. (1996). Revision of the Padua Inventory of obsessive compulsive disorder symptoms: Distinctions between worry and obsessive-compulsive disorder. *Behaviour Therapy*, **24**, 227–240.

Cartwright-Hatton, S. & Wells, A. (1997). Beliefs about worry and intrusions: The meta-cognitions questionnaire and its correlates. *Journal of Anxiety Disorders*, **11**, 279–296.

Chelminski, I. & Zimmerman, M. (2003). Pathological worry in depressed and anxious patients. *Journal of Anxiety Disorders*, **17**, 533–546.

Chorpita, B.F., Tracey, S.A., Brown, T.A., Collica, T.J. & Barlow, D.H. (1997). Assessment of worry in children and adolescents: An adaptation of the Penn State Worry Questionnaire. *Behaviour Research and Therapy*, **35**, 569–581.

Davey, G.C.L (1993). A comparison of three worry questionnaires. *Behaviour Research and Therapy*, **31**, 51–56.

Davey, G.C.L. (1994). Worrying, social problem solving abilities, and social problem solving confidence. *Behaviour Research and Therapy*, **32**, 327–330.

Davey, G.C.L., Hampton, J., Farrell, J.J. & Davidson, S. (1992) Some characteristics of worry: Evidence for worrying and anxiety as separate constructs. *Personality & Individual Differences*, **13**, 133–147.

Davey, G.C.L, Tallis, F. & Capuzzo, N. (1996b) Beliefs about the consequences of worrying. *Cognitive Therapy and Research*, **20**, 599–520.

Di Nardo, P.A. & Barlow, D.H. (1988). *Anxiety Disorders Interview Schedule—Revised (ADIS-R)*. Albany: Center for Stress and Anxiety Disorders.

Di Nardo, P.A., Brown, T.A. & Barlow, D.H. (1994). *The Anxiety Disorders Interview Schedule for DSM-IV (ADIS-IV)*. San Antonio, TX: The Psychological Corporation.

East, M.P. & Watts, F.N. (1994). Worry and the suppression of imagery. *Behaviour Research and Therapy*, **32**, 851–855.

Erickson, T.M. (2002). (Worry levels in various selected and unselected college student groups.) Unpublished raw data.

Erickson, T.M. (2004). (Worry levels in an unselected college student sample.) Unpublished raw data.

Erickson, T.M. & Pincus, A. L. (2005). Using Structural Analysis of Social Behavior (SASB) measures of self and social perception to give interpersonal meaning to symptoms: Anxiety as an exemplar. *Assessment*, **12**, 243–254.

Eysenck, M.W. (1984). Anxiety and the worry process. *Bulletin of the Psychonomic Society*, **22**, 545–548.

Freeman, D. & Garety, P. A. (1999). Worry, worry processes, and dimensions of delusions: An exploratory investigation of a role for anxiety processes in the maintenance of delusional distress. *Behavioural and Cognitive Psychotherapy*, **27**, 47–62.

Freeston, M.H., Ladouceur, R., Rheaume, J., Letarte, H., Gagnon, F. & Thibodeau, N. (1994). Self-report of obsessions and worry. *Behaviour Research and Therapy*, **32**, 29–36.

Freeston, M.H., Rheaume, J., Letarte, H., Dugas, M.J. & Ladouceur, R. (1994). Why do people worry? *Personality and Individual Differences*, **17**, 791–802.

Fresco, D.M., Mennin, D.S., Heimberg, R.G. & Turk, C.L. (2003). Using the Penn State Worry Questionnaire to identify individuals with generalized anxiety disorder: A receiver operating characteristic analysis. *Journal of Behavior Therapy and Experimental Psychiatry*, **34**, 283–291.

Gillis, M.M., Haaga, D.A. & Ford, G.T. (1995). Normative values for the Beck Anxiety Inventory, Fear Questionnaire, Penn State Worry Questionnaire, and Social Phobia and Anxiety Inventory. (1995). *Psychological Assessment*, **7**, 450–455.

Harvey, A., Watkins, E., Mansell, W. & Shafran, R. (2004). *Cognitive processes across psychological disorders. A transdiagnostic approach to treatment and research*. Oxford: Oxford University Press.

Hazlett-Stevens, H., Craske, M.G., Mayer, E.A., Chang, L. & Naliboff, B.D. (2003). Prevalence of irritable bowel syndrome among university students: The roles of worry, neuroticism, anxiety sensitivity and visceral anxiety. *Journal of Psychosomatic Research*, **55**, 501–505.

Hodgson, R.J. & Rachman, S. (1977). Obsessive-compulsive complaints. *Behaviour Research and Therapy*, **15**, 389–395.

Hopko, D.R., Stanley, M.A., Reas, D.L., Wetherell, J.L., Beck, J.G., Novy, D.M. & Averill, P.M. (2003). Assessing worry in older adults: Confirmatory factor analysis of the Penn State Worry Questionnaire and psychometric properties of an abbreviated model. *Psychological Assessment*, **15**, 173–183.

Joorman, J. & Stöber, J. (1997). Measuring facets of worry: A LISREL analysis of the Worry Domains Questionnaire. *Personality and Individual Differences*, **23**, 827–837.

Ladouceur, R., Blais, F., Freeston, M.H. & Dugas, M.J. (1998). Problem solving and problem orientation in generalized anxiety disorder. *Journal of Anxiety Disorders*, **12**, 139–152.

Ladouceur, R., Dugas, M.J., Freeston, M.H., Leger, E., Gagnon, F. & Thibodeau, N. (2000). Efficacy of cognitive-behavioural treatment for generalized anxiety disorder: Evaluation in a controlled clinical trial. *Journal of Consulting and Clinical Psychology*, **68(6)**, 957–964.

Metzger, R.L., Miller, M.L., Cohen, M., Sofka, M. & Borkovec, T.D. (1990). Worry changes decision making: the effect of negative thoughts on cognitive processing. *Journal of Clinical Psychology*, **48**, 76–88.

Meyer, T.J. (1988). Development of a screening questionnaire to identify levels of chronic worry. Unpublished master's thesis, Penn State University, University Park, PA.

Meyer, T.J., Miller, M.L., Metzger, R.L. & Borkovec, T.D. (1990). Development and validation of the Penn State Worry Questionnaire. *Behaviour Research & Therapy*, **28**, 487–495.

Molina, S. & Borkovec, T.D. (1994). The Penn State Worry Questionnaire: Psychometric properties and associated characteristics. In G.C.L. Davey & F. Tallis (Eds), *Worrying: Perspectives on theory, assessment, and treatment* (pp. 265–283). Chichester, UK: John Wiley & Sons, Ltd.

Muris, P., Meesters, C. & Gobel, M. (2001). Reliability, validity, and normative data of the Penn State Worry Questionnaire in 8–12-yr-old children. *Journal of Behavior Therapy and Experimental Psychiatry*, **32**, 63–72.

Newman, M.G., Zuellig, A.R., Kachin, K.E., Constantino, M.J., Przeworski, A., Erickson, T. & Cashman-McGrath, L. (2002). Preliminary reliability and validity of the Generalized Anxiety Disorder Questionnaire-IV: A revised self-report diagnostic measure of generalized anxiety disorder. *Behavior Therapy*, **33**, 215–233.

Nolen-Hoeksema, S. & Morrow, J. (1991). A prospective study of depression and posttraumatic stress symptoms after a natural disaster. The Loma Prieta earthquake. *Journal of Personality and Social Psychology*, **61**, 115–121.

Nolen-Hoeksema, S. & Morrow, J. (1993). Effects of rumination and distraction on naturally occurring depressed mood. *Cognition and Emotion*, **7(6)**, 561–570.

Pallesen, S., Nordhus, I.H., Kvale, G., Havik, O.E., Nielsen, G.H., Johnsen, B.H, Skjøtskift, S. & Hjeltnes, L. (2002). Psychological characteristics of elderly insomniacs. *Scandinavian Journal of Psychology*, **43**, 425–432.

Purdon, C. & Clark, D.A. (1994). Perceived control and appraisal of obsessional intrusive thoughts: a replication and extension. *Behavioural and Cognitive Psychotherapy*, **22(4)**, 269–285.

Roemer, L., Borkovec, M., Posa, S. & Borkovec, T.D. (1995). A self-report diagnostic measure of generalized anxiety disorder. *Journal of Behavior Therapy and Experimental Psychiatry*, **26**, 345–350.

Sanavio, E. (1988). Obsessions and compulsions: The Padua Inventory. *Behaviour, Research and Therapy*, **26**, 169–177.

Scott, E.L., Eng, W. & Heimberg, R.A. (2002). Ethnic differences in worry in a nonclinical population.

Sibrava, N. (2005). (Worry in an unselected student sample.) Unpublished raw data.

Skarborn, M. & Nicki, R. (2000). Worry in pre- and post-retirement persons. *International Journal of Aging and Human Development*, **50**, 61–71.

Spielberger, C. (1983). *State-Trait Anxiety Inventory*. Palo Alto, CA: Consulting Psychologists' Press.

Stanley, M.A., Diefenbach, G.J., Hopko, D.R., Novy, D., Kunik, M.E., Wilson, N. & Wagener, P. (2003). The nature of generalized anxiety in older primary care patients: Preliminary findings. *Journal of Psychopathology and Behavioral Assessment*, **25**, 273–280.

Stanley, M.A., Novy, D.M., Bourland, S.L., Beck. J.G. & Averill, P. M. (2001). Assessing older adults with generalized anxiety: A replication and extension. *Behaviour Research and Therapy*, **39**, 221–235.

Starcevic, V. (1994). Pathological worry in major depression: A preliminary report. *Behaviour Research and Therapy*, **33**, 55–56.

Startup, H.M. & Davey, G.C.L. (2001). Mood-as-input and catastrophic worry. *Journal of Abnormal Psychology*, **110(1)**, 83–96.

Startup, H.M. & Davey, G.C.L (2003). Inflated responsibility and the use of stop rules for catastrophic worrying. *Behaviour, Research and Therapy*, **41**, 495–503.

Startup, H., Freeman, D. & Garety, P.A. (2005). *Catastrophic worry and persecutory delusions*. Manuscript under revision.

Stöber, J. (1998) Worry, problem elaboration and suppression of imagery: the role of concreteness. *Behaviour Research and Therapy*, **36**, 751–756.

Stöber, J. & Bittencourt, J. (1998). Weekly assessment of worry: An adaptation of the Penn State Worry Questionnaire for monitoring changes during treatment. *Behaviour Research and Therapy*, **36**, 645–656.

Tallis, F., Davey, G.C.L., Bond, A. (1994). The Worry Domains Questionnaire. In G.C.L. Davey & F. Tallis (Eds), *Worrying: Perspectives on theory, assessment, and treatment* (pp. 285–299). Chichester, UK: John Wiley & Sons, Ltd.

Tallis, F., Davey, G.C.L. & Capuzzo, N. (1994). The phenomenology of non-pathological worry: a preliminary investigation. In G.C.L. Davey & F. Tallis (Eds), *Worrying: Perspectives on Theory, Assessment and Treatment*. Chichester, UK: John Wiley & Sons, Ltd.

Tallis, F., Eysenck, M.W. & Mathews, A. (1992). A questionnaire for the measurement of nonpathological worry. *Personality and Individual Differences*, **13**, 161–168.

Tallis, F. & de Silva, P. (1992). Worry and obsessional symptoms: a correlational analysis. *Behaviour, Research and Therapy*, **30**, 103–105.

Turner, S.M., Beidel, D.C. & Stanley, M.A. (1992). Are obsessional thoughts and worry different cognitive phenomena? *Clinical Psychology Review*, **12**, 257–270.

van Rijsoort, S., Emmelkamp, P. & Vervaeke, G. (1999). The Penn State Worry Questionnaire and the Worry Domains Questionnaire: Structure, reliability, and validity. *Clinical Psychology and Psychotherapy*, **6**, 297–307.

Watari, K.F. & Brodbeck, C. (2000). Culture, health, and financial appraisals: Comparison of worry in older Japanese Americans and European Americans. *Journal of Clinical Geropsychology*, **6**, 25–39.

Watkins, E. (2004). Appraisals and strategies associated with rumination and worry. *Personality and Individual Differences*, **37**, 679–694.

Wells, A. (1994). A multi-dimensional measure of worry; developmental and preliminary validation of the Anxious Thoughts Inventory. *Anxiety, Stress and Coping*, **6**, 289–299.

Wells, A. (1995). Meta-cognition and worry: A cognitive model of generalized anxiety disorder. *Behavioural and Cognitive Psychotherapy*, **23**, 301–320.

Wells, A. (1997). *Cognitive Therapy of Anxiety Disorders. A Practice Manual and Conceptual Guide*. Chichester, UK: John Wiley & Sons, Ltd.

Wells, A. & Carter, K. (1999). Preliminary test of a cognitive model of generalized anxiety disorder. *Behaviour Research and Therapy*, **37**, 585–594.

Wells, A. & Papageorgiou, C. (1998). Relationships between worry, obsessive-compulsive symptoms and meta-cognitive beliefs. *Behaviour Research and Therapy*, **36**, 899–913.

Wetherell, J.L., Gatz, M. & Craske, M.G. (2003). Treatment of generalized anxiety disorder in older adults. *Journal of Consulting and Clinical Psychology*, **71**, 31–40.

Wisocki, P.A. (1994). The experience of worry among the elderly. In G.C.L. Davey & F. Tallis (Eds), *Worrying: Perspectives on theory, assessment and treatment*. Chichester, UK: John Wiley & Sons, Ltd.

Zigmond, A.S. & Snaith, R.P. (1983). The hospital anxiety and depression scale. *Acta Psychiatrica Scandinavica*, **67**, 361–370.

Chapter 8

THE ANXIOUS THOUGHTS INVENTORY AND RELATED MEASURES OF METACOGNITION AND WORRY

Adrian Wells

Metacognition has recently been pinpointed as a central construct in explaining the development and persistence of psychological disorder (Wells, 2000; Wells & Matthews, 1994). Metacognition refers to the cognitive factors that are involved in the appraisal and control of thinking. It has been divided into two main components of metacognitive knowledge (beliefs and information stored about cognition) and metacognitive regulation (selection and use of strategies to regulate cognition).

The key impetus for its clinical emergence as a construct closely related to psychological disorder is the theoretical framework offered by the Self-Regulatory Executive Function Theory (Wells, 2000; Wells & Matthews, 1994; 1996). An important tenet of this theory is that vulnerability to and maintenance of disorder is linked to the propensity to and activation of a pattern of cognition. This pattern is known as the Cognitive Attentional Syndrome (CAS) and is comprised of perseverative thinking in the form of worry/rumination, attentional strategies of threat monitoring, and coping behaviours that fail to provide adaptive learning experiences that modify dysfunctional beliefs. Essentially the theory argues for examining common cognitive factors across psychological disorders and views the CAS as a factor that interferes with recovery from normally transient negative emotional experiences. The CAS emerges from the patient's metacognitive knowledge (beliefs) about worry/rumination and attention, and from use of dysfunctional strategies for coping many of which are metacognitive in nature. The metacognitive model of GAD reviewed in Chapter 11 is grounded in the S-REF theory, and offers a metacognitive account of the

Worry and Its Psychological Disorders: Theory, Assessment and Treatment. Edited by G. C. L. Davey and A. Wells. © 2006 John Wiley & Sons, Ltd.

internal psychological factors predisposing, precipitating, and sustaining pathological worry.

The metacognitive approach distinguishes between cognition and metacognition, and this distinction is applied to conceptualising the nature of worry. A central idea is that it is not the nature of worry that distinguishes GAD from high levels of normal worry, but it is the patient's appraisal and beliefs about worry (i.e. their metacognitions). In the GAD model worry has been separated into two types that capture the distinction between worry and metacognitions about worry. Type 1 worry refers to worry about social, environmental and physical events (e.g. worrying about relationships), whilst Type 2 worry consists of worry about worry and cognitive functioning (e.g. appraising worry as uncontrollable and harmful).

Scientific investigation of metacognitions in psychological disorder, including pathological worry and GAD has relied on several measures of metacognition. Many of these studies of GAD and worry are reviewed in Chapter 11. The present chapter gives an overview of the measures that provide a useful and effective method of assessing separate types of worry and related metacognitive constructs.

THE ANXIOUS THOUGHTS INVENTORY (AnTI)

Purpose and Description of the AnTI

The AnTI (Wells, 1994) was designed as a multi-dimensional measure of worry aimed at capturing the distinction between content domains of worry and between non-metacognitive (Type 1) and metacognitive (Type 2) concerns.

It is a 22-item self-report measure consisting of three subscales: social worry, health worry, and meta-worry. The social worry subscale consists of nine items, health worry six items, and meta-worry seven items. Examples of items from each subscale are listed below:

Social worry

I worry about saying or doing the wrong thing when among strangers
I worry that people don't like me

Health worry

I worry about having a heart attack or cancer
I worry about my physical health

Meta-worry

I worry that I cannot control my thoughts as well as I would like to
I think I am missing out on things in life because I worry too much

Development of the AnTI

The original item pool for the AnTI was generated from interviews with patients suffering from panic disorder or GAD. Additional items that appeared to be appropriate for the initial factors were adapted from the Beck Depression Inventory (Beck, Ward, Mendelsohn, Mock & Erbaugh, 1961), Maudsley Obsessive-Compulsive Inventory (Rachman & Hodgson, 1980), and one item was used from the Trait anxiety subscale of the State-Trait Anxiety Inventory (Speilberger, Gorsuch, Lushene, Vagg & Jacobs, 1983).

Factor Structure

The AnTI was refined through a series of factor analyses in non-patient samples. The original scale contained items assessing a wider range of content domains than the three domains finally obtained. However, factor analyses showed that a wide range of content domains could be condensed to the three factors of social, health and meta-worry.

Reliability

Alpha coefficients for the scale are reported (Wells, 1994) as .84 for social worry, .81 health worry, and .75 for meta-worry. Six-week test-retest reliability showed test-retest correlations of .76 (social worry), .84 health worry, and .77 (meta-worry).

Convergent Validity (Relationship With Worry Measures)

The AnTI correlates positively with another measure of worry, the Penn State Worry Questionnaire (PSWQ). Wells and Papageorgiou (1998) used two AnTI subscales and found significant correlations with the PSWQ as follows: .58 social worry, and .40 health worry.

Wells (2005) examined relationships between the AnTI subscales and the meta-worry questionnaire (MWQ). Subscale intercorrelations between the MWQ and each AnTI subscale ranged from .18 to .64. AnTI meta-worry correlated most strongly with the MWQ as would be expected.

Construct Validity

Worry is the cognitive component of anxiety and should therefore correlate meaningfully with other anxiety measures. Correlations between AnTI subscales and the trait anxiety subscale of the state-trait anxiety inventory have been reported (Wells, 1994) as: .63 social worry, .36 health worry, .68 meta-worry.

Discriminitive Validity

AnTI subscales discriminate between diagnostic groups. Meta-worry is significantly higher in DSM-IV GAD patients compared with patient groups with panic disorder, social phobia or non-patient controls. As would be expected health worry is highest in the panic group, and social worry highest in social phobics, but GAD patients do not differ from these groups on health or social worry respectively (e.g. Wells & Carter, 2001).

Descriptive statistics for criterion groups

Means and standard deviations for the AnTI subscales in a range of groups are presented in Table 8.1.

Treatment Sensitivity

The AnTI subscales are sensitive to treatment. A case study illustrating the treatmemnt of DSM-III-R GAD with metacognitive therapy showed

Table 8.1   AnTI means and standard deviations (in parentheses) for criterion groups

AnTI subscale	Students (n = 239)	Non-patients (n = 24)	GAD (n = 24)	Social Phobia (n = 24)	Panic Disorder (n = 24)	Major Depression (n = 24)
Social Worry	18.1 (4.5)	17.5 (4.6)	24.0 (5.1)	24.9 (5.7)	18.0 (3.8)	24.1 (6.5)
Health Worry	8.8 (2.8)	10.0 (3.3)	14.3 (3.6)	9.2 (2.7)	15.5 (5.6)	11.0 (4.4)
Meta Worry	11.3 (3.2)	12.8 (3.8)	19.7 (3.9)	15.5 (4.5)	15.7 (4.6)	18.0 (3.7)

Note: Students are unscreened undergraduates, clinical groups are patients diagnosed in accordance with DSM-III-R. Data from Wells, A. (1994). A multi-dimensional measure of worry: Development and preliminary validation of the Anxious Thoughts Inventory. *Anxiety Stress and Coping*, **6**, 289–299; Wells, A. & Carter, K. (2001). Further tests of a cognitive model of Generalized Anxiety Disorder: Metacognitions and worry in GAD, panic disorder, social phobia, depression, and non-patients. *Behavior Therapy*, **32**, 85–102.

substantial reductions in all AnTI subscales with successful treatment (Wells, 1995). An open trial of patients with DSM-IV GAD treated with metacognitive therapy revealed significant reductions in each AnTI subscale pre to post treatment (Wells & King, in press). A randomised treatment trial of metacognitive therapy versus applied relaxation similarly demonstrated changes in AnTI scores that are consistent with patterns of change observed in other outcome measures (Wells, Welford, King, Papageorgiou, Wisely & Mendel, in preparation).

Clinical and Research Utility

The AnTI is brief and easy to administer and has been used in clinical practise as an outcome measure of multiple dimensions of worry. The availability of descriptive data on criterion groups adds to its clinical usefulness. The sensitivity of the instrument to treatment effects and the theoretical importance of meta-worry in the metacognitive theory and treatment mean that the scale is useful conceptually and as a research outcome tool. The AnTI is used increasingly to evaluate the relative contribution of Type 1 and Type 2 worry to pathological and normal worry processes. The AnTI appears to have good reliability and shows good construct, convergent, and discriminative validity.

There are no alternative forms of the AnTI or similar measures offering separate measurement of social, health and meta-worry in a single instrument. Another measure specifically of meta-worry is available (see below), but the items and response format are different.

THE META-WORRY QUESTIONNAIRE (MWQ)

Purpose and Description of the MWQ

Whilst the AnTI consists of a subscale assessing meta-worry, it combines appraisals of uncontrollability with appraisals of danger. Furthermore, it does not assess level of belief in meta-worries. The Meta-Worry Questionnaire (Wells, 2005) was devised to extend the measurement of meta-worry and to specifically measure danger-related meta-worry in the absence of items assessing uncontrollability. The instrument was constructed for testing the metacognitive model in the context of DSM-IV GAD as it avoids potential circularity that would otherwise result from the fact that uncontrollability was included as a diagnostic criterion for GAD in DSM-IV.

The MWQ measures two dimensions of danger-related meta-worry: frequency of meta-worry, and the extent to which the person believes meta-worry when it occurs.

Development of the MWQ

Items for the MWQ were derived as summary statements of beliefs from transcripts of nine patients undergoing metacognitive therapy for GAD. All patients met DSM-IV criteria for GAD as the principal diagnosis. Seven items reflecting the most common danger themes were devised to capture the dimension and these items comprised the final instrument. The items are:

(1) I am going crazy with worrying
(2) My worrying will escalate and I'll cease to function
(3) I'm making myself ill with worrying
(4) I'm abnormal for worrying
(5) My mind can't take the worrying
(6) I'm losing out in life because of worrying
(7) My body can't take the worrying

Factor Structure

Factor analysis of the MWQ in a student sample demonstrated that the instrument had a single factor structure for both the frequency and belief dimensions.

Reliability

Cronbach alpha coefficients for the frequency scale were .88 and were .95 for the belief scale. Corrected-tem total correlations for frequency ranged from .62–.71, and for belief they ranged from .81–.88.

Convergent, Construct, and Discriminant Validity

Both scales of the MWQ appear meaningfully correlated with other measures of metacognition. Moreover, the relationship between MWQ scales and AnTI meta-worry was significantly stronger than the relationship between MWQ scales and either social or health worry. MWQ scales also

Table 8.2   MWQ means and standard deviations (in parentheses) for criterion groups

MWQ subscale	Non-anxious (n = 112)	GAD (n = 11)	Somatic Anxiety (n = 22)
Belief	76.1 (130.1)	242.3 (166.7)	149.5 (168.9)
Frequency	8.6 (2.4)	14.5 (4.8)	11.0 (3.4)

Note: Groups are undergraduate and post-graduate students screened for DSM-IV GAD, somatic anxiety, or no anxiety. Data from Wells, A. (2005). The Metacognitive Model of GAD: Assessment of meta-worry and relationship with DSM-IV Generalized Anxiety Disorder. *Cognitive Therapy and Research*, **29**, 107–121.

show significantly stronger correlations with negative beliefs about worry than with positive beliefs about worry (measured with the metacognitions questionnaire).

Discriminative Validity

The MWQ differentiated non-patients meeting criteria for DSM-IV GAD from two groups of individuals classified as having somatic anxiety, or no anxiety. In this context, individuals with GAD showed significantly higher scores on the frequency scale than either the somatic anxiety or the no anxiety group. Individuals with GAD also obtained the highest scores on the belief scale, which was significantly different from the non-anxious group.

Descriptive Statistics for Criterion Groups

Means and standard deviations for a non-patient sample classified as GAD, somatic anxiety, and no-anxiety on the basis of the GAD-Q are presented in Table 8.2.

THE META-COGNITIONS QUESTIONNAIRE 30 (MCQ-30)

Purpose and Description

The MCQ-30 (Wells & Cartwright-Hatton, 2004) was constructed as a brief measure of individual differences (traits) in positive beliefs about worry, negative beliefs about worry, belief about need to control thoughts, metacognitive monitoring of thoughts, and judgments of cognitive effectiveness. Some of these dimensions are especially relevant to the metacognitive model of GAD and so this instrument has been used in empirical tests of the model and as a component of comprehensive clinical assessment in treatment.

Background Development (The 65 item version)

The MCQ-30 is a derivative of an earlier and longer MCQ scale (Cartwright-Hatton & Wells, 1997). Items of the original MCQ were generated on the basis of semi-structured interviews with a student sample, and on the basis of therapy transcripts of patients treated for GAD, obsessive-compulsive disorder, hypochondriasis and panic disorder.

Participants were questioned about their experience of worry and intrusive thoughts which included questions about the reasons for worrying and the problems associated with worry and intrusions. Items were added aimed at tapping the dimensions of confidence in cognitive functioning and the tendency to monitor thoughts.

The initial item pool was subjected to a series of factor analyses across different samples, culminating in a final 65-item scale of five replicable factors constituting separate subscales. The five subscales assess:

1. positive beliefs about worry (e.g. 'worrying helps me cope'),
2. negative beliefs about worry concerning uncontrollability and danger (e.g. 'When I start worrying I cannot stop'),
3. low cognitive confidence (e.g. 'I have a poor memory'),
4. belief about need to control thoughts and the negative consequences of not doing so in domains of superstition, responsibility and punishment (e.g. 'Not being able to control my thoughts is a sign of weakness'),
5. cognitive self-consciousness (e.g. 'I pay close attention to the way my mind works').

Psychometrics for the 65-item scale are as follows. Internal consistency (Cronbach's alpha) of subscales ranges from 0.72–0.89, with five-week test-retest coefficients of between 0.76 and 0.89 across individual subscales (Cartwright-Hatton & Wells, 1997). The subscales show positive relationships with trait anxiety, and pathological worry (PSWQ, Wells & Papageorgiou, 1998), with the subscale of negative beliefs concerning uncontrollability and danger having the strongest relationship with these anxiety and worry measures. Particular MCQ subscales discriminate patients with GAD or OCD from panic disorder or social phobia. Here GAD and OCD groups endorse higher MCQ negative beliefs concerning uncontrollability and danger.

The 65-item MCQ appears to show good reliability, convergent, construct, and discriminative validity. There is a small amount of evidence that it is responsive to treatment. Papageorgiou and Wells (2000) found in a case replication series that depressed patients showed meaningful reduction in MCQ scores.

MCQ-30

A limitation of the original 65-item MCQ is its significant length. Recently a shortened 30-item version of the MCQ has been developed and evaluated (Wells & Cartwright-Hatton, 2004).

Background Development

To construct the shortened version six items were selected from each of the five MCQ factors. A combination of criteria were used to select items, but principally this was done on the basis of loadings of the items on their respective factors reported in earlier work. The highest loading items selected were required to represent the range of thematic components constituting each factor. The subscale assessing negative beliefs concerning superstition, responsibility and punishment was the most eclectic. The predominant theme is characterised by beliefs concerning need to control thoughts and the negative consequences of not doing so. The six highest loading items reflecting this theme were retained, and the subscale renamed 'need for control'.

Factor Structure

Both exploratory (EFA) and confirmatory factor analyses (CFA) were run to allow for a potentially different latent structure to emerge, and to test the construct validity of the MCQ-30 to determine if the data conformed to the original five-factor model. For the EFA five factors were extracted on the basis of the Scree test and rotated to achieve simple structure. Generally the structure and the composition of the five factors was very similar to that of the original scale. The CFA yielded a significant Chi-square indicating that the five-factor model was not exemplary, however a range of other goodness of fit indices suggested that the model was a good fit supporting the construct validity of the MCQ-30 with reference to the original five-factor model.

Reliability

Cronbach coefficient alpha's for the individual subscales ranged from 0.72–0.93 demonstrating good to excellent internal consistency. Test-retest correlations across an interval of 22–118 days were as follows: Total score = 0.75, positive beliefs = 0.79, uncontrollability/danger = 0.59, cognitive confidence = 0.69, need for control = 0.74, cognitive self-consciousness = 0.87.

Construct Validity

Significant positive correlations between MCQ-30 subscales and theoretically appropriate measures have been found. The relationships are consistent with those obtained using the 65-item version of the questionnaire. Relationships between the uncontrollability/danger subscale and measures of pathological worry (PSWQ) and trait-anxiety were particularly strong ($r = 0.73$ and 0.69). MCQ-30 subscales also correlated positively with a range of obsessive compulsive symptom subscales (Wells & Cartwright-Hatton, 2004).

Discriminative Validity

At the present time there are no published data on the discriminative validity of the MCQ-30. However, these data are available on the 65-item version of the instrument.

Clinical and Research Utility

The MCQ-30 is relatively brief and easy to administer. The original MCQ has been used quite widely in research examining metacognitive predictors of worry, obsessive compulsive symptoms and research on psychotic symptoms.

The MCQ has good reliability and validity, and appears responsive to treatment. It offers a means of quantifying both positive and negative beliefs about worry (amongst other metacognitions) that are meaningful for the conceptualisation of beliefs in GAD.

THE THOUGHT CONTROL QUESTIONNAIRE (TCQ)

Purpose and Description

The aim in developing the TCQ was to construct an instrument to assess individual differences in the use of strategies for controlling unpleasant intrusive thoughts. The literature on thought suppression suggests that trying not to think target thoughts may not be effective (e.g. Purdon, 1999; Wegner, Schneider, Carter & White, 1987). However, Wells and Davies (1994) state that thought suppression describes an aim rather than saying something about the means by which the aim is achieved. Some strategies may be helpful and some may be ineffective when used to control thinking.

Background Development

The initial pool of items was obtained from open-ended semi-structured interviews with 10 patients with a range of Axis I disorders and 10 non-patient controls with no history of treatment for emotional disorders. The interview schedule consisted of seven questions followed by probe items asking for a description of the strategies used to control unpleasant or unwanted thoughts. The patient group consisted of individuals with primary diagnoses of obsessive-compulsive disorder, GAD, or hypochondriasis.

Factor Structure

Initial factor analysis of the TCQ indicated an interpretable six-factor solution of, behavioural distraction, cognitive distraction, social control, worry, punishment, and re-appraisal. Revisions and subsequent administration of the instrument produced the five-factor solution of the current scale in which behavioural and cognitive distraction were combined.

The five-factor solution was replicated in a later study of patients with depression or post-traumatic stress disorder (Reynolds & Wells, 1999).

Reliability

Wells and Davies (1994) report Cronbach coefficient alpha's for the subscales ranging from .64–.79 in a college population of 229 individuals. Test-retest correlations across a six-week period were reported as: Distraction = 0.72, social control = 0.79, worry = 0.71, punishment = 0.64, re-appraisal = 0.67.

Construct Validity

Worry and punishment subscales are positively correlated with a range of emotion disorder measures. Relationships between other TCQ subscales and these measures tend to be negative and non-significant. TCQ worry correlated positively with a measure of social anxiety, whilst social control correlated negatively with social anxiety. Thus, individuals who are socially anxious are less likely to talk to other people as a means of controlling thoughts. Overall the correlations are meaningful and indicate that worry and punishment control strategies may be more maladaptive as indexed by their positive associations with a range of emotional vulnerability measures.

Discriminative Validity

TCQ subscales have been found to differentiate between diagnostic and symptom groups. Amir, Cashman and Foa (1997) found that individuals with a diagnosis of OCD used significantly more punishment, worry, reappraisal, and social control than non-patient controls. In contrast, control subjects used more distraction than patients. The two strongest discriminating strategies were punishment and worry. This finding was replicated by Abramowitz, Whiteside, Kalsy and Tolin (2003).

In a comparison of patients with or without Acute Stress Disorder following road accidents, Warda and Bryant (1998) found that people with ASD endorsed greater use of worry and punishment.

A longitudinal analysis of the predictors of PTSD following traffic accidents conducted by Holeva, Tarrier and Wells (2001) showed that TCQ worry measured at time 1 was a unique simultaneous predictor of the subsequent development of PTSD.

TCQ subscales discriminate patients with a diagnosis of schizophrenia from non-patients. Morrison and Wells (2000) found that the patient group endorsed significantly higher scores on punishment and worry strategies, and significantly lower usage of distraction.

Descriptive Statistics For Criterion Groups

Means and standard deviations for individual TCQ subscales across different diagnostic groups and an undifferentiated non-clinical sample are presented in Table 8.3.

Table 8.3 TCQ means and standard deviations (in parentheses) for criterion groups

TCQ subscale	Students (n = 229)	GAD (n = 20)	Panic Disorder (n = 20)	Major Depression (n = 61)
Distraction	14.6 (3.0)	13.1 (3.4)	14.5 (3.0)	12.3 (3.3)
Social Control	14.0 (3.3)	10.6 (3.0)	13.1 (3.9)	11.6 (3.5)
Worry	10.4 (2.7)	11.7 (3.5)	9.2 (3.0)	11.6 (3.4)
Punishment	10.0 (2.9)	13.3 (3.3)	10.7 (3.6)	11.1 (2.8)
Re-appraisal	14.4 (2.9)	11.3 (4.0)	12.3 (3.9)	12.3 (2.8)

Note: Students are unscreened undergraduates and post-graduates. Clinical groups are patients diagnosed in accordance with DSM-III-R. Data from Wells, A. & Davies, M. (1994). The Thought Control Questionnaire: A measure of individual differences in the control of unwanted thought. *Behaviour Research and Therapy*, **32**, 871–878; Reynolds, M. & Wells, A. (1999). The Thought Control Questionnaire—psychometric properties in a clinical sample, and relationships with PTSD and depression. *Psychological Medicine*, **29**, 1089–1099.

Treatment/Recovery Sensitivity

Reynolds and Wells (1999) examined the sensitivity of the TCQ to recovery in an undifferentiated sample of patients with depression or PTSD. In the recovered, distraction, re-appraisal and social control increased over time, whilst punishment decreased. There was a main effect for worry in which the unrecovered group had higher scores than the recovered group at baseline and at follow-up.

Clinical and Research Utility

The TCQ provides an easy to administer measure of relatively stable individual differences in the use of different strategies for controlling unwanted and distressing thoughts. It has acceptable internal consistency and a stable factor structure that appears replicable across patient and non-patient samples. The subscales correlate meaningfully with related constructs and differentiate groups of patients and non-patients. There appear to be consistent patterns of association supporting the view that two control strategies in particular (worry and punishment) may be dysfunctional. Preliminary indications suggest that the TCQ is responsive to treatment/recovery in anxious and depressed samples.

There are no alternative single sources of measurement of individual differences in adaptive and maladaptive thought control strategies.

SUMMARY AND CONCLUSION

Several measures of worry dimensions and related metacognitive constructs were reviewed in this chapter. These measures have been developed principally as a means of testing the metacognitive model of pathological worry and other disorders. However, each measure provides valuable clinical information in the assessment and formulation of pathological worry and GAD.

The AnTI provides a validated means of assessing three theoretically important dimensions of worry that map onto the distinction made between Type 1 and Type 2 worry. Type 2 worry differentiates GAD patients from other anxiety disorders, and appears to be causally linked to the development of pathological worry and GAD over a time course. Both types of worry as assessed by the AnTI are responsive to treatment effects.

The MWQ offers a clinical advance over the AnTI in that it provides a measure of frequency and belief in meta-worry, which is an important target in metacognitive therapy for GAD. This instrument allows the therapist to track changes in a theoretically important variable that is deemed to have causal significance in the metacognitive model of disorder. The MWQ offers a potential advantage over the AnTI as a research tool in investigating DSM-IV GAD because it excludes uncontrollability related meta-worry, thus avoiding potential circularity.

The MCQ is a multi-component measure of a range of metacognitive beliefs and monitoring tendencies. It is particularly useful in assessing both positive and negative beliefs about worrying. The MCQ-30 benefits from its brevity such that the clinical use of the MCQ-30 becomes more feasible. Dimensions of the MCQ discriminate GAD and OCD patients from other anxious groups. Further descriptive data on criterion groups is required for the MCQ-30.

Assessment of individual differences in use of thought-control strategies is provided by the TCQ. Analysis of the instrument suggests that two subscales of worry and punishment are consistently associated with emotional vulnerability and with a range of psychological disorders. The use of worry to control thoughts appears to be causally linked to the development of post-traumatic stress disorder following trauma.

Further psychometric assessment of the instruments reviewed in this chapter is warranted. In particular, future studies might seek to establish their factor structure in different samples. The emerging literature suggests that assessment and classification of worry and related metacognitions has advanced and will continue to advance psychological formulations of underlying pathogenic mechanisms.

REFERENCES

Abramowitz, J.S., Whiteside, S., Kalsy, S.A. & Tolin, D.A. (2003). Thought control strategies in obsessive compulsive disorder: a replication and extension. *Behaviour Research and Therapy*, **41**, 529–540.

Amir, N., Cashman, L. & Foa, E.B. (1997). Strategies of thought control in obsessive-compulsive disorder. *Behaviour Research and Therapy*, **35**, 775–777.

Beck, A.T., Ward, C.H., Mendelson, M., Mock, J. & Erbaugh, J. (1961). An inventory for measuring depression. *Archives of General Psychiatry*, **4**, 561–571.

Cartwright-Hatton, S. & Wells, A. (1997). Beliefs about worry and intrusions: The Meta-Cognitions Questionnaire and its correlates. *Journal of Anxiety Disorders*, **11**, 279–296.

Holeva, V., Tarrier, N. & Wells, A. (2001). Prevalence and predictors of acute PTSD following road traffic accidents: Thought control strategies and social support. *Behavior Therapy*, **32**, 65–83.

Morrison, A. & Wells, A. (2000). Thought control strategies in schizophrenia: a comparison with non-patients. *Behaviour Research and Therapy*, **38**, 1205–1209.

Papageorgiou, C. & Wells, A. (2000). Treatment of recurrent major depression with Attention Training. *Cognitive and Behavioural Practise*, **7**, 407–413.

Purdon, C. (1999). Thought suppression and psychopathology. *Behaviour Research and Therapy*, **37**, 1029–1054.

Rachman, S.J. & Hodgson, R. (1980). *Obsessions and compulsions*. Englewood Cliffs, NJ: Prentice Hall.

Reynolds, M. & Wells, A. (1999). The Thought Control Questionnaire—psychometric properties in a clinical sample, and relationships with PTSD and depression. *Psychological Medicine*, **29**, 1089–1099.

Speilberger, C.D., Gorsuch, R.L., Lushene, R., Vagg, P.R. & Jacobs, G.A. (1983). *Manual for the State-Trait Anxiety Inventory*. Palo Alto, CA: Consulting Psychology Press.

Warda, G. & Bryant, R.A. (1998). Cognitive bias in acute stress disorder. *Behaviour Research and Therapy*, **36**, 1177–1183.

Wegner, D.M. & Schneider, D.J., Carter, S.R.III. & White, T.L. (1987). Paradoxical effects of thought suppression. *Journal of Personality and Social Psychology*, **53**, 5–13.

Wells, A. (1994). A multi-dimensional measure of worry: Development and preliminary validation of the Anxious Thoughts Inventory. *Anxiety Stress and Coping*, **6**, 289–299.

Wells, A. (1995). Meta-cognition and worry: A cognitive model of generalised anxiety disorder. *Behavioural and Cognitive Psychotherapy*, **23**, 301–320.

Wells, A. (2000). *Emotional Disorders and Metacognition: Innovative Cognitive Therapy*. Chichester, UK: Wiley.

Wells, A. (2005). The Metacognitive Model of GAD: Assessment of meta-worry and relationship with DSM-IV Generalized Anxiety Disorder. *Cognitive Therapy and Research*, **29**, 107–121.

Wells, A. & Carter, K. (2001). Further tests of a cognitive model of Generalized Anxiety Disorder: Metacognitions and worry in GAD, panic disorder, social phobia, depression, and non-patients. *Behavior Therapy*, **32**, 85–102.

Wells, A. & Cartwright-Hatton, S. (2004). A short form of the metacognitions questionnaire: properties of the MCQ 30. *Behaviour Research and Therapy*, **42**, 385–396.

Wells, A. & Davies, M. (1994). The Thought Control Questionnaire: A measure of individual differences in the control of unwanted thought. *Behaviour Research and Therapy*, **32**, 871–878.

Wells, A. & Matthews, G. (1994). Self-consciousness and cognitive failures as predictors of coping in stressful episodes. *Cognition and Emotion*, **8**, 279–295.

Wells, A. & Matthews, G. (1996). Modelling cognition in emotional disorder: The S-REF model. *Behaviour Research and Therapy*, **34**, 881–888.

Wells, A. & Papageorgiou, C. (1998). Relationships between worry, obsessive-compulsive symptoms, and meta-cognitive beliefs. *Behaviour Research and Therapy*, **39**, 899–913.

Wells, A. & King, P. (in press). Metacognitive Therapy for Generalized Anxiety Disorder: An open trial. *Journal of Behavior Therapy and Experimental Psychiatry*.

Wells, A., Welford, M., King, P., Papageorgiou, C., Wisely, J. & Mendel, E. (in preparation). A randomized trial of metacognitive therapy versus applied relaxation in the treatment of GAD.

Chapter 9

ASSESSMENT OF GENERALIZED ANXIETY DISORDER

Cynthia L. Turk and Andrew T. Wolanin

ASSESSMENT OF GENERALIZED ANXIETY DISORDER

Generalized anxiety disorder (GAD) has historically been one of the most difficult disorders to assess and diagnose (Brown, DiNardo, Lehman & Campbell, 2001). One reason for these problems has been the consistent evolution of the diagnostic criteria with each revision of the *Diagnostic and Statistical Manual of Mental Disorders* since GAD was introduced in the third edition (DSM-III; American Psychiatric Association [APA], 1980). The evolving diagnostic criteria also hampered development of theoretical models, which in turn retarded development of instruments consistent with those models. Furthermore, the symptoms of GAD overlap with other psychological disorders and serve as an obstacle for accurate diagnosis (e.g., Brown et al., 2001). For example, the criteria for dysthymia also include symptoms of insomnia, fatigue, and poor concentration. Additionally, differentiating normal and pathological worry can be difficult, given that worry is common in the normal population (Dupuy, Beaudoin, Rhéaume, Ladouceur & Dugas, 2001). It can also be difficult to determine when it is appropriate to give a diagnosis of GAD when other psychopathology is present, given that worry is common among other anxiety and mood disorders (Harvey, Watkins, Mansell & Shafran, 2004).

The goal of this chapter is to provide options for identifying and assessing GAD in adults and to review measures assessing psychological variables that may function as mechanisms of change during treatment according to contemporary theoretical models. Lastly, tools to assess clinically relevant areas such as comorbid symptomatology and quality of life are briefly reviewed.

Worry and Its Psychological Disorders: Theory, Assessment and Treatment. Edited by G. C. L. Davey and A. Wells. © 2006 John Wiley & Sons, Ltd.

Unstructured Clinical Interviews

Unstructured clinical interviewing is common in applied settings. It generally involves the clinician eliciting information from the person based on the chief complaint. This approach creates a situation in which errors are likely to occur, based on bias of the clinician and lack of awareness by the person presenting for treatment (Garb, 1998). For example, a person may present with primary problems of anxiety and fatigue. This person may be diagnosed with an anxiety disorder, when, in reality, the person may have had difficulty spontaneously articulating ruminating thoughts and subjective feelings of depression. Furthermore, clinicians tend to ask confirmatory questions based on their hypothesis of what they believe the diagnosis to be rather than ask questions that may rule out their diagnostic impression (Garb & Boyle, 2003). In this way, unstructured interviewing creates an interaction in which both parties' biases may guide the interview and critical information may be overlooked or underemphasized (Miller, 2003).

Unstructured clinical interviewing is especially unsuited for the diagnosis of GAD. As previously mentioned, the diagnostic criteria of GAD overlap with those of other disorders and are somewhat subjective. These factors, when combined with the subjectiveness of unstructured clinical interviews, increase the likelihood that relevant diagnostic information will be missed or incorrectly emphasized.

Structured Clinical Interviews

Structured clinical interviews provide an advantage over unstructured interviews for several reasons. Structured interviews have known psychometric properties. Structured interviews also provide a structure for a comprehensive assessment of diagnostic categories that is not left up to the judgment of the interviewer (Miller, 2003). Furthermore, some structured clinical interviews provide severity ratings for symptoms, which allows for more specific treatment planning and outcome measurement.

Structured clinical interviews have less flexibility than their unstructured counterparts and may be more time consuming to administer. However, increased accuracy in diagnosis, which is crucial to research and appropriate treatment planning, would seem to outweigh these disadvantages (Miller, Dasher, Collins, Griffiths & Brow, 2001).

Structured Clinical Interview for DSM-IV (SCID)

The Structured Clinic Interview for DSM-IV for Axis I disorders (SCID; First, Spitzer, Gibbon & Williams, 1997) has been updated from the original SCID (Spitzer, Williams, Gibbon & First, 1990). A clinician version (SCID-CV) and a research version (SCID I/P) are available and cover many of the same disorders. However, the research SCID-I/P also assesses for acute stress disorder, minor depressive disorder, mixed anxiety depressive disorder, and binge eating disorder. The SCID-I/P also includes a more thorough assessment of the diagnoses covered in the SCID-CV.

The SCID-I/P begins with an overview of demographic information, which is followed by modules for mood disorders, anxiety disorders, substance use disorders, psychotic disorders, somatoform disorders, eating disorders, and adjustment disorders. The modular format allows for administration of only the sections of interest or significance.

The primary reliability data on the SCID are derived from the version that corresponds to the DSM-III-R (APA, 1987). When two independent interviewers administered this version to a large sample of psychiatric patients, an unsatisfactory kappa of .56 was obtained for a current diagnosis of GAD (Williams et al., 1992).

More recently, Zanarini et al. (2000) completed a reliability study using the DSM-IV version of the SCID-I/P. Interrater reliability was assessed using 27 videotapes viewed by multiple pairs of independent raters. With regard to interrater reliability, a median kappa of .63 for GAD was found. Test-retest reliability was assessed using two different direct interviews of 52 subjects, with one interview occurring at intake and a second blind interview occurring 10 days later. With regard to test-retest reliability, an unsatisfactory median kappa of .44 for GAD was found. Compared to the other diagnoses assessed in this study, GAD had the second lowest interrater reliability and test-retest reliability.

Overall, more data are needed with regard to the reliability of the most recent version of the SCID before any definitive recommendations can be made with regard to its use. However, the very limited data available suggest that the SCID may not be highly reliable with regard to diagnosing GAD.

Anxiety Disorders Interview Schedule (ADIS-IV)

The Anxiety Disorders Schedule for DSM-IV (ADIS-IV; Brown, DiNardo & Barlow, 1994) and the ADIS-IV-Lifetime Version (ADIS-IV-L; DiNardo, Brown & Barlow, 1994) provide a comprehensive diagnostic assessment for each anxiety disorder. The ADIS also assesses disorders that have similar symptoms or are frequently comorbid with anxiety disorders (e.g., mood disorders, substance abuse, hypochondriasis). Other major disorders are ruled out with screening questions (e.g., psychotic disorders).

The GAD section of the ADIS includes dimensional questions about excessiveness and uncontrollability of worry in multiple domains (e.g., work, health, finances) and about severity of associated symptoms of restlessness, fatigue, impaired concentration, irritability, muscle tension, and sleep disturbance. Interference and distress are assessed, and an overall (0–8) clinician's severity rating (CSR) is assigned. A CSR of 4 or higher indicates a clinical diagnosis. When multiple disorders receive a CSR of 4 or higher, the disorder receiving the highest CSR is designated as the "principal" diagnosis and the other disorders are designated as "additional" diagnoses. Brown et al. (2001) found good interrater reliability for the ratings of excessiveness of worry, uncontrollability of worry, and associated symptoms (e.g., muscle tension). Good interrater reliability was also observed for the CSR for GAD ($r = .72$).

The major reliability study of the ADIS-IV-L included 362 individuals seeking treatment at an anxiety specialty clinic who were independently assessed by two highly trained interviewers (Brown et al., 2001). Seventy-six patients were given a principal diagnosis of GAD. Overall, 113 patients were given a current clinical diagnosis of GAD (includes patients with a principal diagnosis of GAD and patients with a principal diagnosis of another disorder but an additional diagnosis of GAD). GAD evidenced fair to good reliability when examined as a current principal diagnosis ($\kappa = .67$) and as a current clinical diagnosis ($\kappa = .65$). Fair interrater reliability was also attained for GAD as a past diagnosis ($\kappa = .65$).

In summary, the ADIS-IV has become the gold standard for the structured clinical assessment of anxiety disorders. The ADIS-IV demonstrates reasonable reliability for the diagnosis of GAD, good reliability for the features of GAD, and good to excellent reliability for the diagnosis of other anxiety disorders (Brown et al., 2001). Its use of dimensional ratings for clinical severity has made it useful for measuring therapeutic change beyond simply documenting the presence or absence of a diagnosis (e.g., Borkovec, Newman, Pincus & Lytle, 2002).

Screening Measures

Generalized Anxiety Disorders Questionnaire-IV (GADQ-IV)

The Generalized Anxiety Disorder Questionnaire-IV (GADQ-IV; Newman et al., 2002) represents a DSM-IV (APA, 1994) revision to the original Generalized Anxiety Disorder Questionnaire (GAD-Q; Roemer, Borkovec, Posa & Borkovec, 1995). The GADQ-IV is a 9-item self-report measure that corresponds to the diagnostic criteria for GAD (with the exception of exclusion criteria). The original GADQ was scored by matching items on the scale to the DSM-III-R (APA, 1987) criteria. Individuals endorsing items consistent with the diagnostic criteria were classified as having GAD. In contrast, with the revised version of the scale, Newman et al. (2002) recommended calculating a total score (range 0–13) and using a cut-off score to determine presence or absence of GAD.

Newman et al. (2002) conducted a series of studies with undergraduates examining the psychometric properties of the GAD-Q-IV. In study 1, students completed the GAD-Q-IV and either an ADIS-IV or ADIS-IV-L at least 10 days later. A cutoff score of 5.7 was identified as achieving the optimal balance between sensitivity and specificity. This cutoff score correctly classified 25 of 30 cases of GAD (83% sensitivity) and 101 of 113 cases without GAD (89% specificity). In study 2, the GAD-Q-IV was more highly correlated with a measure of worry than with a measure of post-traumatic stress and a measure of social anxiety. In study 3, 136 of 148 (92%) undergraduates retained their classification with the GAD-Q-IV after completing the measure twice over a period of two weeks.

In another study, Luterek, Turk, Heimberg, Fresco and Mennin (2002) administered the GAD-Q-IV and the ADIS-IV-L to 31 treatment-seeking individuals with GAD and 53 non-anxious community participants. With a cut-off score of 5.7, 50 of 53 community participants were correctly classified as not having GAD (94.3% specificity), and 31 of 31 participants with GAD were correctly classified as having GAD (100% sensitivity). When GAD classification was based on matching items to the DSM-IV criteria, 51 of 53 community controls were correctly classified as not having GAD (96.2% specificity), and 24 of 31 patients were correctly classified as having GAD (77.4% sensitivity). Although this study has the advantage of including a clinical sample, it is limited in its test of the measure as a screening device since only individuals representing the extremes of the continuum of worry were assessed.

In a recent study that addresses some of the limitations of previous research, Barnes, Haigh and Fresco (2005) administered the GAD-Q-IV and the DSM-IV version of the SCID to 81 consecutive outpatients seeking treatment at a university training clinic. With a cut-off score of 5.7, 30 of 51 patients were correctly classified as not having GAD (58.8% specificity), and 29 of 30 patients with GAD were correctly classified as having GAD (96.6% sensitivity). When GAD classification was based on matching items to the DSM-IV criteria, 37 of 51 patients were correctly classified as not having GAD (72.5% specificity), and 26 of 30 patients were correctly classified as having GAD (86.6% sensitivity).

In summary, the GAD-Q-IV has been widely and productively used in analogue psychopathology research (e.g., Mennin, Heimberg, Turk & Fresco, 2005; Roemer, Salters, Raffa & Orsillo, 2005; Turk, Heimberg, Luterek,

Mennin & Fresco, 2005). However, researchers have varied with regard to whether they have made GAD determinations based on the recommended cut-off score (e.g., Roemer et al., 2005) or based on matching items endorsed on the instrument to the DSM-IV criteria (e.g., Mennin et al., in press). One reason for the conflicting approaches to scoring is due to concerns regarding the validity of the cut score of 5.7 in populations different from the one used to derive it. The original study was conducted at a university in a rural setting with a predominantly Caucasian student body, and the GAD-Q-IV identified a relatively small percentage of students (14%) as having GAD (Newman et al., 2002). However, in other studies with ethnically diverse samples in urban environments, a cutoff score of 5.7 has resulted in approximately a third of respondents being classified as positive for GAD (Roemer et al., 2005; Turk et al., 2005). For GAD, the estimates of its current prevalence in the population are between 1.5% and 3% (Kessler, Walters & Wittchen, 2004). It seems likely that a cut-off score that identifies approximately one-third of unselected college students as having GAD is producing an excess of false positives. Consistent with these observations, Barnes et al.'s (2005) work in a clinical sample seems to suggest that the cut-off score of 5.7 is highly sensitive but lacks specificity. More research is needed to examine the relative utility of the original criterion-matching approach to scoring the GAD-Q-IV and the dimensional scoring system (employing various cut-off scores) in a variety of populations. Overall, more research is needed to understand the psychometric properties of this instrument, as it has already become the instrument most relied upon by psychopathology researchers conducting preliminary tests of their models with analogue undergraduate samples.

Penn State Worry Questionnaire (PSWQ) (see also Chapter 7)

The Penn State Worry Questionnaire (PSWQ; Meyer, Miller, Metzeger & Borkovec, 1990) is a 16-item self report measure that assesses the intensity, uncontrollability, and excessiveness of worry. Two studies have examined its utility as a screening measure for GAD. Fresco, Mennin, Heimberg and Turk (2003) employed a receiver operating characteristic (ROC) analysis to determine that a cut-off score of 53 on the PSWQ maximized both sensitivity and specificity in identifying patients with GAD relative to community controls. In a similar study, Behar, Alcaine, Zuellig and Borkovec (2003) identified a cut-off score of 45 as best differentiating individuals with GAD and community controls. Both studies used carefully diagnosed groups at the extremes of the continuum of worry. Additional research is needed in order to examine the utility of the PSWQ in identifying cases of GAD from unselected samples (e.g., college students, adults from the community) or mixed samples of treatment-seeking individuals relative to a structured clinical interview. Of course, the utility of the PSWQ extends far beyond its possible usefulness as a screening device for GAD. Because of its importance in the assessment of worry, an entire chapter in the current volume has been dedicated to the PSWQ (Chapter 7).

Measures Relating to Contemporary Theoretical Models of GAD

Action and Acceptance Questionnaire (AAQ)

Roemer and Orsillo (2002) have developed a conceptual model of GAD that draws heavily upon the work of Borkovec (e.g., Borkovec, Alcaine & Behar, 2004) and Hayes (e.g., Hayes, Strosahl & Wilson, 1999). According to Borkovec's avoidance theory of worry, the function of worry is to reduce or avoid uncomfortable images, bodily sensations, and emotions by focusing attention on possible future threats (Borkovec et al., 2004). According to Hayes's work in the area of experiential avoidance, many of the problems experienced by patients stem from attempts to control or diminish unwanted internal experiences such as upsetting memories, emotions, or thoughts (Hayes, Strosahl & Wilson, 1999). Attempts to avoid or reduce unwanted internal experiences often lead to increased intrusions of the very things that the individual is trying to avoid, resulting in a cycle of experiential avoidance. Roemer and Orsillo (2002) suggest that GAD is characterized by experiential avoidance, given the avoidant function of worry and the lack of present moment experiencing characteristic of the worry process. Therefore, they have incorporated aspects of Acceptance and Commitment Therapy (ACT; Hayes et al., 1999), which was developed to address the problem of experiential avoidance, into their cognitive-behavioral treatment of GAD.

The Action and Acceptance Questionnaire (AAQ; Hayes et al., 2004) assesses the construct of experiential avoidance (e.g., "When I feel depressed or anxious, I am unable to take care of my responsibilities"). Many versions of this measure have been utilized, with the 9-item and 16-item versions being most frequently employed. A slightly modified 16-item version has been shown to produce two factorially-derived subscales entitled Willingness and Action (Bond & Bunce, 2003). For all versions, participants are asked to respond to questions on a 7-point Likert scale which ranges from 1 (never true) to 7 (always true). Higher scores are indicative of more experiential avoidance, although some studies have also scored this measure in the opposite direction, with higher scores being indicative of greater acceptance of negative internal states and behavioral action despite uncomfortable emotions.

Beginning with a pool of 32 items administered to a large sample of patients at a counseling center, iterative exploratory factor analysis was used to eliminate items and arrive at the 16-item and 9-item versions of the measure (Hayes et al., 2004). Cronbach's alpha for the 9-item version was .70. A confirmatory factor analysis using a large sample of patients from an HMO clinic revealed that the 9-item single factor solution provided a good fit to the data. Across a variety of samples, the AAQ was significantly correlated with related constructs such as thought suppression, thought control, and measures of avoidance. It had moderate positive correlations with measures of psychopathology and a moderate negative correlation with quality of life. In a large sample of undergraduates, test-retest reliability over a period of four months was .64.

The AAQ (17 items) was used as an outcome measure in a small series of case studies (n = 4), which illustrated the potential efficacy of incorporating ACT into cognitive behavioral treatment for GAD (Orsillo, Roemer & Barlow, 2003). The range of scores at pretreatment was 60–89, suggesting significant experiential avoidance. For three of the four patients, change on the AAQ was modest, although, as a group, there was a significant decrease in AAQ from pretreatment to post-treatment. Recent preliminary data from a randomized controlled trial further suggests that the AAQ is responsive to the effects of Roemer and Orsillo's treatment for GAD (Roemer & Orsillo, 2004).

The AAQ may prove to be a useful tool for individuals using the ACT model with GAD patients. However, more psychometric studies involving the AAQ and anxiety disorder patients are needed. The AAQ-II is currently under development in order to address some of the problems with the current versions of the AAQ such as item complexity and the marginal internal consistency that has been observed in some studies ("ACT specific measures," 2005).

Intolerance of Uncertainty Scale (IUS)

Dugas, Gosselin and Ladouceur (2001) have proposed that an important cognitive schema characteristic of GAD is intolerance of uncertainty (see Chapter 12), which they define as an excessive tendency to believe that it is unacceptable if a negative event occurs, even if the probability of its actual occurrence is extremely small. They have developed a promising treatment based on this conceptualization (Ladouceur et al., 2000). The Intolerance of Uncertainty Scale (IUS; Freeston, Rheame, Letarte, Dugas & Ladouceur, 1994) consists of 27 items that target beliefs about the negative aspects of being in an uncertain state (e.g., "The ambiguities in life stress me"). Items are rated on a 5 point scale (1 = not at all characteristic of me; 5 = entirely characteristic of me). A total score is most often calculated although factor scores may be calculated as well. A factor analysis of the English version of the scale yielded four factors: uncertainty is upsetting and stressful, uncertainty leads to inaction, uncertain events are negative and should be avoided, and being uncertain is unfair (Burh & Dugas, 2002).

The IUS is a reliable measure. The French version demonstrated good internal consistency in a non-clinical sample (Freeston et al., 1994) and adequate test-retest reliability in a college sample (Dugas, Freeston & Ladouceur, 1997). The English version was found to have good internal consistency and test-retest reliability in a college sample (Buhr & Dugas, 2002).

The evidence also suggests that the IUS is a valid measure. In a sample of 148 college students, the IUS was significantly correlated with the tendency to interpret ambiguous information as threatening, even after controlling for worry (Hedayati, Dugas, Buhr & Francis, 2003). As expected, the IUS has been shown to be positively correlated with measures of worry (Buhr & Dugas, 2002; Freeston et al., 1994). It also has demonstrated utility in discriminating individuals with GAD from normal controls (Dugas, Gagnon, Ladouceur & Freeston, 1998) as well as individuals with other anxiety disorders (Ladouceur, Dugas, Freeston, Rheaume, Blais, Boisert, Gagnon & Thibodeau, 1999).

In a recent treatment study that included 25 patients with GAD, the pre-treatment scores on the IUS ($M = 73.36$, $SD = 8.64$) were elevated as expected (Dugas et al., 2003). Following a group cognitive behavioral intervention for GAD, the IUS scores reduced considerably ($M = 55.04$, $SD = 17.99$), suggesting that the IUP is sensitive to the effects of treatment.

In conclusion, the IUP is a reliable and valid measure that assesses the theoretical construct of intolerance of uncertainty in individuals with GAD. It has demonstrated utility in both psychopathology studies and treatment outcome research. Lastly, some recent research suggests that the intolerance of uncertainty construct may also be a central theme in other anxiety disorders such as obsessive compulsive disorder (Holaway, Heimberg & Coles, 2005).

The Anxious Thoughts Inventory (AnTI) and Meta-Cognitions Questionnaire (MCQ) (see also Chapter 8)

Wells (2004) has proposed a metacognitive model of the development and maintenance of GAD and has developed a treatment program based on this model (see also Chapters 11 and 15). According to this model, most individuals experience worries about social events and physical symptoms and these worries are normal (Type 1 worry). However, some individuals also experience "worry about worry" or "meta-worry" (Type 2 worry), which Wells (2004) considers most characteristic of GAD. Individuals may engage in Type 2 worry because they hold certain beliefs such as worry is harmful or represents a loss of control. This distinction between Type 1 and Type 2 worry is captured by the Anxious Thoughts Inventory (AnTI; Wells, 1994), a 22-item measure that includes three factor-analytically derived subscales: 1) social worry (e.g., "I worry about making a fool of myself"); 2) health worry (e.g., "I have thoughts about being seriously ill"); and 3) meta-worry, which captures negative thoughts about one's own worry (e.g., "I worry that I cannot control my thoughts as well as I would like to").

In addition to the distinction between Type 1 and Type 2 worry, the metacognitive model of GAD suggests that certain metacognitive processes are central to GAD. To assess these processes, the 65-item Metacognitions Questionnaire (MCQ; Cartwright-Hatton & Wells, 1997) was developed. The MCQ is divided into five factorially-derived subscales which include: positive worry beliefs ("Worrying helps me cope"), beliefs about uncontrollability and danger of worry ("Worrying is dangerous for me"), beliefs about cognitive competence ("I have a poor memory"), general negative beliefs ("Not being able to control my thoughts is a sign of weakness"), and cognitive self-consciousness ("I pay close attention to the way my mind works"). For a review of the psychometric properties of the MCQ and the AnTI, see Chapter 8 in this volume.

Measures associated with other contemporary models of GAD

Other models of GAD have emerged in recent years but none are as closely associated with a particular assessment measure as the models described above. For example, Mennin, Heimberg, Turk and Fresco (2002) have proposed a model that emphasizes the role of emotion regulation deficits in GAD. However, their approach has been to use a variety of instruments to target the various components of their model (Turk, Heimberg & Mennin, 2004).

Other recent theoretical work has emphasized the important role of interpersonal problems in GAD, and treatments for GAD have been developed that address this domain of dysfunction (Crits-Christoph, Connolly & Crits-Christoph, 2004; Newman, Castonguay, Borkovec & Molnar, 2004). Although working from different theoretical models, several groups of researchers (e.g., Crits-Christoph et al., 2004; Borkovec et al., 2002) have relied upon the *Inventory of Interpersonal Problems Circumplex Scales* (IIP-C; Alden, Wiggins & Pincus, 1990) to assess interpersonal problems in GAD and whether treatment has produced interpersonal changes. The most recent version of the scale (IIP-64; Horowitz, Alden, Wiggins & Pincus, 2000) is comprised of 64 items that target a wide range of typical interpersonal difficulties categorized into two domains: 1) interpersonal behaviors that are "hard for you to do" (e.g. trust other people) and 2) those that "you do too much" (e.g., "I put other people's needs before my own too much"). Items are rated using a Likert scale ranging from 0 ("Not at all") to 4 ("Extremely"). The measure includes eight subscales: domineering/controlling, vindictive/self-centered, cold/distant, socially inhibited, nonassertive, overly accommodating, self-sacrificing, and intrusive/needy. In terms of psychometric characteristics, Horowitz et al. (2000) reported acceptable internal consistency and one-week test-retest reliability for the subscales. The IIP-64 was significantly correlated with other measures of interpersonal difficulties (Horowitz et al., 2000).

Assessment of Anxiety

Hamilton Anxiety Rating Scale

The Hamilton Anxiety Rating Scale (HARS; Hamilton, 1959) is a clinician administered measure designed to assess anxious symptomatology among individuals with an anxiety disorder. The HARS is widely used as the gold standard for pharmacological treatment outcomes studies for GAD (e.g., Rickels et al., 2003). In pharmacological studies, HARS scores of greater than 20 are generally considered to indicate significant symptomatology. In administering the HARS, the interviewer uses a 5-point scale (0 = "none"; 4 = "very severe; grossly disabling") to rate 14 symptom categories (e.g. "anxious mood, tensions, fears") in the most widely used version of the scale. Each category is defined by symptomatic criteria (e.g. "worries, anticipates the worst"). However, no specific guidelines beyond the Likert scale are given for determining the severity of the ratings, and the specific language used in the inquiry is determined by the individual administrator. Subscales of psychic anxiety and somatic anxiety may be scored.

The reliability of the HARS has ranged from fair to excellent across studies. When the HARS was administered to anxiety patients by separate interviewers less than 10 days apart, interrater reliability was fair ($r = .65$) and internal consistency was good (alpha = .77 and .81 for the first and second HARS administrations, respectively; Moras, DiNardo & Barlow, 1992). In another study, interrater reliability obtained via live observation was excellent ($r = .96$), as was internal consistency (alpha = .92; Kobak, Reynolds & Greist, 1993). For a sample of patients with GAD, when the HARS was administered by separate interviewers within a seven-day period using a structured interview guide, interrater reliability as assessed by the intraclass correlation coefficient was .79 (Shear et al., 2001).

With regard to validity, the HARS has been found to correlate with self-report measures of anxiety (e.g., Beck & Steer, 1991). Individuals with an anxiety disorder score higher on the HARS than individuals from the community (Kobak et al., 1993). Although the Hamilton depression and anxiety scales were developed to assess these constructs independently, research has generally shown a significant amount of overlap between the two scales (e.g., Diefenbach et al., 2001; Riskind, Beck, Brown & Steer, 1987). This finding of significant scale overlap has held even with a reconstructed version of the Hamilton anxiety and depression scales (see Riskind et al., 1987) intended to make the subscales essentially independent (Diefenbach et al., 2001; Moras et al., 1992).

Beck Anxiety Inventory

The Beck Anxiety Inventory (BAI; Beck Epstein, Brown & Steer, 1988) is a 21-item self-report measure that assesses the severity of anxiety symptoms and is designed to differentiate anxiety from depression. The majority of items are focused on autonomic arousal symptoms such as "heart racing or pounding" or "sweating not due to heat." Research has shown that elevated scores on the BAI may be present in GAD (e.g., Butler, Fennell, Robson & Gelder, 1991); however, the symptoms that are measured by the BAI do not capture the more broad and generalized anxiety symptoms typically associated with GAD (e.g., restlessness, tension). Since the measure's content does not reflect those anxiety symptoms most characteristic of GAD, it should be used cautiously as the sole measure of anxiety or treatment outcome when working with patients with GAD.

State Trait Anxiety Inventory (STAI)

The State Trait Anxiety Inventory (STAI; Speilberger, Gorsuch, Lushene, Vagg & Jacobs, 1983) consists of two 20-item self report scales that measure state and trait anxiety separately. Trait scale, which measures characteristic tendencies to be anxious, was often used in early treatment outcome studies of GAD. Items (e.g., "I get in a state of tension or turmoil as I think over my recent concerns and interests") are rated on a 4-point Likert-type scale based on how the individual generally feels.

The STAI Trait scale appears to have good psychometric properties. It has been found to have excellent internal consistency (αs = .86 to .95 across samples of working adults, students, and military recruits) and good test-retest reliability (e.g., median test-retest correlations of .77 for college students and .70 for high school students) (Spielberger et al., 1983). There is also evidence to support its convergent and discriminant validity (Spielberger et al., 1983). Nevertheless, based on the responses of a sample of patients with anxiety disorders, the STAI Trait was found to have separate lower order factors assessing (1) dysphoric mood and (2) anxiety and worry (Bieling, Antony & Swinson, 1998). The anxiety factor was more highly correlated with other measures of anxiety than measures of depression; the depression factor was more highly correlated with other measures of depression than measures of anxiety. That the STAI Trait taps into depressive symptomatology is not surprising given the content of some items (e.g., "I wish I could be as happy as others seem to be").

In outcome studies of GAD treatment, the STAI Trait has been related to change following intervention (Fisher & Durham, 1999). Given that many patients with GAD experience both anxiety and depression, the STAI Trait may do a reasonable job of assessing change with treatment in part because it may capture improvements of both anxious and depressive symptoms. However, the STAI Trait scale is probably less than ideal if the purpose is to assess the anxiety component of GAD in particular.

Assessment of Depression

GAD is frequently comorbid with depression (e.g., Kessler, DuPont, Berglund & Wittchen, 1999), and it is recommended that any assessment of GAD include an assessment for depressive symptomatology. One option is the *Beck Depression Inventory* (BDI; Beck, Rush, Shaw & Emery, 1979) or BDI-II (Beck, Steer & Brown, 1996), which assesses symptoms of depression including the affective, cognitive, behavioral, somatic, and motivational components as well as suicidal wishes.

Weeks and Heimberg (2004) conducted a study evaluating the psychometric properties of the BDI with a sample of patients with GAD and matched community controls. Within the patient sample, the BDI exhibited good internal consistency (alpha = .85). Patients with GAD scored significantly higher ($M = 16.21, SD = 8.52$) on the BDI compared to control participants ($M = 1.78, SD = 2.02$). Furthermore, individuals with GAD and a comorbid mood disorder scored significantly higher ($M = 22.67, SD = 8.87$) on the BDI than individuals with GAD but no comorbid mood disorder ($M = 14.21, SD = 6.32$). Within the patient sample, the BDI showed a significant positive correlation with a clinician-administered measure of depression. As expected, the BDI did not correlate significantly with measures of generalized anxiety, worry, anxiety sensitivity, or social anxiety. These findings support the use of the BDI to assess depressive symptoms in adults with GAD.

Assessment of Impairment and Quality of Life

Functional impairment describes the extent to which a disorder limits one's ability to fulfill important roles and responsibilities (e.g., parent, employee). Quality of life describes the extent to which a person experiences a subjective sense of well-being. Increasingly, these constructs have been recognized as two distinct indicators of the impact of a mental disorder and the adequacy of treatment (e.g., Hambrick, Turk, Heimberg, Schneier & Liebowitz, 2003).

Questions have been raised regarding whether GAD is an impairing disorder in its own right or whether the impairment seen in GAD is a function of the high levels of comorbidity often observed with the disorder. In their recent review of the literature, Kessler and his colleagues (2004) concluded that "pure" GAD, defined as GAD in the absence of additional disorders, was consistently associated with impairment comparable to the level associated with other anxiety and mood disorders. In a recent study examining patients seeking treatment for GAD, mild to moderate impairment was common across most domains assessed (e.g., educational attainment, career, family relationships) (Turk, Mennin, Fresco & Heimberg, 2000). Such findings argue that measurement of impairment is relevant to a comprehensive assessment of GAD. An example of a widely used, brief measure of impairment is the 4-item self-rated Sheehan Disability Scale (SDS; Sheehan, 1983). The SDS has demonstrated sensitivity to impairment across a wide range of disorder (Olfson et al., 1997), including GAD (Turk et al., 2000).

Because it is often possible to both worry and act, impairment in GAD may be subtle (e.g., reduced but acceptable performance) or even non-existent for some individuals. Regardless of level of impairment, the internal states of worry, anxiety, and tension may nevertheless interfere with quality of life. Turk et al. (2000) found that, although individuals with GAD generally reported mild to moderate impairment across a variety of domains, they reported profound dissatisfaction with their quality of life. Other studies have also found that individuals with GAD report low life satisfaction (e.g., Bourland et al., 2000; Stein & Heimberg, 2004). The Quality of Life Inventory (QOLI; Frisch, 1994; Frisch, Cornell, Villanueva & Retzlaff, 1992) is an example of a self-report instrument that may be used to assess the extent to which individuals perceive themselves as satisfied in the areas of their lives that they deem most important to their happiness. The QOLI has good psychometric properties and normative data are available.

Conclusion

Since its introduction in the DSM-III, our ability to diagnose GAD, assess its features, and measure theoretically important constructs relevant to it has grown dramatically. Despite these advances in the assessment of GAD, more psychometric studies are needed. Ultimately, improved assessment may allow us to better understand the nature of GAD, better customize our treatments to the specific problems of the patient, and increase the effectiveness of our treatments.

REFERENCES

ACT specific measures. (2005). Retrieved February 25, 2005, from http://www.acceptanceandcommitmenttherapy.com/resources/ACT%20Specific%20 Measures.htm.

Alden, L.E., Wiggins, J.S. & Pincus, A.L. (1990). Construction of circumplex scales for the Inventory of Interpersonal Problems. *Journal of Personality Assessment*, **55**, 521–536.

American Psychiatric Association. (1980). *Diagnostic and statistical manual of mental disorders* (3rd ed.). Washington DC: Author.

American Psychiatric Association. (1987). *Diagnostic and statistical manual of mental disorders* (3rd ed. revised). Washington DC: Author.

American Psychiatric Association. (1994). *Diagnostic and statistical manual of mental disorders* (4th ed.). Washington, DC: Author.

Barnes, J.M., Haigh, E.A. & Fresco, D.M. (2005, November). *Screening for generalized anxiety disorder with the GAD-Q-IV.* Poster presented at the Annual Meeting of the Association for Behavioral and Cognitive Therapies, Washington, DC.

Beck, A.T., Epstein, N., Brown, G. & Steer, R.A. (1988). An inventory for measuring clinical anxiety: Psychometric properties. *Journal of Consulting and Clinical Psychology*, **56**, 893–897.

Beck, A.T., Rush, J., Shaw, B.F. & Emery, G. (1979). *Cognitive therapy of depression.* New York: Guilford Press.

Beck, A.T., Steer, R.A. & Brown, G.K. (1996). *Beck Depression Inventory Manual* (2nd ed.). San Antonio: The Psychological Corporation.

Behar, E., Alcaine, O., Zuellig, A.R. & Borkovec, T.D. (2003). Screening for generalized anxiety disorder using the Penn State Worry Questionnaire: A receiver operating characteristic analysis. *Journal of Behavior Therapy and Experimental Psychiatry*, **34**, 25–43.

Bieling, P.J., Antony, M.M. & Swinson, R.P. (1998). The state-trait anxiety inventory, trait version: structure and content re-examined. *Behaviour Research and Therapy*, **36**, 777–788.

Bond, F.W. & Bunce, D. (2003). The role of acceptance and job control in mental health, job satisfaction, and work performance. *Journal of Applied Psychology*, **88**, 1057–1067.

Borkovec, T.D., Alcaine, O. & Behar, E. (2004). Avoidance theory of worry and generalized anxiety disorder. In R.G. Heimberg, C.L. Turk & D.S. Mennin (Eds), *Generalized Anxiety Disorder: Advances in Research and Practice* (pp. 77–108). New York: Guilford Press.

Borkovec, T.D., Newman, M.G., Pincus, A.L. & Lytle, R. (2002). A component analysis of cognitive behavioral therapy for generalized anxiety disorder and the role of interpersonal problems. *Journal of Consulting and Clinical Psychology*, **70**, 288–298.

Bourland, S.L., Stanley, M.A., Snyder, A.G., Novy, D.M., Beck, J.G., Averill, P.M. & Swann, A.C. (2000). Quality of life in older adults with generalized anxiety disorder. *Aging & Mental Health*, **4**, 315–323.

Brown, T.A., DiNardo, P.A. & Barlow, D.H. (1994). *Anxiety Disorders Interview Schedule for DSM-IV*. Albany: Graywind Publications.

Brown, T.A., DiNardo, P.A., Lehman, S.L. & Campbell, L.A. (2001). Reliability of DSM-IV anxiety and mood disorders: Implications for the classification of emotional disorders. *Journal of Abnormal Psychology*, **110**, 49–58.

Buhr, K. & Dugas, M.J. (2002). The Intolerance of Uncertainty Scale: psychometric properties of the English version. *Behaviour Research Therapy*, **40**, 931–45.

Butler, G., Fennell, M., Robson, P. & Gelder, M. (1991). Comparison of behavior therapy and cognitive behavior therapy in the treatment of generalized anxiety disorder. *Journal of Clinical and Consulting Psychology*, **59**, 167–175.

Cartwright-Hatton, S. & Wells, A. (1997). Beliefs about worry and intrusions: The Metacognitions Questionnaire and its correlates. *Journal of Anxiety Disorders*, **11**, 279–296.

Crits-Christoph, P., Connolly-Gibbons, M.B. & Crits-Christoph, K. (2004). Supportive-expressive psychodynamic therapy. In R. Heimberg, C. Turk & D. Mennin (Eds), *Generalized Anxiety Disorder: Advances in Research and Practice* (pp. 294–319). New York: Guilford Press.

Diefenbach, G.J., Stanley, M.A., Beck, J.G., Novy, D.M., Averill, P.M. & Swann, A.C. (2001). Examination of the Hamilton scales in assessment of anxious older adults: Replication and extension. *Journal of Psychopathology and Behavioral Assessment*, **23**, 117–124.

DiNardo, P.A., Brown, T.A. & Barlow, D.H. (1994). *Anxiety Disorders Interview Schedule for DSM-IV—Lifetime Version*. Albany: Graywind Publications.

Dugas, M.J., Freeston, M.H. & Ladouceur, R. (1997). Intolerance of uncertainty and problem orientation in worry. *Cognitive Therapy and Research*, **21**, 593–606.

Dugas, M.J., Gagnon, F., Ladouceur, R. & Freeston, M.H. (1998). Generalized anxiety disorder: A preliminary test of a conceptual model. *Behaviour Research and Therapy*, **36**, 215–226.

Dugas, M.J., Gosselin, P. & Ladouceur, R. (2001). Intolerance of uncertainty and worry: Investigating specificity in a clinical sample. *Cognitive Therapy and Research*, **25**, 551–558.

Dugas, M.J., Ladouceur, R., Leger, E., Freeston, M.H., Langlois, F., Provencher, M.D. & Boisvert, J.M. (2003). Group cognitive-behavioral therapy for generalized anxiety disorder: Treatment outcome and long-term follow-up. *Journal of Consulting and Clinical Psychology*, **71**, 821–825.

Dupuy, J.-B., Beaudoin, S., Rhéaume, J., Ladouceur, R. & Dugas, M.J. (2001). Worry: Daily self-report in clinical and non-clinical populations. *Behaviour Research & Therapy*, **39**, 1249–1255.

First, M.B., Spitzer, R.L., Gibbon, M. & Williams, J.B.W. (1997). *Structured clinical interview for DSM-IV Axis I disorders-clinician version (SCID-CV)*. Washington, DC: American Psychiatric Press.

Fisher, P.L. & Durham, R.C. (1999). Recovery states in generalized anxiety disorder following psychological therapy: An analysis of clinically significant change in the STAI-T across outcome studies since 1990. *Psychological Medicine*, **29**, 1425–1434.

Freeston, M.H., Rheaume, J., Letarte, H., Dugas, M.J. & Ladouceur, R. (1994). Why do people worry? *Personality and Individual Differences*, **17**, 791–802.

Fresco, D.M., Mennin, D.S., Heimberg, R.G. & Turk, C.L. (2003). Using the Penn State Worry Questionnaire to identify individuals with generalized anxiety disorder: A receiver operator characteristic analysis. *Journal of Behavior Therapy and Experimental Psychiatry*, **34**, 283–291.

Frisch, M.B. (1994). *Manual and treatment guide for the Quality of Life Inventory*. Minneapolis, MN: National Computer Systems, Inc.

Frisch, M., Cornell, J., Villanueva, M. & Retzlaff, P. (1992). Clinical validation of the Quality of Life Inventory: A measure of life satisfaction for use in treatment planning and outcome assessment. *Psychological Assessment*, **4**, 92–101.

Garb, H.N. (1998). Studying the clinician: Judgment research and psychological assessment. Washington, DC: American Psychological Association.

Garb, H.N. & Boyle, P.A. (2003). Understanding why some clinicians use pseudoscientific methods: Findings from research and clinical judgment. In: S.O. Lilienfeld, S.J Lynn & J.M. Lohr, *Science and Pseudoscience in Clinical Psychology*. New York: Guilford Press.

Hambrick, J.P., Turk, C.L., Heimberg, R.G., Schneier, F.R. & Liebowitz, M.R. (2003). The experience of disability and quality of life in social anxiety disorder. *Depression and Anxiety*, **18**, 46–50.

Hamilton, M. (1959). The assessment of anxiety states by rating. *British Journal of Psychiatry*, **32**, 50–55.

Harvey, A.G., Watkins, E., Mansell, W. & Shafran, R. (2004). *Cognitive behavioural processes across psychological disorders: A transdiagnostic approach to research and treatment*. Oxford: Oxford University Press.

Hayes, S.C., Stosdahl, K.D. & Wilson, K.G. (1999). *Acceptance and commitment therapy: An experiential approach to behavior change*. New York: Guilford Press.

Hayes, S.C., Strosahl, K.D., Wilson, K.G., Bissett, R.T., Pistorello, J., Toarmino, D., Polunsy, M.A., Dykstra, T.A., Batten, S.V., Bergan, J., Stewart, S.H., Zvolensky, M.J., Eifert, G.H., Bond, F.W., Forsyth, J.P., Karekla, M. & McCurry, S.M. (2004). Measuring experiential avoidance: A preliminary test of a working model. *The Psychological Record*, **54**, 553–578.

Hedayati, M., Dugas, M.J., Buhr, K. & Francis, K. (2003). *The relationship between intolerance of uncertainty and the interpretation of ambiguous and unambiguous information*. Poster presented at the Annual Convention of the Association for the Advancement of Behavior Therapy, Boston, MA.

Holaway, R.M, Heimberg, R.G. & Coles, M.E. (2005). A comparison of intolerance of uncertainty in analogue obsessive compulsive disorder and generalized anxiety disorder. *Journal of Anxiety Disorders*. Manuscript submitted for publication.

Horowitz, L.M., Alden, L.E., Wiggins, J.S. & Pincus, A.L. (2000). *Inventory of Interpersonal Problems: Manual*. San Antonio, TX: The Psychological Corporation.

Kessler, R.C., Dupont, R.L., Berglund, P. & Wittchen, H.-U. (1999). Impairment in pure and comorbid generalized anxiety disorder and major depression at 12 months in two national surveys. *American Journal of Psychiatry*, **156**, 1915–1923.

Kessler, R.C., Walters, E.E. & Wittchen, H.-U. (2004). Epidemiology. In R.G. Heimberg, C.L. Turk & D.S. Mennin (Eds), *Generalized anxiety disorder: Advances in research and practice* (pp. 29–50). New York: Guilford Press.

Kobak, K.A., Reynolds, W.M. & Greist, J.H. (1993). Computerized and clinician assessment of depression and anxiety: Respondent evaluation and satisfaction. *Journal of Personality Assessment*, **63**, 173–180.

Ladouceur, R., Dugas, M.J., Freeston, M.H., Rheaume, J., Blais, F., Boisert, J.M., Gagnon, F. & Thibodeau, N. (1999). Specificity of generalized anxiety disorder symptoms and processes. *Behavior Therapy*, **30**, 191–207.

Ladouceur, R., Dugas, M.J., Freeston, M.H., Léger, E., Gagnon, F. & Thibodeau, N. (2000). Efficacy of a cognitive-behavioral treatment for generalized anxiety disorder: Evaluation in a controlled clinical trial. *Journal of Consulting and Clinical Psychology*, **68**, 957–964.

Luterek, J.A., Turk, C.L., Heimberg, R.G., Fresco, D.M. & Mennin, D.S. (2002, November). *Psychometric properties of the GAD-Q-IV among individuals with clinician-assessed generalized anxiety disorder: An update.* Poster presented at the Annual Meeting of the Association for the Advancement of Behavior Therapy, Reno, NV.

Moras, K., Di Nardo, P.A. & Barlow, D.H. (1992). Distinguishing anxiety and depression: Reexamination of the Reconstructed Hamilton Scales. *Psychological Assessment*, **4**, 224–227.

Mennin, D.S., Heimberg, R.G., Turk, C.L. & Fresco, D.M. (2002). Applying an emotion regulation framework to integrative approaches to generalized anxiety disorder. *Clinical Psychology: Science and Practice*, **9**, 85–90.

Mennin, D.S., Heimberg, R.G., Turk, C.L. & Fresco, D.M. (2005). Preliminary evidence for an emotion dysregulation model of generalized anxiety disorder. *Behaviour Research and Therapy*, **43**, 1281–1310.

Meyer, T.J., Miller, M.L., Metzger, R.L. & Borkovec, T.D. (1990). Development and validation of the Penn State Worry Questionnaire. *Behaviour Research and Therapy*, **28**, 487–495.

Miller, C. (2003). *Interviewing Strategies.* In M. Hersen & S.M. Turner (Eds) *Diagnostic Interviewing 3rd Ed.* New York: Kluwer Academic/Plenum Publishing.

Miller, P.R., Dasher, R., Collins, R., Griffiths, P. & Brown, F. (2001). Inpatient diagnostic assessments: 1. Accuracy of structured vs. unstructured interviews. *Psychiatry Research*, **105**, 255–264.

Newman, M.G., Castanguay, L.G., Borkovec, T.D. & Molnar, C. (2004). Integrative psychotherapy. In R. Heimberg, C. Turk & D. Mennin (Eds), *Generalized Anxiety Disorder: Advances in Research and Practice* (pp. 320–350). New York: Guilford Press.

Newman, M.G., Zuellig, A.R., Kachin, K.E., Constantino, M.J., Przeworski, A., Erickson, T. & Cashman-McGrath, L. (2002). Preliminary reliability and validity of the Generalized Anxiety Disorder Questionnaire-IV: A revised self-report diagnostic measure of generalized anxiety disorder. *Behavior Therapy*, **33**, 215–233.

Olfson, M., Fireman, B., Weissman, M.M., Leon, A.C., Sheehan, D.V., Kathol, R.G., Hoven, C. & Farber, L. (1997). Mental disorders and disability among patients in a primary care group practice. *American Journal of Psychiatry*, **154**, 1734–1740.

Orsillo, S.M., Roemer, L. & Barlow, D.H. (2003) Integrating acceptance and mindfulness into existing cognitive-behavioral treatment for GAD: A case study. *Cognitive & Behavioral Practice*, **10(3)**, 222–230.

Rickels, K., Zaninelli, R., McCafferty, J., Bellew, K., Iyengar, M. & Sheehan, D. (2003). Paroxetine treatment of generalized anxiety disorder: a double-blind, placebo-controlled study. *American Journal of Psychiatry*, **160**, 749–756.

Riskind, J.H., Beck, A.T., Brown, G. & Steer, R.A. (1987). Taking the measure of anxiety and depression: Validity of the reconstructed Hamilton scales. *Journal of Nervous and Mental Disease*, **175**, 474–479.

Roemer, L., Borkovec, M., Posa, S. & Borkovec, T.D. (1995). A self-report diagnostic measure of generalized anxiety disorder. *Journal of Behavior Therapy and Experimental Psychiatry*, **26**, 345–350.

Roemer, L. & Orsillo, S.M. (2002). Expanding our conceptualization of and treatment for generalized anxiety disorder: Integrating mindfulness/acceptance based approaches with existing cognitive behavioral models. *Clinical Psychology: Science and Practice*, **9**, 54–68.

Roemer, L. & Orsillo, S.M. (2004, November). *Acceptance-based behavior therapy for GAD: Preliminary findings from an open trial and a randomized controlled trial.* Paper presented at the annual meeting of the Association for Advancement of Behavior Therapy, New Orleans, LA.

Roemer, L., Salters, K., Raffa, S.D. & Orsillo, S.M. (2005). Fear and avoidance of internal experiences in GAD: Preliminary tests of a conceptual model. *Cognitive Therapy and Research*, **29**, 71–88.

Shear, K.M., Vander Bilt, J., Rucci, P., Endicott, J., Lydiard, B., Otto, M.W., Pollack, M.H., Chandler, L., Williams, J., Ali, A. & Frank, D.M. (2001). Reliability and validity of a Structured Interview Guide for the Hamilton Anxiety Rating Scale (SIGH-A). *Depression and Anxiety*, **13**, 166–178.

Sheehan, D.V. (1983). *The anxiety disease*. NY: Charles Scribner's Sons.

Spielberger, D.D., Gorsuch, R.L., Lushene, R., Vagg, P.R. & Jacobs, G.A. (1983). *Manual for the State-Trait Anxiety Inventory*. Palo Alto, CA: Consulting Psychologist Press.

Spitzer, R.L., Williams, J.B.W., Gibbon, M. & First, M.B. (1990). *Structured Clinical Interview for DSM-III-R, Patient Edition/Non-Patient Edition*, (SCID-P/SCID/NP). Washington, DC: American Psychiatric Press, Inc.

Stein, M.B. & Heimberg, R.G. (2004). Well-being and life satisfaction in generalized anxiety disorder: Comparison to major depressive disorder in a community sample. *Journal of Affective Disorders*, **79**, 161–166.

Turk, C.L., Heimberg, R.G. & Mennin, D.S. (2004). Assessment. In R.G. Heimberg, C.L. Turk, and D.S. Mennin (Eds), *Generalized anxiety disorder: Advances in research and practice* (pp. 219–247). New York: Guilford Press.

Turk, C.L., Heimberg, R.G., Luterek, J.A., Mennin, D.S. & Fresco, D.M. (2005). Emotion dysregulation in generalized anxiety disorder: A comparison with social anxiety disorder. *Cognitive Therapy and Research*, **29**, 89–106.

Turk, C.L., Mennin, D.S., Fresco, D.M. & Heimberg, R.G. (2000). *Impairment and quality of life among individuals with Generalized Anxiety Disorder*. Poster presented at the Annual Meeting of the Association for Advancement of Behavior Therapy, New Orleans, LA.

Weeks, J.A. & Heimberg, R.G. (2005). Evaluation of the psychometric properties of the Beck Depression Inventory (BDI) in a non-elderly adult sample of patients with generalized anxiety disorder. *Depression and Anxiety*, **22**, 41–44.

Wells, A. (1994). A multi-dimensional measure of worry: Development and preliminary evaluation of the Anxious Thoughts Inventory. *Anxiety, Stress, and Coping*, **6**, 289–299.

Wells, A. (2002). A cognitive model of GAD: Metacognitions and pathological worry. In R.G. Heimberg, C.L. Turk, and D.S. Mennin (Eds), *Generalized anxiety disorder: Advances in research and practice* (pp. 161 186). New York: Guilford Press.

Wells, A. & Carter, K. (2001). Further tests of a cognitive model of generalized anxiety disorder: Metacognitions and worry in GAD, panic disorder, social phobia, depression, and nonpatients. *Behavior Therapy*, **32**, 85–102.

Williams, J.B.W., Gibbon, M., First, M.B., Spitzer, R.L., Davies, M., Borus, J., Howes, M.J., Kane, J., Pope, H.G., Rounsaville, B. & Wittchen, H.U. (1992). The Structured Clinical Interview for DSM-III-R (SCID): Multisite test–retest reliability. *Archives of General Psychiatry*, **49**, 630–636.

Zanarini, M.C., Skodol, A.E., Bender, D., Dolan, R., Sanislow, C., Schaefer, E., Morey, L.C., Grilo, C.M., Shea, M.T., McGlashan, T.H. & Gunderson, J.G. (2000). The collaborative longitudinal personality disorders study: Reliability of axis I and II diagnoses. *Journal of Personality Disorders*, **14**, 291–299.

Chapter 10

THE CATASTROPHISING
INTERVIEW PROCEDURE

Graham C.L. Davey

MEASURING PATHOLOGICAL WORRY

Our understanding of worry—both from a theoretical and therapeutic viewpoint—depends importantly on our ability to measure it. In this sense, worry poses some particularly difficult problems, because it is a cognitive activity that is usually directly unobservable under natural conditions. Even if we could observe it, we would still have to decide what feature of worry it was that defined its pathological status. This is problematic, because worry is a perfectly natural process for many people who see it as a necessary part of everyday life that contributes to the solving of personal, social and life problems (Davey, 1994a; Davey, Hampton, Farrell & Davidson, 1992). For those people it is neither a chronic uncontrollable process nor does it cause emotional discomfort.

So what should we be measuring when we want to identify worrying that is pathological? Worry inventories, such as the Penn State Worry Questionnaire (PSWQ) and the Worry Domains Questionnaire (WDQ) (Molina & Borkovec, 1994; Tallis, Davey & Bond, 1994) give an indication of the frequency with which individuals indulge in worry bouts, and this correlates fairly well with measures of relevant psychopathologies such as GAD (Brown et al., 1992). However, while the frequency with which worry occurs is an important variable, of equal importance are more proximal measures that assess the important features of individual worry bouts.

The Worry Bout

While pathological worriers may initiate more worry bouts than nonworriers, it is also important to see how worriers differ from nonworriers in the structure, content and perseveration of their individual worry bouts.

Worry and Its Psychological Disorders: Theory, Assessment and Treatment. Edited by G. C. L. Davey and A. Wells. © 2006 John Wiley & Sons, Ltd.

These features may reveal some insights into the processes that turn 'normal' worry bouts into the perseverative and emotionally uncomforting experiences reported by pathological worriers. Any such measure needs to possess both a quantitative and a qualitative capability. It needs to provide objective numerical data on the important parameters of the worry bout, such as its length, moment-to-moment measures of experienced affect, and possible numerical data on the sequence of events through which the worry bout passes. It also needs to provide qualitative information on the content of the worry bout, its meaning to the worrier, and its effect on the worrier.

Such a measure would serve important functions for both the researcher and the therapist. It would provide the researcher with a tool that could be used in the laboratory for examining the effect of experimental variables on worrying. By providing an objective measure of perseveration, for example, it could be used as a dependent variable for discovering what variables influence the perseveration of a worry bout (Davey & Levy, 1998; Startup & Davey, 2001). For the therapist, it could act as an assessment tool for gauging the tendency to perseverate and catastrophise worries, and to assess whether chronic worrying revealed dysfunctional cognitions that could act to maintain worrying and anxiety.

The Catastrophising Interview Technique

One particular form in which uncontrollable worrying occurs is through the process of catastrophising (Breitholtz, Westling & Ost, 1998; Davey & Levy, 1998; Vasey & Borkovec, 1992). Catastrophising is the tendency of individuals to apply a 'what if . . . ?' questioning style to potential problematic features of their life. Rather than bringing the problem to a satisfactory close, however, this process usually leads the worrier to perceive progressively worse and worse outcomes to the worry topic and to experience greater and greater levels of emotional discomfort as the worry bout proceeds (Davey & Levy, 1998; Kendall & Ingram, 1987; Vasey & Borkovec, 1992).

Using a procedure based on the cognitive therapy technique of decatastrophising (Kendall & Ingram, 1987), Vasey & Borkovec (1992) developed their own catastrophising interview technique. Their method consisted of two phases: a topic generation phase and a catastrophising phase. In the *topic generation* phase, participants were given a 2-min period in which to list all the things that currently worried them, and were then asked to rate (1) the percent time in the previous week that they had worried about each topic, and (2) the significance each topic held for them on a 1–7 scale.

The topic rated as taking the highest percentage of time during the previous week was then selected for the *catastrophising interview procedure*. Vasey & Borkovec's (1992) catastrophising interview procedure had three aspects to it: it measured (1) the number of catastrophising steps until the worry bout ended, (2) the level of emotional discomfort experienced at each catastrophising step, and (3) the conditional likelihood that each of the catastrophising steps they had generated would actually occur.

The catastrophising interview procedure is audio taped and begins with the question 'What is it about _____ that worries you?' where the blank is the selected worry topic. The participant's response is then followed by the question 'What about _____ would you find fearful or bad if it did actually happen?' where the blank is filled by the participant's response to the previous question. This process is repeated until one of three conditions is fulfilled: (1) the participant refuses to continue the interview, (2) the participant is unable to generate any further responses, or (3) the participant repeats the same general response three consecutive times. Participants are asked to rate their current levels of discomfort after each catastrophising step, and then asked to rate the likelihood of each catastrophising step occurring when the sequence of steps they had generated was read aloud to them after the interview by the experimenter.

The catastrophising interview procedure that we have developed in our studies at the University of Sussex is based on that used by Vasey & Borkovec, but has a number of refinements—mainly to facilitate the collection of objective data for research-based experimental studies (e.g. Davey, Startup, MacDonald, Jenkins & Patterson, 2005; Startup & Davey, 2001, 2003). The interview begins with the experimenter asking the question 'What is it that worries you about (X)?', where X is the topic selected for catastrophising (this will vary depending on the purpose of the study). The experimenter then repeats this question but substituting the participant's answer to the first question for X. For example, if the participant's main worry is impending exams, the first question will be 'What is it that worries you about exams?' If the participant replies, 'Because I might fail them', the experimenter then asks 'What is it that worries you about failing exams?' If the participant replies, 'I won't get a good job', the experimenter then asks 'What is it that worries you about not getting a good job?', and so on. This standardised form of questioning is adopted throughout the catastrophising interview to avoid any experimenter bias in the way questions are worded. The catastrophising interview is terminated when the participant admits that they can think of no more responses.

This catastrophising procedure differs in some details from that reported by Vasey & Borkovec (1992). First, participants are asked to write down their response to each catastrophising step on a response sheet. They are encouraged to keep each response no longer than a sentence that fits the appropriate space on the response sheet. This provides a ready hard copy of the participant's responses on each step, and prevents the participant from providing over-elaborated responses that may cover more than a single catastrophising step. Second, at the outset of the catastrophising procedure, all participants are provided with examples of the initial steps in a catastrophising sequence, so that they are aware of what is required.

After the interviews are completed, the response sheets can be analysed by a second experimenter. The second experimenter has no knowledge of the catastrophising interview apart from the response sheet, and will be unaware of any of the PSWQ scores of the participant. This second experimenter calculates the number of steps in each interview. The number of steps is judged according to whichever of the following two criteria is met first: (1) the participant did not give any further answers, or (2) the participant repeats the same or a similar answer three times (cf. Vasey & Borkovec, 1992).

These procedures produce a permanent record of the interview, including the number of steps that occur before closure, and a permanent record of the content of each step that can be used for later analysis. The catastrophising interview procedure thus produces an objective measure of the tendency to perseverate a worry bout (in the form of the number of steps the participant is willing to elaborate before closure), and a record of the responses to each step which can be subjected to content analyses to discover trends in the sequencing of responses or to assess the nature of the cognitions representing worrisome thought.

THE CATASTROPHISING PROCESS: SOME INITIAL FINDINGS

Early studies that used the catastrophising interview procedure to inves-tigate individual worry bouts revealed a number of important differences between the bouts of worriers[1] and nonworriers. For example, Vasey & Borkovec (1992) found that (1) worriers generated significantly more catas-trophising steps than nonworriers, (2) worriers reported a significant in-crease in subjective discomfort as catastrophising progressed, whereas nonworriers did not, (3) worriers reported the events in each catastrophis-ing step as significantly more likely to occur as catastrophising progressed,

---

[1] In the early studies, the term 'worrier' is used primarily in its generic sense and not in relation to specifically defined populations. For example, it may be concluded that worriers indulge more in behaviour X if the frequency of behaviour X is significantly correlated with validated measures of the frequency of worrying.

(4) the content of the worries and the catastrophising steps did not differ significantly between worriers and nonworriers, and (5) catastrophising persistence is independent of the amount of prior time spent worrying about a topic. Table 10.1 shows an example of a catastrophising sequence emitted by a worrier compared with a sequence emitted by a nonworrier. Note the differences in length of the sequence between worrier and nonworrier, the differences in emotional discomfort elicited by each step, and the differences in ratings of likely occurrence of each event. The catastrophising sequence emitted by the worrier also provides a good example of how a single well-defined worry, such as worry about school grades, can be catastrophised into significantly more global and disastrous consequences. In this case, the themes include mental illness, drug dependence, physical deterioration, and finally—the ultimate catastrophe—damnation in hell!

Vasey & Borkovec (1992) concluded from their study that worriers were more adept at answering automatic 'what if . . . ?' questions than nonworriers, i.e. they possessed an automatic questioning style and had a larger stock of answers to these questions in memory. They also identified a streak of self-inadequacy that infiltrated the catastrophising sequences of worriers, and suggested that the increasing levels of emotional discomfort experienced by worriers as catastrophising progressed were the result of the worrier becoming aware of this perceived incompetence or inadequacy as catastrophising progressed. This issue of personal inadequacy and poor self-confidence is a theme that resurfaces in later catastrophising studies (Davey, Jubb & Cameron, 1996; Davey & Levy, 1998, 1999).

Using the catastrophising interview procedure pioneered by Vasey & Borkovec, Davey & Levy (1998) reported a series of six studies that cast further light on the nature of catastrophising in worriers. First, they found that worriers displayed a general iterative style that was (1) independent of whether the worry was a completely new unrehearsed worry or a much-rehearsed old one, and (2) independent of the valency of the iterative task. For example, they asked participants to imagine that they were the Statue of Liberty standing in New York Harbour.[2] They were then asked to imagine they were not happy being the Statue of Liberty, and that they were actually feeling very worried about it. Being the Statue of Liberty was then subjected to the catastrophising interview procedure. Even though none of the participants reported ever worrying about being the Statue of Liberty prior to this study (it might have been indicative of quite different types of psychopathology if they had!), worriers still emitted more catastrophising

---

[2] All studies asking participants to imagine they were the Statue of Liberty were undertaken prior to the important events of 9/11 when the terrorist attack on the World Trade Center occurred!

Table 10.1   Chronic Worrier-Topic: Getting good grades in school

	Discomfort	Likelihood
Catastrophising step		
I won't live up to my expectations.	50	30
I'd be disappointed in myself.	60	100
I'd lose my self-confidence	70	50
My loss of self-confidence would spread to other areas of my life.	70	50
I wouldn't have as much control as I'd like.	75	80
I'd be afraid of facing the unknown.	75	100
I'd become very anxious.	75	100
Anxiety would lead to further loss of self-confidence.	75	80
I wouldn't get my confidence back.	75	50
I'd feel like I wouldn't have any control over my life.	75	80
I'd be susceptible to things that normally wouldn't bother me.	75	80
I'd become more and more anxious.	80	80
I'd have no control at all and I'd become mentally ill.	85	30
I'd become dependent on drugs and therapy.	50	30
I'd always remain dependent on drugs.	85	50
They'd deteriorate my body.	85	100
I'd be in pain.	85	100
I'd die.	90	80
I'd end up in hell.	95	80

Nonworrier-Topic: Getting good grades in school

Catastrophising step

	Discomfort	Likelihood
I might do poorly on a test.	3	20
I'd get a bad grade in theclass.	3	100
That would lower my grade-point average.	2	100
I'd have less of a chance of getting a good job.	2	60
I'd end up in a bad job.	2	80
I'd get a low salary.	2	100
I'd have less money to spend on what I want.	2	100
I'd be unhappy.	2	35
It would be a strain on me.	2	10
I'd worry more.	2	5

This table shows the catastrophising sequences generated by a chronic worrier (Top) and a nonworrier (Below). These sequences were generated using the catastrophic interview procedure in which the individual is first asked 'What is your main worry at the moment?' In this case both participants replied, 'Getting good grades in school'.

By looking at the catastrophising sequences above, we can deduce a number of things about chronic worriers: (1) they produce significantly more catastrophising steps than nonworriers, (2) they experience increasing emotional distress as catastrophising continues, and (3) the content of their catastrophising steps becomes more and more threatening and catastrophic.

After Vasey, M. & Borkovec, T.D. (1992). A catastrophising assessment of worrisome thoughts. *Cognitive Therapy and Research*, **16**, 505–520.

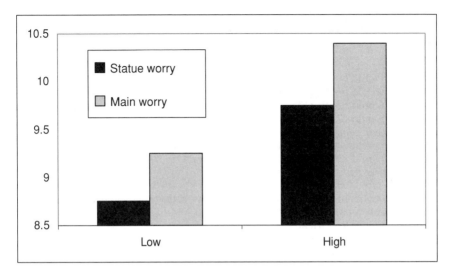

Figure 10.1   Mean number of catastrophising steps emitted by Low and High Worriers to either the 'Statue of Liberty' worry (black bars) or their own current main worry (gray bars). Data taken from Davey G.C.L. & Levy, S. (1998). Catastrophic worrying: personal inadequacy and a perseverative iterative style as features of the catastrophising process. *Journal of Abnormal Psychology*, **107**, 576–586.

steps than nonworriers (Davey & Levy, 1998, Study 2, see Figure 10.1). Even more surprisingly, when asked to indulge in a reverse catastrophising exercise (when participants were asked to say what was *good* about being the Statue of Liberty, and this was subjected to the iterative procedure used in the catastrophising interview), worriers still emitted significantly more steps than nonworriers (Davey & Levy, 1998, Study 4). In these cases, the catastrophising interview procedure has helped to identify the fact that worriers appear to have a *generalized iterative style*—that is, they will iterate any open-ended issue for longer than nonworriers, regardless of whether they have practiced that issue before and regardless of whether it is being iterated in a positive or negative direction! Table 10.2 illustrates examples of the content of 'Statue of Liberty' catastrophising given by a worrier and a nonworrier. The content of the steps emitted by the worrier in Table 10.2 shows many themes that are similar to those given by the worrier in Table 10.1 when they were catastrophising a personal main worry. These common themes often relate to negative outcomes, failure, inadequacy, failure to cope, or loss of self-esteem. Such factors were formally identified in the final two studies reported by Davey & Levy (1998).

With the use of independent raters rating the content of worry topics and the content of steps in the catastrophising procedure, Davey & Levy (1998) found that, when compared to nonworriers, (1) worriers tended to couch

Table 10.2   Catastrophising sequences from the 'Statue of Liberty' worry

Worrier

1. I'm worried about not being able to move.
2. That I would be attacked in some way.
3. That I would not be able to fight back.
4. That I would not be able to control what other people did to me.
5. That I would feel inadequate.
6. That other people would begin to think I was inadequate.
7. That in my relationship with those people I would not be respected.
8. That I would not have any influence over others.
9. That other people would not listen to me.
10. That it would cause a loss of self-esteem.
11. That this loss of self-esteem would have a negative effect on my relationships with others.
12. That I would lose friends.
13. That I would be alone.
14. That I would have no-one to talk to.
15. Because it would mean that I would not be able to share any thoughts/problems with other people.
16. That I would not get advice from others.
17. That none of my problems would be adequately sorted out.
18. That they would remain and get worse.
19. That eventually I would not be able to cope with them.
20. That eventually my problems would have more control over me than I had over them.
21. That they would prevent me from doing other things.
22. That I would be unable to meet new people and make friends.
23. That I would be lonely.

Nonworrier

1. I can't move.
2. I enjoy being free.

their worries in terms of personal inadequacies, and (2) personal inadequacy became a feature of the catastrophising sequence regardless of the topic being catastrophised (i.e. regardless of whether it was a personal or a hypothetical worry) (Davey & Levy, 1998, Studies 5 & 6). A number of studies have already demonstrated that there are no reliable differences in the worry topics reported by worriers and nonworriers (Craske, Rapee, Jackel & Barlow, 1989; Tallis, Davey & Capuzzo, 1994; Vasey & Borkovec, 1992), but there was a clear tendency for worriers to couch their worries in a particular way. Examples of worries rating high on personal inadequacy included 'fear of failure' and 'friendships and loneliness'. Worries rated low on personal inadequacy included 'finding a house' and 'no hot water in halls of residence'. It is possible that the theme of personal inadequacy that appears later in the catastrophising sequence could simply be the result of catastrophising a worry that has initially been couched in terms of personal inadequacy. However, there is more to it than this, because personal inadequacy became a theme in the catastrophising of worriers even when both worriers and nonworriers had been given a hypothetical worry (the Statue of Liberty) that was initially couched in an identical way for both groups. Nevertheless, we must also consider the possibility that the constraints imposed by the catastrophising interview procedure may actually aid identification of features—such as personal inadequacy—that might characterise the individual's catastrophising. For example, when a nonworrier defined a worry as 'finding a house', the sentence limitation imposed on each statement may have influenced the worrier into defining this rather differently as 'I won't be able to find a house'. Even so, the intrusion of information to do with personal inadequacy into the catastrophising process is probably independent of the nature or structure of the interview, because it has subsequently been identified as a central feature of worriers in other studies using other procedures (e.g. Davey, 1994b; Davey, Cameron & Jubb, 1996).

THE CATASTROPHISING INTERVIEW AS A RESEARCH TOOL

The catastrophising interview technique has been a valuable tool in helping to define important differences in the worry bouts of worriers and nonworriers, and this research has been described in detail in the previous section.

However, the technique is useful for more than just defining the differences between populations who pathologically worry and those who do not. It can be used as a quantitative research tool for investigating the role of important variables in generating chronic or pathological worrying, and this is the first step in defining theoretical models of pathological worrying. For those who adopt an experimental approach to understanding psychopathology, the catastrophising interview can provide quantitative data on the effect of an independent variable on worry perseveration. This is the first step in defining the causal factors involved in pathological worrying, and subsequently putting these causal factors together in predictive theoretical models (see Field & Davey, 2005). For example, if we believe that negative mood influences the tendency to perseverate a worry bout, then we can experimentally test this hypothesis by inducing negative mood in our participants, using the catastrophising interview technique to measure the number of steps that the individual will emit, and comparing this with the number of steps emitted by control participants who are not in a negative mood (Johnston & Davey, 1997; Startup & Davey, 2001). This is a method being adopted increasingly in experimental research on worrying, and it is providing a detailed picture of the variables involved in determining worry perseveration. Some of these findings are described below.

The Catastrophising Interview and Worry Perseveration

Negative mood

One of the more obvious features of pathological worriers is that they usually exhibit higher levels of endemic negative mood than nonworriers, and this includes higher levels of both anxiety and depression (Davey, Hampton, Farrell & Davidson, 1992; Metzger, Miller, Chen, Sofka & Borkovec, 1990; Meyer, Miller, Metzger & Borkovec, 1990). However, it is often unclear whether this mood characteristic is a consequence of being a worrier (perhaps via the worrier's frequent inability to bring satisfactory closure to a worry bout), or whether it in some way contributes to the features of pathological worrying.

A study by Johnston & Davey (1997) addressed these issues by using the catastrophising interview to measure catastrophising steps following the induction of a negative, positive or neutral mood. Participants were shown video clips of television news programmes edited to display either positive-, neutral- or negative-valenced material. Participants shown the negatively valenced news bulletin showed significant increases in both anxious and sad mood, and subsequently emitted significantly more steps in the catastrophising interview than participants in the other two groups (see Figure 10.2). All participants were asked to catastrophise their current

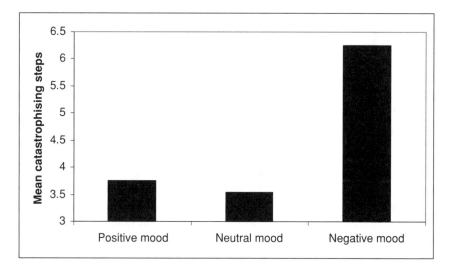

Figure 10.2　Mean number of catastrophising steps emitted by analogue nonclinical participants in pre-experimentally induced positive, neutral or negative moods. After Johnston, W.M. & Davey, G.C.L. (1997). The psychological impact of negative TV bulletins: The catastrophising of personal worries. *British Journal of Psychology*, **88**, 85–91

main worry, and none of these worries were in any way related to the content of the news bulletins they viewed—suggesting that it was the effect of the news bulletin on mood that facilitated perseveration of the worry. Results such as this suggest that negative mood plays some kind of *causal* role in facilitating the perseveration of a worry bout, and is not solely an outcome of worrying (see Chapter 13 for further discussion of the causal role that negative mood plays in worry perseveration).

One plausible explanation for the effect of negative mood on perseveration is that catastrophising is facilitated by mood-congruency effects (Vasey & Borkovec, 1992). That is, the negative mood experienced by worriers may facilitate access to congruent negative information in memory that acts to prolong catastrophising sequences by providing answers to 'what if...?' questions that do not allow the problem-solving task to reach closure (e.g. Davey, 1994a, 1994b). However, a further study by Startup & Davey (2001, Experiment 1) showed that an explanation of the effects of negative mood in mood-congruency terms was unlikely. Like Johnston & Davey (1997), Startup & Davey induced negative, positive and neutral moods in three groups of analogue nonclinical participants and then asked them to catastrophise a worry (in this case, the hypothetical Statue of Liberty worry). The results were identical to those of Johnston & Davey, in which participants in a negative mood catastrophised for longer than those in either a positive or neutral mood. However, Startup & Davey also asked further groups of participants to 'reverse catastrophise', that is, to iterate what was *good* about being the Statue of Liberty (see Chapter 13, p 223). Perhaps surprisingly, this produced an identical pattern of results, where those participants in a negative mood iterated the positive aspects of being the Statue of Liberty for significantly more steps than participants in either a positive or neutral mood. Figure 10.3 illustrates these findings. This pattern of results is quite contrary to mood-congruency explanations, because negative mood also appears to facilitate perseveration at a task requiring the participant to iterate the *positive* qualities of a topic!

So, negative mood not only facilitates perseveration of catastrophising, it also appears to facilitate perseveration at *any* iterative task—regardless of the valency of that task! It is beyond the scope of this chapter to discuss why negative mood has this general effect on iterative tasks, but this will be discussed in significantly more detail in Chapter 13.

Problem-solving confidence

The series of studies described by Davey & Levy (1998) indicate that personal inadequacy and incompetence are themes that constantly intrude into the catastrophising sequences of worriers, and, indeed, worriers also tend to couch their worries in terms of personal inadequacies (Davey & Levy, 1998, Studies 5 & 6). A number of other studies have identified poor

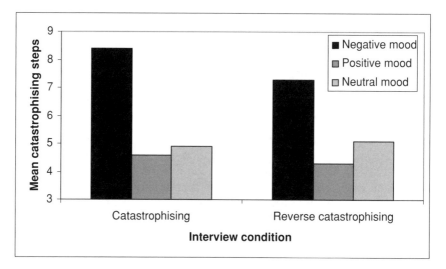

Figure 10.3   The mean number of catastrophising steps emitted by analogue non-clinical participants in either a negative, positive or neutral mood (left hand bars), and the mean number of 'reverse catastrophising' (positive iteration) steps emitted by analogue nonclinical participants in either a negative, positive or neutral mood. Data taken from Startup, H.M. & Davey, G.C.L. (2001). Mood-As-Input and Catastrophic Worrying. *Journal of Abnormal Psychology*, **110(1)**, 83–96. Experiment 1.

problem-solving confidence as a reliable characteristic of worriers, with frequency of worrying being highly correlated with deficiencies in self-perceived problem-solving confidence, poor perceived control over the problem-solving process (Davey, 1994b), and more maladaptive problem orientation in terms of cognitive, emotional and behavioural reactions to the problem (Blankstein, Flett & Batten, 1989; Flett & Blankstein, 1994). However, while worriers tend to exhibit a lack of problem-solving *confidence*, it is not the case that worrying is associated with deficits in problem-solving ability per se (as measured by the Means-Ends Problem-Solving Inventory, MEPS) (Davey, 1994b). Davey (1994b) concluded that worrying does not appear to be associated with deficits in the early stages of problem solving (i.e. solution generation), but does appear to be associated with deficits at later stages in the problem-solving process (e.g. at the level of implementation of the solution).

Just as was the case with the role of negative mood, these studies do not tell us whether poor problem-solving confidence is a consequence of being a worrier (perhaps caused by the vacillations associated with chronic worrying), or whether it has a causal role to play in determining worry perseveration. The use of the experimental method in tandem with the catastrophising interview procedure allows us to address some of these issues.

Davey, Jubb & Cameron (1996) report a study where they experimentally manipulated problem-solving confidence and then examined its effect on worry catastrophising. While they attempted to provide solutions to a list of some real-life problem scenarios, analogue nonclinical participants were given false feedback on their performance that suggested that their solutions were either very poor or very good. Participants who experienced the procedure designed to *decrease* problem-solving confidence (given false feedback that suggested their solutions were very poor) subsequently emitted more steps while catastrophising their main worry than did participants who underwent the procedure to increase problem-solving confidence. These findings suggest that poor problem-solving confidence can have a causal effect on the perseveration of a worry bout, and a subsequent multiple regression analysis demonstrated that measures of poor problem-solving confidence were better predictors of the number of catastrophising steps than measures of self-reported anxiety.

Stop rules for catastrophising

Catastrophising is an open-ended task in the sense that there is no obvious point of closure. The individual who is worrying or catastrophising will therefore tend to continue until they feel that they have met some self-defined goals for completion of the task. To this extent, individuals will tend to have a set of implicit 'stop rules' that they use to help them to define an end to the activity (Martin & Davies, 1998; see Chapter 13). A variety of studies have now identified that worriers appear to deploy what are called 'as many as can' stop rules for worrying (Davey, Startup, MacDonald, Jenkins & Patterson, 2005; Startup & Davey, 2001). That is, they believe they must persevere with a worry bout until they are quite sure that they have addressed all the relevant issues surrounding the worry. These rather stringent stop rules probably derive from the worrier's more general belief schemas, such as beliefs about the utility and value of worrying in helping to avoid future threats and catastrophes (Borkovec & Roemer, 1995; Davey, Tallis & Capuzzo, 1996; Wells, 1995), and beliefs about being responsible for considering all issues surrounding a worry (Startup & Davey, 2003; Wells & Papageorgiou, 1998).

A study by Davey et al. (2005) reports the development of a 'stop rule' checklist which allowed them to measure how strictly an individual adhered to an 'as many as can' stop rule when embarking on a worry bout (the latter was measured by the catastrophising interview procedure). They found that reported use of an 'as many as can' stop rule was significantly related to worry perseveration as measured by the number of steps subsequently emitted during the catastrophising interview procedure. Indeed, scores on the 'as many as can' stop rule checklist were a better predictor of catastrophising perseveration than measures of trait worrying (PSWQ), trait anxiety (STAI Y-2) or measures of state mood prior to catastrophising. This finding suggests that the implicit stop rule deployed at the outset of catastrophising, and the strictness with which it is adhered to, can be a significant determinant of worry perseveration.

There is also evidence that the worrier's use of strict 'as many as can' stop rules can be influenced by their perception of the consequences of the worry task and their beliefs about their role and responsibility in ensuring that the worry task is completed satisfactorily. For example, Davey & Startup (2003) found that high worriers began the catastrophising interview procedure with higher self-reported levels of responsibility towards fully considering all issues involved than did low worriers, and this was the case regardless of whether they were being asked to catastrophise a personal worry or a hypothetical worry. High worriers also emitted significantly more catastrophising steps than low worriers (Experiment 1). A second study experimentally manipulated responsibility by instructing one group of participants that they were going to take part in an interview about dyslexia, and their responses 'may be used to compile a booklet for public distribution ... which may influence the budget received by such students ... ' (2003, p. 499). They were then asked to catastrophise the hypothetical scenario of a close friend or relative suffering from dyslexia (this was the high responsibility group). A second group was simply told that their responses were of no real importance beyond the purpose of the experiment (low responsibility group). As predicted, participants in the high responsibility condition persisted for longer at the catastrophising interview—but only when in a negative mood. This suggests that beliefs about responsibility are themselves not a *sufficient* condition to generate catastrophising perseveration, but that a concurrent negative mood is also important. The theoretical implications of this interaction between independent variables are explored more fully in Chapter 13.

The Catastrophising Interview and Other Psychopathologies

As a research tool, the catastrophising interview technique has been used primarily in the context of research into worry and its related DSM-IV disorder, GAD. This is not surprising because the catastrophising interview technique was developed first and foremost as a means of investigating and measuring the experience of worry. However, it has already begun to be used to investigate the characteristics and dynamics of processes involved in other psychopathologies. As such, its potential for measuring dysfunctional perseveration is useful for investigating any disorder or psychopathological process that involves the compulsive and persistent iteration of thoughts or cognitions.

For example, Harvey and Greenall (2003) used the catastrophising interview procedure to demonstrate that patients with primary insomnia had a significant tendency to persevere with thoughts about the consequences of not sleeping, and that this catastrophising perseveration was associated with increased levels of anxiety and discomfort compared to good sleepers. These findings are consistent with the hypothesis that worry about the consequences of not sleeping may serve to maintain sleep disorders such as primary insomnia.

Watkins and Mason (2002) adapted the catastrophising interview procedure to investigate whether depressed high ruminators used a default 'as many as can' stop rule to determine when they should end a rumination bout. In this study, participants were asked to recall a recent episode of depression and to recall what it was that had made them depressed. The rumination interview then began with the interviewer asking 'Why is it that X makes you feel depressed?' where X was either the initial main topic of depression or the response to the previous step. As predicted, high ruminators emitted significantly more steps during the interview than low ruminators, but high ruminators asked explicitly to use an 'as many as can' stop rule also emitted significantly more steps than high ruminators who were asked to use a less strict 'feel like continuing' stop rule (see Chapter 13). Studies such as this suggest that the factors determining perseveration of a cognitive activity such as worry may be shared by other dysfunctional cognitive activities such as rumination in depression.

The catastrophising interview procedure can provide useful information on perseverative thinking generally, including a measure of the degree of perseveration, the nature of the content of that perseverative thinking, its valence, its effect on the emotional state of the individual, and the individual's perception of the threat posed by the content of the bout as perseveration progresses. To this extent, the catastrophising interview probably has a useful role to play in research on any psychopathology where threats of negative outcomes give rise to compulsive or intrusive thoughts. Such psychopathologies would include health anxiety, contamination fear, pain catastrophising, OCD, specific phobias, amongst many others.

Limitations of the Catastrophising Interview Technique as a Research Tool

While the catastrophising interview technique has a number of advantages as a research tool, it is worth discussing its possible limitations.

First, is the catastrophising interview a faithful analogue of the natural worry bout? Probably not, but it is likely to be as close as we can get to revealing in an objective paradigm the thought processes that underlie worrying and contribute to perseveration. Making each step in the catastrophising interview explicit is not what happens in the natural worry bout, nor are these steps revealed to another person (the interviewer), nor are they normally thrown back at the worrier in the rather explicit terms that the interview procedure does. However, it is an explicit analogue of the worrier's 'what if...?' questioning style and the iterative thinking employed by many worriers. Furthermore, studies using the catastrophising interview procedure have revealed features of the worry process that we know from the use of other methodologies are features of pathological worrying (e.g. the role of negative mood, the perseverative nature of pathological worrying, and the involvement of the worrier's beliefs about their own inadequacies and their inability to solve problems)—so even if the catastrophising interview procedure is not a truly faithful analogue of the worry bout we can still have confidence that it is tapping and measuring features which are important contributors to perseverative worrying.

USES OF THE CATASTROPHISING INTERVIEW TECHNIQUE IN CLINICAL SETTINGS

As well as being an important research tool, the catastrophising interview technique is potentially a useful procedure for clinicians as both an assessment tool and as a means of identifying the types of beliefs and cognitions that may maintain chronic or pathological worrying across a range of disorders. The fact that the interview procedure is based on an original cognitive therapy technique of decatastrophising, suggests that it should lend itself usefully to cognitive behavioural interventions (Kendall & Ingram, 1987).

The Catastrophising Interview as an Assessment Technique

There are clearly no statistical norms associated with the catastrophising interview, and, indeed, it may never be possible to produce any because many of the outcomes of the interview (such as perseveration, content) may depend on the topic being catastrophised and its meaning to the individual. However, there is no reason why it may not prove a useful method for measuring the effect of treatment on any number of anxious disorders where catastrophising is a main feature—especially GAD, primary insomnia, and chronic pain. The interview may also be useful in assessing progress made in the treatment of any disorder where catastrophic cognitions and interpretations are a feature of the acquisition and maintenance of the disorder. Such disorders would include panic disorder, chronic pain, contamination fears, and many forms of specific phobia that are characterised by the catastrophising of phobic outcome beliefs (e.g. contact with a spider in spider phobics) or the catastrophic post-event processing of phobic encounters (e.g. in social phobics).

Successful treatment should indicate a significant pre- to post-treatment decrease in the tendency to perseverate with a catastrophisation, a decrease in the levels of emotional distress elicited by the catastrophisation process, a decrease in the perceived likelihood that events in the catastrophising sequence will actually occur, and a decrease in the intrusion into the catastrophising chain of negative cognitions generally. The use of the catastrophising interview technique in this way provides a measure of how dynamic thought processes relevant to the disorder have been modified by the treatment process—an assessment which is less easy to determine using traditional assessments which measure rather static characteristics of the psychopathology (e.g. measures of trait or dispositional features of the individual).

The Catastrophising Interview as an Intervention Tool

Kendall and Ingram (1987) have argued that an automatic questioning style is an important characteristic of anxiety-related psychopathologies, and the systematic 'what if...?' internal dialogue style of such individuals gives rise to cognitions that maintain anxiety. Kendall and Ingram also noted that such automatic questions 'are not mere indications of a careful and reflective process but, instead, betray a rapid-fire sense of impending incompetence' (Kendall & Ingram, 1987, p. 96). So, the 'rapid-fire' catastrophic questioning style of anxious individuals not only tends to generate anxiety, but also produces and maintains uncertainty—especially about the individual's ability to solve problems and to cope with them—and to generate distorted negative perceptions of the self and the world. There is no doubt, as we have discovered in the previous sections of this chapter, that the views of Kendall and Ingram have been supported by subsequent empirical studies which have revealed negative cognitions, and, in particular, themes of personal inadequacy within catastrophising sequences (Davey & Levy, 1998).

This being the case, the catastrophising interview provides a useful means of helping the client to identify those negative cognitions that may intrude consistently into the catastrophising process. With pathological worriers, this can be done by demonstrating that these negative themes intrude not only across a range of worries, but will probably also intrude into the catastrophising of hypothetical worries. Once identified, these themes can be isolated and challenged using more formal cognitive therapy methods.

In a more direct application of empirical research to treatment, the use of the catastrophising interview technique has identified a number of variables that directly contribute to perseverative worrying. These include negative mood (Johnston & Davey, 1997; Startup & Davey, 2001), feelings of personal inadequacy and poor problem-solving confidence (Davey, Jubb & Cameron, 1996), and the use of implicit 'as many as can' stop rules for worrying (Davey et al., 2005; Startup & Davey, 2003). Clearly, addressing these variables in treatment should ameliorate the perseverative tendencies of the catastrophic worrier. Doing so in the context of the catastrophising interview should provide first-hand experience to the client that dealing with such factors can help to weaken the tendency to perseverative thinking. For example, one prediction from the empirical research is that relaxation training immediately prior to undertaking a catastrophising interview procedure should moderate perseveration (i.e. by reducing negative mood). Being able to exhibit this to an anxious, worrisome client should clearly demonstrate the benefits of relaxation as a means of moderating perseverative worrying.

SUMMARY

This chapter has described the benefits of the catastrophising interview technique as a means of measuring some of the important characteristics of pathological and chronic worrying. It serves as a useful and objective research tool that has enabled us to identify a range of important variables that have a causal influence on perseverative worrying. It also has potential as an assessment and intervention technique that can be used in a variety of clinical settings across a range of anxiety-based disorders that have catastrophising as an important causal and maintaining feature.

ACKNOWLEDGEMENTS

The author would like to thank colleagues Suzy Levy, Benie MacDonald, Helen Startup and Frank Tallis for their invaluable contributions to much of the research described in this chapter, and to the Economic & Social Research Council for its financial support.

REFERENCES

Blankstein, K.R., Flett, G.L. & Batten, I. (1989). Test anxiety and problem-solving self-appraisals of college students. *Journal of Social Behavior and Personality*, **4**, 531–540.

Borkovec, T.D. & Roemer, L. (1995). Perceived functions of worry among general-ized anxiety disorder subjects: Distraction from more emotionally distressing topics. *Journal of Behavior Therapy & Experimental Psychiatry*, **26**, 25–30.

Breitholtz, E., Westling, B.E. & Ost, L.-G. (1998). Cognitions in generalized anxiety disorder and panic disorder patients. *Journal of Anxiety Disorders*, **12**, 567–577.

Brown, T.A., Antony, M.M. & Barlow, D.H. (1992). Psychometric properties of the Penn State Worry Questionnaire in a clinical anxiety disorders sample. *Behaviour Research and Therapy*, **30**, 33–37.

Craske, M.G., Rapee, R.M., Jackel, L. & Barlow, D.H. (1989). Qualitative dimensions of worry in DSM-III generalized anxiety disorder subjects and nonanxious con-trols. *Behaviour Research and Therapy*, **27**, 397–402.

Davey, G.C.L (1994a). Pathological worrying as exacerbated problem solving. In G.C.L. Davey & F. Tallis (Eds), *Worrying: Perspectives on theory, assessment and treatment*. Chichester, UK: John Wiley & Sons, Ltd.

Davey, G.C.L. (1994b). Worrying, social problem solving abilities, and social prob-lem solving confidence. *Behaviour Research and Therapy*, **32**, 327–330.

Davey, G.C.L., Hampton, J., Farrell, J.J. & Davidson, S. (1992). Some characteristics of worry: Evidence for worrying and anxiety as separate constructs. *Personality and Individual Differences*, **13**, 133–147.

Davey, G.C.L., Jubb, M. & Cameron, C. (1996). Catastrophic worrying as a function of changes in problem-solving confidence. *Cognitive Therapy and Research*, **20**, 333–344.

Davey, G.C.L. & Levy, S. (1999). Catastrophising strategies: Internal statements that characterize catastrophic worrying. *Personality and Individual Differences*, **26**, 21–32.

Davey, G.C.L. & Levy, S. (1998). Catastrophic worrying: personal inadequacy and a perseverative iterative style as features of the catastrophising process. *Journal of Abnormal Psychology*, **107**, 576–586.

Davey, G.C.L., Startup, H.M., MacDonald, C.B., Jenkins, D. & Paterson, K. (2004). The use of 'as many as can' versus 'feel like continuing' stop rules during wor-rying. *Cognitive Therapy and Research*, **29**, 155–169.

Davey, G.C.L, Tallis, F. & Capuzzo, N. (1996). Beliefs about the consequences of worrying. *Cognitive Therapy and Research*, **20**, 499–520.

Field, A.P. & Davey, G.C.L. (2004). Experimental methods in clinical research. In J. Miles & P. Gilbert (Eds) *A Handbook of research methods in clinical and health psychology*. Oxford: Oxford University Press.

Flett, G.L. & Blankstein, K.R. (1994). Worry as a component of test anxiety: A multi dimensional analysis. In G.C.L. Davey & F. Tallis (Eds) *Worrying: Perspectives on theory, assessment and treatment*. Chichester, UK: John Wiley & Sons, Ltd.

Harvey, A.G. & Greenall, E. (2003). Catastrophic worry in primary insomnia. *Journal of Behavior Therapy & Experimental Psychiatry*, **34**, 11–23.

Johnston, W.M. & Davey, G.C.L. (1997). The psychological impact of negative TV news bulletins: The catastrophising of personal worries. *British Journal of Psy-chology*, **88**, 85–91.

Kendall, P.C. & Ingram, R.E. (1987). The future for cognitive assessment of anxi-ety: Let's get specific. In L. Michaelson & L.M. Ascher (Eds) *Anxiety and stress disorders: Cognitive-behavioral assessment and treatment*. New York: Guilford Press.

Martin, L.L & Davies, B. (1998). Beyond Hedonism and associationism: A configural view of the role of affect in evaluation, processing, and self-regulation. *Motivation and Emotion*, **22**, 33–51.

Metzger, R.L., Miller, M.L., Cohen, M., Sofka M. & Borkovec, T.D. (1990). Worry changes decision making: The effect of negative thoughts on cognitive process-ing. *Journal of Clinical Psychology*, **48**, 76–88.

Meyer, T.J., Miller, M.L., Metzger, R.L. & Borkovec, T.D. (1990). Development and validation of the Penn State Worry Questionnaire. *Behaviour Research and Therapy*, **28**, 487–495.

Molina, S. & Borkovec, T.D. (1994). The Penn State Worry Questionnaire: psychometric properties and associated characteristics. In G.C.L. Davey & F. Tallis (Eds) *Worrying: Perspectives on theory, assessment and treatment*. Chichester, UK: John Wiley & Sons, Ltd.

Startup, H.M. & Davey, G.C.L. (2001). Mood-As-Input and Catastrophic Worrying. *Journal of Abnormal Psychology*, **110(1)**, 83–96.

Startup, H.M. & Davey, G.C.L. (2003). Inflated responsibility and the use of stop rules for catastrophic worrying. *Behaviour Research and Therapy*, **41**, 495–503.

Tallis, F., Davey, G.C.L. & Bond, A. (1994). The Worry Domains Questionnaire. In G.C.L. Davey & F. Tallis (Eds) *Worrying: Perspectives on theory, assessment and treatment*. Chichester, UK: John Wiley & Sons Ltd.

Vasey, M. & Borkovec, T.D. (1992). A catastrophising assessment of worrisome thoughts. *Cognitive Therapy and Research*, **16**, 505–520.

Wells, A. (1995). Meta-cognition and worry: A cognitive model of generalized anxiety disorder. *Behavioural and Cognitive Psychotherapy*, **23**, 301–320.

Wells, A. & Papageorgiou, C. (1998). Relationships between worry, obsessive-compulsive symptoms and meta-cognitive beliefs. *Behaviour Research and Therapy*, **36**, 899–913.

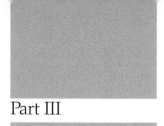

Part III

THEORIES OF CHRONIC AND PATHOLOGICAL WORRY

Chapter 11

THE METACOGNITIVE MODEL OF WORRY AND GENERALISED ANXIETY DISORDER

Adrian Wells

Worry is an important topic for research and theory because the process may contribute to most forms of psychological disorder. The worry process is similar in some respects to other types of perseverative negative thinking, such as depressive rumination. Understanding the psychological underpinnings of worry has contributed to research on depressive thinking (Papageorgiou & Wells, 2004, Papageorgiou, chapter 2 this volume), and post-traumatic stress (Wells & Sembi, 2004, 2005). A central justification for conceptualising the factors that drive pathological worry is that a model of such should lead to the development of more effective treatment of generalised anxiety disorder (GAD). Until recently cognitive-behavioural treatments for this disorder have produced relatively disappointing outcomes (Fisher & Durham, 1999).

In this chapter I present the metacognitive model of GAD and review the evidence for the model. The model was developed to explain the factors giving rise to generalised and repetitive worry that is difficult to control. Before doing so however, in the next section I briefly outline some pertinent features of the metacognitive theory of emotional disorder which gives central prominence to worry as a general factor contributing to psychological pathology, and is the grounding for the GAD model.

METACOGNITION, WORRY, AND PSYCHOLOGICAL DISORDER

The metacognitive theory of emotional disorder (Wells & Matthews, 1994; 1996) implies that worrying emerges not from the general negative social beliefs that individuals hold (e.g. 'I'm worthless, the world is dangerous'),

Worry and Its Psychological Disorders: Theory, Assessment and Treatment. Edited by G. C. L. Davey and A. Wells. © 2006 John Wiley & Sons, Ltd.

but derives from a separate knowledge base. This knowledge base is metacognitive in nature and controls the cognitive system. Metacognitive knowledge consists of negative and positive beliefs about thinking (e.g. 'Some thoughts are harmful; Paying attention to threat will keep me safe; worrying helps me cope'). In this theory maladaptive patterns of thinking such as worry and attentional allocation to threat result from the activation of metacognitive beliefs.

The theory identifies a pattern of cognition that exists across all disorders and is involved in their development and persistence. The pattern, called the Cognitive Attentional Syndrome (CAS), consists of worry/rumination, focusing attention on sources of threat and use of coping strategies that fail to modify negative beliefs. Intense and adhesive self-focused attention is a general marker and feature of this syndrome. The CAS results from the influence of metacognitive beliefs on processing. Such beliefs are plans or programmes for cognition and behaviour in situations, and although not represented verbally can be communicated in verbal form. For example, the hypochondriacal patient believes 'I must pay close attention to my heart in order to stay safe', and the person suffering from Post Traumatic Stress Disorder (PTSD) believes 'I must pay attention to danger in order to be prepared'. Such metacognitive beliefs underlie threat monitoring. Similarly, patients have positive metacognitive beliefs about engaging in worry or ruminative styles of thinking (e.g. 'I must worry about making mistakes in order to maintain control'). In addition, negative beliefs about the meaning and significance of thoughts play a central role in some disorders. For example, the person with PTSD or Obsessive Compulsive Disorder believes that intrusive thoughts are harmful or dangerous. As we shall see positive metacognitive beliefs and especially negative metacognitive beliefs are important contributors to pathological worry in GAD.

Apart from metacognitive beliefs about thinking, the metacognitive theory assigns a central role to use of maladaptive thought control strategies in the development and persistence of disorder. In simple cases these strategies involve trying to suppress particular thoughts. However, other forms of dysfunctional mental regulation can also be identified. For example, individuals may simply not attempt to control their thinking because they believe that negative thinking is part of their personality and cannot be changed. Similarly, the metacognitive belief that thoughts cannot be controlled may lead individuals to transfer the responsibility of controlling cognition onto others. In some cases individuals resort to alcohol or drugs as a means of controlling thoughts. In each of these cases difficulties emerge because control strategies backfire, cause interpersonal problems and/or fail to provide evidence that strengthens perceptions of control.

THE METACOGNITIVE MODEL OF GAD

The metacognitive model of pathological worry and GAD (Wells, 1994, 1995) is based on a distinction between worrying and the negative interpretation of worrying. These have been termed Type 1 and Type 2 worry respectively. Type 2 worry is the negative metacognitive appraisal of worrying as uncontrollable or harmful, I have also used the term meta-worry to refer to this construct.

The model makes a distinction between positive beliefs about worrying and negative beliefs about worrying. The former lead to use of worrying as a coping strategy, whilst the latter lead to negative appraisal of worrying (Meta-worry). Positive beliefs about worrying are considered to be common and not necessarily pathological. However, it is the activation of negative metacognitive beliefs and associated meta-worry that is central to the development of GAD. Whilst the presence of positive beliefs is not in itself a problem, the use of worry as a predominant coping strategy is considered to be problematic as it can interfere with other more useful and adaptive self-regulatory processes. For instance, worry following exposure to stress may interfere with the effective processing and control of intrusions.

The central elements of the model are depicted in Figure 11.1. A run-through of a worry episode will serve to illustrate the components in the model and the nature of dynamic relationships between them.

Triggers for worrying vary, but they are typically events that lead to an intrusive thought. Intrusive thoughts commonly occur as a 'what if?' question (e.g. 'What if I fail?') or sometimes as a negative image such as an image of being involved in an accident.

The trigger activates positive metacognitive beliefs about worrying as a means of coping with the event depicted in the intrusion. Examples of positive beliefs include: 'If I worry about all possibilities I can avoid failure; If I worry I'll do a better job; Worrying about what can go wrong means I'll be prepared'.

As a result Type 1 worrying, consisting of the contemplation of a range of negative outcomes and how to cope, then ensues. Type 1 worrying is predominantly a verbal contemplative process consisting of chains of catastrophising and planning of responses. It is associated with changes in emotion. The person becomes more anxious as negative outcomes are processed, and less anxious as the goal of generating coping options is reached. Type 1 worrying usually persists until the person achieves the goal of worrying. This is often signalled by a 'feeling' that is interpreted as indicating that the person will be able to cope, or an appraisal that most

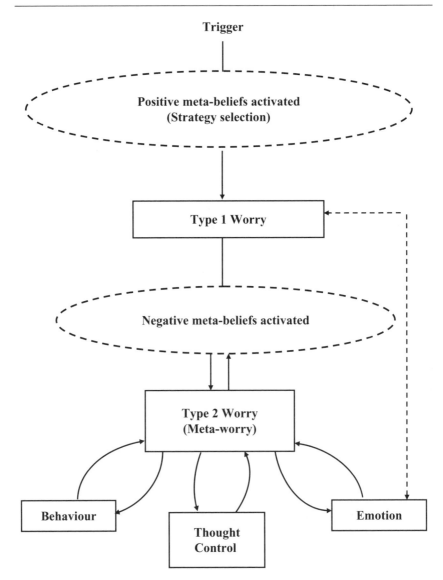

Figure 11.1   The Metacognitive Model of GAD
Reproduced from Wells, A. (1997). *Cognitive Therapy of Anxiety Disorders: A practice manual and conceptual guide*. Chichester, UK: Wiley.

eventualities have been considered. Worrying may also be displaced by distracting demands that are situationally determined.

In pathological worry states such as GAD negative beliefs about worrying are activated during a worry episode. These negative beliefs have two content domains: (1) uncontrollability and (2) danger. The person with GAD believes that worrying is uncontrollable and potentially dangerous for physical psychological or social wellbeing. Examples of these beliefs include: 'Worrying is uncontrollable; I will lose my mind because of worrying; Worrying will cause a heart attack'. Once activated these beliefs give rise to negative interpretation of worrying (meta-worry) and negative interpretation of emotional symptoms as a sign of loss of control or physical/psychological calamity. As a result, anxiety and the sense of threat increases. It then becomes increasingly difficult for the individual to achieve an internal sense that they will cope (because anxiety is not decreasing) and so stop signals for worrying become more elusive.

There are two further mechanisms leading to an escalation and persistence of pathological worry. First, behaviours such as reassurance seeking, avoiding situations that trigger intrusive thoughts maintain negative beliefs about loss of control and the danger of worrying. This is because the individual relies on external factors to control thoughts, or avoids triggers for worrying and opportunities to discover that worrying is harmless.

Second, thought control strategies consisting of trying to suppress thoughts that might trigger worrying are counterproductive and lead to greater awareness of worrying concepts, fuelling the need to worry and beliefs about uncontrollability. Furthermore, the individual does not interrupt the worry process once activated because this is incompatible with beliefs about the need to worry and with beliefs about uncontrollability. Thus, a pattern of thought control that is maladaptive develops because it is aimed at trying to remove the content of thought from consciousness (e.g. do not think about failure) rather than deciding not to engage the Type 1 worry process in response to the intrusion. This pattern prevents the person from discovering that the worry process is controllable. However, even if worry is interrupted this prevents the person discovering that worry is harmless.

An example of the model used as a personal case conceptualisation for an individual with GAD is presented in Figure 11.2.

Empirical Support for the Model

Studies of non-patients scoring high in worrying, and of patients with GAD provide evidence supporting many aspects of the model. Studies that have tested the relationship between metacognitions and worry have relied on measures of positive and negative metacognitive beliefs, and on measures of Type 1 and Type 2 worry. These measures and their psychometric properties are described in Chapter 8. The evidence can be usefully divided into several areas providing support for the main components and processes of the model, each will be considered in turn.

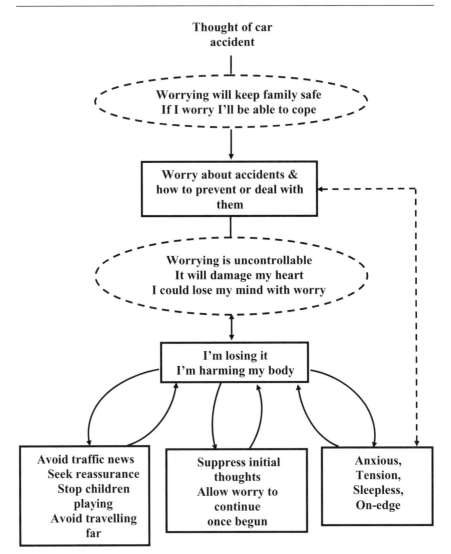

Figure 11.2   An individual case conceptualisation based on the model

Is Pathological Worry Associated With Positive Beliefs About Worrying?

There is strong support for the idea that high worriers (including people with GAD) hold positive beliefs about worrying. Interview studies and studies using self-report measures of beliefs have demonstrated that individuals scoring high in worry, and patients with GAD report positive reasons/beliefs for worrying. Borkovec and Roemer (1995) found that individuals meeting criteria for GAD gave higher ratings for positive reasons for worrying than non-anxious controls. These reasons included the idea that worrying was useful for problem solving, and superstitious ideas about the effects of worrying. Borkovec (1994) summarises five domains of positive reasons for worrying encountered in patients undergoing therapy at the Penn State programme: (1) Superstitious avoidance of catastrophe ('worrying makes it less likely that the feared event will occur'); (2) actual avoidance of catastrophe ('worrying helps to generate ways of avoiding or preventing catastrophe'); (3) avoidance of deeper emotional topics ('worrying about most of the things I worry about is a way to distract myself from worrying about more emotional things...'); (4) coping preparation ('worrying about a predicted negative event helps me to prepare for its occurrence'); (5) motivating device ('worry helps to motivate me to accomplish the work that needs to be done') (pp. 16–17).

Tallis, Davey and Capuzzo (1994) reported the results of a preliminary investigation of the phenomenology of worry in a non-clinical sample. They obtained two factors capturing the perceived benefits of worrying, which were motivation, and preparatory/analytical thinking. These factors appear to reflect positive beliefs about worrying.

Using the metacognitions questionnaire to assess beliefs about worry, Cartwright-Hatton and Wells (1997), provided direct evidence of an association between positive metacognitive beliefs and pathological worrying. Proneness to pathological worry was positively associated with positive beliefs about worry, negative beliefs about uncontrollability and danger, lack of cognitive confidence and trait anxiety when these variables were entered as simultaneous predictors. These data are particularly interesting because positive beliefs made a contribution to worry independently of negative beliefs as would be expected in the model. Cartwright-Hatton and Wells (1997) also compared patients with DSM-III-R GAD, patients with other anxiety disorders and non-patient controls. The GAD patients had similar levels of positive worry beliefs as the other groups. Wells and Carter (2001) compared GAD patients with patients with panic disorder, social phobia, depression and non-patient controls. They showed that the groups did not differ significantly in the endorsement of positive worry beliefs. These results support the idea that pathological worry proneness is associated generally with positive beliefs about worrying, however positive beliefs appear not to distinguish GAD patients from other anxious patients or controls.

Wells and Papageorgiou (1998) tested for the relationship between metacognitive beliefs and pathological worry whilst controlling for overlaps between these variables and obsessive-compulsive symptoms in non-patients. Positive beliefs about worrying and negative beliefs concerning uncontrollability and danger were predictive of worry in this analysis.

There appears to be reliable support for the idea that worriers hold positive beliefs about worrying, and this applies for non-patient samples and for patients with GAD. The finding that individuals hold beliefs about the usefulness of worrying as a coping or self-regulation strategy is consistent with the metacognitive model. Consistent with the model positive metacognitive beliefs are associated with self-report worry measures, and they appear to make a contribution even when negative metacognitions are controlled. However, patients with GAD do not appear to differ from non-patients in the endorsement of positive metacognitive beliefs. This supports the idea that positive beliefs are not unique to GAD but are more generally associated with worrying. According to the metacognitive model it is the strengthening of negative worry beliefs that contributes centrally to the transition from worry to GAD. The evidence supporting the involvement of negative metacognitions is considered next.

Is Pathological Worry and GAD Associated With Negative Metacognitions?

An important aspect of the metacognitive model is the emphasis given to negative metacognitions in the pathogenesis of worry in GAD. In fact the metacognitive model is unique amongst theoretical approaches to GAD in that it is the only one that assigns a role to negative metacognitive beliefs and appraisals. Several studies have focused on testing this predicted relationship. In this section, evidence on meta-worry (Type 2 worry) is reviewed first, and then the evidence on negative metacognitive beliefs is considered.

Type 2 Worry

Type 2 worry (meta-worry) is the negative interpretation of worrying and is therefore a class of negative metacognitive appraisal. Wells and Carter (1999) examined the relative contribution of Type 2 and Type 1 worry to individual differences in pathological worry as measured by the Penn State Worry Questionnaire (PSWQ: Meyer, Miller, Metzger & Borkovec, 1990). In this study Type 1 and Type 2 worry were assessed with the Anxious Thoughts Inventory (AnTI: see Chapter 8). Type 2 worry was uniquely associated with both pathological worrying and problem level associated with worrying, and this relationship was independent of Type 1 worry, trait-anxiety and uncontrollability.

Nassif (1999, study 1) tested the contribution of Type 2 worry to pathological worry in a Lebanese sample, while controlling for trait anxiety and

Type 1 worry. The largest independent contributions to pathological worry were made by Type 2 worry and trait-anxiety. In a second study Nassif (1999) screened non-patients for the presence of DSM-III-R GAD. Of 104 individuals tested, 19 were identified as meeting GAD criteria and 50 as non-anxious. A comparison of these subgroups revealed that the GAD group had significantly higher Type 2 worry scores than the non-anxious group.

The above studies have used the AnTI to assess Type 1 and Type 2 worry. One of the limitations of using this instrument is that it combines negative appraisals about the uncontrollability of worry with appraisals of danger on a single subscale. Whilst this has not been a problem for testing the contribution of Type 2 worry to DSM-III-R defined GAD it introduces a problem of circularity in testing the relationship between Type 2 worry and DSM-IV GAD. This is because uncontrollability of worry was included as a diagnostic feature in DSM-IV. The meta-worry questionnaire (MWQ) was devised to overcome this issue and enable an evaluation of the relationship between DSM-IV defined GAD and Type 2 worry. The MWQ (Wells, 2005; see Chapter 8), measures specifically the danger domain of Type 2 worry and omits the uncontrollability dimension. Using this instrument, danger-related meta-worry was found to be positively correlated with pathological worry (PSWQ), and non-patients meeting criteria for GAD reported significantly higher scores in meta-worry frequency than individuals with somatic anxiety or non-anxious individuals (Wells, 2005).

Nuevo, Montorio and Borkovec (2004) replicated the study by Wells and Carter (1999) and extended it by examining the relationship between meta-worry and worry severity in an elderly sample. Their sample consisted of 105 participants aged 65 years and older (mean age 72.9 years). In this Spanish sample meta-worry consistently emerged as a significant positive predictor of both pathological worry (PSWQ), and interference from worry. The relationships held when Type 1 worries, trait anxiety and uncontrollability of worry were controlled.

These studies provide consistent evidence supporting the idea that negative metacognitions in the form of worry about worry are associated with pathological worrying and distress/disturbance caused by worrying. Evidence of a relatively specific link between meta-worry and GAD in particular has emerged from two of the studies.

Negative Metacognitive Beliefs About Worry

Turning now to review the data on negative metacognitive beliefs concerning the uncontrollability and dangerous consequences of worrying. These studies have used the metacognitions questionnaire (Cartwright-Hatton & Wells, 1997), which is comprised of five subscales, one of which (uncontrollability and danger) is central to the metacognitive model.

In an early study with the MCQ Cartwright-Hatton and Wells (1997) compared patients with DSM-III-R GAD with patients with other anxiety disorders, depressive disorders, obsessive-compulsive disorder (OCD) and non-patient controls. The GAD and OCD groups endorsed significantly greater levels of negative beliefs concerning the uncontrollability and danger of worry and intrusive thoughts than the other groups. The GAD and OCD groups also reported higher levels of negative beliefs about worrying concerning need to control thoughts and themes of superstition and punishment than non-patients.

Wells and Papageorgiou (1998) tested the relationship between metacognitive beliefs and pathological worry whilst controlling for the possible overlap between worry and obsessive-compulsive symptoms. Negative beliefs concerning uncontrollability and danger contributed significantly to pathological worry, even when positive beliefs and obsessive symptoms were controlled.

Davis and Valentiner (2000) showed that GAD subjects had higher scores than non-anxious and non-worried anxious groups on two negative metacognitive belief dimensions: uncontrollability and danger, and negative beliefs concerning need for control of thoughts, superstition responsibility and punishment.

Wells and Carter (2001) examined the specificity of negative metacognitive beliefs to GAD. They compared beliefs across groups of patients meeting DSM-III-R criteria for GAD, panic disorder, social phobia, and included a non-patient group. There were no differences between groups in the endorsement of positive beliefs about worry. Significant differences emerged in negative belief ratings. Patients with GAD had significantly higher beliefs in the uncontrollability and danger domain than the other groups. When Type 1 worry was treated as a covariate these differences remained significant, suggesting that differences in uncontrollability and danger metacognitions were not simply a function of differences in the frequency of Type 1 worry.

A study by Ruscio and Borkovec (2004) is particularly interesting in its evaluation of differences in the experience of worry and appraisal of worry among high worriers with and without GAD. They compared high worriers with and without GAD on the characteristics of worry and beliefs about worry as measured by the MCQ. This study allowed for a test of whether differences between high worriers with and without GAD could be attributed to group differences in actual worry, in beliefs about worry, or in both dimensions. Comparison of these groups revealed similar experiences and consequences of worry in both groups following worry induction. There appeared to be more substantial differences in beliefs about worry, with GAD participants endorsing higher negative beliefs about uncontrollability and danger. The study is notable for separating the danger and uncontrollability dimensions and demonstrating differences in both dimensions. Interesting differences between high worriers with and without GAD, and an unselected sample were also found on other metacognitive dimensions such that positive beliefs about worry appeared universal, general awareness of thoughts appeared to vary with worry severity, and negative beliefs about worry appeared distinctive of GAD.

In summary, the evidence clearly supports a positive association between negative metacognitions and pathological worry and GAD. Moreover, consistent with predictions of the metacognitive model elevated negative metacognitive appraisal and beliefs about worry appears to be distinctive of GAD. These data do not however, address questions of the causal status of metacognitions in GAD. In the next section we examine this issue.

Is There a Causal Role of Negative Metacognitions in the Development of GAD?

Evidence of a causal link between negative metacognitions and GAD has begun to emerge, but the quantity of data lags behind that from cross-sectional studies. Nassif (1999, study 2) examined the longitudinal predictors of pathological worry and GAD. Participants completed measures of pathological worry, metacognitions and the presence of GAD on two occasions, 12–15 weeks apart. Logistic regressions predicting the presence of GAD or no-anxiety at time two on the basis of metacognitions assessed at time 1 showed the following:

(1) Type 2 but not Type 1 worry predicted the presence of GAD at time 2, when GAD status at time 1 was controlled.
(2) MCQ negative beliefs concerning uncontrollability and danger predicted the presence of GAD at time 2, when GAD status, trait anxiety, and Type 1 worry at time 1 were controlled. Analysis of the prospective predictors of pathological worry (PSWQ) showed that uncontrollability and danger were positively associated with worry at time 2 when worry measured at time 1 was accounted for.

In summary, there is a small amount of evidence at the present time to support a causal role of negative metacognitive beliefs. As we will see later, there is also evidence to support the idea that use of worry as a coping strategy causes subsequent symptoms of failure in self-regulation.

Is Pathological Worry or GAD Associated With Ineffective Thought Control Strategies?

There is little evidence on the nature of thought control strategies used specifically by individuals with pathological worry or GAD. Evidence from other sources suggests that some strategies may be counterproductive (e.g. Purdon, 1999). One way to approach this issue is to maintain the assumption that worry itself is a maladaptive thought control or self-regulation strategy. Research with the Thought Control Questionnaire (Wells & Davies, 1994) shows that worry and punishment, when measured as individual differences in thought control strategies, are positively associated with psychological disorder (Abramowitz, Whiteside, Kalsy & Tolin, 2003; Amir, Cashman & Foa, 1997; Reynolds & Wells, 1999; Warda & Bryant, 1998).

A small number of studies have explored the effects of suppressing worry. Becker, Rinck, Roth and Margraf (1998) reported that GAD patients experienced an enhancement of thoughts when suppressing thoughts of their main worry. However, Mathews and Milroy (1994) did not find effects of suppression in participants classified as high or low worriers on the basis of the PSWQ. More generally, the literature on the effects of thought suppression suggests that asking people to attempt not to think a certain thought is often ineffective (Purdon, 1999; Wegner, Schneider, Carter & White, 1987). This may be particularly problematic for people who have negative beliefs about thoughts, since it will heighten fear of negative consequences.

Further evidence of the use of ineffective thought control strategies (or combinations of strategy) can be found in a study by Purdon (2000). The metacognitive model suggests that as a result of the co-existence of positive and negative beliefs about worry, there will be oscillation or conflict in the control of worry and the engagement in worry. Purdon examined the in-vivo negative appraisal of worrying in non-patients and found that they were associated with greater attempts to control thoughts. However, positive beliefs about worry emerged as simultaneous predictors of a reduced motivation to get rid of thoughts.

Does Worry-based Coping Lead to Negative Outcomes in Self-regulation?

The metacognitive model of GAD leads to a hypothesis that the use of worrying as a coping strategy can eventually create its own problems that lead to intrusive thoughts and impaired self-regulation. This is one pathway in which worrying could culminate in the development of negative metacognitive beliefs and a spiralling of pathological worry.

There are a range of ways that worrying may be problematic for self-regulation and emotional wellbeing. It may bias cognitive processes for the detection or recall of negative material, may maintain activation of negative beliefs and may distract from or divert processing resources away from activity required to change beliefs or to support emotional processing (Borkovec & Inz, 1990; Wells & Matthews, 1994; Wells 2000).

Early exploration of the effects of worrying (Borkovec, Robinson, Pruzinsky & De Pree, 1983), examined the effects of periods of 30, 15 or 0 minutes of worry in high and low worriers. During a five-minute breathing task that followed worry periods, high worriers reported more anxiety, more depression, less task-focused attention and more negative thoughts during the task than low worriers. York, Borkovec, Vasey and Stern (1987) later demonstrated that participants had more negative thought intrusions after the induction of worry than after a neutral condition.

Unintended intrusive images have been conceptualised as a symptom of failed emotional processing following stressful experiences (Rachman, 1979; Foa and Kozac, 1986). Several studies have explored the effects of worry following exposure to a stressful stimulus. Two initial studies explored the effects of worry on intrusive images after exposure to a stressful film. In both studies groups of participants were asked to watch a film about a workshop accident, and were then instructed to engage in brief periods of different types of thinking. Butler, Wells and Dewick (1995) asked participants to either: settle down (control condition), to image the events in the film, or to worry about the film. Those asked to worry reported more intrusive images about the film over a subsequent three-day monitoring period compared to participants in the other two conditions. Wells and Papageorgiou (1995) used four post-film mentation conditions: settle down, worry about the film, worry about usual concerns, distraction, or image the film. The results showed that participants who worried reported most intrusions, and the frequency of intrusions was incremental across conditions in a way that had been predicted on the basis of a theoretical co-joint mechanism.

Hazlett-Stephens (1997) investigated the effects of worrying in speech-anxious participants asked to give five consecutive speeches. Whilst individuals in the control conditions displayed habituation of subjective anxiety over repeated exposures, individuals in the worry condition who worried prior to each exposure did not. Mellings and Alden (2000) examined post-event worry/rumination in high socially anxious subjects and found that it predicted the recall of negative self-relevant information, negative bias in self-judgments, and recall of anxiety sensations on a subsequent occasion involving anticipation of a social interaction.

Individual differences in the use of worry to control more upsetting thoughts (as measured with the Thought Control Questionnaire; Wells and Davies, 1994), is positively associated with symptoms of acute stress and PTSD in several studies. Warda and Bryant (1998) investigated thought control strategies in victims of motor vehicle accidents who had either acute stress disorder (ASD) or not. Those people with ASD reported higher scores on the use of worry, and use of punishment to control thoughts compared with non-ASD subjects. In addition, worry and punishment control strategies were positively correlated with scores on measures of depression, anxiety, intrusive thoughts and avoidance. Holeva, Tarrier and Wells (2001) found that individual differences in worry based thought control strategies were positively associated with the severity of symptoms of acute stress disorder following motor-vehicle accidents, and worry was a longitudinal predictor of the subsequent development of PTSD when acute stress symptoms at the time of first assessment were controlled.

In summary, the results of worry-manipulation studies and of studies examining correlates of individual differences in use of worry to deal with more upsetting thoughts provide data consistent with the metacognitive hypothesis. It appears that worrying has a number of potentially deleterious effects. It increases the subsequent experience of thought intrusions during neutral tasks, and following exposure to stress. Endorsement of worry as a coping strategy is associated with symptoms of acute stress in cross-sectional analyses, and appears to be causally linked to the development of PTSD in a longitudinal study. It appears reasonably safe to conclude that there is evidence that worrying is associated with negative outcomes, and that use of worry as a coping strategy is likely to present its own problems as predicted. Evidence from the manipulation of worry and from prospective analysis in PTSD is especially important since it is consistent with a negative causal effect of worrying on emotional and cognitive self-regulation.

Summary of the Evidence

To sum up the scientific status of the model, it should be acknowledged that evidence of the causal status of metacognitive beliefs is as yet limited by the small number of studies conducted so far. However, the evidence that is available supports a causal role of negative metacognitive beliefs in the development of GAD. There is strong evidence from a variety of different sources to support many of the central predicted components and processes in the model.

Reliable relationships have been found between both positive and negative metacognitions and pathological worry in samples drawn from different cultural backgrounds. The negative appraisal of worry appears to be a better predictor of pathological worry than the frequency of worry in other content domains, or the experience of worry. There exists good evidence of the specificity of negative metacognitions to pathological worry, and to GAD defined by DSM-III-R and DSM-IV. Positive metacognitive beliefs, in contrast, do not appear to be specific to GAD.

The evidence reviewed provides strong support for the idea that worrying may be problematic for cognitive-emotional self-regulation, and therefore it is not a particularly effective coping strategy. Individual differences in use of worry to control thoughts are positively associated with psychological vulnerability in both cross sectional and prospective analyses. The results of studies that have manipulated worrying and the results of prospective analyses support a causal effect of worry on negative cognitive and emotional outcomes.

Finally, there is support from a small number of studies that individuals high in pathological worry or GAD tend to show patterns of thought control that may not be particularly effective or beneficial. Furthermore, negative appraisal of worrying in situations appears to be associated with greater attempts to control thoughts, whilst positive beliefs reduce the motivation to get rid of them; a pattern of potential conflict in regulation that is predicted by the model.

These studies address questions relating to different aspects of the metacognitive model of pathological worry and GAD, and as a set they provide a good level of support for its central tenets.

IMPLICATIONS FOR TREATING GAD AND UNCONTROLLABLE WORRY

The metacognitive approach provides a unique emphasis in the focus of treatment for GAD. It suggests that an important target of intervention should be modification of dysfunctional negative metacognitions concerning uncontrollability and danger. As described in detail in Chapter 15 a range of strategies have been developed for this purpose.

Although the presence of positive beliefs about worrying is deemed to be normal, the model suggests that these should be weakened because they underlie an inflexible over-use of worrying as a coping strategy in GAD.

This approach suggests that it is not necessary, and it will not be highly effective to focus on challenging individual Type 1 worries, or to teach patients to control somatic symptoms of anxiety through relaxation methods. This is because challenging Type 1 worry content does not tackle the underlying psychological factors that drive uncontrollable worry. Reappraisal strategies that focus on 'rationalising' Type 1 worries, and relaxation methods that increase self-control of anxiety run the risk of providing new coping behaviours that support a 'near miss' mind set in which the individual can believe they have narrowly avoided the danger of worrying and anxiety this time, but catastrophe might strike next time. Consistent with this view standardised analysis of treatment outcome studies suggest that multi-component cognitive-behavioural packages based on anxiety management methods lead to inconsistent and often modest levels of recovery (see Fisher, Chapter 20).

WIDER APPLICATIONS OF METACOGNITIVE THEORY AND TREATMENT

Earlier in this chapter I briefly alluded to the fact that the metacognitive model of GAD is based on a wider theory of the psychological factors involved in the genesis of emotional disorder. According to the Self-Regulatory Executive Function (S-REF) theory (Wells & Matthews, 1994, 1996), disorder is associated with the activation of a cognitive-attentional syndrome that locks individuals into psychological disturbance. The syndrome consists of perseverative negative thinking in the form of worry/rumination, attentional strategies of threat monitoring, and coping behaviours that fail to lead to correction of faulty knowledge. The syndrome is fuelled by the person's metacognitions such as the belief that it is necessary to maintain vigilance for danger, to think negatively in order to be prepared, and beliefs about the negative meaning/consequences of thoughts/emotions.

GAD is viewed as a basic manifestation of this generic process. It follows from this that the treatment developed for GAD can provide basic and core ingredients that should be of benefit in constructing treatments of other disorders, such as depression, post-traumatic stress, social anxiety and obsessional rumination. Indeed, metacognitive treatments for these disorders are available, and have been described elsewhere (Wells, 1997, 2000; Wells and Papageorgiou, 2004; Wells & Sembi, 2004). The implementation of these treatments for GAD, social phobia and PTSD are described by King in Chapter 19, and the similarities and differences between worry and depressive rumination are considered further in the chapter by Papageorgiou (Chapter 2, this volume).

Explaining the Uncontrollability of Worry

A central feature of pathological worry, and worry in GAD is that it is perceived as uncontrollable. One way to explain this is that it is based on an inaccurate appraisal of the potential controllability of worry. The metacognitive theory assumes that worrying is potentially controllable by patients, but there are several potential pathways leading to appraisals of uncontrollability:

(1) The repeated use of worry as a means of coping leads to diminished awareness of the pervasiveness of the activity. Such lack of objective meta-awareness leads to impediments in recognising the process of worrying when activated.

(2) The idea of interrupting worry runs contrary to the person's lay beliefs about worrying. For example, the person believes that it is a part of his/her personality and therefore has to be endured.

(3) The co-existence of positive and negative beliefs about worry underlies conflicting or vacillating motivations to engage with or suppress the thoughts that trigger worrying. Such a process fails to provide unambiguous experiences of control.

(4) Individuals lack knowledge of the nature of worry. Not realising that it is a response to other intrusive thoughts, they assume erroneously that it possesses the uncontrollable characteristics of unintended intrusive thoughts that trigger the activity. That is, individuals confuse the involuntary initiation of worrying with its volitional execution.

(5) Patients use self-regulation strategies that are counterproductive for reducing worry. For example, some individuals use information search to try and discount worrying thoughts but the strategy can backfire and increase awareness of potential threat.

(6) Negative appraisal/beliefs about worry lead to elevated emotional arousal (anxiety), and/or heightened attention to mental events. Each can increase the likelihood/awareness of intrusions, contributing to appraisals of diminished control.

(7) Worrying can divert processing resources away from other internal processing operations required for the control of cognition and for emotional processing. As a result intrusive thoughts and emotional symptoms persist contributing to appraisals of diminished control.

This list represents a range of factors that individually or in combination could underlie appraisals of uncontrollability. A central theme in this argument is that patients lack awareness of the potential control that they have over worry, and several factors could contribute to that diminished awareness. Patients attending the Manchester GAD clinic are often asked what leads them to believe that worrying is uncontrollable. They typically state that it is because attempts to control worry are usually ineffective. They have not considered that the reason for this ineffectiveness may rest with use of ineffective strategies. Moreover, they report experiences of worry being controlled by external factors such as the provision of reassurance, or the problem that was causing worry is removed by circumstances. Whilst these external factors can be an effective means of terminating individual worries, an over-reliance on them creates a problem of lack of experiences of effective internal control.

CONCLUSION

In this chapter I have described the metacognitive model of pathological worry and GAD, and reviewed the empirical evidence supporting the model. The implications of the model for treating GAD were briefly outlined, and the use of the metacognitive approach in a wider therapeutic context was introduced. Discussion of the metacognitive treatment of GAD is resumed in Chapter 15 where it is presented in detail.

This chapter also considered the issue of the apparent uncontrollability of pathological worry, and several candidate factors contributing to that appraisal arising from the metacognitive analysis were considered. Uncontrollability can be anchored in dysfunctional metacognitive knowledge, effects of thought-control strategies, effects of worry on emotional processing, the effects of meta-appraisals on monitoring of internal events and the effects of negative meta-appraisals on emotion, which modulates lower level processing giving rise to intrusive thoughts.

The metacognitive model of GAD provides a framework for understanding the difficult to control and pervasive worry process seen in this disorder by formulating it as a function of dysfunctional metacognitions. Such an approach rests principally on an important distinction between cognition and metacognition. The model is unique in the emphasis given to negative appraisal of worrying, or Type 2 worry, and negative beliefs about uncontrollability and danger. As we have seen there appears to be a degree of dissociation between such metacognitions and the actual characteristics of worry. Thus, it appears not so much the nature of worry but metacognitions concerning worry that distinguish normal and pathological types of this activity.

Research on metacognitive factors associated with GAD and pathological worry provide consistent support for many aspects of the model. Further studies are now needed to test the causal role of negative metacognitions in the development of pathological worry and GAD.

REFERENCES

Abramowitz, J.S., Whiteside, S., Kalsy, S.A. & Tolin, D.F. (2003). Thought control strategies in obsessive-compulsive disorder: a replication and extension. *Behaviour Research and Therapy*, **41**, 529–540.

Amir, N., Cashman, L. & Foa, E.B. (1997). Strategies of thought control in obsessive compulsive disorder. *Behaviour Research and Therapy*, **35**, 775–777.

Becker, E.M., Rinck, M., Roth, W.T. & Margraf, J. (1998). Don't worry and beware of white bears: Thought suppression in anxiety patients. *Journal of Anxiety Disorders*, **12**, 39–55.

Borkovec, T.D. (1994). The nature, functions and origins of worry. In: G.C.L. Davey & F. Tallis (Eds). *Worrying: Perspectives in Theory, Assessment and Treatment*. New York: John Wiley & Sons, Inc, pp. 5–34.

Borkovec, T.D. & Inz, J. (1990). The nature of worry in Generalised Anxiety Disorder: A predominance of thought activity. *Behaviour Research and Therapy*, **28**, 153–158.

Borkovec, T.D., Robinson, E., Pruzinsky, T. & DePree, J.A. (1983). Preliminary exploration of worry: Some characteristics and processes. *Behaviour Research and Therapy*, **21**, 9–16.

Borkovec, T.D. & Roemer, L. (1995). Perceived functions of worry among generalised anxiety subjects: Distraction from more emotionally distressing topics? *Behaviour Therapy and Experimental Psychiatry*, **26**, 25–30.

Butler, G., Wells, A. & Dewick, H. (1995) Differential effects of worry and imagery after exposure to a stressful stimulus: A pilot study. *Behavioural and Cognitive Psychotherapy*, **23**, 45–56.

Cartwright-Hatton, S. & Wells, A. (1997). Beliefs about worry and intrusions: The Meta-Cognitions Questionnaire and its correlates. *Journal of Anxiety Disorders*, **11**, 279–296.

Davis, R.N. & Valentiner, D.P. (2000). Does meta-cognitive theory enhance our understanding of pathological worry and anxiety? *Personality and Individual Differences*, **29**, 513–526.

Fisher, P.L. & Durham, R.C. (1999).Recovery rates in generalised anxiety disorder following psychological therapy: An analysis of clinically significant change in STAI-T across outcome studies since 1990. *Psychological Medicine*, **29**, 1425–1434.

Foa, E.B. & Kozak, M.J. (1986). Emotional processing and fear: Exposure to corrective information. *Psychological Bulletin*, **99**, 20–35.

Hazlett-Stephens, H. (1997). *The role of relaxation in the reduction of fear: An investigation of speech anxiety*. Paper presented at the Annual Meeting of the Association for the Advancement of Behavior Therapy, Miami.

Holeva, V., Tarrier, N. & Wells, A. (2001). Prevalence and predictors of acute stress disorder and PTSD following road traffic accidents: Thought control strategies and social support. *Behavior Therapy*, **32**, 65–83.

Mathews, A. & Milroy, R. (1994). Effects of priming and suppressing of worry. *Behaviour Research and Therapy*, **32**, 843–850.

Mellings, T.M.B. & Alden, L.E. (2000). Cognitive processes in social anxiety: the effects of self-focus, rumination and anticipatory processing. *Behaviour Research and Therapy*, **38**, 243–257.

Meyer, T.J., Miller, M.L., Metzger, R.L. & Borkovec, T.D. (1990). Development and validation of the Penn State Worry Questionnaire. *Behaviour Research and Therapy*, **28**, 487–495.

Nassif, Y. (1999). *Predictors of pathological worry*. Unpublished M.Phil. Thesis. University of Manchester, UK.

Nuevo, R., Montorio, I. & Borkovec, T.D. (2004). A test of the role of metaworry in the prediction of worry severity in an elderly sample. *Journal of Behavior Therapy and Experimental Psychiatry*, **35**, 209–218.

Papageorgiou, C. & Wells, A. (2004). Nature, functions, and beliefs about depressive rumination. In: C. Papageorgiou & A. Wells (Eds). *Depressive Rumination: Nature, Theory and Treatment*. Chichester, UK: John Wiley & Sons, Ltd.

Purdon, C. (1999). Thought suppression and psychopathology. *Behaviour Research and Therapy*, **37**, 1029–1054.

Purdon, C. (2000). Metacognition and the persistence of worry. Paper presented at the annual conference of the British Association of Behavioural and Cognitive Psychotherapy, Institute of Education, London, UK.

Rachman, S.J. (1980). Emotional processing. *Behaviour Research and Therapy*, **18**, 51–60.

Reynolds, M. & Wells, A. (1999). The Thought Control Questionnaire–psychometric properties in a clinical sample, and relationships with PTSD and depression. *Psychological Medicine*, **29**, 1089–1099.

Ruscio, A.M. & Borkovec, T.D. (2004). Experience and appraisal of worry among high worriers with and without generalized anxiety disorder. *Behaviour Research and Therapy*, **42**, 1469–1482.

Tallis, F., Davey, G.C.L. & Capuzzo, N. (1994). The phenomenology of non-pathological worry: a preliminary investigation. In G.C.L. Davey & F. Tallis (Eds) *Worrying: Perspectives on theory, assessment, and treatment*. Chichester, UK: John Wiley & Sons, Ltd.

Warda, G. & Bryant, R.A. (1998). Cognitive bias in acute stress disorder. *Behaviour Research and Therapy*, **36**, 1177–1183.

Wegner, D.M., Schneider, D.J., Carter, S.R. III. & White, T.L. (1987). Paradoxical effects of thought suppression. *Journal of Personality and Social Psychology*, **53**, 5–13.

Wells, A. (1994). Attention and the control of worry. In G.C.L. Davey & F. Tallis (eds), *Worrying: Perspectives on theory, assessment and treatment*. (pp. 91–114). Chichester, UK: John Wiley & Sons, Ltd.

Wells, A. (1995). Metacognition and worry: A cognitive model of generalised anxiety disorder. *Behavioural and Cognitive Psychotherapy*, **23**, 301–320.

Wells, A. (1997). *Cognitive Therapy of Anxiety Disorders: A practice manual and conceptual guide*. Chichester, UK: John Wiley & Sons, Ltd.

Wells, A. (2000). *Emotional Disorders and Metacognition: Innovative Cognitive Therapy*. Chichester, UK: John Wiley & Sons, Ltd.

Wells, A. (2005). The Metacognitive Model of GAD: Assessment of meta-worry and relationship with DSM-IV Generalized Anxiety Disorder. *Cognitive Therapy and Research*, **29**, 107–121.

Wells, A. & Carter, C. (1999). Preliminary tests of a cognitive model of Generalised Anxiety Disorder. *Behaviour Research and Therapy*, **37**, 585–594.

Wells, A. & Carter, K. (2001). Further tests of a cognitive model of Generalized Anxiety Disorder: Metacognitions and worry in GAD, panic disorder, social phobia, depression, and non-patients. *Behavior Therapy*, **32**, 85–102 .

Wells, A. & Davies, M. (1994) The Thought Control Questionnaire: A measure of individual differences in the control of unwanted thought. *Behaviour Research and Therapy*, **32**, 871–878.

Wells, A. & Matthews, G. (1994) Self-consciousness and cognitive failures as predictors of coping in stressful episodes. *Cognition and Emotion*, **8**, 279–295.

Wells, A. & Matthews, G. (1996). Modelling cognition in emotional disorder: The S-REF model. *Behaviour Research and Therapy*, **34**, 881–888.

Wells, A. & Papageorgiou, C. (1995) Worry and the incubation of intrusive images following stress. *Behaviour Research and Therapy*, **33**, 579–583.

Wells, A. & Papageorgiou, C. (1998). Social phobia: Effects of external attention focus on anxiety, negative beliefs and perspective taking. *Behavior Therapy*, **29**, 357–370.

Wells, A. & Papageorgiou, C. (2004). Metacognitive Therapy for Depressive Rumination. In: C. Papageorgiou & A. Wells (Eds). *Depressive Rumination: Nature, Theory and Treatment*. Chichester, UK: John Wiley & Sons, Ltd.

Wells, A. & Sembi, S. (2004). Metacognitive Therapy for PTSD: A preliminary investigation of a new brief treatment. *Journal of Behavior Therapy and Experimental Psychiatry*, **35**, 307–318.

York, D., Borkovec, T.D., Vasey, M. & Stern, R. (1987). Effects of worry and somatic anxiety induction on thoughts, emotion and physiological activity. *Behaviour Research and Therapy*, **25**, 523–526.

Chapter 12

A COGNITIVE MODEL OF GENERALIZED ANXIETY DISORDER: THE ROLE OF INTOLERANCE OF UNCERTAINTY

Naomi Koerner and Michel J. Dugas

Research on general and specific cognitive constructs and their role in the aetiology of various anxiety disorders has dramatically enhanced theoretical conceptualizations and treatments for these conditions. However, generalized anxiety disorder (GAD) has posed a great challenge, which is reflected in the fact that numerous individuals fail to attain full remission following treatment for this condition (see Borkovec, Newman & Castonguay, 2003). Initial psychosocial treatments for GAD consisted of interventions aimed at reducing anxiety and tension, but did not directly address GAD's core symptom—excessive and uncontrollable worry. The emergence of cognitive-behavioral therapies based on frameworks that were more theoretically cohesive and specific to worry represented a significant advancement in the field. Indeed, there now exist several empirically-supported models of GAD that have led to important changes in its treatment (e.g., Borkovec & Newman, 1999; Dugas, Gagnon, Ladouceur & Freeston, 1998; Wells & Carter, 1999).

In this chapter, we describe a cognitive model of GAD that our group developed and has been systematically validating and extending since the early 1990s. The model, as it currently stands, has four components. At the cornerstone is a construct we have termed *intolerance of uncertainty*, a higher-order process that is thought to lead to worry directly, and via three other processes: positive beliefs about worry, negative problem orientation (which results in poor problem-solving), and cognitive avoidance. In the following paragraphs, we describe the research on intolerance of uncertainty and each of the other processes in turn; we then conclude with a discussion of promising future directions for our model.

Worry and Its Psychological Disorders: Theory, Assessment and Treatment. Edited by G. C. L. Davey and A. Wells. © 2006 John Wiley & Sons, Ltd.

INTOLERANCE OF UNCERTAINTY: A KEY PROCESS INVOLVED IN WORRY

Researchers in various fields have taken a keen interest in the ways in which individuals respond to and cope with uncertainty. Several explanatory models of behavior in situations involving risk and uncertainty have been developed as a result (e.g., Hock & Krohne, 2004; Sorrentino & Roney, 2000). Whereas some individuals cope well with and even *embrace* the uncertainties of life, others appear to be highly uncomfortable with, and even *threatened* by them, and as such, make every attempt to eliminate uncertainties from their lives.

Based on anecdotal accounts from patients, we hypothesized that GAD may be driven and maintained by a fundamental intolerance for uncertainty, which is a dispositional characteristic that manifests as strong, negative, cognitive-affective reactions and futile attempts to control uncertain situations and events. For example, some of our patients with GAD reported that when faced with a problem, they preferred a negative outcome to an uncertain one. Other patients reported feeling overwhelmed by relatively minor problems, and that even when they could identify the most appropriate solution, they would delay implementing it because it was not the "perfect solution." Finally, we observed that the use of certain general cognitive techniques seemed to be ineffective for patients with GAD. For example, the re-evaluation of the probability of occurrence of a feared outcome often did little in the way of reducing worry and anxiety, because unless the probability could be nullified, patients reported that they could not help worrying.

Relatedly, two lines of empirical work substantiated our clinical observations of a relationship between worry and difficulty tolerating uncertainty. First, early research by Pennsylvania State University researchers suggested that worry always seemed to concern the uncertain future (Borkovec, Robinson, Pruzinsky & DePree, 1983). Then, subsequent work by Tallis and colleagues (Tallis & Eysenck, 1994; Tallis, Eysenck & Mathews, 1991) provided initial evidence that worriers appear to experience great difficulty solving problems under conditions of ambiguity, due to their "elevated evidence requirements."

Our clinical observations combined with the findings described above led us to develop the construct of intolerance of uncertainty (IU), which we define as a dispositional characteristic that results from a set of fundamental beliefs about uncertainty. Broadly speaking, IU affects how an individual perceives, interprets, and responds to uncertain situations on a cognitive, emotional, and behavioral level. Individuals who are intolerant of uncertainty believe that uncertainty is stressful and upsetting, that being uncertain about the future is unfair, that unexpected events are negative and should be avoided, and that uncertainty interferes with one's ability to function (Buhr & Dugas, 2002). IU is the central component of our model of GAD because we believe that the cognitive, emotional, and behavioral reactions and responses of patients with GAD are to a great extent, motivated by a fundamental belief that uncertainty is intolerable, which in turn leads to a strong resistance to accepting that uncertainty is almost always indelible.

In our initial work, it was important to establish the degree to which worry and IU shared a unique relationship, since a number of cognitive processes appear to be present to some extent in many anxiety disorders. In a non-clinical investigation, we found that IU was more highly related to worry than to obsessive-compulsive symptoms and panic sensations (Dugas, Gosselin & Ladouceur, 2001). Furthermore, IU maintained a significant unique relationship with worry, even when controlling for variance due to the relationships between worry and other anxiety-related processes such as perceived responsibility and anxiety sensitivity (Dugas et al., 2001). In a related study, we found that IU was more highly correlated with worry than with depressive symptoms and depresso-typic cognitions in a non-clinical sample (Dugas, Schwartz & Francis, 2004). Finally, in a third non-clinical study, we found that worry was more highly related to IU than to other processes known to be associated with anxiety such as perfectionism, need for control, and intolerance of ambiguity (Buhr & Dugas, in press). In clinical studies of GAD, similar results have been found, in that patients with GAD report higher levels of IU than do patients with panic disorder (Dugas, Marchand & Ladouceur, 2005), patients with other anxiety disorders (Ladouceur et al., 1999), and non-clinical controls (Dugas, Gagnon, et al., 1998).

To substantiate the prominent role of IU in our conceptual model, we sought to further examine the potential for a causal relationship between IU and worry. In a laboratory study involving the manipulation of IU, participants in the increased IU group reported more worry than those in the decreased IU group following the experimental procedure (Ladouceur, Gosselin & Dugas, 2000). Moreover, using time-series analysis on daily self-monitoring ratings, we have found that in individuals receiving cognitive-behavioral therapy for GAD, changes in IU tend to precede changes in worry over the course of treatment (Dugas & Ladouceur, 2000; Dugas, Langlois, Rhéaume & Ladouceur, 1998).

Taken together, although these findings are by no means sufficient by themselves to assert that IU *causes* excessive and uncontrollable worry, it is not unreasonable to presume that IU may play some role in its development. We hypothesize that IU may promote the maintenance and development of worry through two possible pathways. One possibility is that IU directly leads to chronic worry by promoting the operation of cognitive biases. Another possibility is that IU fosters high worry in an indirect manner—via the subsidiary processes of positive beliefs about worry, negative problem orientation, and cognitive avoidance.

INTOLERANCE OF UNCERTAINTY: DIRECT LINKS WITH WORRY

Research by other groups suggested early on that worry and GAD may be associated with hypervigilance and negative evaluative biases (see MacLeod & Rutherford, 2004 for a review). This processing style may manifest in the form of automatic attentional biases for stimuli that are negative in tone and implication (Bradley, Mogg, White, Groom & de Bono, 1999; Mathews, Mogg, Kentish & Eysenck, 1995; Mogg, Bradley & Williams, 1995). The activation and imposition of threatening interpretations of stimuli or events where there is a potential for a relatively benign interpretation has also been shown in persons with GAD (Eysenck, Mogg, May, Richards & Mathews, 1991; Mogg, Bradley, Miller & Potts, 1994). When considering these findings, it seems reasonable to presume then, that cognitive processing biases may play a role in the perpetuation of worry (MacLeod & Rutherford, 2004). However, it must be borne in mind that the biases found in GAD are not necessarily specific to this disorder, considering that similar biases are associated with other anxiety disorders (see MacLeod, 1999) and to some degree, with high trait anxiety (MacLeod & Rutherford, 2004). Therefore, although the evidence appears compelling, it may be that enhanced encoding and evaluative biases are a non-specific feature of anxiety disorders. Although this is useful for advancing conceptualizations of the mechanisms delineating adaptive from non-adaptive anxiety, a move from a phenomenological level of investigation, to one that is *process-oriented* may be required to enhance our current understanding of specific anxiety conditions such as GAD.

We hypothesize that a strong inclination toward being intolerant of uncertainty may indeed promote a heightened sensitivity to stimuli or situations that are relatively innocuous. This sensitivity (among other factors) may explain how it is that individuals with GAD come to develop the multitude of worries they present with. Specifically, the fundamental beliefs that underlie IU (e.g., "uncertainty is dangerous," "uncertainty is intolerable," "I can't deal with uncertainty") tend to be more extensive and are activated at a lower threshold in individuals with GAD than in people with other anxiety disorders (Dugas, Buhr & Ladouceur, 2004). That uncertainty is so troubling for these individuals may indicate that what constitutes "threat" for patients with GAD may be different relative to patients with other anxiety disorders. Specifically, uncertainty and ambiguity may be perceived as more unpleasant by individuals with GAD than by those with other anxiety disorders. With this conceptualization of IU in mind, we have begun to investigate information processing using basic tasks that assess biases in a theoretically cogent way.

Our preliminary investigations have demonstrated that individuals who are intolerant of uncertainty process stimuli that are ambiguous or denotative of uncertainty *differently* than do individuals who are more tolerant of uncertainty. In a study in which undergraduate students were asked to rate the threat value of written scenarios that were either positively-valenced, negatively-valenced, or ambiguous, high-IU individuals tended to rate ambiguous scenarios as more threatening, compared to low-IU individuals. Furthermore, although individuals who were high on IU tended to perceive *all* scenarios as more threatening relative to those low on IU, this between-group difference was most pronounced when scenarios were ambiguous (Dugas et al., 2005; Hedayati, Dugas, Buhr & Francis, 2003). These initial findings are interesting for a number of reasons. First, the fact that the ambiguous stimuli (i.e., those involving *potential* threat) led to the greatest interpretive differences between the groups is in line with current information processing theories such as Mogg and Bradley's (1998) cognitive-motivational analysis, which suggest that enhanced encoding of mild or innocuous stimuli may be a more valid marker of cognitive bias than, for example, sensitive responding to threat stimuli. Second, it is important to note that the relationship between IU and the tendency to interpret ambiguous scenarios as threatening remained significant after accounting for variance shared with worry, anxiety, and depression. This finding represents a first step toward linking this interpretive bias with a *specific* cognitive process known to be highly related to worry. In other words, the bias is not merely the result of high levels of negative affect.

In a related, but separate study aimed at investigating processing of uncertainty-relevant information (Dugas et al., 2005), undergraduate students viewed words denoting uncertainty (e.g., "uncertain," "possibility") and matched neutral words (e.g., "unnatural," "personality") and were asked to make a judgment about the familiarity of each word (to ensure that they focused on each word without using memorization strategies). Subsequently, participants were given a free recall task to write down all the words they remembered seeing. The results showed that in relation to the total number of words recalled, individuals high on IU remembered more words denoting uncertainty than did individuals low on IU. To our knowledge, this is the first study to reveal biases for *uncertainty-related* stimuli in individuals who resemble, at least cognitively, individuals with GAD.

Taken together, these studies suggest that a heightened sensitivity to ambiguous and uncertainty-relevant information may characterize individuals who are prone to worry. The most salient aspect of the study on interpretive bias in particular is that ambiguity, and not unambiguous threat, led to the greatest interpretive differences between the high IU and low IU groups, which is entirely consistent with our conceptualization of GAD. Interestingly, these findings parallel those of an earlier study, which examined the relationship between IU and performance in tasks varying in ambiguity (Ladouceur, Talbot & Dugas, 1997). Specifically, we found that level of IU was correlated with the number of cues required before responding in a *moderately* ambiguous task, but was unrelated to performance in tasks that were unambiguous or highly ambiguous.

INTOLERANCE OF UNCERTAINTY: INDIRECT LINKS WITH WORRY

We have described a possible pathway by which intolerance of uncertainty might directly promote excessive worry. Alternatively, IU might perpetuate high levels of worry via its relationship with three other processes: positive beliefs about worry, negative problem orientation, and cognitive avoidance. In this section, each of these relationships will be described in turn.

Intolerance of Uncertainty and Positive Beliefs about Worry

Wells (2004) has described metacognition as those "cognitive processes, strategies, and knowledge that are involved in the regulation and appraisal of thinking itself." Most of our research (e.g., Dugas, Gagnon, et al., 1998; Francis & Dugas, 2004) has concentrated on one type of metacognition: positive beliefs about worry, which have also been investigated by other groups (Borkovec & Roemer, 1995; Davey, Tallis & Capuzzo, 1996). Findings from our group indicate that excessive worry is related to at least five different kinds of positive beliefs. The first two types of beliefs center on the notion that worrying is functionally adaptive: worrying helps one to problem solve more effectively, and increases one's motivation to get things done. A third type of belief is that worrying dampens emotional reactions (surprise, disappointment) to future negative outcomes. A fourth type of belief that has been reported is that worry can directly alter the course of events. Finally, a fifth belief is that worrying represents a positive aspect of one's personality in that it shows that one is well-intentioned and caring (Bakerman, Buhr, Koerner & Dugas, 2004; Francis & Dugas, 2004; Holowka, Dugas, Francis & Laugesen, 2000). In a recent non-clinical investigation (Bakerman et al., 2004), we found that among the five types, the belief that worry represents a positive personality trait appears to be the strongest predictor of worry. As might be expected, individuals with GAD have been shown to hold positive beliefs about worry to a greater extent than people from the general population (Dugas, Gagnon, et al., 1998).

Worry and positive beliefs about worry are maintained via both positive and negative reinforcement. Positive reinforcement plays a role when worrying precedes a favourable outcome such as finding a solution to a problem. Negative reinforcement is involved when worrying is associated with the non-occurrence of an unfavourable outcome (i.e., a worry scenario). Negative reinforcement appears to play a prominent role in the maintenance of worry given that worry scenarios often have a very low probability of occurring (Borkovec, Hazlett-Stevens & Diaz, 1999). Furthermore, most positive beliefs about worry contain the notion that worrying can help an individual prepare for the worst and maintain control, if not of a potentially problematic situation, then of potential negative emotions in the event that one's "worst case scenario" does materialize. Thus, beliefs that worry can be used unconsciously or deliberately to somehow alter the outcome of an unclear situation or to mitigate one's own negative reaction to such a situation may all be manifestations of IU.

Intolerance of Uncertainty and Negative Problem Orientation

The relationship between worry and various aspects of problem-solving has been investigated by many researchers (e.g., Davey, Jubb & Cameron, 1996; Metzger, Miller, Cohen, Sofka & Borkovec, 1990; Tallis et al., 1991). Our work suggests that the problem-solving difficulties of individuals with GAD originate mainly from having a *negative problem orientation* (Dugas, Freeston & Ladouceur, 1997; Dugas, Letarte, Rhéaume, Freeston & Ladouceur, 1995; Robichaud & Dugas, 2005a; 2005b). Negative problem orientation, the third component of our GAD model, refers to a set of dysfunctional attitudes and perceptions related to the problem-solving process. Specifically, negative problem orientation includes perceptions of problems as threats, a lack of self-confidence in one's problem-solving abilities, a tendency toward becoming easily frustrated when attempting to problem solve, and negative views of the outcomes of one's problem-solving efforts (D'Zurilla, Nezu & Maydeu-Olivares, 1998). If one has a negative problem orientation, this will surely have a detrimental impact on the course of problem solving; which is why it may appear as though individuals with GAD have extremely poor problem-solving skills.

Research has shown that patients with GAD have a more negative problem orientation than patients with other anxiety disorders (Ladouceur et al., 1999) and non-clinical controls (Dugas, Gagnon, et al., 1998). Furthermore, negative problem orientation appears to have greater specificity to worry than to depression (Robichaud & Dugas, 2005b). Negative problem orientation may even have a causal role in worry. Davey, Jubb and Cameron (1996) showed that a decrease in problem-solving confidence, an element of problem orientation, leads to an increase in catastrophic worrying. Thus, there is sufficient evidence supporting a relationship between negative problem orientation and worry, but how does it relate to IU? Early studies by other researchers provided initial evidence for a possible relationship between IU and problem-solving difficulties (Tallis & Eysenck, 1994). Because some degree of uncertainty is inherent to most problems, it is easy to see how individuals with GAD could become frustrated and overwhelmed with solving even minor problems. If one is already intolerant of uncertainty and in addition, has a negative problem orientation, then this can interfere with the problem-solving process, which would have the effect of maintaining worry or even exacerbating it unnecessarily.

Intolerance of Uncertainty and Cognitive Avoidance

Cognitive avoidance refers to the implementing of primarily covert strategies to curtail distressing thoughts and mental images. An aspect of GAD that makes it particularly challenging to conceptualize and treat, is that although avoidance is part and parcel of the clinical picture of all anxiety disorders, the pattern of avoidance seen in GAD is particularly complex. Very often, individuals with GAD are not able to report what, why, or even how they avoid. According to the avoidance theory (Borkovec, Alcaine & Behar, 2004; Borkovec, Ray & Stöber, 1998), individuals with GAD may be attempting to avoid the invocation of threatening mental images and the uncomfortable somatic arousal that accompanies this imagery (see Chapter 14).

The avoidance theory suggests that the constant implementation of avoidant strategies is "effective" for bringing short-term relief from the arousal associated with the evocation of threatening mental imagery, but ultimately becomes an impediment to complete emotional processing (Borkovec et al., 1998). It has been suggested that worry has a suppressive effect (Borkovec & Hu, 1990) on mental imagery and somatic arousal; however, the exact mechanisms of this relationship remain speculative (Borkovec et al., 1998), particularly since other types of cognitive activity have also been shown to be associated with reduced imagery vividness (East & Watts, 1994). One compelling hypothesis that has been forwarded is that worry does not directly prevent the occurrence of emotional images, nor does it reduce their frequency; rather it may simply dampen their detectability (East & Watts, 1994) or their vividness and "concreteness" (Stöber, 1998). This reduces the intrusive quality of the images, which would in turn, have the effect of reducing somatic reactivity (Stöber, 1998).

Like Borkovec and colleagues, we believe that cognitive avoidance plays an important role in GAD. Our earlier work focused on the relationship between worry and one particular cognitive strategy—thought suppression, and the results have shown that the degree to which one engages in thought suppression reliably distinguishes patients with GAD from non-clinical controls (Dugas, Gagnon, et al., 1998). However, we are now beginning to investigate the relationship between worry and cognitive avoidance more closely. We will describe three lines of research we have undertaken to improve our understanding of this construct and its role in excessive worry.

Fear of emotional arousal and worry

Although Borkovec and colleagues have long suggested that worry is associated with reduced processing of emotion, in recent years, research on "emotional" avoidance seems to have burgeoned in the field (see, e.g., Mennin, Heimberg, Turk & Fresco, 2002; Roemer & Orsillo, 2002). Explanatory models implicating emotion regulation deficits in GAD are currently being developed and tested (Mennin et al., 2002). We recently completed a series of studies also aimed at investigating the relationship between worry and avoidance of emotional experience. The first study sought to investigate the relationships between worry and various aspects of emotion to determine whether high worriers have difficulties with particular domains related to the experience of emotion. In a non-clinical study (Bakerman, Buhr & Dugas, 2003), relationships were examined between the tendency to worry and fear of positive and negative emotions, maladaptive emotion regulation strategies, and experiential avoidance. High levels of worry showed the strongest correlations with fear of anxiety and experiential avoidance.

Because fear of anxiety and experiential avoidance are likely to be factors in a number of emotional disorders, we conducted a second study to explore the specificity of the relationship between worry and these affective processes in a non-clinical sample (Bergevin, Koerner & Dugas, 2003). The results showed that relative to symptoms of other anxiety disorders and depression, worry shared the strongest relationship with fear of anxiety and experiential avoidance. Furthermore, fear of anxiety appeared to have greater specificity to worry than did experiential avoidance.

With that, we conducted a third study (Otis, Buhr & Dugas, 2003) to investigate the specificity of the relationships between worry, and fear of anxiety and experiential avoidance, beyond those shared between worry and the four cognitive constructs already known to be predictors of excessive worry in our model. First, the findings from the specificity study were corroborated, in that the unique contribution of fear of anxiety to the prediction of worry was larger than that of experiential avoidance. Second, fear of anxiety and experiential avoidance made a significant contribution to the prediction of worry above and beyond the contributions of age, sex, and the four processes in our model of GAD.

Taken together, these studies support the hypothesis that avoidance of emotional experiences, as the work of others (Mennin et al., 2002) has suggested, may indeed be an important factor in excessive worry. Contrarily, however, the avoidance may not pertain to emotions *in general*; rather the set of studies described above appears to be pointing to fear of *anxious arousal* as a specific factor involved in high-level worry.

Investigation of cognitive avoidance strategies

GAD may be associated with a fairly vast variety of avoidance strategies that are largely internally or covertly generated. What is more, behavioral avoidance may also be part of the coping repertoire, but may be more subtle and erratic than in other anxiety disorders. Our work up until recently concentrated on one form of cognitive avoidance—thought suppression. Worriers, however, may use a number of other strategies to evade distressing cognitions, including: substitution of thoughts, conversion of threatening mental images into verbal-linguistic thought, behavioral avoidance of external cues that act as triggers for thoughts of feared outcomes, and distraction (Gosselin et al., 2002; Sexton, Dugas & Hedayati, 2004). The empirical examination of these diverse forms of cognitive avoidance is an important and necessary step in the progression of our conceptual model of GAD, since thought suppression may not necessarily be unique to GAD. Suppression may in fact be common to *many* emotional disorders (Becker, Rinck, Roth & Margraf, 1998; Purdon, 1999). If GAD is to be considered distinguishable from other anxiety disorders, it seems particularly pertinent to identify the avoidance strategies that differentiate individuals with GAD from persons with anxiety disorders that are characterized by other forms of distressing cognitions, such as OCD and post-traumatic stress disorder. We have yet to examine the specificity of these various cognitive avoidance strategies to worry.

Worry and negative beliefs about anxiety

One interesting hypothesis is that perhaps the use of cognitive avoidance by persons with GAD is motivated by different fears, as compared to individuals who experience other forms of intrusions. Suppression of intrusions by an individual with OCD might be brought on by thought-action fusion beliefs or beliefs surrounding the controllability of thoughts (Purdon, 1999), whereas for persons with GAD, the avoidance of certain thoughts and mental images might be motivated by a different set of beliefs. Based on our research on fear of anxiety, one possibility is that individuals with GAD may have strong negative beliefs about the experience of anxious arousal, which may promote increased worry and the use of strategies to inhibit the experience of it. We are exploring this hypothesis in a study of the relationship between cognitive avoidance and beliefs about the negative consequences of anxiety (Sexton & Dugas, 2004).

Although we have shown that fear of anxious arousal plays an important role in worry, it is unclear whether it is a factor that aggravates worry only in individuals who are already intolerant of uncertainty. If this is the case, this would differ substantially from recent models of GAD that suggest that avoidance of emotional experience (Mennin et al., 2002) and the presence of metacognitive beliefs (Wells, 2004) are primary factors in the development and maintenance of GAD.

THE ROLE OF COMPETING COGNITIVE-MOTIVATIONAL STATES IN THE MAINTENANCE OF WORRY

Over the course of our research, it has become increasingly apparent that one way of conceptualizing excessive worry, is as the result of competing cognitive-motivational states (Dugas & Koerner, 2005). Paradoxical processes become more comprehensible within a framework that considers GAD-type worry as an expression of various cognitive-motivational conflicts that, for the individual become difficult to manage. Based on our newly refined formulation, what follows is a discussion of hypotheses that we are interested in addressing in our future research.

We propose that this formulation might be useful for making sense of how people with GAD can display excessive levels of vigilant *and* avoidant behavior. As discussed earlier, IU promotes enhanced attention toward stimuli and situations that are ambiguous or that are suggestive of uncertainty. However, due to the sensitivity of IU, many stimuli and situations are labelled "dangerous," which can fuel inordinate attempts to control the feared outcomes triggered by these. We hypothesize that this IU-driven process of detecting, interpreting, and approaching potentially problematic situations may manifest in excessively vigilant behavior.

Paradoxically, people with GAD report holding the belief that uncertainty is stressful and upsetting and therefore should be *avoided* (Buhr & Dugas, 2002), which suggests that the need to attain certainty may be costly. What could be motivating the need to avoid that which is uncertain or unknown? Our work and the work of others (e.g., Borkovec, Ray & Stöber, 1998), as was described earlier, suggests that while worry may represent an attempt to engage in some sort of problem solving, individuals with GAD typically do not fully elaborate on their worry scenarios because it may lead to the evocation of threatening mental images and anxious arousal. This might indeed motivate the use of cognitive avoidance strategies. Thus opposing motivations may drive IU and cognitive avoidance. Oscillating between vigilant and avoidant coping might become cognitively and emotionally demanding, *enhance* worry and anxiety, and eventually lead to the exhaustion and demoralization that is often described by GAD patients. Because of the potentially complex relationship between IU and cognitive avoidance, we are turning our efforts toward gaining a better understanding of the factors that might mediate the relationship between these two processes.

A framework that views excessive worry as the expression of competing motivations can also explain the simultaneous presence of opposite metacognitive beliefs in persons with GAD. In our model, the holding of positive beliefs about worry is an important contributory and maintenance factor in excessive worry. However, it is known that worriers also hold beliefs about the *negative* consequences of worrying (Holowka et al., 2000; Wells, 2004; Wells & Carter, 1999), namely that worrying interferes with being effective, amplifies problems, and causes emotional distress (Davey, Tallis, et al., 1996). We hypothesize that while the belief that worrying is helpful and personally advantageous promotes its maintenance, when worry is experienced as uncontrollable, negative beliefs about worry may be activated. The individual then becomes caught in a dilemma because if he or she stops worrying, this might lead to the loss of certain benefits (e.g., feelings of control, positive perceptions of self as a "caring" person); but if he or she continues to worry, this might lead to heightened levels of distress, and functional interference. Although most of our work on metacognition has focused on positive beliefs about worry, a deeper examination of the unique and combined contributions of positive and negative beliefs about worry to the development and maintenance of GAD is a direction that would be fruitful for our model.

CONCLUSION

In everyday life, we are required to make many choices, appraisals, and decisions, usually with an insufficient amount of information, a limited timeframe, conflicting emotions, and some degree of uncertainty with regard to the outcome. Yet, most individuals manage to deal with these constraints and are able to make decisions of minor or major significance with relative ease under such conditions. However, for individuals with GAD, this process can be tremendously distressing. In this chapter, we discussed our group's empirically-supported model of the factors involved in excessive and uncontrollable worry. The model's central process, intolerance of uncertainty, was described as a dispositional characteristic that results from a set of acutely sensitive deep-seated beliefs that become activated in response to situations that are ambiguous or in which the outcome is uncertain. Three other processes that are thought to interact with IU to maintain and possibly produce chronic worry are subsumed under it in the model: beliefs about the usefulness of worry, a negative problem orientation, and the tendency to engage in cognitive avoidance. We proposed that conceptualizing worry as the expression of competing cognitive-motivational states might help organize disparate findings in the literature on GAD and may stimulate new hypotheses with regard to the factors that contribute to and maintain worry. In Chapter 17, we describe a cognitive-behavioral treatment for GAD that our group has developed and systematically tested, based on the research discussed here.

REFERENCES

Bakerman, D., Buhr, K. & Dugas, M.J. (2003, March). *Examination of the relationship between worry and fear of emotional arousal and experiential avoidance.* Article presented at the national conference of the Anxiety Disorders Association of America. Toronto, ON.

Bakerman, D., Buhr, K., Koerner, N. & Dugas, M.J., (2004, November). *Exploring the link between positive beliefs about worry and worry.* Article presented at the annual convention of the Association for Advancement of Behavior Therapy, New Orleans, LA.

Becker, E.S., Rinck, M., Roth, W.T. & Margraf, J. (1998). Don't worry and beware of white bears: Thought suppression in anxiety patients. *Journal of Anxiety Disorders*, **12**, 39–55.

Bergevin, M., Koerner, N. & Dugas, M.J. (2003, November). *Fear of anxiety and experiential avoidance in excessive worry: Specificity in a nonclinical sample.* Poster presented at the annual convention of the Association for Advancement of Behavior Therapy, Boston, MA.

Borkovec, T.D., Alcaine, O. & Behar, E. (2004). Avoidance theory of worry and generalized anxiety disorder. In R.G. Heimberg, C.L. Turk & D.S. Mennin (Eds), *Generalized anxiety disorder: Advances in research and practice* (pp. 77–108). New York: Guilford Press.

Borkovec, T.D., Hazlett-Stevens, H. & Diaz, M.L. (1999). The role of positive beliefs about worry in generalized anxiety disorder and its treatment. *Clinical Psychology and Psychotherapy*, **6**, 126–138.

Borkovec, T.D. & Hu, S. (1990). The effect of worry on cardiovascular response to phobic imagery. *Behaviour Research and Therapy*, **28**, 69–73.

Borkovec, T.D. & Newman, M.G. (1999). Worry and generalized anxiety disorder. In A.S. Bellack & M. Hersen (Series Eds) & P. Salkovskis (Vol. Ed.), *Comprehensive clinical psychology: Vol. 4. Adults: Clinical formulation and treatment* (pp. 439–459). Oxford: Elsevier Science.

Borkovec, T.D., Newman, M.G. & Castonguay, L.G. (2003). Cognitive-behavioral therapy for generalized anxiety disorder with integrations from interpersonal and experiential therapies. *CNS Spectrums,* **8**, 382–389.

Borkovec, T.D., Ray, W.J. & Stöber, J. (1998). Worry: A cognitive phenomenon intimately linked to affective, physiological, and interpersonal behavioral processes. *Cognitive Therapy and Research,* **22**, 561–576.

Borkovec, T.D., Robinson, E., Pruzinsky, T. & DePree, J.A. (1983). Preliminary exploration of worry: Some characteristics and processes. *Behaviour Research and Therapy,* **21**, 9–16.

Borkovec, T.D. & Roemer, L. (1995). Perceived functions of worry among generalized anxiety disorder subjects: Distraction from more emotional topics? *Journal of Behavior Therapy and Experimental Psychiatry,* **26**, 25–30.

Bradley, B.P., Mogg, K., White, J., Groom, C. & de Bono, J. (1999). Attentional bias for emotional faces in generalized anxiety disorder. *British Journal of Clinical Psychology,* **38**, 267–278.

Buhr, K. & Dugas, M.J. (2002). The Intolerance of Uncertainty Scale: Psychometric properties of the English version. *Behaviour Research and Therapy,* **40**, 931–945.

Buhr, K. & Dugas, M.J. (in press). Investigating the construct validity of intolerance of uncertainty and its unique relationship with worry. *Journal of Anxiety Disorders.*

D'Zurilla, T.J., Nezu, A.M. & Maydeu-Olivares, A. (1998). *Manual for the Social Problem-Solving Inventory—Revised.* North Tonawanda, New York: Multi-Health Systems.

Davey, G.C.L., Jubb, M. & Cameron, C. (1996). Catastrophic worry as a function of changes in problem-solving confidence. *Cognitive Therapy and Research,* **20**, 333–344.

Davey, G.C.L., Tallis, F. & Capuzzo, N. (1996). Beliefs about the consequences of worrying. *Cognitive Therapy and Research,* **20**, 499–520.

Dugas, M.J., Buhr, K. & Ladouceur, R. (2004). The role of intolerance of uncertainty in etiology and maintenance. In R.G. Heimberg, C.L. Turk & D.S. Mennin (Eds), *Generalized anxiety disorder: Advances in research and practice* (pp. 143–163). New York: Guilford Press.

Dugas, M.J., Freeston, M.H. & Ladouceur, R. (1997). Intolerance of uncertainty and problem orientation in worry. *Cognitive Therapy and Research,* **21**, 593–606.

Dugas, M.J., Gagnon, F., Ladouceur, R. & Freeston, M.H. (1998). Generalized anxiety disorder: A preliminary test of a conceptual model. *Behaviour Research and Therapy,* **36**, 215–226.

Dugas, M.J., Gosselin, P. & Ladouceur, R. (2001). Intolerance of uncertainty and worry: Investigating specificity in a nonclinical sample. *Cognitive Therapy and Research,* **25**, 551–558.

Dugas, M.J., Hedayati, M., Karavidas, A., Buhr, K., Francis, K. & Phillips, N.A. (2005). Intolerance of uncertainty and information processing: Evidence of biased recall and interpretations. *Cognitive Therapy and Research,* **29**, 57–70.

Dugas, M.J. & Koerner, N. (2005). Cognitive-behavioral treatment for generalized anxiety disorder: Current status and future directions. *Journal of Cognitive Psychotherapy: An International Quarterly,* **19**, 61–81.

Dugas, M.J. & Ladouceur, R. (2000). Treatment of GAD: Targeting intolerance of uncertainty in two types of worry. *Behavior Modification,* **24**, 635–657.

Dugas, M.J., Langlois, F., Rhéaume, J. & Ladouceur, R. (1998, November). Intolerance of uncertainty and worry: Investigating causality. In J. Stöber (chair),

Worry: New findings in applied and clinical research. Symposium: Association for Advancement of Behavior Therapy, Washington, DC.

Dugas, M.J., Letarte, H., Rhéaume, J., Freeston, M. H. & Ladouceur, R. (1995). Worry and problem-solving: Evidence of a specific relationship. *Cognitive Therapy and Research*, **19**, 109–120.

Dugas, M.J., Marchand, A. & Ladouceur, R. (2005). Further validation of a cognitive-behavioral model of generalized anxiety disorder: Diagnostic and symptom specificity. *Journal of Anxiety Disorders*, **19**, 329–343.

Dugas, M.J., Schwartz, A. & Francis, K. (2004). Intolerance of uncertainty, worry, and depression. *Cognitive Therapy and Research*, **28**, 835–842.

East, M.P. & Watts, F.N. (1994). Worry and the suppression of imagery. *Behaviour Research and Therapy*, **32**, 851–855.

Eysenck, M.W., Mogg, K., May, J., Richards, A. & Mathews, A. (1991). Bias in interpretation of ambiguous sentences related to threat in anxiety. *Journal of Abnormal Psychology*, **100**, 144–150.

Francis, K. & Dugas, M.J. (2004). Assessing positive beliefs about worry: Validation of a structured interview. *Personality and Individual Differences*, **37**, 405–415.

Gosselin, P., Langlois, F., Freeston, M.H., Ladouceur, R., Dugas, M.J. & Pelletier, O. (2002). Le Questionnaire d'Evitement Cognitif (QEC): Développement et validation auprès d'adultes et d'adolescents [The Cognitive Avoidance Questionnaire (CAQ): Development and validation among adult and adolescent samples]. *Journal de thérapie comportementale et cognitive*, **12**, 24–37.

Hedayati, M., Dugas, M.J., Buhr, K. & Francis, K. (2003, November). *The relationship between intolerance of uncertainty and interpretation of ambiguous and unambiguous information.* Poster presented at the annual convention of the Association for Advancement of Behavior Therapy, Boston, MA.

Hock, M. & Krohne, H.W. (2004). Coping with threat and memory for ambiguous information: Testing the repressive discontinuity hypothesis. *Emotion*, **4**, 65–86.

Holowka, D.W., Dugas, M.J., Francis, K. & Laugesen, N. (2000, November). *Measuring beliefs about worry: A psychometric evaluation of the Why Worry-II questionnaire.* Poster presented at the annual convention of the Association for Advancement of Behavior Therapy, New Orleans, LA.

Ladouceur, R., Dugas, M.J., Freeston, M.H., Rhéaume, J., Blais, F., Boisvert, J.M., et al. (1999). Specificity of generalized anxiety disorder symptoms and processes. *Behavior Therapy*, **30**, 191–207.

Ladouceur, R., Gosselin, P. & Dugas, M.J. (2000). Experimental manipulation of intolerance of uncertainty: A study of a theoretical model of worry. *Behaviour Research and Therapy*, **38**, 933–941.

Ladouceur, R., Talbot, F. & Dugas, M.J. (1997). Behavioral expressions of intolerance of uncertainty in worry. *Behavior Modification*, **21**, 355–371.

MacLeod, C. (1999). Anxiety and anxiety disorders. In T. Dalgleish & M.J. Power (Eds), *Handbook of cognition and emotion* (pp. 447–477). Chichester: John Wiley & Sons, Ltd.

MacLeod, C. & Rutherford, E. (2004). Information processing approaches: Assessing the selective functioning of attention, interpretation, and retrieval. In R.G. Heimberg, C.L. Turk & D.S. Mennin (Eds), *Generalized anxiety disorder: Advances in research and practice* (pp. 109–142). New York: Guilford Press.

Mathews, A., Mogg, K., Kentish, J. & Eysenck, M. (1995). Effect of psychological treatment on cognitive bias in generalized anxiety disorder. *Behaviour Research and Therapy*, **33**, 293–303.

Mennin, D., Heimberg, R.G., Turk, C.L. & Fresco, D.M. (2002). Applying an emotion regulation framework to integrative approaches to generalized anxiety disorder. *Clinical Psychology: Science and Practice*, **9**, 85–90.

Metzger, R.L., Miller, M.L., Cohen, M., Sofka, M. & Borkovec, T.D. (1990). Worry changes decision making: The effect of negative thoughts on cognitive processing. *Journal of Clinical Psychology*, **46**, 78–88.

Mogg, K. & Bradley, B.P. (1998). A cognitive-motivational analysis of anxiety. *Behaviour Research and Therapy*, **36**, 809–848.

Mogg, K., Bradley, B.P., Miller, T. & Potts, H. (1994). Interpretation of homophones related to threat: Anxiety or response bias effects? *Cognitive Therapy and Research*, **18**, 461–477.

Mogg, K., Bradley, B.P. & Williams, R. (1995). Attentional bias in anxiety and depression: The role of awareness. *British Journal of Clinical Psychology*, **34**, 17–36.

Otis, C., Buhr, K. & Dugas, M.J. (2003, November). *The role of fear of anxiety and experiential avoidance in excessive worry*. Poster presented at the annual meeting of the Société Québécoise pour la Recherche en Psychologie. Montreal, Quebec, Canada.

Purdon, C. (1999). Thought suppression and psychopathology. *Behaviour Research and Therapy*, **37**, 1029–1054.

Robichaud, M. & Dugas, M.J. (2005a). Negative problem orientation (Part I): Psychometric properties of a new measure. *Behaviour Research and Therapy*, **43**, 391–401.

Robichaud, M. & Dugas, M.J. (2005b). Negative problem orientation (Part II): Construct validity and specificity to worry. *Behaviour Research and Therapy*, **43**, 403–412.

Roemer, L. & Orsillo, S.M. (2002). Expanding our conceptualization of and treatment for generalized anxiety disorder: Integrating mindfulness/acceptance-based approaches with existing cognitive-behavioral models. *Clinical Psychology: Science and Practice*, **9**, 54–68.

Sexton, K.A. & Dugas, M.J. (2004, November). *An investigation of the factors leading to cognitive avoidance in worry*. Poster presented at the annual convention of the Association for Advancement of Behavior Therapy, New Orleans, LA.

Sexton, K.A., Dugas, M.J. & Hedayati, M. (2004, November). *The Cognitive Avoidance Questionnaire: Validation of the English translation*. Article presented at the annual convention of the Association for Advancement of Behavior Therapy, New Orleans, LA.

Sorrentino, R.M. & Roney, C.J.R. (2000). *The uncertain mind: Individual differences in facing the unknown*. Philadelphia: Psychology Press.

Stöber, J. (1998). Worry, problem elaboration and suppression of imagery: The role of concreteness. *Behaviour Research and Therapy*, **36**, 751–756.

Tallis, F., Eysenck, M. & Mathews, A. (1991). Elevated evidence requirements and worry. *Personality and Individual Differences*, **12**, 21–27.

Tallis, F. & Eysenck, M.W. (1994). Worry: Mechanisms and modulating influences. *Behavioural and Cognitive Psychotherapy*, **22**, 37–56.

Wells, A. (2004). A cognitive model of GAD: Metacognitions and pathological worry. In R.G. Heimberg, C.L. Turk & D.S. Mennin (Eds), *Generalized anxiety disorder: Advances in research and practice* (pp. 164–186). New York: Guilford Press.

Wells, A. & Carter, K. (1999). Preliminary tests of a cognitive model of generalized anxiety disorder. *Behaviour Research and Therapy*, **37**, 585–594.

Chapter 13

A MOOD-AS-INPUT ACCOUNT OF PERSEVERATIVE WORRYING

Graham C.L. Davey

HOW DO WE EXPLAIN PATHOLOGICAL WORRYING?

All theoretical endeavours need to begin with an attempt to establish what it is about the phenomenon that needs to be explained. Important questions about pathological worry that seek theoretical answers are of the following kind: (1) why do worriers continue with a worry episode for significantly longer than nonworriers (Vasey & Borkovec, 1992; Startup & Davey, 2001)? (2) Why does emotional discomfort increase during a worry bout for pathological worriers, but not for nonworriers (e.g. Vasey & Borkovec, 1992)? And (3) why do pathological worriers perceive their worry as being uncontrollable, when nonworriers do not (Davey, Tallis & Capuzzo, 1994; Wells, 1995)? Such differences between pathological worriers and nonworriers will be the defining elements of any theory that attempts to explain pathological worrying.

These differences between worriers and nonworriers are not just confined to the activity of worrying, and similar differential features between normal and pathological behaviour can be found in a number of anxious psychopathologies—especially those that have come to be known as the *perseverative psychopathologies*. A number of prominent psychopathologies are characterised by the dysfunctional perseveration of certain thoughts, behaviours or activities. Examples include pathological worrying, which is the current cardinal diagnostic feature of Generalised Anxiety Disorder (GAD) (DSM, 4th ed., DSM-IV; American Psychiatric Association, 1994); obsessive compulsive disorder (OCD) in which individuals indulge in perseverative bouts of activities such as checking, washing or obsessive thoughts; and rumination, which has been recognised as an important maintaining factor in depression (Nolen-Hoeksema & Morrow, 1993). In almost all examples of these psychopathologies the perseveration is viewed

Worry and Its Psychological Disorders: Theory, Assessment and Treatment. Edited by G. C. L. Davey and A. Wells. © 2006 John Wiley & Sons, Ltd.

as excessive, out of proportion to the functional purpose that it serves, and a source of emotional discomfort for the individual concerned. Interestingly, there is a significant degree of comorbidity between the disorders that support these perseverative activities (Andrews, Stewart, Morris-Yates, Holt & Henderson, 1990; Brown, Dowdall, Cote & Barlow, 1994; Butler, Fennel, Robson & Gelder, 1991; Parkin, 1997), with one implication of this being that there may be some common elements to the psychological mechanisms that underlie perseveration across these various disorders.

Given that dysfunctional perseveration is one of the critical defining features of pathological worrying, then an understanding of the causes of this perseveration would seem to be an important starting point for any theory attempting to explain it. But 'explanations' can be couched at many different levels, and these are not necessarily mutually exclusive explanations. For example, it is quite reasonable to ask what *functions* pathological worry serves—presumably, if it has a function, then this will serve to maintain the activity. Many contemporary theories of worry do indeed try to explain it at least partially in these terms, and these include accounts which stress that worry functions (1) to avoid the processing of distressing phobic imagery (Borkovec, 1994; Borkovec & Lyonfields, 1993), (2) to help prevent the occurrence of future catastrophes (Borkovec & Roemer, 1995; Davey, Tallis & Capuzzo, 1996; Roemer, Molina & Borkovec, 1997; Wells, 1995), (3) to generate 'what if . . . ?' questions in an attempt to reduce uncertainty about future threats (Dugas, Freeston & Ladouceur, 1997; Dugas, Gagnon, Ladouceur & Freeston, 1998), and (4) to increase sensitivity to worry triggers and provide a means of coping with future threats (Wells, 1995; Wells & Hackman, 1993).

While such functional models are useful in identifying the factors that might maintain pathological worrying, and in identifying what can best be described as the purpose of worrying for the pathological worrier, they are less helpful in describing the detail of the actual mechanisms that give rise to specific bouts or episodes of perseverative worrying. Some theories have begun to identify by experimental means causal relationships between the central constructs of those theories and pathological worrying (e.g. Dugas, Gagnon, Ladouceur & Freeston, 1998), but they still do not specifically identify *how* such causal relationships are mediated (see Davey, 2003). The details of how causal relationships are mediated will be found in *proximal* explanations of the activity of worrying, which attempt to describe the causal interactions between variables which determine the onset, duration and sequential properties of worry bouts. These proximal explanations will not be competing with functional explanations, but they elaborate explanation on another level of detail. Indeed, explanations in terms of proximal mechanisms may not need to address functional explanations in any way. This is because functionality may develop opportunistically as a consequence of the basic processes that give rise to individual perseverative bouts of worry. For example, it may be that the individual perseverative worry bouts of worriers are governed by a generalised iterative style generated by a combination of basic cognitive processes (e.g. Davey & Levy, 1998). However, worriers may then find that their perseverative worry bouts have added value in that they may serve other functions, such as preventing the processing of disturbing phobic imagery (Borkovec & Lyonfields, 1993). This gives the process a functionality that is not inherent in the description of the proximal mechanism itself.

The remainder of this chapter will describe our attempts to elaborate the details of a proximal explanation of pathological worrying in terms of the mood-as-input hypothesis (Martin & Davies, 1998; Startup & Davey, 2001). This model attempts to explain the perseveration of individual worry bouts in terms of the dynamic interactions between concurrent mood and the implicit 'stop rules' used by the worrier. The following sections will describe the development of this model and the role of critical variables in determining the perseveration of individual worry bouts.

THE MOOD-AS-INPUT HYPOTHESIS AND PATHOLOGICAL WORRYING

What is the Mood-as-Input Hypothesis?

The mood-as-input hypothesis represents a rather specific way of conceptualising the motivating effects of moods (Martin, Achee, Ward & Harlow, 1993) and has been extended by Sanna, Turley and Mark (1996), George and Zhou (2002) and Martin and Davis (1998). Rather than being intrinsically linked to certain default processing strategies (such as mood-congruent processing), the mood-as-input hypothesis proposes that it is an individual's interpretation of their mood rather than the mood *per se* that has particular performance implications. Mood in this view assumes more of a secondary role, the function of which is derived from 'top down', 'configural' interpretations based on the goal at hand (Martin & Davis, 1998). For example, during the course of task performance, people may ask themselves, either explicitly or implicitly, 'Have I reached my goal?' People in positive moods would tend to answer yes, whereas people in negative moods would tend to answer no. That is, people in a positive mood are likely to interpret their positive affect as a sign that they have attained or made progress toward their goal (Hirt, McDonald & Melton, 1996; Martin et al., 1993). In contrast, in a negative mood, individuals may interpret their negative affect as a sign that they have not attained or made progress toward their goal and so continue to persist at the task (Frijda, 1988; Martin et al., 1993; Schwarz & Bless, 1991).

This approach assumes that mood can have differential effects on behaviour depending on the nature of the task that is being carried out, the stop rules associated with that task, and how the information conveyed by the mood is interpreted in the context of the task (Martin & Davies, 1998). For example, if catastrophic worrying is viewed as an attempt to problem solve, and the individual sees solving the problem as being of uppermost importance (Davey, 1994), then the 'mood-as-input' hypothesis would predict that negative mood would be interpreted as evidence that the problem-solving process was not yet complete (e.g. 'I still feel negative, so I cannot have completed the problem-solving task satisfactorily'). Thus, rather than determining how information is processed, the mood-as-input hypothesis states that mood provides information about whether the task has been successfully completed or not.

This type of account can be explained by describing a study conducted by Martin, Achee, Ward and Harlow (1993). They induced either positive or negative moods in their participants and asked them to generate a list of birds' names. Half of the participants were told to stop generating the names of birds when they no longer felt like doing it (a 'feel like continuing' stop rule), whereas the other half were asked to stop when they thought they had generated as many as they could (an 'as many as can' stop rule). They found that the effect of mood on the generation task was dependent on the stop rule that the participant was asked to use: for those using the 'feel like continuing' stop rule, participants in the positive mood persisted at the task for significantly longer than those in the negative mood. However, for participants using the 'as many as can' stop rule, participants in a negative mood persisted for significantly longer than those in the positive mood. Martin et al. (1993) interpret these effects in mood-as-input terms. For example, participants in a negative mood interpret their mood in relation to the stop rule: in the 'feel like continuing' condition their negative mood tells them to stop. In the 'as many as can' condition their negative mood tells them they are not satisfied with the number of items they have generated on the task, and so they persist at the task for longer.

Figure 13.1 provides a schematic representation of the predictions derived from mood-as-input hypothesis. This indicates that perseveration at a task will occur under two explicit conditions: (1) when the individual has deployed an 'as many as can' stop rule and is in a concurrent negative mood, or (2) when the individual has deployed a 'feel like continuing' stop rule and is in a concurrent positive mood.

This type of explanation can be applied fairly readily to worrying, and in particular to the perseverative worrying that is characteristic of the

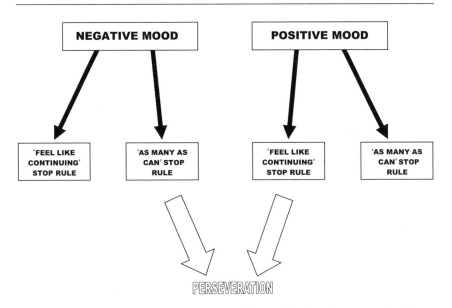

Figure 13.1   A schematic representation of the predictions from mood-as-input hypothesis. Perseveration at an open-ended activity can result from a configuration of either negative mood and 'as many as can' stop rules or positive mood and 'feel like continuing' stop rules

catastrophising of pathological worriers. For instance, worrying is an open-ended task that has no obvious or clear end point. This being the case, individuals commencing a worry bout will usually bring their own set of implicit stop rules to the task, and the individual will have to make some decisions during the course of the worry episode about whether to continue or to stop (depending on whether they feel their criteria for stopping have been met). Worrying is also an iterative task very similar to the tasks used by Martin and colleagues in their initial demonstration of mood-as-input effects. This suggests that the factors determining perseveration at an item generation task will also be relevant to worry perseveration.

When applied to catastrophic worrying, the mood-as-input hypothesis assumes that worriers are in a significantly more negative mood state than nonworriers, and that they use relatively stringent 'as many as can' stop rules for judging whether to terminate the catastrophising task (cf. Davey, Field & Startup, 2003; Startup & Davey, 2001). Thus, when catastrophising, worriers are continually asking themselves (either implicitly or explicitly) whether they have successfully dealt with the problem, but their negative mood provides them with information that they have not and this results in perseveration at the task. A look at Figure 13.1 indicates that there is another route to perseveration, but this is through the configuration of 'feel like continuing' stop rules and concurrent positive mood. It is highly unlikely that this is a configuration that is relevant to understanding the behaviour of pathological worriers, because such individuals are rarely in a positive mood at the outset of a worry bout, and they are not usually inclined to commence a worry bout using a rule that advises them to 'stop when they feel like it' (Davey, Startup, MacDonald, Jenkins & Paterson, 2004; Startup & Davey, 2001). For these reasons, we will concentrate on the mood-as-input prediction that perseveration at a catastrophising task in pathological worriers is determined by the deployment of 'as many as can' stop rules in the context of a concurrent negative mood.

Basic Research on Mood-as-Input and Pathological Worrying

The catastrophising interview procedure

Before investigating how various proximal variables interact to cause worry perseveration, we need to have a suitable measure of a worry bout that provides an objective estimate of its perseveration. To this end, we have normally adopted the catastrophising interview procedure as the relevant worry task on which to explore the effects of various experimental manipulations (see Chapter 10 for a fuller discussion of the catastrophising interview procedure). This task is an open-ended one which allows the participant to fully explore the worry topic, it has a structure which reflects the natural iterative style of worriers, and it provides an objective measure of perseveration in the form of the number of iterative steps that the individual is willing to elaborate before ending the bout.

The role of mood in catastrophic worrying

One obvious feature of pathological worriers is that they experience endemic negative mood which is normally at significantly higher levels than is experienced by nonworriers (Davey, Hampton, Farrell & Davidson, 1992; Metzger, Miller, Chen, Sofka & Borkovec, 1990; Meyer, Miller, Metzger & Borkovec, 1990), and this negative mood will often manifest itself as higher levels of both anxiety and depression. It is often tempting to view these higher levels of anxiety and depression as simply the outcomes of the disorder suffered by pathological worriers. If an individual cannot bring closure to worry bouts and is constantly bombarded by potential threats that actively need to be processed, then it is quite reasonable to suppose that anxiety is a natural product of this hypervigilant processing and depression the result of a perceived failure to control it. However, negative moods may be much more than just an experienced outcome of pathological worrying, and may actively contribute to the perseveration of that activity.

Our own experience of worry suggests that it seems to be an activity that we indulge in more frequently when we are feeling negative—for example, when we are tired, suffering aches and pains, having just had an unresolved argument, or simply when we are anxiously awaiting challenging events such as an interview or an examination. What is interesting about these occasions is that the causes of the negative emotions that seem to promote worrying are usually unrelated to the content of the worry. This can be illustrated in a study by Johnston and Davey (1997). In this study, participants were shown video clips of television news programmes edited to display positive-, neutral- or negative-valenced material. After viewing one of these edited bulletins, participants were then asked to catastrophise one of their current main worries. Those participants shown the negatively valenced news bulletin showed significant increases in both anxious and sad mood, and emitted significantly more steps in the catastrophising interview than participants in either the positive or neutral conditions. This occurred even though the content of their worry bout was entirely unrelated to the topic presented in the edited news bulletin they viewed. This and similar studies (e.g. Startup & Davey, 2001, 2003) demonstrate that negative mood has a *causal* effect on worry perseveration, and is not simply the experienced outcome of worrying.

So how does experienced negative mood cause the perseveration of worry bouts? One early explanation of this effect was in terms of mood congruency. That is, the negative mood being experienced may facilitate the access and retrieval of congruent negative information in memory (e.g. Vasey and Borkovec, 1992; Bower, 1981), and this negative information may be used to feed the iterative 'what if . . . ?' questioning style typical of worrying. However, there is evidence that is clearly contrary to a mood congruency explanation of this kind. First, Davey and Levy (1998, Study 4) found that chronic worriers would also perseverate for longer than nonworriers at a *positive* iteration task—even though they reported being in a significantly greater negative mood than nonworriers. A positive iterative task is where the participant is asked to iterate what it is that is positive or good about a situation or topic using the catastrophising interview procedure (sometimes known as the 'reversed catastrophising' procedure). These results appear to be difficult to interpret in mood congruency terms, because those participants in a more negative mood (chronic worriers) are persevering for longer iterating the positive features of a topic than are participants in a more positive mood (nonworriers).

Secondly, Startup and Davey (2001, Experiment 1) induced negative, positive and neutral moods in three groups of analogue, nonclinical

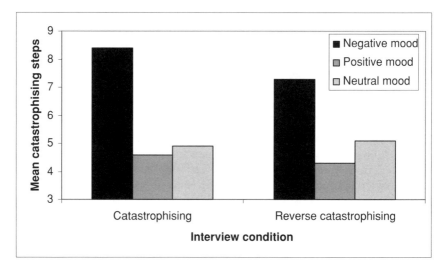

Figure 13.2   The mean number of catastrophising steps emitted by analogue non-clinical participants in either a negative, positive or neutral mood (left hand bars), and the mean number of 'reverse catastrophising' (positive iteration) steps emitted by analogue nonclinical participants in either a negative, positive or neutral mood Data taken from Startup, H.M. & Davey, G.C.L. (2001). Mood-As-Input and Catastrophic Worrying. *Journal of Abnormal Psychology*, **110(1)**, 83–96, Experiment 1.

participants. They then asked half the participants in each condition to catastrophise a worry, and the other half to 'reverse catastrophise' (to iterate what was *good* about a topic). The number of steps emitted in each condition is shown in Figure 13.2. The left-hand panel of the figure shows the conventional effect of negative mood on catastrophising, where participants in a negative mood emit more steps than those in either a positive or a neutral mood. However, the right hand panel shows the effect of the mood manipulation on the reverse catastrophising task. Perhaps surprisingly, those participants in a negative mood emitted significantly more steps on this positive iteration task than those in either a positive or a neutral mood. What these results imply is that negative mood causes perseveration at an iterative task *regardless of the valency* of that task. These findings are not at all easy to incorporate into a mood congruency explanation that claims that perseveration should be facilitated only when there is a congruency between the valency of the material being iterated and the mood under which the task is being conducted.

These findings seem to indicate that negative mood will generate perseveration at any open ended task, and that the valency of the task is not important. These findings are quite consistent with the mood-as-input account, which suggests that mood (1) is not simply an experienced outcome of psychopathology, (2) is not simply intrinsically linked to certain default processing strategies (such as mood congruency), but (3) acts as information which is interpreted in the context of the task.

The next section of this chapter looks at one of the important features of the task that determines how mood will be interpreted. This is the nature of the implicit 'stop rules' that individuals deploy at the outset of an open-ended task such as worrying.

The role of stop rules in catastrophic worrying

The item generation task conducted by Martin, Achee, Ward and Harlow (1993), and described on p. 220 of this chapter, shows how the perseverative effects of a concurrent mood can be influenced dramatically by the nature of the stop rules deployed at the outset of the task. If an individual is asked to undertake an item generation task using 'as many as can' stop rules (to do the task until they feel they have generated as many items as they can), then they persevere for significantly longer in a negative mood than in a positive mood. If, however, they are asked to undertake the task using an explicit 'feel like continuing' stop rule (to continue with the task until they feel like stopping), they persist for significantly longer if they are in a positive than in a negative mood. According to mood-as-input hypothesis, concurrent mood is used to judge whether the goals defined by the deployed stop rules have been met. In the case of an 'as many as can' stop rule, positive mood implies the strict achievement goals defined by the stop rule have been met (and the task should be terminated), whereas a negative mood implies they have not (and so the individual should persevere with the task). Using a 'feel like continuing' stop rule, negative mood implies the task is no longer enjoyable (and should be terminated), but a positive mood means it is enjoyable (and so should continue).

Given that we know that pathological worriers are normally in negative moods (at least compared to nonworriers), then we would only predict perseverative worrying in worriers if they are deploying rather strict 'as many as can' stop rules.

There is good evidence from a number of different sources to suggest that pathological worriers do indeed deploy strict 'as many as can' stop rules at the outset of a worry bout. For example, both pathological worriers and individuals diagnosed with GAD hold strong beliefs that worrying is a necessary process that must be undertaken fully and properly in order to avoid future catastrophes (Borkovec, Hazlett-Stevens & Diaz, 1999; Borkovec & Roemer, 1995; Breitholtz, Westling & Ost, 1998; Davey, Tallis & Capuzzo, 1996; Wells, 1995); they also possess elevated evidence requirements for decision making (Tallis, Eysenck & Mathews, 1991) that would indicate that they should explore all possibilities before terminating a worry bout. In addition, trait worry measures have been shown to be related to measures of perfectionism (Frost, Lahart & Rosenblate, 1990; Pratt, Tallis & Eysenck, 1997), feelings of responsibility for negative outcomes (Wells & Papageorgiou, 1998), intolerance of uncertainty (Dugas, Freeston & Ladouceur, 1997; Ladouceur, Talbot & Dugas, 1997), and inflated concerns over mistakes (Stober & Joorman, 2001). All of these dispositional attributes are ones that would indicate that worriers would be driven to deploy 'as many as can' stop rules at the outset of worrying in order to ensure that their worrying will meet the rather important goals that worriers require of it.

There is now some evidence that worriers do indeed deploy strict 'as many as can' stop rules at the outset of a worry bout—either implicitly or explicitly. Davey et al. (2005) developed a worry stop rule check list which allowed some assessment of the types of internal statements that individuals used to determine whether they should continue or abort their worry bout. These statements fell into two main types which corresponded reasonably well to either 'as many as can' stop rules or 'feel like continuing stop rules'. Examples of 'as many as can' stop rule statements include 'I feel I must focus on every conceivable solution to this worry' and 'I must sort out what is worrying me'. Examples of 'feel like continuing' stop rule statements include 'I just don't feel like worrying about this for much longer' and 'I feel it is rather pointless to continue worrying for much longer'. Davey et al. (2005) conducted two studies in which they investigated (1) the extent to which the endorsement of 'as many as can' stop rules was related to trait measures associated with chronic worrying, and (2) the extent to which the use of 'as many as can' stop rules was related to perseveration in a catastrophising interview task.

The results of the first study indicated that scores on the 'as many as can' stop rule sub-scale were highly correlated with a variety of worry-relevant variables, including measures of trait worry (PSWQ), beliefs about both the positive and negative consequences of worrying (as measured by the Consequences of Worry Scale—Davey, Tallis & Capuzzo, 1996), and measures of shame and guilt. Scores on the 'feel like continuing' stop rule sub-scale were unrelated to any of the predictor variables investigated. These findings suggest that the deployment of 'as many as can' stop rules is significantly related to worry frequency. They also suggest that 'feel like continuing' stop rules are entirely unrelated to measures of worry frequency, and appear to be orthogonal to, rather than on the same dimension as, 'as many as can' stop rules. A subsequent regression analysis indicated that, although the use of 'as many as can' stop rules is best predicted by PSWQ scores, scores on both the negative and positive scales of the Consequences of Worry Scale (COWS) independently predicted additional variance in stop rule scores. This suggests that the stop rules used by worriers may be closely linked to, or derived from, the more stable, global beliefs that worriers have about the nature of worrying. This in turn suggests that 'as many as can' stop rule measures are not just another measure of worry frequency and intensity (because sub-scales of the COWS predict additional variance in stop rule scores over and above measures of worry frequency), but are probably derived from other meta-cognitive constructs that maintain beliefs in the need to worry (e.g. Davey, Tallis & Capuzzo, 1996; Wells, 1995).

The second study conducted by Davey et al. (2005) found that the reported use of 'as many as can' stop rules was significantly related to perseveration in a worry catastrophising task (as measured by the number of catastrophising steps emitted in a catastrophising interview procedure). In fact, scores on the 'as many as can' stop rule sub-scale were a better predictor of catastrophising perseveration than measures of trait worry (PSWQ), trait anxiety (measured by the STAI Y-2), or measures of state mood taken prior to catastrophising.

These studies clearly indicate that ' as many as can' stop rules are used by chronic worriers, they appear to be related to beliefs about the important functions that the worry process serves, and their reported usage is associated with perseveration on a catastrophising task. They certainly indicate that the deployment of 'as many as can' stop rules is significantly related to worry traits, worry frequency and worry perseveration—but do they exert a *causal* influence on worry perseveration?

If it is the deployment of 'as many as can' stop rules at the outset of a worry bout that contributes significantly to the perseveration observed in worriers, then we should be able to manipulate perseveration in the worrier simply by manipulating their use of stop rules. This was demonstrated in an experiment by Startup and Davey (2001, Experiment 3).

Startup and Davey (2001) compared worriers and nonworriers on a catastrophising task when they were explicitly asked to use either an 'as many as can' stop rule or a 'feel like continuing' stop rule. They found that manipulating the deployed stop rule had differential effects for worriers and nonworriers. Asking participants to use an 'as many as can' stop rule resulted in worriers generating significantly more catastrophising steps than nonworriers. However, when participants were asked to use a 'feel like continuing' stop rule, worriers emitted slightly fewer steps than nonworriers (see Figure 13.3). These findings have some important implications. First, they suggest that worriers do not have a perseverative iterative style that is independent of the stop rules they deploy (Davey & Levy, 1998; Kendall & Ingram, 1987). Secondly, they suggest that the nature of the stop rules deployed does have a causal influence on perseveration. Interestingly, in this

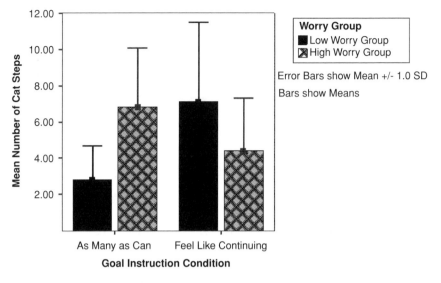

Figure 13.3   Mean number of catastrophising steps emitted by high worriers (hatched bars) and low worriers (black bars) following an instruction to use either 'as many as can' or 'feel like continuing' stop rules
After Startup, H.M. & Davey, G.C.L. (2001). Mood-As-Input and Catastrophic Worrying. *Journal of Abnormal Psychology*, **110(1)**, 83–96, Experiment 3.

study, worriers and nonworriers differed significantly on mood measures prior to catastrophising—worriers were significantly more depressed, and there was a trend towards them also being more anxious. This can explain the pattern of perseveration found in Figure 13.3. Under 'as many as can' stop rules, the higher levels of negative mood experienced by worriers will tend them to persist with the task compared with nonworriers. However, when using a 'feel like continuing' stop rule, their higher levels of negative mood will tend them towards stopping sooner than nonworriers.

If worrying is an important problem-solving activity for all those who indulge in it (e.g. Davey, 1994), then it is likely that both worriers and nonworriers will deploy 'as many as can' stop rules when they worry. This is supported by the fact that Davey et al. (2005) found significant correlations between the use of 'as many as can' stop rules and worry frequency across a nonselected participant sample, but no relationship at all between 'feel like continuing' stop rules and worry frequency. The way in which worriers and nonworriers differ in their stop rule use may not be in the qualitative type of stop rule they deploy, but in the strictness with which they deploy 'as many as can' stop rules. This appears to be supported by the fact that worriers possess elevated evidence requirements (Tallis, Eysenck & Mathews, 1991), and higher levels of perfectionism (Frost, Marten, Lahart & Rosenblate,

1990; Pratt, Tallis & Eysenck, 1997) and intolerance of uncertainty (Dugas, Freeston & Ladouceur, 1997) than nonworriers.

Startup and Davey (2003) reported the results of two studies designed to investigate whether worriers possess characteristics that would contribute to the use of relatively strict 'as many as can' stop rules for catastrophic worrying. Experiment 1 indicated that worriers began a catastrophising interview with higher self-reported levels of responsibility towards fully considering all the issues involved than did nonworriers. This elevated sense of responsibility persisted throughout the catastrophising process, and was associated with the generation of significantly more catastrophising steps. In Experiment 2, Startup and Davey asked nonselected, nonclinical participants to catastrophise a hypothetical worry about a friend who suffered from dyslexia. They manipulated responsibility levels at the outset of catastrophising by telling half of the participants that the content of their catastrophising might be used in a booklet to help people with dyslexia (high responsibility condition), the remaining participants were told their responses had no real importance beyond the purpose of the experiment (low responsibility group). Also prior to the catastrophising interview, participants were subjected to either a negative, positive or neutral mood induction. Figure 13.4 illustrates the pattern of perseveration at the

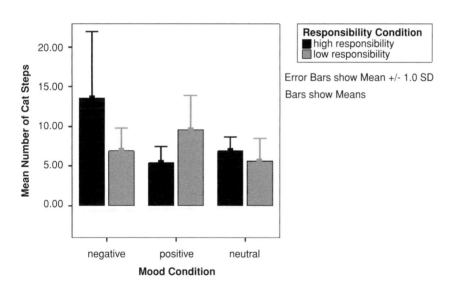

Figure 13.4   Mean number of catastrophising steps for participants in either a high responsibility condition (black bars) or a low responsibility condition (grey bars) following either negative, positive, or neutral mood induction
After Startup, H.M. & Davey, G.C.L (2003). Inflated responsibility and the use of stop rules for catastrophic worrying. *Behaviour Research and Therapy*, **41**, 495–503, Experiment 2.

catastrophising task across all six conditions. This indicates that elevated levels of responsibility did indeed have a facilitative causal effect on perseveration, but only in participants that were in a concurrent negative mood. The reverse pattern of findings in participants in a positive mood indicates that responsibility or strictness of 'as many as can' stop rules does not fuel perseveration independently of mood valency, and that whether stop rule goals have been achieved are interpreted in the context of the information supplied by the valency of the individual's concurrent mood.

So far, we have talked of stop rules and mood being relatively independent contributors to the process that generates perseveration. However, we do have to consider the possibility that mood and stop rule may not be entirely independent of each other. For example, there is indirect evidence to suggest that mood may influence the kinds of stop rules an individual deploys, and the strictness with which they evaluate whether stop rule goals have been met. Negative mood has a number of important effects on information processing and goal-setting which suggest that negative mood is likely to facilitate the deployment of 'as many as can' stop rules. First, negative mood induces comparatively higher performance standards than positive or neutral mood (Scott & Cervone, 2002), causing individuals to become relatively dissatisfied with any given level of imagined performance (Cervone, Kopp, Schaumann & Scott, 1994). Negative mood also promotes a more systematic and deliberate information-processing style than positive or neutral mood (Ambady & Gray, 2002; Batra & Stayman, 1990; Tiedens & Linton, 2001), which is also likely to facilitate the deployment of 'as many as can' stop rules which define rather strict criteria for goal attainment. This being the case, it is likely that the worrier's endemic negative mood will not only provide negative information about the attainment of goals during the worry bout, but it will also define more stringent goals for closure by raising performance standards and facilitating the systematic processing of information relevant to the worry.

The Mood-as-Input Model of Pathological Worrying

The model

Figure 13.5 provides a schematic illustration of the important factors that a mood-as-input account predicts will affect the perseveration of a worry bout. This model supposes that pathological worriers bring a negative mood to the worry bout and at the outset either explicitly or implicitly deploy strict 'as many as can' stop rules. They then continually use their concurrent mood as information to determine whether the strict stop rule-defined goals of the worry bout have been met. Since this concurrent mood is inherently negative, this implies that the goals have not been met and

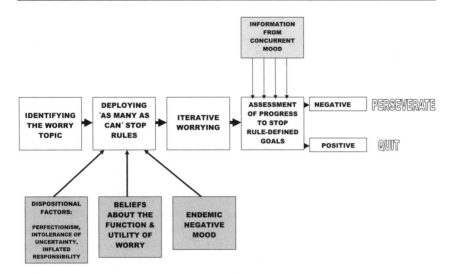

Figure 13.5   A schematic illustration of the important factors that a mood-as-input account predicts will affect the perseveration of a worry bout. See text for further elaboration

that the individual should persevere with the worry bout. The grey boxes indicate factors which probably contribute to the deployment of strict 'as many as can' stop rules, and these include dispositional factors such as perfectionism and intolerance of uncertainty, both of which have been shown to be highly associated with pathological worrying (Dugas, Freeston & Ladouceur, 1997; Frost, Marten, Lahart & Rosenblate, 1990; Pratt, Tallis & Eysenck, 1997; Stober & Joorman, 2001) and which imply that any goals for the worry bout should be sufficient to eliminate uncertainty and to achieve the best possible solution prior to closure. These factors also include the global beliefs developed by worriers that worrying is an essential and useful activity that needs to be undertaken in order to avoid future catastrophes (Borkovec, Hazlett-Stevens & Diaz, 1999; Borkovec & Roemer, 1995; Davey, Tallis & Capuzzo, 1996; Wells, 1995). Such ingrained metacognitions will not only determine that worrying should be undertaken on a regular basis, but that a worry bout should continue until effective solutions are defined or threats and problems are eliminated. This will require the setting of relatively strict 'as many as can' stop rules.

Predictions from the model

The mood-as-input model makes a number of testable predictions about perseverative worrying, many of which have been discussed at p. 220–221. The most obvious prediction is that perseverative worrying will occur in worriers following the deployment of 'as many as can' stop rules while in a concurrent negative mood.[1] However, more interestingly, the hypothesis also predicts that perseveration will only occur when *both* these factors are present. Perseveration will not necessarily occur when 'as many as can' stop rules are deployed in the absence of a negative mood, and negative mood will not generate perseveration unless the goals of worrying are implicitly or explicitly defined by 'as many as can' stop rules. These predictions have been upheld in laboratory-based studies that have manipulated one or both of these factors (Startup & Davey, 2001, 2003). This implies that dispositional factors which may determine the deployment of 'as many as can' stop rules—such as perfectionism, intolerance of uncertainty, inflated responsibility, etc.—will only generate perseverative worrying when a concurrent negative mood is present. This, of course, has implications for those models of perseverative psychopathologies that stress the importance of these dispositional constructs (e.g. Dugas, Gagnon, Ladouceur & Freeston, 1998; Salkovskis, Wroe, Gledhill, Morrison, Forrester, Richards, Reynolds & Thorpe, 2000; Shafran & Mansell, 2001), and such models will need to take into account that these constructs depend on the presence of negative mood for their explanatory effectiveness.

A further implication of the mood-as-input hypothesis is that worriers do not have an inherent iterative style or dispositional characteristic that generates perseverative worrying or catastrophising. It is a combination of their deployed stop rule and their negative mood that generates perseveration and catastrophising. To this extent, worriers can be turned into nonworriers and vice versa (at least in the laboratory!) by manipulating stop rules and moods, and this has been demonstrated in at least one study (Startup & Davey, 2001, Experiment 3—see Figure 13.3). This has some very clear ramifications for the treatment of pathological or catastrophic worrying. Either attempting to change the mood state under which worrying occurs, or the nature of the 'as many as can' stop rules normally deployed by worriers should have ameliorative effects on perseveration.

Some critical issues for mood-as-input explanations
of pathological worrying

While most of the experimental data appear to support mood-as-input hypothesis as an explanation of perseverative or catastrophic worrying, there are still some critical issues surrounding the mood-as-input account that need to be resolved.

---

[1] The mood-as-input hypothesis also predicts that perseveration will occur following the deployment of 'feel like continuing' stop rules in a concurrent positive mood, but as we discussed earlier in this chapter, this is a configuration that has no natural relevance to anxious psychopathology.

First, most of the research on mood-as-input and worrying has been carried out on nonclinical analogue populations. We now need to extend the predictions of the mood-as-input hypothesis to clinical populations. In particular, the need to identify whether individuals diagnosed with GAD deploy 'as many as can' stop rules when worrying, and whether manipulating their stop rules and mood will influence worry perseveration in ways predicted by the model.

Second, most research on mood-as-input and worrying describes results that are consistent with predictions from the model (Davey et al., 2005; Startup & Davey, 2001, 2003) – but there is no independent evidence yet available that individuals are actually using their concurrent mood as information when assessing the progress of their worry bout. Such evidence is needed in order to confirm that the mood-as-input process actually exists and operates in the way that the model says it does. In addition, we need to be sure that other cognitive or psychological processes that do not allude to mood being used as information cannot explain findings consistent with mood-as-input predictions.

Third, if the valency of a mood is used as information to assess the progress of a worry bout, do all similar valenced moods have the same informational effect? For example, is anxious mood comparable in information value to sad mood, or even angry mood? All are negative moods, but does each convey slightly different information about the worry process and its goals (e.g. George & Zhou, 2002; Raghunathan & Pham, 1999)?

Fourth, is the mood-as-input process more important at some stages rather than others in the aetiology of pathological worrying? It is interesting that many anxiety-based disorders begin to develop during periods of severe stress in an individual's life (Barlow, 2002), and the nature of the disorder is often unrelated to the specific nature of the stressor. If an individual suffering a stressful life episode (and as a result experiencing negative affect) also possesses dispositional characteristics which might give rise to the deployment of 'as many as can' stop rules while problem-solving, worrying, ruminating etc., then the conditions are suitable for the perseveration of these activities. In this way, mood-as-input processes may play a significant role in the development of a perseverative psychopathology such as pathological worrying.

There are still many features of worrying, and in particular catastrophic worrying that the mood-as-input model does not immediately address. For example, (1) what causes themes of personal inadequacy to constantly intrude into the catastrophising sequences of worriers, and do these intrusions contribute to perseveration (Davey & Levy, 1998)? (2) Most pathological worriers do eventually end a worry bout, but what leads them to do this? Has their mood changed from negative to positive, have they abandoned their 'as many as can' stop rules for 'feel like continuing' stop rules, or has some other process intervened to end the bout? All we know at present is that mood-as-input processes appear to contribute to perseveration, but this does not obviously explain why worriers actually end the bout. (3) Worriers appear to experience more and more emotional discomfort as their catastrophising progresses (Vasey & Borkovec, 1992), and this would suggest that the increasing levels of negative mood should be interpreted as stronger and stronger evidence to continue worrying. This appears to be contrary to mood-as-input predictions because, although worriers appear to have persevered with the bout for longer than nonworriers, negative mood is apparently at its strongest at the point when the worrier abandons the bout.

In summary, it is highly unlikely that the mood-as-input hypothesis will describe all of the processes involved in beginning and ending a bout of perseverative worrying in a pathological worrier. However, it does begin to help understand the factors that contribute to perseveration at the proximal level, and it provides clear and testable predictions that can serve as the basis for future research into a range of perseverative psychopathologies, including pathological worrying.

SUMMARY

This chapter has described the mood-as-input hypothesis and its contribution to our understanding of some of the processes that generate perseverative and catastrophic worrying. It is a model that attempts to explain pathological worrying at the proximal level of the individual worry bout, and the experimental evidence described in this chapter is generally supportive of predictions derived from the model. The model now needs to be extended to clinical populations with perseverative psychopathologies, and research needs to focus on collecting evidence describing how individuals evolve the types of stop rule they deploy during their perseverative activities and how they may use various negative moods as information.

REFERENCES

Ambady, N. & Gray, H.M. (2002). On being sad and mistaken: Mood effects on the accuracy of thin-slice judgments. *Journal of Personality & Individual Differences*, **83**, 947–961.

American Psychiatric Association (1980). *Diagnostic and statistical manual of mental disorders*. Washington.

Andrews, G., Stewart, G., Morris-Yates, A., Holt, P. & Henderson, S. (1990). Evidence for a general neurotic syndrome. *British Journal of Psychiatry*, **157**, 6–12.

Barlow, D.H. (2002). *Anxiety and its disorders*. New York: Guilford.

Batra, R. & Stayman, D.M. (1990). The role of mood in advertising effectiveness. *Journal of Consumer Research*, **17**, 203–214.

Borkovec, T.D. (1994). The nature, functions and origins of worry. In G.C.L. Davey & F. Tallis (Eds), *Worrying: Perspectives on theory, assessment and treatment* (pp. 5–33). Chichester, UK: John Wiley & Sons, Ltd.

Borkovec, T.D., Hazlett-Stevens, H. & Diaz, M.L. (1999). The role of positive beliefs about worry in generalized anxiety disorder and its treatment. *Clinical Psychology & Psychotherapy*, **6**, 126–138.

Borkovec, T.D. & Lyonfields, J.D. (1993). Worry: Thought suppression of emotional processing. In H. Krohne (Ed.) *Vigilance and avoidance*. Toronto: Hogrefe and Huber Publishers.

Borkovec, T.D. & Roemer, L. (1995). Perceived functions of worry among generalized anxiety disorder subjects: Distraction from more emotionally distressing topics. *Journal of Behavior Therapy & Experimental Psychiatry*, **26**, 25–30.

Bower, G.H. (1981). Mood and memory. *American Psychologist*, **36**, 129–148.

Breitholtz, E., Westling, B.E. & Ost, L.-G. (1998). Cognitions in generalized anxiety disorder and panic disorder patients. *Journal of Anxiety Disorders*, **12**, 567–577.

Brown, T.A., Dowdall, D.J., Cote, G. & Barlow, D.H. (1994). Worry and obsessions: The distinction between generalized anxiety disorder and obsessive–compulsive disorder. In G.C.L. Davey & F. Tallis (Eds) *Worrying: Perspectives on theory, assessment and treatment*. Chichester, UK: John Wiley & Sons, Ltd.

Butler, G., Fennell, M., Robson, P. & Gelder, M. (1991). A comparison of behavior therapy and cognitive behavior therapy in the treatment of generalized anxiety disorder. *Journal of Consulting & Clinical Psychology*, **59**, 167–175.

Cervone, D., Kopp, D.A., Schaumann, L. & Scott, W.D. (1994). Mood, self-efficacy, and performance standards: Lower moods induce higher standards for performance. *Journal of Personality & Social Psychology*, **67**, 499–512.

Davey, G.C.L. (1994). Pathological worrying as exacerbated problem solving. In G.C.L. Davey & F. Tallis (Eds), *Worrying: Perspectives on theory, assessment and treatment*. Chichester, UK: John Wiley & Sons Ltd.

Davey, G.C.L. (2003). Doing clinical psychology research: What is interesting isn't always useful. *The Psychologist*, **16**, 412–416.

Davey, G.C.L., Field, A.P. & Startup, H.M. (2003). Repetitive and iterative thinking in psychopathology: Anxiety-inducing consequences and a mood-as-input mechanism. In R. Menzies and P. de Silva (Eds) *Obsessive-compulsive disorder: Theory, research and treatment*. Chichester, UK: John Wiley & Sons, Ltd.

Davey, G.C.L., Hampton, J., Farrell, J.J. & Davidson, S. (1992). Some characteristics of worry: Evidence for worrying and anxiety as separate constructs. *Personality and Individual Differences*, **13**, 133–147.

Davey, G.C.L. & Levy, S. (1998). Catastrophic worrying: personal inadequacy and a perseverative iterative style as features of the catastrophising process. *Journal of Abnormal Psychology*, **107**, 576–586.

Davey, G.C.L., Startup, H.M., MacDonald, C.B., Jenkins, D. & Paterson, K. (2004). The use of 'as many as can' versus 'feel like continuing' stop rules during worrying. *Cognitive Therapy and Research*, **29**, 155–169.

Davey, G.C.L, Tallis, F. & Capuzzo, N. (1996). Beliefs about the consequences of worrying. *Cognitive Therapy and Research*, **20**, 499–520.

Dugas, M.J., Freeston, M.H. & Ladouceur, R. (1997). Intolerance of uncertainty and problem orientation in worry. *Cognitive Therapy and Research*, **21**, 593–606.

Dugas, M.J., Gagnon, F., Ladouceur, R. & Freeston, M.H. (1998). Generalized anxiety disorder: A preliminary test of a conceptual model. *Behaviour Research and Therapy*, **36**, 215–226.

Frijda, N.H. (1988). The laws of emotion. *American Psychologist*, **43**, 349–358.

Frost, R.O., Marten, P., Lahart, C. & Rosenblate, R. (1990). The dimensions of perfectionism. *Cognitive Therapy and Research*, **14**, 449–468.

George, J.M. & Zhou, J. (2002). Understanding when bad moods foster creativity and good ones don't: The role of context and clarity of feelings. *Journal of Applied Psychology*, **87**, 687–697.

Hirt, E.R., Melton, R.J., McDonald, H.E., Harackiewicz, J.M. (1996). Processing goals, task interest, and the mood-performance relationship: a mediational analysis. *Journal of Personality and Social Psychology*, **71**, 245–261.

Johnston, W.M. & Davey, G.C.L. (1997). The psychological impact of negative TV news bulletins: The catastrophising of personal worries. *British Journal of Psychology*, **88**, 85–91.

Kendall, P.C. & Ingram, R.E. (1987). The future for cognitive assessment of anxiety: Let's get specific. In L. Michaelson & L.M. Ascher (Eds) *Anxiety and stress disorders: Cognitive-behavioral assessment and treatment*. New York: Guilford Press.

Ladouceur, R., Talbot, F. & Dugas, M.J. (1997). Behavioral expressions of intolerance of uncertainty in worry: Experimental findings. *Behavior Modification*, **21**, 355–371.

Martin, L.L & Davies, B. (1998). Beyond hedonism and associationism: A configural view of the role of affect in evaluation, processing, and self-regulation. *Motivation and Emotional*, **22**, 33–51.

Martin, L.L., Ward, D.W, Achee, J.W & Wyer, R.S. (1993). Mood as input: People have to interpret the motivational implications of their moods. *Journal of Personality and Social Psychology*, **63**, 317–326.

Metzger, R.L., Miller, M.L., Cohen, M., Sofka, M. & Borkovec, T.D. (1990). Worry changes decision making: The effect of negative thoughts on cognitive processing. *Journal of Clinical Psychology*, **48**, 76–88.

Meyer, T.J., Miller, M.L., Metzger, R.L. & Borkovec, T.D. (1990). Development and validation of the Penn State Worry Questionnaire. *Behaviour Research and Therapy*, **28**, 487–495.

Nolen-Hoeksema, S. & Morrow, J. (1993). Effects of rumination and distraction on naturally occurring depressed mood. *Cognition and Emotion*, **7(6)**, 561–570.

Parkin, R. (1997). Obsessive-compulsive disorder in adults. *International Review of Psychiatry*, **9**, 73–81.

Pratt, P., Tallis, F. & Eysenck, M. (1997). Information-processing, storage characteristics and worry. *Behaviour Research and Therapy*, **35**, 1015–1023.

Raghunathan, R. & Pham, M.T. (1999). All negative moods are not equal: Motivational influences of anxiety and sadness on decision making. *Organizational Behavior and Human Decision Making*, **79**, 56–77.

Roemer, L., Molina, S. & Borkovec, T.D. (1997). An investigation of worry content among generally anxious individuals. *Journal of Nervous and Mental Disease*, **185**, 314–319.

Salkovskis, P.M., Wroe, A.L., Gledhill, A., Morrison, N., Forrester, E., Richards, C., Reynolds, M. & Thorpe, S. (2000). Responsibility attitudes and interpretations are characteristic of obsessive compulsive disorder. *Behaviour Research and Therapy*, **38**, 347–372.

Sanna, C.J., Turley, K.J. & Mark, M.M. (1996). Expected evaluation, goals, and performance: Mood as input. *Personality and Social Psychology Bulletin*, **22**, 323–335.

Schwarz, N. & Bless, H. (1991). Happy and mindless, but sad and smart? The impact of affective states on analytic reasoning. In J. Forgas (Ed.) *Emotion and Social Judgements*, pp. 55–71. London: Pergamon.

Scott, W.D. & Cervone, D. (2002). The impact of negative affect on performance standards: Evidence for an affect-as-information mechanism. *Cognitive Therapy and Research*, **26**, 19–37.

Shafran, R. & Mansell, W. (2001). Perfectionism and psychopathology: A review of research and treatment. *Clinical Psychology Review*, **21**, 879–906.

Startup, H.M. & Davey, G.C.L. (2001). Mood-as-input and catastrophic worrying. *Journal of Abnormal Psychology*, **110(1)**, 83–96.

Startup, H.M. & Davey, G.C.L. (2003). Inflated responsibility and the use of stop rules for catastrophic worrying. *Behaviour Research and Therapy*, **41**, 495–503.

Stober, J. & Joormann, J. (2001). Worry, procrastination, and perfectionism: Differentiating amount of worry, pathological worry, anxiety, and depression. *Cognitive Therapy and Research*, **25**, 49–60.

Tallis, F., Eysenck, M.W. & Mathews, A. (1991). Elevated evidence requirements and worry. *Personality and Individual Differences*, **12**, 505–520.

Tiedens, L.Z. & Linton, S. (2001). Judgment under emotional certainty and uncertainty: The effects of specific emotions on information processing. *Journal of Personality and Social Psychology*, **81**, 973–988.

Vasey, M. & Borkovec, T.D. (1992). A catastrophising assessment of worrisome thoughts. *Cognitive Therapy and Research*, **16**, 505–520.

Wells, A. (1995). Meta-cognition and worry: A cognitive model of generalized anxiety disorder. *Behavioural and Cognitive Psychotherapy*, **23**, 301–320.

Wells, A. & Hackman, A. (1993). Imagery and core belief in health anxiety: content and origins. *Behavioural and Cognitive Psychotherapy*, **21**, 265–273.

Wells, A. & Papageorgiou, C. (1998). Relationships between worry, obsessive-compulsive symptoms and meta-cognitive beliefs. *Behaviour Research and Therapy*, **36**, 899–913.

Chapter 14

THE COGNITIVE AVOIDANCE THEORY OF WORRY

Nicholas J. Sibrava and T.D. Borkovec

When we began experimental research on worry, we defined the process as "a chain of thoughts and images, negatively affect-laden and relatively uncontrollable; it represents an attempt to engage in mental problem-solving on an issue whose outcome is uncertain but contains the possibility of one or more negative outcomes; consequently, worry relates closely to the fear process" (Borkovec, Robinson, Pruzinsky & DePree, 1983, p. 10). Since then, much has been learned about worry and its severe clinical manifestation in generalized anxiety disorder (GAD), leading to refinements in the ways we see and understand chronic worrying. The present chapter reviews much of the basic research on the nature, functions, and origins of worry as that research bears on an early theoretical view of this process, the cognitive avoidance model of worry.

From clinical experience in treating GAD for two decades and from the basic research literature, we would summarize the central cognition of GAD as, "The world is potentially dangerous and I may not be able to cope with whatever comes from the future, so I must anticipate all bad things that might happen so that I can avoid them or prepare for them." As an important cognitive feature of human anxiety and like all anxious responding, the trigger of worrisome activity is the perception of threat. When humans perceive threat, they naturally engage in activities to eliminate it. Mowrer's (1947) two-stage learning theory of fear and avoidance posited that we become fearful of things that have been associated with punishment (classical aversive conditioning), and we are negatively reinforced for emitting behaviors that remove us from the experience of the fear and from the conditional stimuli that elicited the conditional fear (operant conditioning). The result is the preservation of anxious meanings associated with the conditional stimuli, because avoidance precludes repeated exposures to those stimuli that are necessary for extinction. This learning

Worry and Its Psychological Disorders: Theory, Assessment and Treatment. Edited by G. C. L. Davey and A. Wells. © 2006 John Wiley & Sons, Ltd.

model served as a foundation for the evolution of exposure therapies for many anxiety disorders, and it served as the starting point for our attempts to understand worry. We were curious about whether this cognitive process might function as a negatively reinforced avoidance response to threat detection. Early findings (Borkovec et al., 1983; Pruzinsky & Borkovec, 1990) that worry, like fear, incubates (i.e., moderate durations of worrying result in an increase in negative thought intrusions) encouraged this speculation.

Our field has long known that cognitive processes can serve anxiety-maintaining avoidant functions. For example, images containing avoidance responses to phobic-hierarchy scenes can eliminate extinction or even cause increases in anxious meanings associated with the phobic stimulus (Grayson & Borkovec, 1978; Borkovec, 1972; 1974). From a James-Lange position (Fehr & Stern, 1970), this makes sense: How we respond to a stimulus contributes to the future meaning of that stimulus. Indeed, if we suppress even a neutral thought, that thought acquires anxious meaning ("I suppress it; therefore, it must be dangerous.") (Roemer & Borkovec, 1994). Thus, worry in response to internal or external cues will result in increases in that cue's threatening meaning.

THE PRIMARY AVOIDANT FUNCTION OF WORRY

The most fundamental way in which worry is a cognitive avoidance response resides in the following facts. Worrying focuses on possible, but nonexistent, future bad things that might happen. Furthermore, people have little control over many of the things about which they worry. Because the perceived danger does not now exist and because no effective fight-or-flight response exists to avoid the threat, humans are left with only mental attempts to solve the problem.

This psychological circumstance is reflected in what we know about the psychophysiological state of GAD clients and the causal effects of acute worry on psychophysiology. People suffering from GAD display increased muscle tension at rest and in response to challenge or threat, but other peripheral physiology does not show activation different from normals (Hoehn-Saric & McLeod, 1990; Hoehn-Saric, McLeod & Zimmerli, 1989). They do display, however, a reduction in the range of variability of cardiovascular and skin conductance activity relative to controls. Hoehn-Saric concluded that GAD clients are characterized by autonomic inflexibility and the inhibition of sympathetic activation. Later research showed that these effects may be due to chronic parasympathetic deficiency and the causal ability of acute worrying to suppress parasympathetic tone (Thayer, Friedman & Borkovec, 1996; Lyonfields, Borkovec

& Thayer, 1995). However, this effect may be limited to people suffering from GAD, given that high worriers who do not meet GAD criteria do not always show vagal deficiency (Davis, Montgomery & Wilson, 2002). Several observations follow from these effects. First, they likely somatically reflect the psychological state that worry creates among GAD individuals: Without an available fight-or-flight response, the default evolutionary defensive response is a freezing response (increased muscle tension and reduced variability) (Gray, 1987). This phenomenon may also relate to frequent reports of procrastination among GAD clients and laboratory-demonstrated effects of both chronic worry status and acute worry inductions on delayed reaction times when making decisions (Metzger, Miller, Cohen, Sofka & Borkovec, 1990; Tallis, Eysenck & Mathews, 1991). Second, this psychophysiology is the likely foundation for DSM-IV changes (American Psychiatric Association, 1994) in the associated symptoms necessary for diagnosing GAD: Nearly all of the DSM-III-R (American Psychiatric Association, 1987) symptoms deleted from DSM-IV are mediated by the autonomic nervous system. The empirical reason for this was that those symptoms were not being reported by most with GAD (Marten, Brown, Barlow, Borkovec, Shear & Lydiard, 1993). These symptoms are likely not reported because clients notice little variability and thus would have difficulty detecting them. The remaining symptoms (restless or keyed up or on edge, easily fatigued, difficulty concentrating, irritability, sleep disturbance, and muscle tension) are mediated primarily by the central nervous system (see also Noyes, Woodman, Garvey, Cook, Suelzer, Clancy & Anderson, 1992). Third, laboratory manipulations known to suppress parasympathetic tone (isometric grip tasks, recall of past aversive events, anticipation of a threat, and mental arithmetic tasks; Grossman, Stemmler & Meinhardt, 1990) reflect the chronic state of GAD. Fourth, decreased parasympathetic tone is associated with poor attentional control and predicts poor development of pro-social behavior in children (Porges, 1992). Consequently, pervasive attentional bias to threat found to be characteristic of GAD (MacLeod, Campbell, Rutherford & Wilson, 2004) and rigidity and nonadaptiveness in their interpersonal relationships (discussed later) may be grounded in their distinctive psychophysiology. Finally, Thayer, Friedman, Borkovec, Johnsen & Molina (2000) showed that many physiological characteristics of GAD, including the development of orienting responses to neutral stimuli paired with aversive words, provide a reasonable foundation for understanding their attentional proclivities, hypervigilance, and rapid avoidance of threat cues.

As long as we perceive danger, we mentally continue to search for ways to avoid it or prepare ourselves to cope with it, should we be unable to avoid it. This is an evolutionarily understandable response: The mind returns to problems not yet solved: it forgets problems that have been solved

(Zeigarnik, 1927). Given this reasonableness of worry, the most significant question is not why people worry, but why some people perceive so much threat and/or feel that they may not cope with feared events that might happen.

Beyond this most basic reason for viewing worry as cognitive avoidance, research suggests that worry also plays additional avoidant functions. Before describing these, we describe what is known about the nature of worry.

THE NATURE OF WORRY

Phenomenologically, worry involves mostly verbal-linguistic thought. When we worry, we are talking to ourselves. Mentation sampling (e.g., Borkovec & Inz, 1990; Freeston, Dugas & Ladouceur, 1996) indicates that control participants report mostly (and positively valenced) imagery during relaxation, whereas GAD clients report greater, negatively valenced thought, and their thought/imagery ratios normalize after psychotherapy. Furthermore, worry increases the amount of thinking even in the nonanxious people. Apparently, the predominance of thought in worry is not just subjective: Brain wave recordings show that worry and GAD are both associated with increased left-hemisphere frontal beta activation (Borkovec, Ray & Stöber, 1998; Carter, Johnson & Borkovec, 1986).

This is not to say that images are not also occurring during worry. Thinking about worrisome topics no doubt primes brief images of possible bad things that may happen, providing further perceptions of threat and motivation to shift to thinking to reduce the affective and physiological effects of those images, as described later. Moreover, as Stöber (1998) pointed out, Paivio's (1986) dual-coding account of mental activity indicates that thoughts and images can occur in parallel. Either human beings do not attend much to periodic catastrophic images during worry, or their occurrence merely further motivates thought-based cognitive avoidance (i.e., thinking about how to avoid the image-represented, possible bad events). Research on imagery suggests where in the imagery process this occurs. A created image fades unless a refresher mechanism is engaged to keep that image in mind (Kosslyn, 1983). In this model, worry would preclude the engagement of the refresher mechanism. Recent support for the avoidance of aversive imagery among high versus low worriers was reported by Laguna, Ham, Hope and Bell (2004). Their dichotic listening task presented worry or neutral imagery scripts to the attended ear and neutral words to the unattended ear. Worriers recalled a greater number of unattended neutral words during the worry scripts, indicating that they were actively avoiding the worry script content.

The distinction between thought and imagery is fundamental to additional elements of the cognitive avoidance theory. Imagery is closely connected to efferent command into affect, physiology, and behavior, whereas thought is not. Imagining an emotional scene will produce a strong physiological response and a pattern of physiological responding (and affect) very similar to what occurs in the actual event; verbally articulating a description of the same scene mentally, however, elicits very little physiological response (Vrana, Cuthbert & Lang, 1986). The evolutionary reason for little connection between thought and efferent command is self-evident: If every thought was immediately expressed in behavior, thinking would lose its adaptive value for freely experimenting with possible choices and thinking through their consequences before acting. The fundamental problem of this characteristic for anxiety disorders in general and GAD in particular is this: If anxiety must be fully emotionally processed for change to occur, as Foa and Kozak (1986) argued in their account of exposure therapy and extinction, then worry (as predominantly thought-based) will preclude emotional processing. Secondly, this logic provides the basis for positing another avoidant function for worry. By shifting to worrisome thinking in response to threat cues (either in the external environment or in periodic images of possible catastrophic events), humans can reduce the somatic activation aspects of anxious experiencing.

SECONDARY AVOIDANT FUNCTIONS OF WORRY

Suppression of Somatic Reactions

Several lines of empirical evidence emerge that support the proposition that worry is an avoidance response that suppresses aversive images, thereby reducing somatic activation and emotional processing and thus contributing to the maintenance of anxious meanings. Early evidence demonstrated that worrying just before repeated presentations of phobic images eliminates cardiovascular responses to those presentations and precludes change over repeated exposures. Phobic participants who thought relaxing thoughts before each image, on the other hand, displayed strong responses to initial images and declines in response over repeated presentations. A third group thinking neutral thoughts fell between the former two groups (Borkovec & Hu, 1990). These results were subsequently partially replicated (Peasley-Miklus & Vrana, 2000) or fully replicated (Borkovec, Lyonfields, Wiser & Deihl, 1993) with additional evidence that it was not merely thought, but worrisome thought, that interferes with cardiovascular response to feared images. The significance of these findings is that heart rate reaction is an index of emotional processing (Foa & Kozak, 1986). Although the one published study utilizing the same design but employing repeated *in vivo* exposures (Hazlett-Stevens & Borkovec, 2001) failed to find similar cardiovascular differences (likely due to the high physiological activation elicited by real-life encounters with a complex and physiologically demanding speech performance), subjective anxiety failed to decline among speech-anxious participants who worried before each speech presentation, whereas participants who relaxed or engaged in neutral thinking showed declines in reports of anxiety. Castaneda and Segerstrom (2004) have recently shown that high-worry phobics displayed reduced physiological reactions to actual presentations of the phobic object in comparison to the strong responses of low-worrier phobics.

Related findings expand cognitive avoidance in worry to the more general construct of experiential avoidance in emotional disorders (see Hayes et al., 1996). Participants high on the experiential avoidance measure showed attenuated heart rate to unpleasant film clips compared to participants low on the measure, even though they reported subjectively greater emotion to both pleasant and unpleasant stimuli (Sloan, 2004). Similarly, Roemer's research (Roemer, Salters, Raffa & Orsillo, 2005; Salters-Pedneault, Tull & Roemer, 2004) indicates that worry and GAD are associated with a tendency to react to any emotional experience as if that internal experience were threatening and to engage in avoidance of those experiences. These results fit with Mennin et al.'s (2005) emotional dysregulation model of GAD, which asserts four factors in its development: heightened emotional intensity, lack of understanding of emotional experience, fear of emotions, and nonadaptive management responses. Support for increased emotional experience has emerged from brainwave evidence: GAD clients display increased gamma activation in the posterior region, especially the left posterior associated with negative affect, and that gamma (especially in the right posterior region associated with positive affect) moves toward normalization after cognitive behavioral therapy (CBT) (Ray, Oathes, Yamasaki, Blai, Aikins, Molnar & Borkovec, 2000).

Evidence also indicates that worrying after exposure to emotional material (a stressor film) interferes with emotional processing such that anxious meanings are preserved (seen in increased cognitive intrusions over succeeding days) (Butler, Wells & Dewick, 1995; Wells & Papageorgiou, 1995). In addition to the fact that thinking is not closely tied to efferent command, other possible mechanisms suggested for the interference of worry on emotional processing include: (a) Worry requires attentional resource allocation, making it difficult to attend to something else; (b) worry reduces the mismatch between information expected and information received (see Gray's (1982) model of anxiety); (c) it is more difficult to shift from worrisome thinking to other internal or external stimuli; and (d) the repetitive thoughts of worry (Molina, Borkovec, Peasley & Person, 1998) create semantic satiation (Smith, 1984), whereby words involved become remote from their other associative network (especially emotional) connections (Borkovec, Alcaine & Behar, 2004).

The above research contributes to the view that worry is not only a long-term attempt to mentally figure out how to avoid future catastrophes or to prepare oneself but also has immediate avoidant effects on aspects of anxious experience. Worrying reduces somatic or physiological reactions to emotional material that would otherwise be experienced in neutral or relaxed states. Thus, worry is a negatively reinforced avoidant behavior, whether or not individuals are aware of the impact of internal or external threat cues on their bodily reactions. However, humans do have some awareness of this feature. One commonly-held belief by both GAD and nonanxious individuals about the benefits of worry is that it prepares them for the worst, should bad events actually occur (Borkovec & Roemer, 1995).

The Abstractness of Worry

The thought-based nature of worry, given its relative isolation from emotion, has provided a basis for inferring its short-term avoidant function. The deployment of abstract thought in response to perceived threat reduces some aspects of negative emotional experience. Further research has elaborated on the abstract quality of worry. Stöber (Stöber, 1998; Stöber & Borkovec, 2002; Stöber, Tepperwien & Staak, 2000) found that worry is more abstract and less concrete (less image-producing) than other types of thinking, the degree to which this is true relates to how much the worry topic is of concern to the person, and concreteness associated with worries increases after CBT in GAD clients. He argues that the shift in worry to abstract processing of emotional information is one of the mechanisms by which worry functions to avoid aversive images and their arousing effects. This feature of worry reflects a subset of a broader and significant phenomenon captured in emerging theories (e.g., Philippot, Baeyens, Douilliez & Francart, 2004; Teasdale & Barnard, 1993) and research (e.g., Harvey, 2000; Philippott et al., 2004; Watkins & Teasdale, 2001) on dual-level information processing accounts of emotional disturbance in general. Two systems of information processing are posited. The schematic (or implicational) level is not accessible to consciousness but contains abstracted information from past historical events, especially as it relates to emotional experiences. The propositional level is consciously accessible and contains concrete, episodic information. Research that has manipulated these two modes of processing emotional information found predictable, differential effects. Dealing with information abstractly generates greater emotion and lessened emotional processing than does dealing with the information at the propositional level. Future research stemming from these theoretical accounts holds great promise for understanding the maintenance of emotional disturbance and for developing more effective therapies for facilitating emotional processing.

Further Evidence of Reduced Emotional Processing

We have recently become interested in the interactive effects of worry and other forms of recurrent negative thinking, and research in this area provides further evidence for worry's interference with emotional processing. When humans engage in negative thinking, the content of those thoughts likely fluctuates between worries about the future, images of past traumatic or other bad events, and rumination about past loss or failure. This is a reasonable assumption, because worries must be based on past experiences, and trauma recall and depressive rumination are meaningful to some extent because of their implications for the future. It would also provide an explanation for why each process generates the other as well as both anxious and depressed moods (e.g., Andrews & Borkovec, 1988; Nolen-Hoeksema, 2000; Reynolds & Brewin, 1998). Behar, Zuellig, and Borkovec (2005) tested the main and interactive effects of worry and trauma recall inductions (counterbalanced within participants) on certain cognitive and affective states. In two studies, the design was replicated on unselected participants and on three groups of selected participants (GAD, posttraumatic stress disorder, and nonanxious control). As predicted, thought samples revealed greater thought than imagery in worry, whereas the opposite was found during trauma recall. Both inductions led to increases in anxiety and depression, but trauma recall generated greater depression than worry in both experiments, and worry generated greater anxiety in the second experiment where the majority of participants suffered from anxiety. The important finding for our purposes is that interactive effects supported the role of worry in the mitigation of the emotional processing of trauma: Worrying preceding trauma induction lessened the subjective anxiety experienced during the largely imagery-based trauma recall, compared to when trauma recall preceded worry. Trauma recall also had a causal influence on emotional experience during subsequent worrying: Greater anxiety occurred during worry if it was preceded by a trauma recall induction. Imagining a past trauma appears to provide a reminder that catastrophes do happen, thus increasing the subjective probability and threat value of future bad events when they are worried about.

Likely, future brain imaging will reveal further processes and structures in the brain influenced by worrisome activity. In the only known study using this method, Hoehn-Saric et al. (in press) found that worry inhibited the very neural regions usually activated by fear stimuli (the right amygdala [the most basic structure involved in emotional processing], the hippocampus, and insula).

A final domain of related research comes from Jones and Davey (1990). What is particularly astonishing is that this investigation demonstrated that worry suppresses emotional processing in a way that is opposite to the anxiety-maintaining effects discussed thus far. Specifically, worry prevents unconditional stimulus rehearsal effects, i.e., the reestablishment of an aversive conditional stimulus/conditional fear response after that fear response has been extinguished and after subsequent presentations of the unconditional stimulus alone.

Positive Beliefs about Worry

Further evidence for the avoidant functions of worry and its frequent negative reinforcement comes from investigations on beliefs about the positive functions of worry (e.g., Freeston, Rheaume, Letarte, Dugas & Ladouceur, 1994; Tallis, Davey & Capuzzo, 1994; Wells, 2004). In our own work (Borkovec & Roemer, 1995), we identified with GAD clients six reasons why worry might have beneficial consequences. It was important to identify early in therapy any such beliefs and deal with them right away, because any perceived rewards for worrisome activity would make it more difficult for them to be motivated to eliminate worrying from their lives. A questionnaire based on these beliefs was given to GAD as well as nonanxious control groups. Both equally felt that five of the beliefs were true for them: Worry helps to determine ways of avoiding bad events, to prepare for them, to superstitiously reduce their likelihood, to problem solve, and to motivate performances. The sixth belief significantly distinguished the groups in replicated studies: Worries distract GAD clients from more emotional topics that they did not want to think about.

Most, perhaps all, of these beliefs reflect negatively reinforced avoidant behavior. This conclusion is based on what we know empirically about how often feared events contained in worry actually happen. GAD clients have monitored their daily worries and have rated eventual outcomes in terms of whether things turned out better or worse than feared and whether they coped with the outcomes better or worse than feared (Borkovec, Hazlett-Stevens & Diaz, 1999). The vast majority of worries turned out well, and clients coped quite well with even the few bad things that did happen. Thus, worry is most often followed by the nonoccurrence of feared events (as in figuring out ways to avoid bad events, superstitiously or otherwise) or by the removal of negative internal states (as in preparing for the worst, problem solving, distraction from more emotional topics, and motivation). These data also provide an explanation for the most fundamental reason for what maintains worry. Worrisome activity in order to solve the perceived problem is routinely associated with the problem never materializing. In addition, the results indicate that GAD clients live many emotional (and psychophysiological) lives up in their heads, even though most will not occur in reality.

ORIGINS OF PATHOLOGICAL WORRY AND GAD

As mentioned earlier, worry is an understandable mental response to perceived threat to which no behavioral solution exists. Although most people worry under such circumstances, why pathological worrying emerges in some people and not others is an important question. What leads to the development of perceptions of so much threat about the future and/or felt inability to cope with the future? Three ideas have been offered thus far to answer this question.

Dugas and colleagues have offered the notion that an excessive intolerance of uncertainty of any type predisposes an individual to shift from normal worrying to excessive and uncontrollable worrying (see Chapter 12). This concept is interesting, given the work of Davey and colleagues on the related areas of catastrophizing interview methods and his mood-as-input hypothesis about possible mechanisms of the development of pathological worry (see Chapters 10 and 13 for more detailed description of these two domains). An alternative model by Wells and colleagues suggests that meta-worry and negative beliefs about worry are the primary contributors to the creation of severe, nonadaptive worrying. This work is described completely in Chapter 11 of this volume.

Our own research on this issue has focused on interpersonal factors in the etiology of GAD. Interpersonal connections in GAD have long been apparent: Worry correlates most highly with social evaluative fears (Borkovec, et al., 1983), social phobia is one of the most common comorbid conditions for GAD (Brown & Barlow, 1992), the majority of worrisome topics fall into an interpersonal category (Roemer, Molina & Borkovec, 1997), and the more frequent occurrences of past trauma reported by GAD clients involve mostly catastrophes to significant others as opposed to non-interpersonal catastrophes (Roemer, Molina, Litz & Borkovec, 1997). Our most exciting leads in this domain, however, come from two interrelated areas of investigation: developmental childhood experiences and current adult interpersonal problems.

Bowlby's (1982) attachment theory suggests that diffuse anxiety problems (like GAD) are the understandable consequence of insecure attachment in childhood. If primary care-givers do not provide an emotionally secure base, then children will not freely explore, learn from, and develop self-confidence in coping with the world. On a questionnaire assessing certain aspects of attachment and in replicated studies, GAD clients reported greater degrees of enmeshed, role-reversed relationship with their primary care givers than controls, but not greater rejection (Cassidy, 1995; Zuellig, Newman, Kachin & Constantino, 1997). The retrospective, self-report, and correlational nature of these findings suggest cautious interpretation, but they lead to an intriguing hypothesis about the possible origins of pathological worry. In a role-reversed relationship, the mother was not reliably there to take care of the child; indeed, the child had to take care of the mother. The child was therefore required to look out for him/herself and for the mother. Such a child would naturally feel that the world is dangerous, that he/she may not be able to cope with future events, and that he/she must anticipate the future for him/herself and the mother in order to survive and to obtain love and approval. Cassidy (personal communication, March, 2005) recently conducted preliminary analyses on Adult Attachment Interviews obtained from our GAD clients. The results thus far indicate that: (a) the majority of GAD clients were insecurely attached in childhood, (b) the predominating form of insecure attachment involved the "disorganized attachment" category (an inability to form a coherent strategy of processing childhood experiences), and (c) the majority of a separate group of GAD clients receiving the interview at follow-up when they no longer met GAD criteria were securely attached. Whether the latter reflects a mood-memory effect or the fact that therapy actually changed the clients' working models remain rival hypotheses for future research. However, the best available assessment for determining attachment has revealed that our clients were insecurely attached in ways that would be conducive to the development of a pervasive adult perception of potential dangers in the future and of low confidence in coping abilities.

These attachment findings relate compellingly to what we discovered about the interpersonal lives of our clients. Cluster analysis of the Inventory of Interpersonal Problems (Horowitz, Rosenberg & Bartholomew, 1993) revealed that nearly two-thirds were overly nurturing and intrusive in their interpersonal relationships (Pincus & Borkovec, 1994). Their attempts to satisfy their interpersonal needs involve taking care of everyone, so much so that it causes problems in their relationships. So they not only worry about things related to themselves. They also worry about, and take on the concerns of, others, magnifying the domains of their worrisome activity. The combination of the attachment results and these findings reflect well the underlying theory of interpersonal psychotherapy: Our clients have learned in childhood to take care of mother in order to get her love and approval, and they nonadaptively continue to engage in this pattern with significant others in adulthood. The fact that the degree of interpersonal problems negatively predicted short-term and long-term clinical gains after CBT led us to pursue the targeting of interpersonal functioning in therapy (see Chapter 16 in this volume).

CORE FEARS IN GAD?

The above considerations lead to the question of whether or not a core fear or limited set of core fears underlie GAD. GAD is characterized by its diffuse nature and the absence of circumscribed anxiety-provoking stimuli. Identification of core fears would allow the therapeutic application of imaginal and/or in vivo exposure techniques that are so effective with other anxiety disorders.

Contained within our chapter are hints of what such fears might be. Given that 50% of GAD clients have experienced at least one traumatic event (Roemer et al., 1997), exposure methods used with PTSD might be an important treatment element for those clients. Second, Dugas and colleagues suggest the central importance of fears of uncertainty, and this led to interventions targeting this fear (Ladouceur, Dugas, Freeston, Leger, Gagnon & Thibodeau, 2000). Third, Wells' approach highlights the contribution of worry about worry (meta-worry), and he has formulated treatments to deal with this hypothetically crucial process. Fourth, the interpersonal therapy, incorporated recently into our CBT, is grounded in the notion that the predominant fears of GAD clients center on interpersonal situations and the clients' failures to get their interpersonal needs met (Newman, Castonguay, Borkovec & Molnar, 2004).

As described earlier, a further possibility is that GAD clients fear emotional experience in general. A decade ago, they were found to score highly on alexithymia (difficulties in identifying and describing emotional experience (Abel, 1994; Yamas, Hazlett-Stevens & Borkovec, 1997). Although this could be due to their spending so much time in thought and thus pay little attention to affects, they also may be actively avoiding emotions (see Mennin et al., 2005; Salters-Pedneault et al., 2004). If fear and avoidance of emotions are contributors to worry and GAD maintenance, then repeated exposures to emotions (both positive and negative) may be a wise therapeutic strategy. Partly based on this hypothesis, we have incorporated emotional deepening methods from experiential therapy into our CBT approach with GAD (see Newman et al., 2004).

EPILOGUE

Accumulated evidence suggests that worry functions as a cognitive avoidance response, both to perceived threats in the future and to aversive images or other internal experiences, like emotions. The consequence is the preclusion of emotional processing and thus the maintenance of anxious meanings. Worry is pervasive throughout the anxiety disorders (Barlow, 1988) and in mood disorders (Chelminski & Zimmerman, 2003). Consequently, what we learn about worry and its effective treatment will likely have implications for understanding these other disorders and for therapy developments for their amelioration.

Recent developments also promise to broaden our understanding of emotional disorders. The last few years have seen an increase in investigations devoted to identifying similarities and differences in the nature and functions of different forms of negative recurrent thinking. Worry, depressive rumination, and trauma recall represent three examples, each of which has been typically associated with specific disorders (GAD, depression, and posttraumatic stress disorder, respectively). Yet each is generative of the others, all are likely to occur during any negative thinking episode, and interactive effects may occur between them when they do occur during an emotional episode (McLaughlin, Sibrava, Behar & Borkovec, in press). Each process is characterized by the perception of a problem to be solved, and each has been associated in one way or another with avoidant functions as well as failures in emotional processing. Continued research and theory development in this domain similarly promises to advance our knowledge about emotional problems and how best to treat them.

ACKNOWLEDGEMENT

Preparation of this chapter was supported in part by the National Institute of Mental Health Grant MH-58593.

REFERENCES

Abel, J.L. (1994, November). *Alexithymia in an analogue sample of generalized anxiety disorder and non-anxious matched controls*. Paper presented at the annual meeting of the Association for the Advancement of Behavior Therapy, San Diego, CA.

American Psychiatric Association (1987). *Diagnostic and statistical manual of mental disorders-revised 3rd ed.*. Washington, DC: Author.

American Psychiatric Association (1994). *Diagnostic and statistical manual of mental disorders* (4th ed.). Washington, DC: Author.

Andrews, V.H. & Borkovec, T.D. (1988). The differential effects of inductions of worry, somatic anxiety, and depression on emotional experience. *Journal of Behavior Therapy and Experimental Psychiatry*, **19**, 21–26.

Barlow, D.H. (1988). *Anxiety and its disorders: The nature and treatment of anxiety and panic*. New York: Guilford Press.

Behar, E., Zuellig, A.R. & Borkovec, T.D. (2005). Thought and imaginal activity during worry and trauma recall. *Behavior Therapy*, **36**, 157–168.

Borkovec, T.D. (1972). Effects of expectancy on the outcome of systematic desensitization and implosive treatments for analogue anxiety. *Behavior Therapy*, **3**, 29–40.

Borkovec, T.D. (1974). Heart-rate process during systematic desensitization and implosive therapy for analogue anxiety. *Behavior Therapy*, **5**, 636–641.

Borkovec, T.D., Alcaine, O. & Behar, E. (2004). Avoidance theory of worry and generalized anxiety disorder. In R.G. Heimberg, C.L. Turk & D.S. Mennin (Eds), *Generalized anxiety disorder: Advances in research and practice*. New York: Guilford Press.

Borkovec, T.D., Hazlett-Stevens, H. & Diaz, M.L. (1999). The role of positive beliefs about worry in generalized anxiety disorder and its treatment. *Clinical Psychology & Psychotherapy*, **6**, 126–138.

Borkovec, T.D. & Hu, S. (1990). The effect of worry on cardiovascular response to phobic imagery. *Behaviour Research and Therapy*, **28**, 69–73.

Borkovec, T.D. & Inz, J. (1990). The nature of worry in generalized anxiety disorder: A predominance of thought activity. *Behaviour Research & Therapy*, **31**, 321–324.

Borkovec, T.D., Lyonfields, J.D., Wiser, S.L. & Deihl, L. (1993). The role of worrisome thinking in the suppression of cardiovascular response to phobic imagery. *Behaviour Research and Therapy*, **31**, 321–324.

Borkovec, T.D., Ray, W.J. & Stöber, J. (1998). Worry: A cognitive phenomenon intimately linked to affective, physiological, and interpersonal behavior. *Cognitive Therapy & Research*, **22**, 561–576.

Borkovec, T.D., Robinson, E., Pruzinsky, T. & DePree, J.A. (1983). Preliminary exploration of worry: Some characteristics and processes. *Behaviour Research & Therapy*, **21**, 9–16.

Borkovec, T.D. & Roemer, L. (1995). Perceived functions of worry among generalized anxiety disordered subjects: Distraction from more emotional topics? *Journal of Behavior Therapy & Experimental Psychiatry*, **26**, 25–30.

Bowlby, J. (1982). *Attachment and loss*. New York: Basic Books.

Brown, T.A. & Barlow, D.H. (1992). Comorbidity among anxiety disorders: Implications for treatment and DSM-IV. *Journal of Consulting and Clinical Psychology*, **60**, 835–844.

Butler, G., Wells, A., Dewick, H. (1995). Differential effects of worry and imagery after exposure to a stressful stimulus. *Behavioural & Cognitive Psychotherapy*, **23**, 45–56.

Carter, W.R., Johnson, M.C. & Borkovec, T.D. (1986). Worry: An electrocortical analysis. *Advances in Behaviour Research and Therapy*, **8**, 193–204.

Cassidy, J.A. (1995). Attachment and generalized anxiety disorder. In D. Cicchetti & S. Toth (Eds), *Emotion, cognition, and representation* (pp. 343–370). Rochester, NY: University of Rochester Press.

Castaneda, J.O. & Segerstrom, S.C. (2004). Effect of stimulus type and worry on physiological response to fear. *Journal of Anxiety Disorders*, **18**, 809–823.

Chelminski, I. & Zimmerman, M. (2003). Pathological worry in depressed and anxious patients. *Anxiety Disorders*, **17**, 533–546.

Davey, G.C.L., Jubb, M. & Cameron, C. (1996). Catastrophic worrying as a function of changes in problem-solving confidence. *Cognitive Therapy & Research*, **20**, 333–344.

Davis, M., Montgomery, I. & Wilson, G. (2002). Worry and heart rate variables: Autonomic rigidity under challenge. *Journal of Anxiety Disorders*, **6**, 639–659.

Dugas, M.J., Gagnon, F., Ladouceur, R. & Freeston, M.H. (1998). Generalized anxiety disorder: A preliminary test of a conceptual model. *Behaviour Research & Therapy*, **36**, 215–226.

Fehr, F.S. & Stern, J.A. (1970). Peripheral physiological variables and emotion: The James-Lange theory revisited. *Psychological Bulletin*, **74**, 411–424.

Foa, E.D. & Kozak, M.J. (1986). Emotional processing of fear: Exposure to corrective information. *Psychological Bulletin*, **99**, 20–35.

Freeston, M.H., Dugas, M.J. & Ladouceur, R. (1996). Thoughts, images, worry, and anxiety. *Cognitive Therapy & Research*, **20**, 265–273.

Freeston, M.H., Rheaume, J., Letarte, H., Dugas, M.J. & Ladouceur, R. (1994). Why do people worry? *Personality & Individual Differences*, **17**, 791–802.

Gray, J.A. (1982). Precis of "The neurophysiology of anxiety: An enquiry into the functions of the septo-hippocampal system". *Behavioral and Brain Sciences*, **5**, 469–534.

Gray, J. (1987). *The psychology of fear and stress*. Cambridge: Cambridge University Press.

Grayson, J.B. & Borkovec, T.D. (1978). The effects of expectancy and imagined response to phobic stimuli on fear reduction. *Cognitive Therapy and Research*, **2**, 11–24.

Grossman, P., Stemmler, G. & Meinhardt, E. (1990). Paced respiratory sinus arhythmia as an index of cardiac parasympathetic tone during varying behavioral tasks. *Psychophysiology*, **27**, 404–416.

Harvey, A.G. (2000). Pre-sleep cognitive activity in insomnia: A comparison of sleep-onset insomniacs and good sleepers. *British Journal of Clinical Psychology*, **39**, 275–286.

Hayes, S.C., Wilson, K.G., Gifford, E.V., Follette, V.M. & Stosahl, K. (1996). Experiential avoidance and behavioral disorders: A functional dimensional approach to diagnosis and treatment. *Journal of Consulting and Clinical Psychology*, **64**, 1152–1168.

Hazlett-Stevens, H. & Borkovec, T.D. (2001). Effects of worry and progressive relaxation on the reduction of fear in speech phobia: An investigation of situational exposure. *Behavior Therapy*, **32**, 503–517.

Hoehn-Saric, R. & McLeod, D.R. (1988). The peripheral sympathetic nervous system: Its role in normal and pathological anxiety. *Psychiatric Clinics of North America*, **11**, 375–386.

Hoehn-Saric, R., McLeod, D.R. & Zimmerli, W.D. (1989). Somatic manifestations in women with generalized anxiety disorder. *Archives of General Psychiatry*, **46**, 1113–1119.

Horowitz, L.M., Rosenberg, S.E. & Bartholomew, K. (1993). Interpersonal problems, attachment styles, and outcome in brief dynamic therapy. *Journal of Consulting and Clinical Psychology*, **61**, 549–560.

Johnston, W.M. & Davey, G.C.L. (1997) The psychological impact of negative TV news bulletins: The catastrophising of personal worries. *British Journal of Psychology*, **88**, 85–91.

Jones, T. & Davey, G.C.L. (1990). The effects of cued UCS rehearsal on the retention of differential "fear" conditioning: An experimental analogue of the "worry" process. *Behaviour Research and Therapy*, **28**, 159–164.

Kosslyn, S.M. (1983). *Ghosts in the mind's machine: Creating and using images in the brain*. New York: W.W. Norton.

Ladouceur, R., Dugas, M.J., Freeston, M.H., Leger, E., Gagnon, F. & Thibodeau, N. (2000). Efficacy of a cognitive-behavioral treatment for generalized anxiety disorder: Evaluation in a controlled clinical trial. *Journal of Consulting and Clinical Psychology*, **68**, 957–964.

Laguna, L.B., Ham, L.S., Hope, D.A. & Bell, C. (2004). Chronic worry as avoidance of arousal. *Cognitive Therapy and Research*, **28** (2), 269–281.

Lyonfields, J.D., Borkovec, T.D. & Thayer, J.F. (1995). Vagal tone in generalized anxiety disorder and the effects of aversive imagery and worrisome thinking. *Behavior Therapy*, **26**, 457–466.

MacLeod, C., Campbell, L., Rutherford, E. & Wilson, E. (2004). The causal status of anxiety-linked attentional and interpretive bias. In J. Yiend (Ed.), *Cognition, emotion, and psychopathology*. Cambridge, UK: Cambridge University Press.

Marten, P.A., Brown, T.A., Barlow, D.H., Borkovec, T.D., Shear, M.K. & Lydiard, R.B. (1993). Evaluation of the ratings comprising the associated symptom criterion of DSM-III-R generalized anxiety disorder. *Journal of Nervous and Mental Disease*, **181**, 676–682.

McLaughlin, K., Sibrava, N., Behar, E. & Borkovec, T.D. (in press). Recurrent negative thinking in emotional disorders: Worry, depressive rumination, and trauma recall. In S. Sassaroli, G. Ruggerio & R. Lorenzini (Eds), *Worry, need of control, and other core cognitive constructs in anxiety and eating disorders*. Milan: Raphael Cortina Publisher.

Mennin, D.S., Heimberg, R.G., Turk, C.L., Fresco, D.M. (2005). Preliminary evidence for an emotion dysregulation model of generalized anxiety disorder. *Behaviour Research and Therapy*, **28**, 153–158.

Metzger, R.L., Miller, M.L., Cohen, M., Sofka, M. & Borkovec, T.D. (1990). Worry changes decision making: The effect of negative thoughts on cognitive processing. *Journal of Clinical Psychology*, **46**, 78–88.

Molina, S., Borkovec, T.D., Peasley, C. & Person, D. (1998). Content analysis of worrisome streams of consciousness in anxious and dysphoric participants. *Cognitive Therapy and Research*, **2**, 109–123.

Mowrer, O.H. (1947). On the dual nature of learning—a re-interpretation of "conditioning" and "problem-solving." *Harvard Educational Review*, **17**, 102–148.

Newman, M.G., Castonguay, L.G., Borkovec, T.D. & Molnar, C. (2004). Integrative psychotherapy. In R.G. Heimberg, C.L. Turk & D.S. Mennin (Eds), *Generalized anxiety disorder: Advances in research and practice*. New York: Guilford Press.

Nolen-Hoeksema, S. (2000). The role of rumination in depressive disorders and mixed anxiety/depressive symptoms. *Journal of Abnormal Psychology*, **109**, 504–511.

Noyes, R., Jr., Woodman, C., Garvey, M.J., Cook, B.L., Suelzer, M., Clancy, J. & Anderson, D.J. (1992). Generalized anxiety disorder vs. panic disorder: Distinguishing characteristics and patterns of comorbidity. *Journal of Nervous & Mental Disease*, **180**, 369–379.

Paivio, A. (1986). *Mental representations: A dual coding approach*. New York: Oxford University Press.

Philippot, P., Baeyens, C., Douilliez, C. & Francart, B. (2004). Cognitive regulation of emotion: Application to clinical disorders. In P. Philippot & R.S. Feldman (Eds). *The regulation of emotion*. New York: Laurence Erlbaum Associates.

Pincus, A.L. & Borkovec, T.D. (1994, June). *Interpersonal problems in generalized anxiety disorder: Preliminary clustering of patients' interpersonal dysfunction*. Paper presented at the Annual Meeting of the American Psychological Society, New York, NY.

Peasley-Miklus, C. & Vrana, S.R. (2000). Effect of worrisome and relaxing thinking on fearful emotional processing. *Behaviour Research and Therapy*, **38**, 129–144.

Porges, S.W. (1992). Autonomic regulation and attention. In B.A. Campbell, H. Hayne & R. Richardson (Eds), *Attention and information processing in infants and adults* (pp. 201–223). Hillside, NJ: Erlbaum.

Pruzinsky, T. & Borkovec, T.D. (1990). Cognitive and personality characteristics of worriers. *Behaviour Research and Therapy*, **28**, 507–512.

Ray, W.J., Oathes, D., Yamasaki, A., Blai, A., Aikins, D., Molnar, C. & Borkovec, T.D. (2000, October). *Generalized anxiety disorder clients show normalized EEG patterns after psychotherapy*. Paper presented at the annual meeting of the Society for Psychophysiological Research, San Diego.

Reynolds, M. & Brewin, C.H. (1998). Intrusive cognitions, coping strategies and emotional responses in depression, post-traumatic stress disorder and a non-clinical population. *Behaviour Research and Therapy*, **36**, 135–147.

Roemer, L., Molina, S., Litz, B.T. & Borkovec, T.D. (1997). A preliminary investigation of the role of previous exposure to potentially traumatizing events in generalized anxiety disorder. *Depression and Anxiety*, **4**, 134–138.

Roemer, L. & Borkovec, T.D. (1994). Effects of suppressing thoughts about emotional material. *Journal of Abnormal Psychology*, **103**, 467–474.

Roemer, L., Molina, S. & Borkovec, T.D. (1997). An investigation of worry content among generally anxious individuals. *The Journal of Nervous and Mental Disease*, **185**, 314–319.

Roemer, L., Salters, K., Raffa, S.D. & Orsillo, S.M. (2005). Fear and avoidance of internal experiences in GAD: preliminary tests of a conceptual model. *Cognitive Therapy and Research*, **29(1)**, 71–88.

Salters-Pedneault, K., Tull, M.T. & Roemer, L. (2004). The role of avoidance of emotional material in the anxiety disorders. *Applied and Preventive Psychology*, **11**, 95–114.

Sloan, D.M. (2004). Emotion regulation in action: emotional reactivity in experiential avoidance. *Behaviour Research and Therapy*, **42**, 1257–1270.

Smith, L.C. (1984). Semantic satiation affects category membership decision time but not lexical priming. *Memory and Cognition*, **12**, 483–488.

Stöber, J. (1998). Worry, problem-solving, and suppression of imagery: The role of concreteness. *Behaviour Research & Therapy*, **36**, 751–756.

Stöber, J. & Borkovec, T.D. (2002). Reduced concreteness of worry in generalized anxiety disorder: Findings from a therapy study. *Cognitive Therapy & Research*, **26**, 89–96.

Stöber, J., Tepperwien, S. & Staak, M. (2000). Worrying leads to reduced concreteness of problem elaborations: Evidence for the avoidance theory of worry. *Anxiety, Stress & Coping*, **13**, 217–227.

Startup, H.M. & Davey, G.C.L. (2001). Mood-as-input and catastrophic worrying. *Journal of Abnormal Psychology*, **110(1)**, 83–96.

Tallis, F., Davey, G.C.L. & Capuzzo, N. (1994). The phenomenology of nonpathological worry: A preliminary investigation. In G.C.L. Davey & F. Tallis (Eds), *Worrying: Perspectives on theory, assessment and treatment* (pp. 61–89). Chichester, UK: John Wiley & Sons, Ltd.

Tallis, F., Eysenck, M. & Mathews, A. (1991). Elevated evidence requirements and worry. *Personality and Individual Differences*, **12**, 21–27.

Teasdale, J.D. & Barnard, P.J. (1993). *Affect, cognition and change*. London: Lawrence Erlbaum.

Thayer, J.F., Friedman, B.H. & Borkovec, T.D. (1996). Autonomic characteristics of generalized anxiety disorder and worry. *Biological Psychiatry*, **39**, 255–266.

Thayer, J.F., Friedman, B.H., Borkovec, T.D., Johnsen, B.H. & Molina, S. (2000). Phasic heart period reactions to cued threat and nonthreat stimuli in generalized anxiety disorder. *Psychophysiology*, **37**, 361–368.

Vasey, M.W. & Borkovec, T.D. (1992). A catastrophizing assessment of worrisome thoughts. *Cognitive Therapy & Research*, **16**, 505–520.

Vrana, S.R., Cuthbert, B.M. & Lang, P.J. (1986). Fear imagery and text processing. *Psychophysiology*, **23**, 247–253.

Watkins, E. & Teasdale, J.D. (2001). Rumination and overgeneral memory in depression: Effects of self-focus and analytic thinking. *Journal of Abnormal Psychology*, **110**, 353–357.

Wells, A. (2004). A cognitive model of GAD: Metacognition and pathological worry. In R.G. Heimberg, C.L. Turk & D.S. Mennin (Eds), *Generalized anxiety disorder: Advances in research and practice*, pp. 164–186. New York: Guilford Press.

Wells, A. & Papageorgiou, C. (1995). Worry and the incubation of intrusive images following stress. *Behaviour Research & Therapy*, **33**, 549–583.

Yamas, K., Hazlett-Stevens, H. & Borkovec, M. (1997, November). *Alexithymia in generalized anxiety disorder*. Paper presented at the annual meeting of the Association for the Advancement of Behavior Therapy, Miami.

Zeigarnick, B. (1927). Uber das Behalten von erledigten und unerledigten handlungen. *Psychologische Forschung*, **9**, 1–85.

Zuellig, A.R., Newman, M.G., Kachin, K.E. & Constantino, M.J. (1997, November). *Childhood attachment styles in adults with generalized anxiety disorder or panic disorder*. Paper presented at the 31st Annual Meeting of the Association for Advancement of Behavior Therapy, Miami, FL.

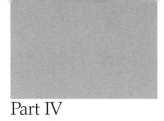

Part IV

TREATMENT METHODS

Chapter 15

METACOGNITIVE THERAPY FOR WORRY AND GENERALISED ANXIETY DISORDER

Adrian Wells

The metacognitive model of pathological worry and Generalised Anxiety Disorder is the basis of a specific new form of treatment. This treatment differs from existing cognitive-behavioural approaches in focusing exclusively on metacognitive appraisals, beliefs and strategies. The model on which treatment is based is backed by an accumulating database, which was reviewed earlier in Chapter 11.

In this chapter the metacognitive treatment (Wells, 1995, 1997) is described. Treatment consists of using the metacognitive model to construct an idiosyncratic case formulation, and we will examine the process of doing such. This initial stage of treatment is followed by socialisation, which includes shifting the patient to a metacognitive understanding of the presenting problem. Treatment then proceeds through a series of stages that are presented in a specific sequence. First, negative metacognitive beliefs about the uncontrollability of worry are challenged, second metacognitive beliefs about the danger of worry and associated emotion are targeted for modification, and third positive beliefs about the need to worry in order to cope are tackled. The final stage of treatment consists of the introduction of relapse prevention strategies. In this chapter I will briefly describe how each of these stages is implemented.

Typically, Metacognitive Therapy is conducted in sessions held once a week, and lasting 45–60 minutes each. Homework is a crucial component of treatment, and enables patients to run behavioural experiments aimed at modifying beliefs in erroneous metacognitions. A course of treatment usually spans 6–12 sessions.

Worry and Its Psychological Disorders: Theory, Assessment and Treatment. Edited by G. C. L. Davey and A. Wells. © 2006 John Wiley & Sons, Ltd.

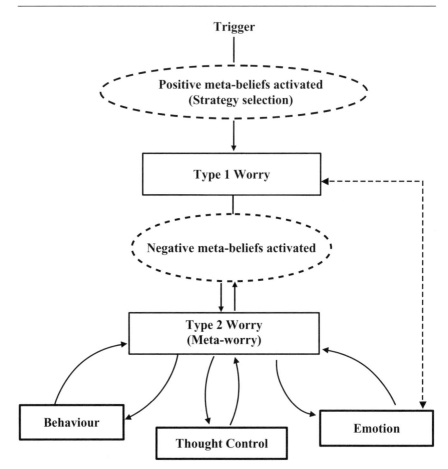

Figure 15.1   The Metacognitive Model of GAD
Reproduced from Wells, A. (1997). *Cognitive Therapy of Anxiety Disorders: A practice manual and conceptual guide*. Chichester, UK: Wiley.

SYNOPSIS OF THE METACOGNITIVE MODEL

A basic tenet of the metacognitive model is that the development and persistence of pathological worry and GAD are linked to dysfunctional metacognitive appraisals and beliefs, and unhelpful self-regulation strategies. The model is presented in Figure 15.1. The trigger for an episode of worrying is a negative thought often in the form of a 'what if' question (e.g. 'what if I have an accident?'). Sometimes the trigger takes the form of a negative image or memory, which activates tacit positive metacognitive beliefs about worrying. These beliefs support the implementation of worry as a means of coping with anticipated danger and are exemplified by the beliefs 'I must worry in order to be able to cope in the future, If I worry I will be prepared, Worrying stops me making mistakes, Worrying keeps me in control'.

Activation of positive metacognitive beliefs leads to maintenance of chains of thinking in which a range of potential calamities and coping strategies are contemplated. This Type 1 worry process is characterised by a predominance of verbal catastrophising. Thus, Type 1 worrying is a covert coping strategy. It impacts on the person's emotional response as depicted by the bi-directional dotted line in Figure 15.1. It can lead to an intensification of anxiety or low mood as a range of negative ideas are generated. However, it can reduce anxiety, when for example it is used to shift internal processing away from more distressing images, and when it is successful in a person achieving their goal of 'knowing' they can cope. Achievement of the goal is signalled by subjective states such as 'feeling' that one can cope, or a state of 'knowing' that all possibilities have been contemplated.

During the Type 1 worry process in GAD negative metacognitive beliefs are activated leading to negative interpretation of worrying and of associated symptoms. Negative metacognitive beliefs fall into two basic categories: (1) the belief that worry is uncontrollable, and (2) beliefs about the dangers of worrying. The dangers include the physical, psychological and social consequences of worrying. Examples of each type of belief include; 'I have no control over worrying; Worrying can damage my body; If I worry too much I will lose my mind; Worrying is abnormal and people will reject me if they know I worry'. The negative interpretation (called Type 2 worry) intensifies the person's sense of threat and results in increased anxiety. Anxiety symptoms may be misinterpreted as a sign of imminent danger, such as loss of mental control, and under these circumstances anxiety increases and panic attacks are likely.

In an attempt to deal with worrying the person with pathological worry or GAD uses unhelpful coping strategies. For example, behaviours include seeking reassurance, avoiding situations that might trigger worrying, using alcohol and searching for information. These responses are prone to backfire and contribute to a persistence of the problem. For instance, reassurance seeking can give rise to ambiguous or conflicting information that can provide further grounds for worrying. The effective termination of worrying through reassurance from others removes opportunities to discover that worry can be controlled by the self. Similarly, avoidance of situations that might trigger worrying deprives the individual of opportunities to discover that worrying can be controlled, and prevents the person from discovering that even if worry is not controlled it does not culminate in the feared catastrophe. Information search, such as 'surfing the net' is used by some people in an attempt to discover that there is nothing to worry about. Unfortunately, this is likely to reveal more potential threats that act as triggers for worrying.

A further pattern of strategies for dealing with worry is important too. Typically in GAD there are inconsistent attempts to interrupt worry once it is activated, thus preventing the individual discovering that worry can be regulated effectively. This is because the person believes worry is uncontrollable, or it is part of the personality and cannot be controlled. It also results from conflicting motivations to control worry caused by conflict between positive and negative metacognitive beliefs. If control attempts are used, these are often directed at suppressing thoughts that trigger worrying. However, suppression is not particularly effective, and so choice of ineffective strategies or combinations of strategy prevent the individual discovering that worry can be controlled. Even on the occasions when it is controlled effectively, this raises the problem of preventing the individual discovering that worry is harmless.

STRUCTURE OF TREATMENT

Metacognitive Therapy (MCT) aims to conceptualise and modify negative metacognitive appraisals and beliefs about worry, and increase the flexible use of alternative strategies for dealing with triggers. The latter consists of modifying positive beliefs about the need to worry and introducing alternative plans for processing.

Following general assessment, the process of treatment commences with case conceptualisation, it is followed by socialisation to the model, and then proceeds with direct metacognitive modification. The modification of metacognitive beliefs follows a particular sequence in which negative beliefs about uncontrollability are challenged, next negative beliefs about danger, and finally positive beliefs about worry are modified. The final stage of treatment is relapse prevention consisting of consolidation of knowledge and examination of alternative strategies for dealing with triggers. Figure 15.2 presents a schematic overview of the focus of individual sessions in a typical course of MCT, however the precise number of sessions required in each case depends on the rate of patient progress.

It is important that the therapist introduces challenging of danger metacognitions only when uncontrollability has been effectively challenged. Similarly, challenging positive metacognitions is introduced only after danger metacognitions have been removed. Progress towards these sub-goals is monitored at each session with the Generalized Anxiety Disorder Scale

	Session Number											
	1	2	3	4	5	6	7	8	9	10	11	12
Formulation	●											
Socialisation	●	●										
Uncontrollability	●	●	●	●								
Danger				●	●	●	●	●	●			
Positive								●	●	●	●	
Relapse Prevention											●	●

Figure 15.2 Schematic overview of the typical structure of a course of MCT

(GADS: Wells, 1997). A case study describing the implementation of this treatment is presented by King in Chapter 19.

ASSESSMENT INSTRUMENTS

Treatment outcome is normally measured with a range of self-report instruments. Anxiety and mood are assessed with the Beck Anxiety Inventory (BAI: Beck, Epstein, Brown & Steer, 1988), and the Beck Depression Inventory (BDI: Beck, Ward, Mendelson, Mock & Erbaugh, 1961). Worry is assessed with the Penn State Worry Questionnaire (PSWQ: Meyer, Miller, Metzger & Borkovec, 1990) and the Anxious Thoughts Inventory (AnTI: Wells, 1994). The worry measures are administered at pre-treatment and post-treatment. At each session the BAI, BDI and the Generalized Anxiety Disorder Scale (GADS: Wells, 1997) are used.

The GADS provides a summary measure of worry, avoidance, coping behaviours and level of belief in negative and positive metacognitions in the past week. It is a useful source of information that can be used in case formulation, and it provides a means of assessing changes in symptoms and metacognitive beliefs during treatment.

CASE FORMULATION

The metacognitive model (Figure 15.1) is used as a template for constructing an individual patient case formulation. To achieve this the therapist first asks the patient to identify a recent episode of distressing worry, and structured questioning proceeds as a means of building the case formulation.

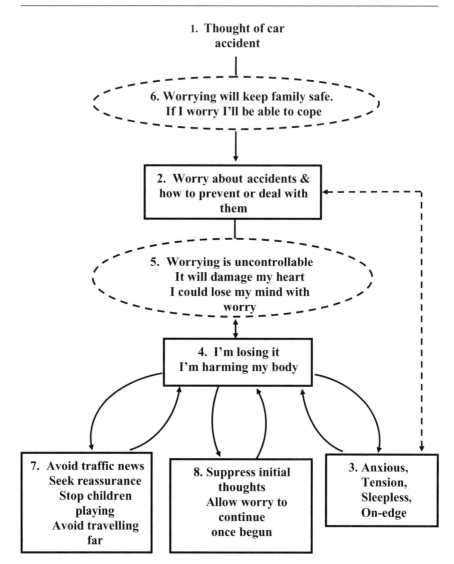

Figure 15.3 Numerical sequence for case formulation questions and an example formulation

The sequence, structure and content of questioning as it relates to each component in the model in Figure 15.3 is as follows:

(1) Think of the last time you suffered from a distressing episode of worrying. What was the first thought that triggered your worrying (was it a negative thought, image, or memory)?

(2) When you had that thought what did you go on to worry about?
(3) When you were worrying like that, how did that make you feel emotionally? What symptoms did you have?
(4) When you felt like that, did you have any negative thoughts about your worry and your feelings? Did you think anything bad could happen if you continued to worry? What is the worst that could happen?
(5) How much do you believe worrying is uncontrollable. How much do you believe worrying is harmful? In what way could it be harmful?
(6) Do you think there are any advantages to worrying? Can worrying help you in any way?
(7) When you were worrying, did you do anything to try and stop it or prevent bad things from happening? What did you do? Do you ever try to deal with your worries by asking for reassurance, avoiding situations, searching for information, using alcohol?
(8) Do you try to control your worrying thoughts more directly by trying not to think about things that might trigger worry? Have you ever tried the strategy of choosing not to worry when you have a negative thought?

SOCIALISATION

The next step is socialisation, consisting of presenting the formulation with the goal of helping the patient to understand that the problem is not predominantly an issue of worry but a problem of beliefs about worry and use of unhelpful coping strategies. Socialisation also provides a simple overview of the course and nature of MCT. It is an important initial procedure in enabling the patient to begin to construct an explanation of their problem.

The therapist draws out the formulation for the patient and brings to their attention the presence of positive and negative beliefs about worrying. It is emphasised that treatment will initially focus on exploring negative beliefs, worry about worry and the unhelpful ways the patient tries to deal with worry. Socialisation questions are used to illustrate the role of beliefs about worry. For example the patient is asked: 'If you only believed that worrying was a good thing, how much of a problem would you have?', and 'If you discovered that worrying can be controlled how much of a problem would worry be?'.

Socialisation continues with discussion of the effectiveness of the patient's behaviours and thought control strategies. The therapist asks how effective the strategies have been, and points to the fact that they do not work since the patient still has a problem with worrying. It is suggested that the problem may partially rest with strategies that are unhelpful in the long term, and this is demonstrated with a thought-suppression experiment. The patient is asked to 'try not to think about a yellow rabbit for the next three minutes'. Typically, the patient reports that this is difficult to achieve and the therapist uses this experience to explain how some thought control strategies can backfire and fail to provide evidence that worry can be controlled. However, the therapist explains that the goal of treatment is not to provide more effective means of controlling worry but to use this as a stepping-stone in changing negative beliefs about worry. Following socialisation, the next therapeutic task is commencement of modification of negative metacognitive beliefs concerning uncontrollability.

MODIFYING UNCONTROLLABILITY METACOGNITIONS

Verbal reattribution methods are used to weaken belief in uncontrollability metacognitions. The therapist questions the patient's evidence that worry is uncontrollable. This is normally met with the response that having a problem with worry is evidence that it cannot be controlled. The therapist suggests the problem is that ineffective strategies have been used, and draws attention to the presence of positive beliefs about worry that may lead to conflicting views about controlling it.

Further weakening of belief in uncontrollability is achieved by reviewing evidence of effective control. For example, the patient is asked what typically happens to his/her worry if they have to perform a task such as answering the telephone. Worry is usually displaced by such activities and this can be interpreted as evidence that worry can be controlled. Further questioning is used to determine how worry episodes stop if they are truly uncontrollable.

The most powerful procedures for challenging uncontrollability beliefs are worry-postponement experiments. These are introduced by suggesting that the patient conduct an experiment for homework in which worry is postponed. The task is described as follows:

I'd like you to try an experiment for homework. Normally when you have a negative thought you engage in worry in an attempt to deal with the problem. I would like you to try something different. When you first notice a thought that would trigger worry, I want you to acknowledge the presence of the thought, and tell yourself that you will not worry about it now but save your worry until later in the day. Set aside a time later in the day, say between 7pm and 7.15pm, which you can use as your worry time. When that time arrives you may deal with your negative thoughts by worrying, but this is not compulsory and most people decide not to use it. It is important that you don't confuse postponing your worry with the act of trying not to think a thought. I'm asking you to allow an initial thought that triggers worry to remain in your mind but you are choosing not to engage with it by worrying and trying to work it out. If you try not to think the thought or push it out of your mind that is unhelpful and produces the effect like the yellow rabbit experience earlier. Do you understand the distinction between postponing the worry activity and trying to remove the initial concern from your mind?

If the patient does not grasp the distinction readily, exercises are practised in session to allow the patient to do so. For example, the patient can be asked to think of the yellow rabbit and allow the thought to remain in consciousness without engaging with it in any way, merely watching the thought as a passive observer. This strategy is labelled as 'detached mindfulness' (Wells and Matthews, 1994). Detached mindfulness can then be practised with a recent worry trigger.

During the course of verbal reattribution, and following the practise of the worry postponement experiment for homework, the therapist asks for subjective belief ratings in the uncontrollability metacognition (e.g. 'How much do you now believe that worrying is uncontrollable, on a scale of zero per cent to one-hundred per cent convinced?'). Experiments are refined and repeated until the uncontrollability belief is at zero. In particular, subsequent experiments encourage the patient to deliberately worry more in situations to determine if they can actually lose control of worrying.

MODIFYING DANGER METACOGNITIONS

Next, negative metacognitive beliefs concerning the danger of worrying are modified. Initially by verbal reattribution methods. This involves questioning the evidence for believing that worry is harmful, questioning the mechanism, reviewing counter-evidence, and learning of new information.

In questioning the mechanism it is often possible to uncover erroneous beliefs about the effects of worry on the body and provide corrective information. For instance, one patient believed that worrying raised blood pressure and this would lead to health problems. However, during close questioning by the therapist it transpired that the patient's blood pressure was normal despite worrying (counterevidence), and the therapist went on to make the distinction between chronically elevated blood pressure linked to disease processes and the transient increases associated with anxiety. Transient increases were also equated with similar effects experienced during exercise, which can protect against cardiac risk.

The therapist also provides corrective information about worry and anxiety. For example, some people confuse worry with the concept of stress, whereas worry is a response to stress in as much as it represents the person's coping strategy. The nature of anxiety can be de-catastrophised by drawing attention to the fact that it is part of the person's survival mechanism. How good would such a mechanism be if it caused physical or mental harm? One particular patient worried that her worry and anxiety would cause a heart attack. The therapist asked her if she had seen any medical dramas on television recently, and what had been done to re-start a person's heart once it had stopped beating. She remembered that electric shocks were given, and with a little more prompting realised that Adrenaline had been injected into the heart muscle to restart it. A discussion then followed to review the fact that Adrenaline is released during worry and anxiety, and this was incompatible with the idea that worry and anxiety would stop the heart.

Verbal methods are followed by direct behavioural experiments to test negative beliefs about the danger of worrying. Examples of such experiments include worrying more in order to try and lose control of thinking, engaging in physical exercise during a worry episode to determine if this leads to a specific physical calamity, thinking 'crazy thoughts' in order to determine if thinking can cause mental breakdown, and so on. In each case the experiment is tailored to test the patient's idiosyncratic feared outcome. One experiment asks the patient to push their worrying to new high levels. Later the patient is asked to attempt the worry-more experiment during a naturally occurring distressing worry episode in order to obtain unambiguous disconfirmation of negative beliefs about the specific dangers of worrying.

MODIFYING POSITIVE METACOGNITIVE BELIEFS

Once negative metacognitions concerning danger have been modified the therapist moves on to weakening positive metacognitions. Questioning the evidence supporting positive beliefs, and asking the patient why they have a problem with worrying if it is helpful are used as provisional techniques for weakening these beliefs.

Several specific strategies for weakening positive beliefs have been devised in MCT. These include the mismatch strategy, and worry modulation experiments (Wells, 1997). In the former the therapist obtains a detailed description of a patient's worry and then compares this against a description of the events that actually transpired in a worried-about situation. The aim here is to help the patient to see how the worry script is distorted and presents a catastrophic picture of the world that does not match reality. Once this is apparent the therapist then asks the question: 'If your worry does not match reality, how useful can it really be?'. The mismatch strategy can be used retrospectively for a situation recently encountered, and set up prospectively in which the patient is asked to think about a future situation that they are worrying about (e.g. going on holiday). The catastrophic script of worries is written out for this event in the session, and the patient is asked to follow through with the activity. A reality-script is then written summarising the events that occurred in the situation, and the worry script is compared with the reality-script in order to challenge the usefulness of worry.

A further strategy is the worry-modulation experiment. Here the patient is asked to reduce worrying on some occasion and increase worrying on a different occasion to determine if positive outcomes occur when worry is greater. This is configured as a behavioural experiment to test the prediction that worrying facilitates coping, increases positive outcomes, or enhances positive self-control. For example, a patient believed that worrying increased the quality of his work performance. He predicted that if he spent a day not worrying at work that he would make more mistakes. After implementing the experiment he discovered, contrary to his prediction, that the number of mistakes he made did not change, however he felt better when he worried less.

The mini-survey can also be used. Here the patient is invited to survey several people, some of them are considered to be high worriers and some low worriers. In this scenario the prediction is that if worry increases positive outcomes such as ability to cope, then high worriers will view themselves as better at coping than low worriers.

RELAPSE PREVENTION

In the final sessions of treatment attention focuses increasingly on relapse prevention. The GADS offers an important source of information concerning change and residual pathological processes, and it is prudent for the therapist to closely inspect ratings on this instrument during treatment and the relapse prevention phase. Residual avoidance, and remaining negative and positive metacognitive beliefs (i.e. those not at zero per cent), should be targeted. More of the same strategies as used earlier in treatment may be required to eliminate residual beliefs.

Two further components of relapse prevention are developing the therapy blueprint, and consolidating alternative strategies for dealing with negative thoughts/stress. The blueprint consists of a summary of the material covered during treatment and includes a copy of the case formulation. It consists of a list of idiosyncratic negative and positive metacognitive beliefs and a summary of evidence against them. The blueprint contains a description of alternative strategies for dealing with stress and negative thoughts. Alternative strategies include, using detached mindfulness, worry postponement, doing rather than thinking and re-writing worry scripts. The idea of doing rather than thinking is introduced as acting in the absence of detailed thought or planning. Re-writing worry scripts consists

of introducing the strategy of responding to negative thoughts with positive imagery that aim to rapidly finish-out negative thoughts with positive
endings. These strategies are introduced to broaden the response repertoire of individuals, and it is important to determine that they will not be
used maladaptively in a way that prevents modification of dysfunctional
metacognitive beliefs.

DEALING WITH CO-MORBIDITY

The metacognitive theory on which GAD treatment is based is a theory of
generic pathological processes. It follows that metacognitive therapy for
GAD could be a first line intervention in co-morbid presentations involving GAD and other disorders. For example, a case of GAD and depression may be formulated using the GAD model and expanded to include
positive and negative metacognitions concerning depressive thinking (i.e.
rumination) in addition to metacognitions about worry. In a case of GAD
with social phobia, treatment of GAD may be followed by treatment of
social phobia using the appropriate model (e.g. Clark and Wells, 1995).
The targeting of worry processes rather than more specific social phobia
processes is recommended initially because worry processes are important
in the maintenance of both disorders. However, the precise nature of treatment must take account of factors such as risk. If patients have high levels
of hopelessness appraisals or suicidality, direct intervention in these areas
is an initial imperative.

EFFECTIVENESS OF MCT

Evidence of the effectiveness of MCT in the treatment of pathological worry
and GAD has begun to emerge. In an open trial Wells and King (in press)
treated ten consecutively referred patients meeting DSM-IV criteria for
GAD. Patients received 3–12 weekly sessions and were followed-up over
12 months. Patients showed significant reductions in measures of anxiety,
worry and depressed mood. Both Type 1 and Type 2 worry improved
as did trait anxiety. Applying Jacobsen criteria for recovery to the trait-
anxiety data showed that 87.5% of patients met criteria for recovery at post
treatment and at 6- and 12-month follow-up this was 75%. Post treatment
effect sizes ranged from 1.18–2.86 across measures.

The data from a randomised trial of MCT versus applied relaxation have
shown similar outcomes for MCT (Wells et al., in preparation). These data
have been independently analysed for clinical significance by Fisher (see
Chapter 20). In this analysis MCT produced recovery rates of 80% with a
further 10% of patients improved on the basis of trait anxiety scores. On

the basis of the Penn State Worry Questionnaire (PSWQ) these statistics were 80% of patients recovered and 20% improved at post treatment. At 12-month follow-up 70% were recovered based on trait-anxiety, and this was 80% based on the PSWQ.

SUMMARY AND CONCLUSIONS

The metacognitive model provides a conceptual framework for developing individual case formulations and guiding the focus of cognitive-behavioural change strategies. The metacognitive treatment developed in the context of this model provides a unique emphasis on modifying negative and positive metacognitive beliefs. To meet this objective a range of special techniques have been developed. The structure of therapy and some of the techniques used in implementing MCT were described in this chapter.

Treatment follows a specific sequence and proceeds on the basis of an individual case formulation. Ongoing monitoring of change in metacognitive and behavioural factors aided by the GADS is an important index of therapeutic effects and provides a guide to factors that should be targeted. Metacognitive change is achieved through a combination of particular verbal and behavioural strategies that aim to weaken existing metacognitive beliefs and build alternative beliefs about worry as a controllable and benign thinking process that is not necessary for coping.

Initial indications suggest that MCT is a brief and highly effective treatment for GAD. It appears to produce recovery or improvement that is stable over a 12-month post-treatment period.

Metacognitive therapy is not confined to the treatment of GAD. The model on which it is based is derived from a generic theory of psychological disorder, which gives central importance to worry/rumination. It follows from this that the techniques developed in MCT for worry and GAD should be useful in the treatment of other disorders. Such developments of metacognitive therapy and metacognitive techniques are emerging in the treatment of Post-Traumatic Stress Disorder (Wells & Sembi, 2004a, b), hypochondriasis (Papageorgiou & Wells, 1998), depression (Wells & Papageorgiou, 2004), obsessive-compulsive disorder (Fisher & Wells, 2005), and social phobia (Wells & Papageorgiou, 2001).

REFERENCES

Beck, A.T., Epstein, N., Brown, G. & Steer, R.A. (1988). An inventory for measuring clinical anxiety: psychometric properties. *Journal of Consulting and Clinical Psychology*, **56**, 893–897.

Beck, A.T., Ward, C.H., Mendelson, M., Mock, J. & Erbaugh, J. (1961). An inventory for measuring depression. *Archives of General Psychiatry*, **4**, 561–571.

Clark, D.M. & Wells, A. (1995). A cognitive model of social phobia. In: R.G. Heimberg, M.R. Liebowitz, D.A. Hope & R.R. Schneier (Eds). *Social Phobia: Diagnosis, Assessment and Treatment*. New York: Guilford Press.

Fisher, P.L. & Wells, A. (2005). Experimental modification of beliefs in obsessive-compulsive disorder: a test of the metacognitive model. *Behaviour Research and Therapy*, **43**, 821–829.

Meyer, T.J., Miller, M.L., Metzger, R.L. & Borkovec, T.D. (1990). Development and validation of the Penn State Worry Questionnaire. *Behaviour Research and Therapy*, **28**, 487–495.

Papageorgiou, C. & Wells, A. (1998). Effects of attention training in hypochondriasis: An experimental case series. *Psychological Medicine*, **28**, 193–200.

Wells, A. (1994). A multi-dimensional measure of worry: Development and preliminary validation of the Anxious Thoughts Inventory. *Anxiety, Stress and Coping*, **6**, 289–299.

Wells, A. (1995). Meta-cognition and worry: A cognitive model of generalised anxiety disorder. *Behavioural and Cognitive Psychotherapy*, **23**, 301–320.

Wells, A. (1997). *Cognitive Therapy of Anxiety Disorders: A practice manual and conceptual guide*. Chichester, UK: John Wiley & Sons, Ltd.

Wells, A. (2000). *Emotional Disorders and Metacognition: Innovative Cognitive Therapy*. Chichester, UK: John Wiley & Sons, Ltd.

Wells, A. & King, P. (in press). Metacognitive Therapy for Generalized Anxiety Disorder: An open trial. *Journal of Behavior Therapy and Experimental Psychiatry*.

Wells, A. & Matthews, G. (1994) Self-consciousness and cognitive failures as predictors of coping in stressful episodes. *Cognition and Emotion*, **8**, 279–295.

Wells, A. & Papageorgiou, C. (2001). Brief cognitive therapy for social phobia: A case series. *Behaviour Research and Therapy*, **39**, 713–720.

Wells, A. & Papageorgiou, C. (2004). Metacognitive Therapy for Depressive Rumination. In: C. Papageorgiou & A.Wells (Eds). *Depressive Rumination: Nature, Theory and Treatment*. Chichester, UK: John Wiley & Sons, Ltd.

Wells, A. & Sembi, S. (2004a). Metacognitive Therapy for PTSD: A preliminary investigation of a new brief treatment. *Journal of Behavior Therapy and Experimental Psychiatry*, **35**, 307–318.

Wells, A. & Sembi, S. (2004b). Metacognitive Therapy for PTSD: A Core Treatment Manual. *Cognitive and Behavioral Practice*, **11**, 365–377.

Wells, A., Welford, M., King, P., Papageorgiou, C., Wisely, J. & Mendel, E. (in prep). A randomized trial of metacognitive therapy versus applied relaxation in the treatment of GAD.

Chapter 16

APPLIED RELAXATION AND COGNITIVE THERAPY FOR PATHOLOGICAL WORRY AND GENERALIZED ANXIETY DISORDER

T.D. Borkovec

The dawn of experimental research on worry occurred in the early 1980s (Borkovec, Robinson, Pruzinsky & DePree, 1983). At the same time, generalized anxiety disorder (GAD), the first diagnostic disorder to explicitly contain worry as a defining characteristic, emerged in DSM-III (American Psychiatric Association, 1980), and the first therapy outcome investigation for this new disorder, involving a cognitive behavioral therapy (CBT) approach (Barlow et al., 1984), was reported. With the publication of DSM-III-R (American Psychiatric Association, 1987) and DSM-IV (American Psychiatric Association, 1994), worry became the central defining feature of GAD. Since these origins, a vast amount of basic and applied research, reflected in the content of this volume, has been generated. There are very good reasons behind this explosion of research and treatment development: (a) Worry is a pervasive phenomenon throughout the anxiety and mood disorders (Barlow, 1988) and is a common and problematic experience even in normal populations; (b) GAD has a fairly high prevalence rate but more importantly is one of the most common comorbid conditions among the anxiety and mood disorders (Brown & Barlow, 1992); (c) GAD may be the basic anxiety disorder out of which emerges other anxiety and mood disorders (Brown, Barlow & Liebowitz, 1994); and (d) worry predominantly involves the most highly evolved information processing system (i.e., abstract thought), functions as a cognitive avoidance response to perceived threat, and precludes the emotional processing of anxiety and other emotions, thus contributing to the maintenance of emotional difficulties (see Chapter 14, this volume). For all of these reasons, the pursuit of basic knowledge about worry and GAD is very likely to contribute a great deal to our understanding of anxiety and mood disorders as well

Worry and Its Psychological Disorders: Theory, Assessment and Treatment. Edited by G. C. L. Davey and A. Wells. © 2006 John Wiley & Sons, Ltd.

as of the nature of being a human being, and the development of increasingly effective interventions for pathological worry and GAD is likely to contribute considerably to our methods of treating several of the Axis I disorders. The latter possibility is reinforced by the fact that successful treatment of GAD is associated with the amelioration of most comorbid anxiety and mood disorders (Borkovec, Abel & Newman, 1995), even though those disorders were not explicitly targeted in optimal ways by the employed interventions.

Over the past two decades, various CBT methods have been applied to the treatment of GAD, but most of these intervention packages have involved four basic elements: self- monitoring, relaxation training, cognitive therapy, and the rehearsal of the resulting coping responses in the therapy sessions and in daily life. The present chapter will describe these basic components of CBT for worry and GAD, along with brief discussions of some of the additional intervention methods that have periodically been incorporated into the basic CBT approach. The chapter will end with a description of the latest developments that are occurring in the pursuit of more effective ways of intervening with this difficult-to-treat disorder.

BASIC COGNITIVE BEHAVIORAL INTERVENTIONS FOR GAD

Awareness and Self-Monitoring

Most theoretical orientations to psychotherapy emphasize the importance of clients becoming increasingly aware of their stuck, habitual patterns of responding. Modern cognitive theory and research support the usefulness of people becoming aware of automatic processing so that they can engage in new (initially effortful) strategic responding in order to change habitual behavior. The initial foundation of most CBT approaches with adult anxiety disorders involves self-monitoring to create this awareness. Clients are typically taught to pay attention to internal (cognitive, affective, and somatic) and external events as they are occurring during anxious episodes and to identify causal connections among these events.

The purpose of this is twofold. First, it is important for clients to become aware of what triggers anxiety for them and how they react to those triggers in ways that contribute to the development and maintenance of their anxiety. Second, by observing their reactions, they can learn to identify the earliest occurrence of shifts in their internal state in an anxious direction. By so doing, they will later be able to intervene at the beginning of anxious episodes by strategically deploying new coping skills at the earliest possible moment. The earlier that they choose to react differently and more adaptively, the more effective the coping responses will be.

Teaching clients to self-monitor takes place both in the therapy session and in their daily lives. In sessions, in order to observe and learn about their anxiety, the therapist asks clients to recall and relive recent anxious or worrisome episodes and to describe, moment to moment, the sequence of reactions that they are experiencing as their anxious process develops. The therapist also watches for any verbal or nonverbal indications of incipient anxiety while clients are talking and frequently stops them to query about noticed internal reactions and what thoughts, images, and behaviors are contained in those reactions. Emphasis is placed on identifying the earliest indication that anxiety or worry is beginning to take place. Clients are also asked to monitor their internal states and the events associated with them during daily living in order to learn more about what is initiating anxious responding and how they are sequentially reacting in ways that contribute to and maintain that anxiety. From the first session and thereafter, the therapist creates a 0–100-point scale, anchored on one end by complete tranquility and on the other by the most anxious and worried the client has ever been. The therapist frequently asks clients throughout therapy sessions to rate their in-the-moment experience in order to inform both the therapist and themselves how their anxiety fluctuates, in response to what stimuli, and to what degree. Later in therapy as new coping skills are being learned, the same scale is used to assess the in-the-moment effectiveness of coping applications.

Self-monitoring and its consequential increases in awareness of one's moment-to-moment internal and external environments also serve another important function. They are the first experiences provided to clients designed to teach them the meaning of "present moment." As the therapist and clients make use of recalling anxious experiences and discussing worrisome topics in order to observe incipient anxiety cues and their impact on the rating scale, the therapist periodically points out that the anxiety is being generated solely by the clients' thoughts and images, that these cognitions always refer to the nonexistent future or a past that no longer exists, and that there can be no anxiety (or depression) if one is focused only on the present moment. Objectively observing what is happening internally and externally in each present moment without reacting in habitual and nonadaptive ways to those events is a foundational skill for distinguishing the reality of the present from the illusions of the future and the past.

Relaxation Techniques

Relaxation training has been central to the treatment of diffuse anxiety problems for many decades. Recent research on the psychophysiological characteristics of GAD has reinforced the use of both relaxation strategies in general and progressive muscular relaxation in particular. Both the tonic condition of GAD and the phasic effects of worry are associated with reduced variability in peripheral physiological functioning, deficiency in parasympathetic tone, and excessive muscle tension (Hoehn-Saric & McLeod, 1988; Hoehn-Saric, McLeod & Zimmerli, 1989; Thayer, Friedman & Borkovec, 1996). The reason for these characteristics appears to reside in the psychological state that GAD clients create for themselves in their worrying: They are anxious about nonexistent future events, and because there is no effective behavioral avoidance response to remove the threat under this circumstance, sympathetic activation of the fight-or-flight system may be suppressed and replaced by a freezing response (Gray, 1987).

Several types of relaxation training have historically been used, including progressive muscle relaxation; slowed, paced, diaphragmatic breathing; pleasant imagery; and mediational techniques. Progressive relaxation (Bernstein, Borkovec & Hazlett-Stevens, 2000) begins with the systematic tensing and releasing of various muscle groups throughout the body and the attending to the resulting sensations of relaxation that are so produced. Over sessions, muscle groups are combined to make the technique more efficient and generative of a deeply relaxed state in a briefer period of time. Eventually, tensing and releasing of muscles is eliminated altogether, and clients learn to create relaxation by merely recalling how the muscles felt before when they were released ("relaxation by recall"). Breathing methods involve learning to slow one's breathing down, to breathe more deeply, and to breathe from the stomach rather than the chest. Imaginal relaxation involves the vivid creation of a scene that is generative of feelings of relaxation, safety, tranquility, and comfort. Meditational techniques provide a focusing device (such as a single word, like "calm," that is spoken upon each exhalation of breath). There are good reasons to teach GAD clients several of these techniques. Some methods are more effective than others for some clients, different methods are found to be useful under different circumstances or for different symptoms, relaxation-induced anxiety (common in diffusely anxious individuals; F. Heide & Borkovec, 1984) is less likely if clients have more than one relaxation method available to them (F.J. Heide & Borkovec, 1983), and multiple relaxation skills maximize choice and flexibility.

Most importantly, applied relaxation is taught (Öst, 1987). Clients learn to deploy their relaxation responses as soon as incipient anxiety or worry is detected in the course of their self-monitoring. Clients practice such applications both during the therapy hour and in their daily lives as a homework assignment. In early sessions, therapists will frequently interrupt clients whenever there is an indication of increased anxiety and instruct them to briefly elicit a relaxation response in order to return to a tranquil state. Later in therapy, they are encouraged to do this on their own any time they detect an anxiety cue during the session. They are further instructed to generate relaxation responses in their daily lives (a) whenever they notice incipient anxiety or worry, (b) before, during, and after stressful events, and (c) frequently during the day, even when they are not feeling anxious, in order to cultivate a more relaxed life-style in general.

The clients' experiences with the peacefulness, calmness, and tranquility generated by deep relaxation are also their first experiences within therapy (and eventually in their daily life applications) of pleasant present moments. Just as they are learning that their cognitions impact on (cause) their emotional states, they are learning that there are things that they can do to create (cause) more adaptive and enjoyable states.

Cognitive Therapy

Traditional cognitive therapy methods

Because GAD and worry are associated with frequent (and inaccurate) predictions that bad events might happen in the future, traditional cognitive therapy methods (e.g. Beck & Emery, 1985) have long been employed. Self-monitoring, both in session and in daily life, includes the identification of thoughts, images, and ways of perceiving that are associated with anxious and worrisome responding, and core beliefs about the self, the world, and the future eventually become apparent from the common themes revealed by the monitoring of these thoughts. Cognitive therapy proceeds with (a) assessments of the accuracy of these thoughts and beliefs, using logic, probability, and evidence; (b) the generation of alternative thoughts and beliefs that are more accurate; (c) practicing the use of these new perspectives whenever anxiety or worry are detected; and (d) the testing of the old and new perspectives through behavioral experiments designed to acquire evidence for their inaccuracy or accuracy.

In the process of cognitive therapy, the therapist often uses a Socratic method of questioning, designed to lead clients to new conclusions about the way things actually are instead of the way they might think that they are. Clients do not often think through their worries and anxieties, so de-catastrophizing methods can be particularly useful. When discussing a worry, the therapist asks what outcome the client fears might happen, and then asks what would be bad about that outcome. The same question is asked for each underlying feared outcome that the client generates until they determine what the worst outcome would be. For each of these steps, logic analysis and search for evidence are employed, followed by the creation of alternative outcomes that are more likely and the identification of coping resources that might be available at each step. It is not uncommon that clients realize at the end of this process that the feared outcomes are unlikely to happen, would not be as bad as they thought even if they did occur, and would be coped with quite well.

Worry outcome diary

A significant method for having GAD clients test their worrisome predictions makes use of the Worry Outcome Diary. Clients write down in their diary each worry they detect during the day as well as what they are afraid might happen. Each evening, they review all of their past entries. For any worry that had an outcome on that day, they rate whether the outcome and their ability to cope with the outcome were better than predicted, as bad as they predicted, or worse than predicted. They are asked to vividly imagine the outcomes in order to fully process the information that reality has presented to them. Data from the diaries of clients in one of our clinical trials indicated that most of the things about which they worry turn out better than expected, and when bad events do occur, they cope with them better than expected (Borkovec, Hazlett-Stevens & Diaz, 1999).

Expectancy-free living

Traditional cognitive therapy aims at replacing inaccurate thoughts and beliefs with more accurate cognitions. GAD clients in their characteristic worrying are making frequent predictions that bad events are likely to happen. Certainly making more accurate predictions helps them to reduce the amount of anxiety that they are experiencing. One further step beyond such helpful changes involves letting go of predictions and expectations altogether. Decades of research in the fields of cognitive and social psychology have demonstrated that preconceptions of any type influence both selective attention to present-moment environmental information and interpretations of that information. The frequent consequence of such influences is confirmatory bias; human beings will tend to attend to and interpret information in a way that supports their pre-existing beliefs. This means that accurately perceiving, processing, and learning about reality in the present moment is more challenging than one might think. In order to maximize accurate perception and learning in any given present moment then, it would be best to minimize preconceptions, including predictions. So later on in therapy, the therapist encourages clients to practice entering each new present moment with a minimum of expectation about what that present moment will bring. In this way, cognitive therapy, like self-monitoring and relaxation techniques, leads to an emphasis on living in the present moment.

Intrinsic motivation

Once a person is spending more time in the present moment, additional cognitive perspectives can be brought to bear not merely for facilitating a reduction in anxiety and worry but also for creating joy. The therapist works with clients to identify what values they have that are near and dear to their hearts, and they then practice applying these values to whatever present moments (e.g., work tasks or interpersonal interactions) occur. A major advantage exists for engaging environments from these value-guided perspectives. The behaviors and ways of being guided by deeply held values are reinforcing in and of themselves, and thus the new value-oriented perspectives elicit positive affective states. With greater focus on the present moment, the task at hand, the pleasantness of engaging the task as generated by the intrinsic perspective, the less likely will be anxiety and worry. And when all of these characteristics are combined, there is a maximization of the probability of skilled performance in the situation and thus an increased likelihood of achieving any extrinsic outcomes that might be available. Somewhat paradoxically, a focus on valued present-moment process, instead of future outcome, makes the outcome more likely.

Imagery Rehearsal of Coping Strategies

Several clinical trials evaluating CBT for GAD have included in-session imaginal rehearsals of developing coping responses. Rather than using imagery as a repeated exposure technique to extinguish anxiety, imaginal rehearsal techniques (e.g., self- control desensitization, Goldfried, 1971 and anxiety management training, Suinn & Richardson, 1971), employ imagery in order to provide opportunities to repeatedly practice new, adaptive coping strategies. In self-control desensitization, for example, after the client is deeply relaxed, an image containing some of the external and internal anxiety cues characteristic of a client's daily experience (including worry) is presented. As soon as the client notices actual anxiety occurring in response to this image and signals this by raising the index finger, he/she immediately practices generating relaxation responses as well as cognitive shifts, viewing the situation in terms of the alternative, adaptive, and more accurate perspectives that were developed during the cognitive therapy portions of the session. As the imagery process continues, the client indicates by dropping the index finger that he/she is continuing to imagine the scene but is no longer experiencing anxiety. The client continues to imagine being in the scene and coping successfully with it for a while, and then the therapist has him/her turn off the scene and deepen the relaxation. The same image is then presented repeatedly in this way in order to develop stronger habit strength for the coping responses in association

Table 16.1   Sequence of self-control desensitization steps

Therapist Presents	Anxiety Is Signaled	Anxiety Is Not Signaled
I. Hierarchy image with anxiety cues	Go to row II upon anxiety signal	Go to row II after 60 secs.
II. Relaxation & cognitive coping imagery	When anxiety signal stops, go to row III	Go to row IV after 20 secs.
III. Continued coping imagery	After 20 secs, go to row IV	
IV. Post-image relaxation	20 secs.	20 secs.
V. Repeat image, using steps I–IV, until client is no longer experiencing anxiety in response to anxiety cue image and/or rapidly eliminates any anxiety that does occur.		

with the anxiety cues. Once clients are unable to experience anxiety in response to the imaginal presentation of these anxiety cues and/or they can efficiently and rapidly eliminate any anxiety that does occur, further images containing a new set of internal and external anxiety cues are presented. Table 16.1 gives the sequence of self-control desensitization as our research group has implemented it in past clinical trials.

The duration of any of the above phases is not important. What is important is to make sure that clients have repeated opportunities to practice detecting anxiety and worry, to rehearse their new coping skills in response to those internal cues for the sake of increasing their habit strength, and to experience success in each of those rehearsals.

ADDITIONAL INTERVENTION METHODS

Stimulus Control Treatment

One of the earliest behavioral interventions developed specifically for worry involves the application of the principle of stimulus control. When operant behaviors are enacted, they become associated with the environments in which they occur. These environments then set the occasion for future occurrences of those behaviors, making them more likely to be emitted in the presence of the associated environments. Both internal and external stimuli can come to serve such discriminative functions. The mood/memory effect is an example of internal stimulus control. (Bower, 1981). Worry (viewed as an internal, voluntary, operant behavior) can occur at any time and in any place. Consequently, the more one worries, the more the worrying is likely to become associated with an increasing number of external and internal stimuli; it is under poor stimulus control. Deliberately limiting the stimulus conditions under which the nonadaptive behavior occurs is a useful method for achieving greater stimulus control of, and thus reduction in, the behavior. Such stimulus control methods have been successfully applied in the past to several problematic behaviors, including sleep-incompatible behaviors that contribute to the development of insomnia (Bootzin & Epstein, 2000).

The original stimulus control program for worry (Borkovec, Wilkinson, Folensbee & Lerman, 1983) involved four instructions:

(1) Learn to identify worrisome thoughts and other thoughts that are unnecessary or unpleasant. Distinguish these from necessary or pleasant thoughts related to the present moment.
(2) Establish a half-hour worry period to take place at the same time and in the same location each day.
(3) When you catch yourself worrying, postpone the worry to the worry period and replace it with attending to present-moment experience.
(4) Make use of the half-hour worry period to worry about your concerns and to engage in problem-solving to eliminate those concerns.

Although telling a worrier not to worry is not an effective instruction, it does turn out that worriers are able to postpone their worrying with relative ease. The worrying readily returns, however, and so worriers need to repeatedly follow these instructions upon each occurrence of worrisome process.

As clients learn the cognitive therapy methods described earlier, they make use of their worry period to apply those techniques in order to reduce their perception of threats that typically initiates worrisome sequences.

There is also an alternative method for achieving stimulus control which many clients find preferable. This technique involves identifying a specific time of the day (e.g., upon awakening until finishing breakfast) or a particular place (e.g., the living room) that will be designated a "worry-free zone." Clients are instructed to postpone any worrying detected inside of this zone to any time or place outside of that zone. As they begin to notice the lessening of the tendency to worry within their worry-free zone, they choose additional times or places to be worry-free. Over the weeks, the zones increase until they cover nearly every time of the day or all of the places in which they live.

Exposure Therapy

GAD is not as characterized by circumscribed feared situations as are the other anxiety disorders. If it were, or if we someday discover a core fear or limited set of core fears in GAD, then exposure techniques that have been found to be so effective in the treatment of the other anxiety disorders could be incorporated into CBT methods for GAD. At the present time, however, we do not know whether such core fears exist or what their content might be. It is for this reason that CBT approaches to this disorder have emphasized coping oriented methods as opposed to mastery methods.

This is not to say that exposure techniques are not relevant to the treatment of GAD. These methods should be included any time specific, anxiety-provoking situations do exist for a client. There are two forms in which such specific external triggers may be found in GAD clients. First, Butler (B. Butler, Cullington, Hibbert, Klimes & Gelder, 1987) has pointed out that they sometimes engage in subtle avoidance behaviors that are revealed only through careful questioning of clients about situations that they hesitate to enter or prefer not to enter (e.g., often deciding not to attend social gatherings, or preferring spouse to interact with others). Second, GAD has a very high rate of comorbid anxiety disorders associated with it; social phobias and specific phobias are the most common (Brown & Barlow, 1992). When comorbid anxiety disorders exist, then repeated exposure techniques usefully become an element of a complete CBT treatment approach for such clients. During these exposures, clients can still make use of their relaxation and cognitive coping responses before, during, and after the exposures.

Behavioral Activation

GAD clients frequently have comorbid mood disorders (Brown & Barlow, 1992), and worry generates both anxious and depressed states (Andrews & Borkovec, 1988). Consequently, encouraging clients to engage in pleasant activities is likely to be quite useful. Butler's CBT treatment trials for GAD (Butler et al., 1987; Butler, Fennell, Robson, & Gelder, 1991) have included such a behavioral component. The inclusion of intrinsically motivated behaviors (described earlier) also exemplifies an element of treatment that potentially increases positive affective states and thus can impact on the depressive moods so often accompanying GAD.

EFFICACY RESEARCH

Chapter 20 provides an up-to-date review of the effectiveness of CBT with GAD clients, and should serve as the basis for the most recent, valid conclusions about treatment efficacy. However, several prior reviews have clearly documented the effectiveness of this form of treatment for GAD (e.g., Chambless & Gillis, 1993; Borkovec & Ruscio, 2001; Borkovec & Whisman, 1996), and CBT is recognized as an empirically supported treatment for the disorder based on criteria-meeting randomized clinical trials (Chambless & Ollendick, 2001). In summary of these earlier reviews, CBT has typically been found to generate the largest within-group and between-group effect sizes at both post-therapy and long-term follow-up assessments compared to nonspecific, alternate treatment, and component control conditions, and at post-therapy assessments compared to waiting-list no-treatment conditions. CBT has also been typically associated with the lowest drop-out rate, and therapeutic improvements are typically maintained at long-term follow-up assessments. Some ambiguity exists with regard to CBT's superiority over one of its component conditions (e.g., cognitive therapy only or relaxation training only), given that only a minority of direct experimental comparisons have found significant differences. Whether a component condition yields as much improvement as the full CBT package or less improvement may, however, be a function of length of treatment: Those investigations finding greater change in CBT than in a component condition involved fewer sessions of treatment, whereas those finding no differences had lengthier treatment (Borkovec, Newman, Pincus & Lytle, 2002). Given that anxiety involves the interactions over time of several levels of information processing and responding, it may be the case that targeting one of these response systems (e.g., cognitive process, or somatic process) and providing sufficiently long practice of a relevant coping response for that response system will eventually result in changes in the other response systems.

NEW THERAPEUTIC DEVELOPMENTS

Although research supports the efficacy of CBT, many GAD clients are not returned to normal levels of anxious experience. Indeed, based on the empirical literature, Dave Barlow has concluded that GAD is the most difficult anxiety disorder to treat. In recent years, exciting new interventions, grounded in basic research knowledge about worry and GAD, have been emerging and are in the process of being experimentally evaluated. Two of these new approaches (Wells' metacognitive therapy for worry, and Dugas' treatment methods targeting intolerance of uncertainty) come squarely from the cognitive therapy tradition and are described in detail in this volume in Chapters 11 and 12, respectively. Another set of developing techniques have been drawn from the mindfulness tradition (e.g., Kabat-Zinn et al., 1992) and from related methods contained within Acceptance and Commitment Therapy and integrated with CBT (Roemer & Orsillo, 2002).

A third emerging trend has been the targeting of interpersonal functioning. Considerable evidence has accumulated to indicate that worry and

GAD have intimate connections to the interpersonal realm. Worry correlates most highly with social evaluative fears and less so with nonsocial
stimuli (Borkovec, Robinson et al., 1983), social phobia is one of the most
frequent comorbid conditions associated with GAD (Brown & Barlow,
1992), the most frequent worry topics are interpersonally related (Roemer,
Molina, & Borkovec, 1997), GAD clients show significant rigidity and
nonadaptiveness in their interpersonal relationships (Pincus & Borkovec,
1994), and degree of interpersonal problems negatively predicts the therapeutic outcomes of intrapersonally focused CBT for GAD (Borkovec et
al., 2002). Crits-Christoff, Connolly, Azarian, Crits-Christoff, and Shappell
(1996) have found some uncontrolled evidence for the potential usefulness of supportive-expressive therapy in an open trial with GAD clients.
My own research group (with collaborators, Michelle Newman and Louis
Castonguay) is nearing the completion of an experimental comparison of our CBT approach versus our CBT combined with an Interper-
sonal/Emotional Processing Therapy element. This latter element was
based on Safran and Segal's (1990) integration of CBT with interpersonal
and experiential therapy methods and was adapted specifically for GAD
clients by Michelle Newman. Below is an outline of these new therapy
methods. More in-depth description of them can be found in Newman,
Castonguay, Borkovec and Molnar (2002).

I. Goals: To facilitate client identification of interpersonal needs and fears,
   and to help client to develop better interpersonal behaviors to satisfy
   those needs.
II. Methods:
   (a) Exploration of out-of-session interpersonal relationships and exper-
       iments between sessions.
   (b) Accessing and modifying cognitive processes in an emotionally im-
       mediate way.
       1. Moment-to-moment attention to what is emotionally alive for the
          client.
       2. Use of interpersonal markers for cognitive/affective exploration.
   (c) Use of the therapeutic relationship for exploring cognitive/affective
       processes and for challenging interpersonal schemas.
       1. Use of the therapist's own feelings to generate hypotheses about
          client's interpersonal patterns.
       2. Importance of detection and successful resolution of ruptures in
          the therapeutic alliance.
   (d) Social skills training.

Upon completion of our current outcome trial, we will be able to determine whether the addition of the interpersonal and experiential techniques
yields significantly superior outcomes compared to CBT alone.

CONCLUSION

Remarkable progress has occurred in our understanding of pathological worry and its severe clinical manifestation in GAD. CBT approaches have been developed and experimentally evaluated over the past two decades, resulting in interventions that we clinicians can apply with confidence, knowing that these approaches indeed contain active therapeutic ingredients for the treatment of disorders in which worry and chronic anxiety play a predominant role. Our work has not been completed, however, because in clinical trial research not all clients are found to return to normal levels of anxiety and worry. Furthermore, we have yet to explore the potential applicability of these methods to the other anxiety and mood disorders that contain recurrent negative thinking as a part of the problem. Given the importance of GAD and its central worry characteristic for understanding emotional psychopathologies and their treatment, I am confident that continued research efforts will result in significant further gains in our ability to provide relief to those who suffer from emotional problems.

ACKNOWLEDGEMENT

Preparation of this chapter was supported in part by the National Institute of Mental Health Grant MH-58593.

REFERENCES

Andrews, V.H. & Borkovec, T.D. (1988). The differential effects of induction of worry, somatic anxiety, and depression on emotional experience. *Journal of Behavior Therapy and Experimental Psychiatry*, **19**, 21–26.

American Psychiatric Association (1980). *Diagnostic and Statistical Manual—3rd Edition*. Washington, DC.

American Psychiatric Association (1987). *Diagnostic and Statistical Manual—Revised 3rd Edition*. Washington, DC.

American Psychiatric Association (1994). *Diagnostic and Statistical Manual—4th Edition*. Washington, DC.

Barlow, D.H. (1988). *Anxiety and its disorders: The nature and treatment of anxiety and panic*. New York: Guilford Press.

Barlow, D.H., Cohen, A.S., Waddell, M., Vermilyea, J.A., Klosko, J.S., Blanchard, E.B. & DiNardo, P.A. (1984). Panic and generalized anxiety disorders: Nature and treatment. *Behavior Therapy*, **15**, 431–449.

Beck, A.T. & Emery, G. (1985). *Anxiety disorders and phobias: A cognitive perspective*. New York: Basic Books.

Bernstein, D.A., Borkovec, T.D. & Hazlett-Stevens, H. (2000). *New directions in progressive relaxation training: A guidebook for helping professionals*. Westport, CT: Praeger Publishers.

Bootzin, R.R. & Epstein, D.R. (2000). Stimulus control instructions. In K.L. Lichstein & C.M. Morin (Eds), *Treatment of late-life insomnia* (pp. 167–184). Thousand Oaks, CA: Sage.

Borkovec, T.D., Abel, J.L. & Newman, H. (1995). The effects of therapy on comorbid conditions in generalized anxiety disorder. *Journal of Consulting and Clinical Psychology*, **63**, 479–483.

Borkovec, T.D., Hazlett-Stevens, H. & Diaz, M.L. (1999). The role of positive beliefs about worry in generalized anxiety disorder and its treatment. *Clinical Psychology and Psychotherapy*, **6**, 126–138.

Borkovec, T.D., Newman, M.G., Pincus, A. & Lytle, R. (2002). A component analysis of cognitive behavioral therapy for generalized anxiety disorder and the role of interpersonal problems. *Journal of Consulting and Clinical Psychology*, **70**, 288–298.

Borkovec, T.D., Robinson, E., Pruzinsky, T. & DePree, J.A. (1983). Preliminary exploration of worry: Some characteristics and processes. *Behaviour Research and Therapy*, **21**, 9–16.

Borkovec, T.D. & Ruscio, A. (2001). Psychotherapy for generalized anxiety disorder. *Journal of Clinical Psychiatry*, **62**, 37–45.

Borkovec, T.D. & Whisman, M.A. (1996). Psychological treatment for generalized anxiety disorder. In M.R. Mavissakalian & R.F. Prien (Eds), *Long-term treatments of anxiety disorders* (pp. 171–199). Washington, DC: American Psychiatric Association.

Borkovec, T.D., Wilkinson, L., Folensbee, R. & Lerman, C. (1983). Stimulus control applications to the treatment of worry. *Behaviour Research and Therapy*, **21**, 247–251.

Bower, G.H. (1981). Mood and memory. *American Psychologist*, **36**, 129–148.

Brown, T.A. & Barlow, D.H. (1992). Comorbidity among anxiety disorders: Implications for treatment and DSM-IV. *Journal of Consulting and Clinical Psychology*, **60**, 835–844.

Brown, T.A., Barlow, D.H. & Liebowitz, M.R. (1994). The empirical basis of generalized anxiety disorder. *American Journal of Psychiatry*, **151**, 1272–1280.

Butler, B., Cullington, A., Hibbert, G., Klimes, I. & Gelder, M. (1987). Anxiety management for persistent generalized anxiety. *British Journal of Psychiatry*, **151**, 535–542.

Butler, G., Fennell, M., Robson, P. & Gelder, M. (1991). Comparison of behavior therapy and cognitive behavior therapy in the treatment of generalized anxiety disorder. *Journal of Consulting and Clinical Psychology*, **59**, 167–175.

Chambless, D.L. & Gillis, M.M. (1993). Cognitive therapy of anxiety disorders. *Journal of Consulting and Clinical Psychology*, **61**, 248–260.

Chambless, D.L. & Ollendick, T.H. (2001). Empirically supported psychological interventions: Controversies and evidence. *Annual Review of Psychology*, **52**, 685–716.

Crits-Christoff, P., Connolly, M.B., Azarian, K., Crits-Christoff, K. & Shappell, S. (1996). An open trial of brief supportive-expressive psychotherapy in the treatment of generalized anxiety disorder. *Psychotherapy*, **33**, 418–431.

Goldfried, M.R. (1971). Systematic desensitization as training in self-control. *Journal of Consulting and Clinical Psychology*, **37**, 228–234.

Gray, J. (1987). The psychology of fear and stress, 2nd ed. Cambridge: Cambridge University Press.

Heide, F. & Borkovec, T.D. (1984). Relaxation-induced anxiety: Mechanisms and theoretical implications. *Behaviour Research and Therapy*, **22**, 1–12.

Heide, F.J. & Borkovec, T.D. (1983). Relaxation-induced anxiety: Paradoxical anxiety enhancement due to relaxation training. *Journal of Consulting and Clinical Psychology*, **51**, 171–182.

Hoehn-Saric, R. & McLeod, D.R. (1988). The peripheral sympathetic nervous system: Its role in normal and pathological anxiety. *Psychiatric Clinics of North America*, **11**, 375–386.

Hoehn-Saric, R., McLeod, D.R. & Zimmerli, W.D. (1989). Somatic manifestations in women with generalized anxiety disorder: Physiological responses to psychological stress. *Archives of General Psychiatry*, **46**, 1113–1119.

Kabat-Zinn, J., Massion, A.O., Kristeller, J., Peterson, L.G., Fletcher, K.E., Pbert, L., Lenkerking, W.R. & Santorelli, S.F. (1992). Effectiveness of a meditation-based stress reduction program in the treatment of anxiety disorders. *American Journal of Psychiatry*, **149**, 936–943.

Newman, M.G., Castonguay, L.G., Borkovec, T.D. & Molnar, C. (2002). Integrative therapy for generalized anxiety disorder. In R.G. Heimberg, C.L. Turk & D.S. Mennin (Eds), *Generalized anxiety disorder: Advances in research and practice* (pp. 320–350). New York: Guilford Press.

Öst, L. (1987). Applied relaxation: Description of a coping technique and review of controlled studies. *Behaviour Research and Therapy*, **25**, 397–409.

Pincus, A.L. & Borkovec, T.D. (1994, June). *Interpersonal problems in generalized anxiety disorder: Preliminary clustering of patients' interpersonal dysfunction*. Unpublished Paper presented at the annual meeting of the American Psychological Society, New York, NY.

Roemer, L., Molina, S. & Borkovec, T.D. (1997). The nature of generalized anxiety disorder: Worry content. *Journal of Nervous and Mental Disease*, **185**, 314–319.

Roemer, L. & Orsillo, S.M. (2002). Expanding our conceptualization of and treatment for generalized anxiety disorder: Integrating mindfulness/acceptance-based approaches with existing cognitive-behavioral models. *Clinical Psychology: Science and Practice*, **9**, 54–68.

Safran, J. & Segal, Z. V. (1990). *Interpersonal process in cognitive therapy*. New York: Basic Books.

Suinn, R.M. & Richardson, F. (1971). Anxiety management training: A nonspecific behavior therapy program for anxiety control. *Behavior Therapy*, **2**, 498–510.

Thayer, J.F., Friedman, B.H. & Borkovec, T.D. (1996). Autonomic characteristics of generalized anxiety disorder and worry. *Biological Psychiatry*, **39**, 255–266.

Chapter 17

A COGNITIVE-BEHAVIORAL TREATMENT TARGETING INTOLERANCE OF UNCERTAINTY

Melisa Robichaud and Michel J. Dugas

Generalized Anxiety Disorder (GAD) is a chronic anxiety condition that has received increasing attention in the last decade, since the introduction of excessive worry as the cardinal feature of GAD in the DSM-IV (American Psychiatric Association, 1994). As noted by several authors (e.g., Dugas, 2002; Wells, 2004), early treatment interventions were only moderately successful, and relied primarily on somatic management and general cognitive-behavioral techniques rather than a disorder-specific treatment package. However, a number of theoretically-driven treatment models have emerged recently to address the specific symptomatology of GAD (e.g., Borkovec & Newman, 1999; Roemer & Orsillo, 2002; Wells & Carter, 1999, see also Chapters 15 and 16). The protocol described herein is based on a cognitive model of GAD that posits etiological and maintaining roles for four processes: intolerance of uncertainty, positive beliefs about worry, negative problem orientation, and cognitive avoidance (see Dugas et al., 1998; Dugas, Marchand, & Ladouceur, 2005). As definitions of these constructs have been elaborated upon elsewhere in this volume (see Chapter 12), the following chapter will focus discussion on the four processes in terms of their clinical application within the context of treatment. In addition, process-specific assessment measures and efficacy findings for the treatment protocol will be addressed.

A COGNITIVE-BEHAVIORAL TREATMENT PROTOCOL FOR GAD

The following cognitive-behavioral treatment (CBT) package has been used for GAD in both a group and individual format, consisting of

Worry and Its Psychological Disorders: Theory, Assessment and Treatment. Edited by G. C. L. Davey and A. Wells. © 2006 John Wiley & Sons, Ltd.

approximately 12 to 16 sessions (see Dugas et al., 2003; Ladouceur et al., 2000). The core treatment components include: (1) psycho education about CBT and GAD; (2) worry awareness training; (3) coping with uncertainty; (4) re-evaluating beliefs about the usefulness of worry; (5) improving problem orientation and problem-solving ability; (6) processing core fears through imaginal exposure; and (7) relapse prevention. Although the treatment components target all four processes described in our model, the importance of learning to tolerate and accept uncertainty is a consistent theme that runs through all sessions.

Psycho Education about CBT and GAD

As is typical of most cognitive-behavioral packages, the first session is designed to familiarize patients with the principles of CBT. The therapist introduces the format of sessions, including the structured and directive nature of CBT, the time-limited nature of treatment, the active collaboration between therapist and patient, the focus on present symptomatology (i.e., the "here and now"), and the weekly assignment of between-session exercises. The diagnostic criteria for GAD are reviewed, and the patient is made aware that the target of treatment is excessive worry. Although somatic symptoms are discussed in session, the therapist explains that these symptoms are addressed *indirectly*. That is, reductions in worry lead to concomitant reductions in associated somatic symptoms.

In terms of psycho education, the rationale for treatment begins with an explanation of the cycle of excessive worry, using our current model in an illustrative fashion (see Figure 17.1). However, given the relative complexity of the model, particularly upon initial presentation, it is presented in a step-wise fashion (i.e., one treatment target at a time) throughout treatment. As new targets are introduced to patients (e.g., intolerance of uncertainty), they are incorporated into the model, allowing for a progressively richer understanding of GAD and excessive worry. As such, in early sessions, the therapist initially describes a "stripped-down" model that involves the following components:

$$\text{Trigger} \rightarrow \text{"What if}\ldots\text{?"} \rightarrow \text{Worry} \rightarrow \text{Anxiety} \rightarrow$$
$$\text{Demoralization/Exhaustion}$$

It is explained to patients that the worry cycle begins with a *trigger* that can be external (e.g., reading the newspaper) or internal (e.g., feeling of nausea). This trigger then leads to a *"what if..."* question, such as "what if my husband gets into a car accident while driving to work?" These "what if"

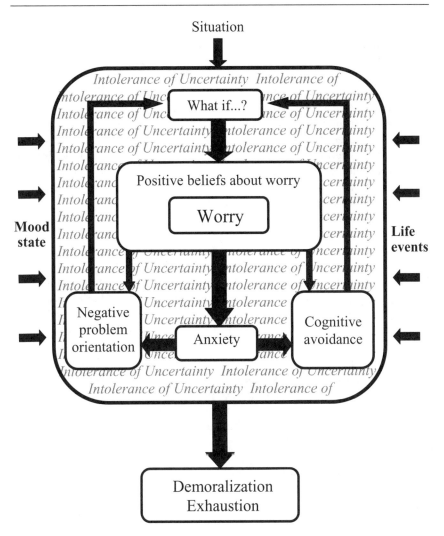

Figure 17.1   Cognitive-behavioral model of generalized anxiety disorder
From Dugas, M.J., Gagnon, F., Ladouceur, R. & Freeston, M.H. (1998). Generalized
Anxiety Disorder: A preliminary test of a conceptual model. *Behaviour Research and
Therapy*, **36**, 215–226.

questions set *worries* into motion. For example, "if my husband gets injured,
how will I cope? If he died, I would be all alone, and I would have to raise
the kids by myself, and I might lose my job and be unable to pay the rent . . ."
These worries are often associated with *anxiety*, which includes physiological sensations (e.g., muscle tension) as well as emotional discomfort (e.g.,
irritability). From the outset therefore, a distinction is made between worry

as a cognitive phenomenon and anxiety as an emotional and physiological response. Worry is defined to patients as a thought process related to uncertain negatively-valenced events in the future, which is accompanied by anxiety. Patients are encouraged to generate personal examples of a triggered worry cycle, allowing them to "see themselves" in the model. The chronic and longstanding nature of the disorder is highlighted by the final component of the model. It is explained to patients that experiencing repeated worry cycles over a period of months or years typically leads to feelings of *demoralization and exhaustion* (see Butler, Fennel, Robson & Gelder, 1991). A goal of treatment is therefore to recognize and break the worry cycle, in order to decrease both worry and feelings of anxiety, demoralization, and exhaustion.

Worry Awareness Training

The first step in targeting excessive worry is recognizing it once it occurs. As an initial between-session exercise, patients are charged with recording their worries in a worry diary three times a day at a predetermined time. The purpose of this task is two-fold: (1) by paying attention to their worries, patients can become increasingly adept at identifying them early on in the worry cycle; (2) monitoring daily worries will allow patients to recognize whether any worry topics recurrently emerge. Patients are also asked to separate their worries into two categories: worries that pertain to current problems (e.g., argument with a friend for having missed a lunch date), and those related to hypothetical situations (e.g., worries about a spouse one day getting ill). The therapist emphasizes the importance of distinguishing between both types of worries, as treatment interventions differ accordingly. For some patients, separating their worries into two categories can be a difficult exercise because it involves making decisions that involve uncertainty (the categories are not always mutually exclusive). When this happens, the therapist can draw attention to the importance of moving ahead with decision-making in the face of uncertainty. In this way, the patient begins to learn to cope with uncertainty, which is not only the next treatment component, but also the consistent theme of treatment.

Coping with Uncertainty

Beginning in the second or third session, the therapist introduces the concept of intolerance of uncertainty (IU) by adding it as a background to the illustrative model of GAD. The therapist explains that IU is the "fuel" for the engine of worry, and that people who are intolerant of uncertainty are more likely to worry because uncertainty leads to more "what if" questions among worriers. That is, whenever a situation occurs that contains any element of uncertainty, it can serve as a trigger for "what if" questions and begin the worry cycle. Since daily life is fraught with uncertainty, encountering uncertainty-laden triggers is inevitable. The following allergy model is used to better explain the concept of IU: "When people have a medical allergy, for example an allergy to pollen, they have an extreme reaction when exposed to even a tiny amount of the substance (e.g., violent coughing and sneezing). In a similar fashion, individuals with GAD can be said to have an 'allergy' to uncertainty, since they have a strong reaction when exposed to even a small amount of uncertainty (i.e., excessive worry and anxiety)."

In terms of treatment intervention, the therapist presents the following dilemma to patients: Given that intolerance of uncertainty plays a major role in worry, what can be done to change this? Logically, there are two options available, that is, to either reduce uncertainty or to increase tolerance to uncertainty. The therapist encourages the patient to realize that attempting to reduce uncertainty is an exercise in futility, as uncertainty in life is inescapable. Moreover, GAD patients are made aware that a great deal of time and energy is spent trying to reduce, eliminate, or avoid uncertainty, typically to little avail. As such, if uncertainty is unavoidable, the alternative option of increasing tolerance to uncertainty becomes the primary target of treatment. The therapist provides the patient with a list of behaviors typically carried out in an attempt to reduce or avoid uncertainty (see Table 17.1). The between-session exercise involves completing behavioral experiments where the patient in fact seeks out uncertainty. For example, rather than re-reading a low priority e-mail several times before

Table 17.1   Examples of Manifestations of Intolerance of Uncertainty

Types of Behaviours
• Avoiding doing certain things because the "outcome" is uncertain
• Finding imaginary obstacles for not doing certain things
• Procrastinating
• Not delegating tasks to others because of uncertainty that others will not do it "right"
• Only partially committing to a task, a project, or a relationship
• Seeking a great deal of information (reading, asking advice) before making a decision
• Questioning a decision because of uncertainty about whether it is the "right" or "perfect" decision
• Looking for reassurance from others
• Reassuring oneself with exaggerated optimism
• Double-checking or redoing things several times to be certain that they are correct
• Over-protecting others, doing things for them

sending it in order to ensure that there are no mistakes, the patient can send the e-mail immediately after writing it without being certain if there are indeed any errors. These types of behavioral experiments are completed throughout treatment, thereby allowing patients to develop a momentum, and to progressively tolerate increasingly uncertain situations that might be construed as more difficult or anxiety provoking. The importance of accepting uncertainty as a part of life and learning to tolerate it is reinforced throughout treatment, with all subsequent treatment interventions being tied in to this primary concept.

Re-evaluating the Usefulness of Worry

In this stage of treatment, the role of positive beliefs about the function of worry is introduced into the model of GAD. It is explained to patients that their beliefs about the usefulness of certain behaviors can greatly influence the likelihood of perpetuating those behaviors. A useful analogy to illustrate this point is the following: "If I have the oil in my car changed regularly and my car has been running well for several years, I might believe that changing the oil is useful, so I'll keep doing it. Similarly, the more a person believes that worry is useful, the more likely he or she will be to continue worrying." The therapist also discusses the contributory role of intolerance of uncertainty in maintaining positive beliefs about worry. Specifically, individuals who are intolerant of uncertainty are more likely to think that worry serves a positive function, as it allows them to predict or plan for every possible eventuality, thereby potentially eliminating uncertainty. Research from our group (Francis & Dugas, 2004; Holowka et al., 2000) suggests that GAD patients typically endorse positive beliefs according to the following five themes: (1) worry is a positive personality trait; (2) worry aids in problem solving; (3) worry serves a motivating function; (4) worry protects me from negative emotions; and (5) worry, in and of itself, can prevent bad things from happening (see Table 17.2 for examples of these beliefs). So long as patients believe that their worries serve a purpose, they are likely to be ambivalent about reducing their worries. As a consequence, patients are encouraged to generate personal examples of their own "useful" worries, in order to determine through cognitive and behavioral challenging whether they are in fact beneficial.

Challenges to positive beliefs are directed toward the personal example of a "positive" worry generated by the patient. For example, if the patient states, "worrying about my children shows that I am a good parent," it is this belief that should be challenged, rather than the general belief "worry is a positive personality trait." The therapist uses a variety of strategies to challenge the belief, including the "lawyer-prosecutor role play." In this

Table 17.2   Challenges to Specific Positive Beliefs about the Function of Worry

---

Worry is a positive personality trait (e.g., worry shows that I am a good parent)
- What else defines a caring parent?
- Is there anything else you do that shows you are a caring parent?
- Do you know any "good" parents who don't worry excessively?
- Have you suffered any costs because of your worries? (i.e., Do others see your worry as negative trait?)

Worry aids in problem solving (e.g., worrying about work helps me to come up with better solutions)
- Do you solve your work problems by worrying, or are you just going over the problem in your head?
- Are you confusing a thought (worry) with an action (problem solving)?

Worry serves a motivating function (e.g., worrying about school motivates me to do well)
- Do you know any other students who do well and don't worry as much as you?
- Does your worry dramatically improve your performance, or are there negative consequences? (i.e., Do you experience concentration or memory problems? Do the time and effort involved in worrying take away from your study time?)

Worry protects against negative emotions (e.g., "If I don't worry about my health, I'll be unprepared")
- Has anything bad ever happened to you that you had worried about before? How did you feel? Do you think you were buffered from the pain?
- Has worrying about potential negative events protected you against current negative emotions, or has thinking about things that may never happen actually increased your negative emotions?

Worry, in and of itself, prevents negative outcomes (e.g., when I don't worry about work I don't do a good job)
- Has anything bad happened at work even though you worried?
- Were you really not worrying when things don't go well, or are you just remembering it that way?
- Could you test this theory through a behavioral experiment?

---

role play, the patient is first asked to take on the role of a lawyer who must convince the members of a jury that the worry is useful. Once all arguments have been exhausted, the patient then plays the role of a prosecutor who must convince the members of the jury that the worry is in fact not useful. Consistent with the principles of motivational interviewing (see Miller & Rollnick, 2002), the therapist uses Socratic questioning to help patients reconsider the actual usefulness of worrying when playing the role of the prosecutor. Examples of questions related to particular beliefs are presented in Table 17.2. The goal of this phase of treatment is to allow patients to begin to question the actual usefulness of their worries in order to reduce ambivalence and increase treatment compliance.

Improving Problem Orientation and Problem-Solving Ability

The third component introduced to patients is negative problem orientation. A distinction is made from the outset between problem-solving ability and beliefs surrounding problem solving. The therapist explains that people with GAD are more likely to have a negative problem orientation, that is, to hold dysfunctional attitudes about problem solving. Negative problem orientation includes the tendency to doubt one's problem-solving ability, to view problems as threatening, and to be pessimistic about the outcome of problem solving. As a result of these beliefs, excessive worriers are less likely to solve their problems, and less effective when actually using their problem-solving skills. The therapist discusses the nature of problems as uncertain future events without a readily available solution, and thereby logically links negative problem orientation to intolerance of uncertainty. The consequences of having a negative problem orientation include feelings of frustration and anxiety when confronted with problems, a tendency to procrastinate or avoid problems, as well as an increase in "what if" triggers since problems often remain unsolved or engender new problems.

The goal for the patient in this treatment phase is to develop a more positive orientation toward problems. The therapist explains that it is human nature to avoid threatening situations and approach opportunities. As such, so long as patients view problems as purely threatening and doubt their own abilities, they will necessarily refrain from solving their problems even if they are good problem solvers. In order to shift patient attitudes toward a more balanced orientation, several strategies are employed. The first intervention is to assist the patient in discriminating between the problematic situation and his or her own negative emotions surrounding the problem. Patients typically experience difficulty in recognizing problems, as they incorrectly identify their emotions as the problem (e.g., frustration, anxiety), rather than the objective situation (e.g., communication problems with the boss). The therapist describes using negative emotions as "cues" to the presence of problems (e.g., "I'm frustrated because of the problem with my boss at work"), and asks the patient to write a list of ongoing problems in order to identify them as soon as they occur. The therapist then addresses the patient's negative problem perception by explaining that problems are a normal part of life that necessarily require time and effort, and are not attributable to personal deficits. A third strategy is to target the appraisal of problems as purely threatening. The therapist makes a distinction between viewing "threat" and "opportunity" as opposite ends of a continuum rather than as discrete categories. The patient is charged with attempting to find a challenging aspect, or opportunity, in the problem so as to move the situation away from 100% threatening on the continuum, and toward a balance between threat and opportunity. For example, a work problem with the boss might be seen as an opportunity to increase communication skills or to improve the working environment. In this manner, although the threatening aspects of the situation are not ignored, the patient can see a benefit to solving the problem.

The second component of this treatment phase involves problem-solving training. The therapist explains that this skill is a rational and effortful process that is best performed in a "pen and paper" format initially. Problem solving involves the acquisition and mastery of five problem-solving steps: (1) problem definition, (2) goal formulation, (3) generation of alternative solutions, (4) decision-making, and (5) solution implementation and verification (see D'Zurilla & Nezu, 1999, for a thorough description of these steps along with strategies for problem-solving training). For the first step, the therapist explains that an effective problem definition is concrete and specific. The problem statement should incorporate what the situation is, what the ideal situation would be, and the obstacle(s) preventing attainment of the ideal situation. The challenge in defining problems is in extricating secondary or assumptive information. For example, if the problem is communication difficulties with an employer, adding the statement "my boss doesn't like me" into the definition is not based on fact and should not be included. In the second step, patients establish realistic goals that are defined in specific behavioural terms and logically address the defined problem. If long-term goals are described, it is recommended that short-term, more easily attainable goals are included as well. For the third step, the therapist explains the rules of brainstorming (i.e., deferment of judgment, quantity and variety of solutions) in order to assist the patient in coming up with multiple potential solutions that are more creative than those typically generated through habit and convention. Patients are encouraged to come up with "wild" solutions as well as practical ones, since several mediocre solutions can later be combined to create one ideal solution. Once the patient has at least 12 solution alternatives, the next step is to select a solution that best fits the problem. The emphasis is placed on choosing the best solution, not the perfect one. The criteria for decision-making include the time and effort involved in carrying out the solution, the personal and social consequences to the individual in both the short and long term, and the likelihood of the chosen solution actually solving the problem. Generally speaking, the best solution is the one that has the most advantages and the fewest disadvantages based on these criteria. The final component entails planning all the steps involved in carrying out the solution, actually implementing it, and monitoring progress to ascertain whether the problem is in fact solved. This step can be particularly challenging for GAD patients, since actually carrying out a chosen solution requires a great deal of tolerance of uncertainty. The therapist uses a sample problem as an illustrative example to work through each of the problem-solving steps (e.g., "I don't seem to be able to make ends meet at the end of every month"), and explains that this set of skills is most relevant to *worries related to current problems* as they are often under the individual's control and can therefore be resolved. For problems that do not appear to be under the patient's control, the therapist should encourage the formulation of emotion-focused goals (i.e., finding ways to adapt to a difficult situation) rather than instrumental goals (i.e., actually trying to modify the situation). Discussion of problem-solving training is also linked to prior treatment phases, specifically to challenges to the usefulness of worry and the concept of intolerance of uncertainty. If patients agree that worry is not particularly useful, problem solving can be viewed as a more productive strategy when encountering problematic situations. In addition, because of the uncertainty inherent in problem solving, practicing this set of skills is a continuation of the tolerance of uncertainty experiments discussed early on in treatment.

Processing Core Fears

This component of treatment integrates the final process, cognitive avoidance, into the model of GAD, and is most pertinent to *worries about hypothetical situations*. Imaginal (or cognitive) exposure is used to allow patients to vividly experience their core fears through threatening mental imagery. The therapist makes illustrative use of graphs depicting the avoidance, neutralization, and exposure curves to explain that attempting to avoid or neutralize a threatening mental image maintains and strengthens worry in the long term. However, sustained functional exposure to a feared stimulus results in a decrease in anxiety through emotional processing. Moreover, as shown by Borkovec and colleagues (e.g., Borkovec, Ray & Stöber, 1998), worry is essentially a form of avoidance, as thinking in "thoughts" (i.e., lexical mental activity) rather than images emotionally distances the individual from feared outcomes and leads to a decrease in physiological responding (Lang, 1985), thereby maintaining the fear by interfering with emotional processing (see Foa & Kozak, 1986, for a discussion of the parameters of successful emotional processing of fear) (see Chapters 14 and 16).

Using the worry diary, the patient chooses a recurrent worry about a hypothetical situation (e.g., "my spouse will get cancer"). The therapist then assists the patient in identifying the core fear underlying the worry (e.g., "I'll be alone for the rest of my life") through the catastrophizing interview procedure (see Vasey & Borkovec, 1992, and Chapter 10 for a description of this technique). An exposure scenario is subsequently developed by the patient, describing the feared outcome in vivid sensory detail. The therapist verifies that no neutralizing elements are incorporated into the scenario, and that the script is in the first-person present tense in order to enhance visual imagery. The patient's script is then recorded onto a looped audiotape or compact disc, making sure to read it slowly, with appropriate pauses and emotional tone. The patient conducts daily exposures to the script, typically lasting between 30 and 60 minutes, noting anxiety ratings with SUDS levels (subjective units of distress) before and after exposure (following exposure, the patient also retrospectively notes the level of anxiety attained at the peak of exposure). Imaginal exposure is continued for approximately two to three weeks, until the core fear has been processed and worry related to the topic is reduced. The link between cognitive exposure and intolerance of uncertainty is underscored, as excessive worriers typically avoid thinking of their feared outcomes in detail due to the intrinsic uncertainty in threatening hypothetical situations.

Relapse Prevention

The final phase of treatment involves the consolidation of acquired skills by preparing the patient for potential challenges and pitfalls following cessation of treatment. The therapist reviews all major treatment interventions, and encourages the patient to continue practicing the skills taught in session, as well as to reward him or herself frequently for successes. The patient is reminded that enduring changes to thinking patterns can take time, and to expect dips in progress on occasion. Specifically, the therapist integrates negative mood states and stressful life events into the model of GAD, noting that during times of stress or change, it is expected that worry and anxiety levels might briefly increase. The emphasis is placed on brainstorming ways to handle increases in worry and anxiety using the strategies acquired in treatment. The therapist also distinguishes between a lapse, which represents a situationally induced increase in symptoms, and a relapse, which is a return of symptom levels observed prior to treatment.

ASSESSMENT OF THE COGNITIVE PROCESSES INVOLVED IN GAD

Given that our model of GAD assumes primary roles for intolerance of uncertainty, positive beliefs about the usefulness of worry, negative problem orientation, and cognitive avoidance, the assessment of these processes among patients with GAD is warranted. Although diagnostic interviews and self-report worry measures are essential for a valid diagnosis of GAD, additional assessment with process measures can provide important information about treatment mechanisms and progress. The following is a list of self-report measures that directly target the processes described in our model.

Intolerance of Uncertainty

The Intolerance of Uncertainty Scale (IUS; French Version: Freeston et al., 1994; English translation: Buhr & Dugas, 2002) is a 27-item self-report measure that reflects the beliefs that unexpected events are negative and should be avoided, and that uncertainty is unfair, stressful, and leads to the inability to act. The English version of the IUS displays excellent internal consistency ($\alpha = .94$), good test-retest reliability at five weeks ($r = .74$), and evidence of convergent and discriminant validity (Buhr & Dugas, 2002).

Positive Beliefs about the Usefulness of Worry

The Why-Worry II (WW-II; French version: Langlois et al., 1999; English translation: Holowka et al., 2000) is a 25-item self-report inventory that assesses the five dimensions of positive beliefs about the usefulness of worry. The English version of the measure displays high internal consistency ($\alpha = .93$), good test-retest reliability at six weeks ($r = .80$) and convergent and divergent validity with other measures of positive and negative beliefs about worry (Holowka et al., 2000).

Negative Problem Orientation

The Negative Problem Orientation Questionnaire (NPOQ; French version: Gosselin, Pelletier & Ladouceur, 2001; English translation: Robichaud & Dugas, 2005) is a 12-item self-report measure that assesses the dysfunctional cognitive set of negative problem orientation. The NPOQ is unifactorial, and displays excellent internal consistency ($\alpha = .92$), high test-retest reliability at five weeks ($r = .80$), and good convergent and discriminant validity with measures of psychological distress and problem solving (Robichaud & Dugas, 2005).

Cognitive Avoidance

The Cognitive Avoidance Questionnaire (CAQ; Gosselin et al., 2002; English translation: Sexton, Dugas & Hedayati, 2004) is a 25-item scale that assesses the tendency to use the following cognitive avoidance strategies: substitution of disturbing thoughts, transformation of mental images into verbal thoughts, distraction, avoidance of threatening stimuli, and thought suppression. The French version of the measure displays excellent reliability and validity (Gosselin et al., 2002), and preliminary analyses of the English version suggest good internal consistency ($\alpha = .74$ to $.95$ for the five subscales), as well as convergent validity with other measures of cognitive avoidance (Sexton et al., 2004) (see Chapters 7 through to 10 for other methods of measuring and assessing worry and GAD).

TREATMENT OUTCOME STUDIES

The efficacy of our treatment protocol for GAD has been investigated in two randomized controlled trials. Ladouceur and colleagues (2000) studied treatment outcome for 26 GAD patients who received the protocol on an individual basis. A wait-list control condition was used for comparison. Statistically significant differences between the treatment and control conditions were found on all study measures, including a self-report measure of worry (Penn State Worry Questionnaire; PSWQ) and a clinician-administered rating of GAD symptoms (Anxiety Disorders Interview Schedule for DSM-IV; ADIS-IV). Statistically and clinically significant changes emerged at post-treatment, with 62% reaching a high endstate functioning and 77% of participants no longer meeting diagnostic criteria for the disorder. Moreover, treatment gains were maintained at one year follow-up, with 58% of participants retaining high endstate functioning and 77% continuing to meet criteria for full remission. In terms of the model components, scores on a self-report measure of intolerance of uncertainty showed significant reductions at post-treatment, as well as at six- and 12-month follow-ups.

The efficacy of the treatment protocol was also assessed when administered in a group context of four to six participants (Dugas et al., 2003). A total of 52 GAD patients received the treatment package, with a wait-list control condition used for comparison. Significant differences between the treatment and control conditions emerged on all study measures, including the ADIS-IV, the PSWQ, and measures of somatic symptoms, anxiety, and depression. In addition, intolerance of uncertainty scores were significantly decreased at post-treatment as well as at six-, 12-, and 24-month follow-ups. Sixty-five percent (65%) of patients reached high endstate functioning at post-treatment, and 60% no longer met diagnostic criteria for GAD. Interestingly, additional improvements were noted two years after treatment, with 72% of participants meeting high endstate functioning, and 92% no longer qualifying for a diagnosis of GAD. However, although the treatment protocol displayed promising results in a group context, there was a notable difference in drop-out rates according to the format of therapy (0% in individual treatment, 10.2% in group treatment), suggesting that the treatment may be helpful for a greater proportion of patients when delivered on an individual basis. Despite this, findings from both efficacy studies appear to be superior to those found for general CBT packages that are not derived from a theoretically-driven model of GAD.

CONCLUSION

The goal of this chapter was to present a treatment protocol based on an empirically-supported model of GAD that includes the following main components:

– Worry awareness training
– Coping with uncertainty
– Re-evaluating beliefs about the usefulness of worry
– Improving problem orientation and problem-solving ability
– Processing core fears through imaginal exposure

All components of our model have been empirically linked to excessive worry and are individually targeted in session, with intolerance of uncertainty receiving primary importance. The findings to date suggest that the treatment has good efficacy, and that treatment gains are maintained over extended periods of time. However, given that the treatment has yet to be compared to other empirically-derived treatments for GAD (e.g., Newman et al., 2004; Wells, 2004), conclusions about comparative efficacy await further study. Nonetheless, the results of our treatment studies underscore the importance of continued research on specific cognitive, behavioral, and affective processes involved in the development and maintenance of GAD, in order to further refine and enhance treatment interventions specifically targeted to the disorder.

REFERENCES

American Psychiatric Association (1994). *Diagnostic and statistical manual of mental disorders* (4th ed.). Washington, DC: Author.

Borkovec, T.D. & Newman, M.G. (1999). Worry and generalized anxiety disorder. In A.S. Bellack & M. Hersen (Series Eds) & P. Salkovskis (Vol. Ed.), *Comprehensive clinical psychology: Vol. 4. Adults: Clinical formulation and treatment* (pp. 439–459). Oxford: Elsevier Science.

Borkovec, T.D., Ray, W.J. & Stober, J. (1998). Worry: A cognitive phenomenon intimately linked to affective, physiological, and interpersonal behavioral processes. *Cognitive Therapy and Research, 22,* 561–576.

Buhr, K. & Dugas, M.J. (2002). The Intolerance of Uncertainty Scale: Psychometric properties of the English version. *Behaviour Research and Therapy*, **40**, 931–946.

Butler, G., Fennell, M., Robson, P. & Gelder, M. (1991). A comparison of behavior therapy and cognitive behavior therapy in the treatment of generalized anxiety disorder. *Journal of Consulting and Clinical Psychology*, **59**, 167–175.

Dugas, M.J. (2002). Generalized anxiety disorder. In M. Hersen (Ed.), *Clinical behavior therapy: Adults and children* (pp. 125–143). New York: John Wiley & Sons, Inc.

Dugas, M.J., Gagnon, F., Ladouceur, R. & Freeston, M.H. (1998). Generalized Anxiety Disorder: A preliminary test of a conceptual model. *Behaviour Research and Therapy*, **36**, 215–226.

Dugas, M.J., Ladouceur, R., Léger, E., Freeston, M.H., Langlois, F., Provencher, M.D. & Boisvert, J.M. (2003). Group cognitive-behavioral therapy for generalized anxiety disorder: Treatment outcome and long-term follow-up. *Journal of Consulting and Clinical Psychology*, **71**, 821–825.

Dugas, M.J., Marchand, A. & Ladouceur, R. (2005). Further validation of a cognitive-behavioral model of generalized anxiety disorder: Diagnostic and symptom specificity. *Journal of Anxiety Disorders*, **19**, 329–343.

D'Zurilla, T.J. & Nezu, A.M. (1999). *Problem-solving therapy: A social competence approach to clinical intervention*. New York: Springer Publishing.

Foa, E.D. & Kozak, M.J. (1986). Emotional processing of fear: Exposure to corrective information. *Psychological Bulletin*, **1**, 20–35.

Francis, K. & Dugas, M.J. (2004). Assessing positive beliefs about worry: Validation of a structured interview. *Personality and Individual Differences*, **37**, 405–415.

Freeston, M.H., Rhéaume, J., Letarte, H., Dugas, M.J. & Ladouceur, R. (1994). Why do people worry? *Personality and Individual Differences*, **17**, 791–802.

Gosselin, P., Langlois, F., Freeston, M.H., Ladouceur, R., Dugas, M.J. & Pelletier, O. (2002). Le Questionnaire d'Evitement Cognitif (QEC): Développement et validation auprès d'adultes et d'adolescents. [The Cognitive Avoidance Questionnaire: Development and validation among adult and adolescent samples.] *Journal de thérapie comportementale et cognitive*, **12**, 24–37.

Gosselin, P., Pelletier, O. & Ladouceur, R. (2001, July). *The Negative Problem Orientation Questionnaire (NPOQ): Development and validation among a non-clinical sample*. Poster session presented at the annual meeting of the World Congress of Behavioral and Cognitive Therapies, Vancouver, BC.

Holowka, D.W., Dugas, M.J., Francis, K. & Laugesen, N. (2000, November). *Measuring beliefs about worry: A psychometric evaluation of the Why Worry-II questionnaire*. Poster presented at the annual convention of the Association for the Advancement of Behavior Therapy, New Orleans, LA.

Ladouceur, R., Dugas, M.J., Freeston, M.H., Léger, E., Gagnon, F. & Thibodeau, N. (2000). Efficacy of a cognitive-behavioral treatment for generalized anxiety disorder: Evaluation in a controlled clinical trial. *Journal of Consulting and Clinical Psychology*, **68**, 957–964.

Lang, P.J. (1985). The cognitive psychophysiology of emotion: Fear and anxiety. In A.H. Tuma & J.D. Maser (Eds). *Anxiety and the anxiety disorders* (pp. 131–170). Hillsdale, NJ: Erlbaum.

Langlois, F., Gosselin, P., Laberge, M., Tremblay, M., Léger, E., Provencher, M. & Ladouceur, R. (1999, May). *Les croyances erronées face aux inquiétudes: Validation de la version révisée du questionnaire Pourquoi S'Inquieter? (PSI-II)* [Erroneous beliefs about worry: Validation of the revised version of the Why Worry Questionnaire (WW-II)]. Poster presented at the annual meeting of l'Association Francophone de la Formation et de la Recherche en Thérapie Comportementale et Cognitive, Lyon, France.

Miller, W.R. & Rollnick, S. (2002). *Motivational interviewing: Preparing people for change* (2nd ed.). New York: Guilford Press.

Newman, M.G., Castonguay, L.G., Borkovec, T.D. & Molnar, C. (2004). Integrative psychotherapy. In R.G. Heimberg, C.L. Turk & D.S. Mennin (Eds), *Generalized anxiety disorder: Advances in research and practice* (pp. 320–50). New York: Guilford Press.

Robichaud, M. & Dugas, M.J. (2005). Negative problem orientation (part I): Psychometric properties of a new measure. *Behaviour Research and Therapy*, **43**, 391–401.

Roemer, L. & Orsillo, S.M. (2002). Expanding our conceptualization of and treatment for generalized anxiety disorder: Integrating mindfulness/acceptance-based approaches with existing cognitive-behavioral models. *Clinical Psychology: Science and Practice*, **9**, 54–68.

Sexton, K.A., Dugas, M.J. & Hedayati, M. (2004, November). *The Cognitive Avoidance Questionnaire: Validation of the English translation.* Poster session presented at the annual convention of the Association for Advancement of Behavior Therapy, New Orleans, LA.

Vasey, M.W. & Borkovec, T.D. (1992). A catastrophizing assessment of worrisome thoughts. *Cognitive Therapy and Research*, **16**, 505–520.

Wells, A. (2004). A cognitive model of GAD: Metacognitions and pathological worry. In R.G. Heimberg, C.L. Turk & D.S. Mennin (Eds), *Generalized anxiety disorder: Advances in research and practice* (pp. 164–186). New York: Guilford Press.

Wells, A. & Carter, K. (1999). Preliminary tests of a cognitive model of generalized anxiety disorder. *Behaviour Research and Therapy*, **37**, 585–594.

Chapter 18

PHARMACOLOGICAL TREATMENTS FOR WORRY: FOCUS ON GENERALISED ANXIETY DISORDER

Ian M. Anderson and Marisha E. Palm

INTRODUCTION

Studies of pharmacological treatment have not targeted worry and only recently has worry been reported as an outcome (as item 1 of the Hamilton Anxiety Rating Scale, HAMA). In DSMIV worry is emphasised as a core symptom of Generalised Anxiety Disorder (GAD), but other physical symptoms of anxiety are also required. Ruscio and Borkovec (2004) found that subjects with GAD differed from non-GAD worriers (matched on worry severity) in experiencing less control over negative intrusive thoughts and greater worry-related somatic hyperarousal negative beliefs. Whether pharmacological treatment has primary or secondary effects on excessive worry is unclear, because worry is poorly measured and symptom clusters tend to improve in parallel.

Before reviewing drug treatment studies of GAD, we will briefly consider the neurobiology of worry and the methodology of treatment trials of GAD.

THE NEUROBIOLOGY OF ANXIETY AND WORRY

Anxiety is a complex of physiological, behavioural, emotional and (in humans) cognitive processes/reactions related to brain mechanisms of aversion and defence (e.g. Deakin & Graeff, 1991; McNaughton & Corr, 2004) involving neural circuits ranging from brainstem to cortex. Anxiety-provoking events (threats) can be thought of as immediate or future, actual or potential, close or distant. Different facets of the defence/aversion

Worry and Its Psychological Disorders: Theory, Assessment and Treatment. Edited by G. C. L. Davey and A. Wells. © 2006 John Wiley & Sons, Ltd.

reaction reflect the involvement of different brain regions and circuitry in response to the type of threat. For example, immediate, actual, close threats may lead to freezing or fighting whereas future, potential, distant threats are likely to lead to avoidance.

Important brain regions include the peri-aqueductal grey in the midbrain (unconditioned and panic reactions), subcortical areas including amygdala (associative learning, integration of sensory and emotion-related information, output to effector regions), hippocampus (learning, memory, context), hypothalamus (autonomic and endocrine responses), basal ganglia (muscular tension), cingulate/prefrontal cortex (reinforcer and threat evaluation, decision-making, social evaluation, cognition) (Deakin & Graeff, 1991; LeDoux, 2000; McNaughton & Corr, 2004; Nutt, 2001).

There are reciprocal connections between cortical and subcortical areas of the brain. For example when the amygdala is activated, arousal systems are triggered, focusing cortical processing and ensuring vigilance for potential danger. However, the information content is imprecise (LeDoux, 2000) and higher-level cognitive processes are needed to specify the problem and appropriate action. Because of the asymmetry of subcortical-cortical connections it has been suggested that thoughts can easily trigger negative emotions, but they struggle to deactivate subcortical regions (LeDoux, 2000), although in humans, the prefrontal cortex can go some way towards inhibition of emotion via language systems (Gray & McNaughton, 2003). Worry appears adaptive if it results in deactivation of subcortical anxiety-related circuits (e.g. by finding a solution to a real threat) but maladaptive if it reinforces subcortical overactivity without finding a resolution.

This formulation suggests interventions can occur at different 'levels' of the system, both anatomically and conceptually (mind versus brain). Optimising treatment for individual patients may require combining pharmacological and psychological treatment which work at different levels of the problem.

It is possible that different treatments have different efficacy on one or more facets of the syndrome of GAD. We will therefore explore whether there are differential effects of different drugs in clinical studies.

PHARMACOTHERAPY OF GAD

Acute reduction of anxiety with alcohol, sedative and narcotic drugs is rewarding which helps explain their widespread use and their major drawback, addictive potential. Benzodiazepines and barbiturates act on the major brain inhibitory system involving γ-aminobutyric acid (GABA), and can be considered as archetypal anxiolytics with sedative, hypnotic and addictive properties. Although it was originally thought that anxiety reduction was related to sedation, the advent of newer non-sedative treatments such as buspirone and the selective serotonin reuptake inhibitors (SSRIs) has shown this not to be true. These act on monoamine pathways, particularly those involving serotonin (5-HT) and noradrenaline (Nutt, 2001), which are implicated in anxiety. As these drugs are not associated with the psychomotor impairments, sedation and addiction potential of benzodiazepines they offer the potential for longer-term treatment, extremely important in a chronic disorder such as GAD.

IDENTIFICATION OF STUDIES AND METHODS

Given that treatment trials are liable to be confounded by placebo effects (see below), we concentrate on published randomised placebo-controlled trial (RCT) evidence. RCTs were identified by searching MEDLINE and EMBASE up until April 2005 using the search term ('generalized anxiety' OR 'generalised anxiety') AND (treatment OR *therapy); Limits: Human. In addition review articles were searched for references including guidelines (e.g. Bandelow et al., 2002) and a recent systematic review (Mitte et al., 2005). Studies were included if patients met accepted diagnostic criteria (Research Diagnostic Criteria (RCD), DSMII onward or ICD10), were randomised to different treatments with a placebo arm and involved a drug that is available, or likely to be available, for prescription. Trials of short-acting benzodiazepines used as hypnotics were excluded. The main findings of these placebo-controlled studies are in Tables 18.1–18.4.

METHODOLOGICAL ISSUES IN DRUG TREATMENT TRIALS OF GAD

Comorbidity is common with GAD, especially depression and other anxiety disorders (Kessler et al., 2001), making it difficult to find patients with 'pure GAD'. The coexistence of anxiety and depressive symptoms leads to boundary problems between the two diagnoses (Brown et al., 2001). GAD studies vary in the strictness of the exclusion criteria applied although most exclude major depression and panic disorder and many studies have a requirement for low depression ratings. This may limit the generalisability of RCTs for clinical practice where significant depression is common. When anxiety and depression coexist guidelines emphasise the treatment of depression first (e.g. National Institute for Clinical Excellence, 2004a), i.e. prescribing an antidepressant if drug therapy is used although it can be seen from Tables 18.1–18.4 that benzodiazepines and buspirone also improve depression when used in GAD with significant levels of depression.

The studies differ in the criteria used for inclusion, both in the version of DSM applied and in the minimum severity (defined by Hamilton Anxiety Rating Scale, HAMA, scores). The diagnosis of GAD has changed from DSM-III through DSM-IIIR to DSM-IV; from a residual anxiety disorder lasting one month to one requiring six months of uncontrollable worry with less focus on somatic symptoms (Brown et al., 1994; Rickels & Rynn, 2001). Most of the studies with benzodiazepines used DSM-III/III-R whereas studies with newer antidepressants have used DSM-IV, increasing the difficulty in making efficacy comparisons between compounds.

In GAD studies the response rates to placebo were frequently greater than 40% and these high rates decrease the assay sensitivity of a trial (Schweizer & Rickels, 1997). High response rates to placebo appear common in some anxiety disorders (Piercy et al., 1996) and seem higher than the average rates (30%) in depression (Walsh et al., 2002). Response to placebo includes a response to non-specific elements in the trial (i.e. a true 'placebo-response') as well as confounds including spontaneous improvement, measurement errors and regression towards the mean (Guess et al., 2002). These factors argue strongly for closely matching placebo-treatments for any putative active intervention (including specific psychological treatments).

Drug studies in GAD have generally been of short duration whereas it is increasingly recognised that the optimum management of psychiatric disorders requires taking a medium to long-term view. This raises particular difficulties with regard to prescribing benzodiazepines which are now only recommended and licensed for short-term use in the UK (see also National Institute for Clinical Excellence, 2004b).

Finally, a serious weakness in the empirical evidence is a lack of comparative trial data between best current pharmacological and psychological treatments.

RATING SCALES IN DRUG TREATMENTS OF GAD

The universally used primary measure of efficacy in GAD treatment studies is the observer-rated 14-item HAMA (Hamilton, 1959), often analysed as two subscales purporting to reflect psychic anxiety and somatic symptoms. The psychic anxiety subscale is the total of items 1 (worry and anticipatory anxiety), 2 (tension including emotionality, startle and restlessness), 3 (fears), 4 (insomnia), 5 (concentration and memory) and 6 (depressed mood) and usually item 14 (behaviour at interview encompassing appearance and bodily expressions of anxiety). The somatic subscale is the sum of items 7 to 13 covering pain, sensory, cardiovascular, respiratory, gastrointestinal, genitourinary, autonomic symptoms, occasionally together with item 14 when it has not been counted in the psychic anxiety subscale. Studies usually do not report how they calculated the subscales.

Since the advent of DSM-IV, items 1 and 2 and/or their combined score have increasingly been analysed independently as they assess core symptoms of anxiety, but in practice they parallel the psychic anxiety subscale and usually the total score. The HAMA was developed before the current classification of anxiety disorders and lacks specificity for GAD but appears sensitive to change. It has a weighting towards physical symptoms and the somatic subscale may be confounded by side-effects of drugs (Maier et al., 1988).

The Clinical Global Impression (CGI) scale (Guy, 1976) is a commonly used outcome measure. A global judgment regarding patients' severity of illness is made on a scale between 1 and 7 and therefore doesn't provide any information about discrete symptoms.

A variety of other scales are used in the studies as secondary outcome measures, including functioning and quality of life in some recent studies. It is difficult to draw overall conclusions because of the lack of systematic use of secondary measures and their general tendency to improve in parallel with the HAMA.

We found no use scales specifically assessing worry in these studies so it is difficult to assess the impact of treatment on worry itself. Future studies would benefit from including measures such as the Penn State Worry Questionnaire (PSWQ) (Meyer et al., 1990) and the Anxious Thoughts Inventory (Wells, 1994).

EFFICACY OF DRUG TREATMENT IN GAD

Benzodiazepines, most commonly diazepam, have become the standard active comparator in recent GAD studies, in spite of limitations with their use. Newer antidepressants are increasingly becoming established as the treatment of choice in GAD. We concentrate on efficacy but comment on tolerability and discontinuation and also consider comparisons derived from non-placebo-controlled RCTs.

Benzodiazepines

Benzodiazepines act at the $GABA_A$-benzodiazepine receptor complex in the brain where they increase the effect of the inhibitory neurotransmitter, GABA (Nutt, 2001).

Table 18.1 Placebo-controlled trials of benzodiazepines in Generalised Anxiety Disorder (excluding studies with non-benzodiazepine active comparators)

Study	Diagnosis, entry severity, study duration	Drugs (N)	Outcome and response rate where reported	Comments
Castillo et al., 1987	DSMIII. HAMA >17. 8 weeks	Placebo (33) Alprazolam 1–3mg (31) CBZ 10–60mg (32)	Alprazolam = Clobazam = Placebo 63% 69% 62%	Advantage to active drugs at week 1 due to improvement on HAMA somatic subscale
Chouinard et al., 1982	RDC. No minimum HAMA. 8 weeks	Placebo (14) Alprazolam 0.5–3mg (15)	Alprazolam ≥ Placebo	Efficacy on both HAMA subscales
Cohn & Wilcox 1984	DSMIII. HAMA >25. 16 weeks	Placebo (32) Alprazolam 1–4.5mg (72) Lorazepam 1–4.5mg (73)	Alprazolam = Lorazepam > Placebo	Continued improvement on alprazolam
Fontaine et al., 1983, 1984	DSMIII. HAMA >19. 4 weeks (+3 week abrupt v gradual drug withdrawal)	Placebo (16) Diazepam 15mg (16) Bromazepam 18mg (16)	Bromazepam > Diazepam > Placebo	Efficacy on both HAMA subscales. Return of anxiety on withdrawal, rebound when abrupt

Study	Criteria	Treatment (n)	Result	Comments
Pourmotabbed et al., 1996	DSMIII. HAMA >17. 6 weeks (+ 2 week withdrawal)	Placebo (10) Diazepam 15mg (11)	Diazepam > Placebo to 3 weeks, no difference at endpoint	Greater efficacy on HAMA somatic than psychic subscale. Return of anxiety on withdrawal.
Power et al., 1985	RDC. HAMA >14.6 week (+1 week abrupt withdrawal)	Placebo (11) Diazepam 15mg (10)	Diazepam > Placebo	Rebound anxiety on withdrawal
Scarpini et al., 1988	DSMIII. HAMA >17. 2 weeks	Placebo (45) Ketazolam 15mg (47)	Ketazolam > Placebo 20% 55%	Efficacy on both HAMA subscales
Wilcox et al., 1994	DSMIIIR. HAMA > 20. 4 weeks	Placebo (10) Adinazolam 30/60/90mg (30)	Adinazolam > Placebo 0% 28%	
Zung, 1987	DSMIII. No minimum HAMA. 3 weeks	Placebo (86) Clorazepate 7.5–30mg (103)	Clorazepate > Placebo	Clorazepate improved depression scores

HAMA: Hamilton Anxiety Rating Scale.

Most studies with benzodiazepines lasted four–eight weeks with nearly all patients diagnosed on the basis of DSM-III or DSM-III-R. As a group, benzodiazepines are more effective than placebo and benefits appear as early as one week in a number of studies. In some small studies this was not maintained (Castillo et al. 1987; Chouinard et al., 1982; Pourmotabbed et al., 1996) due to continued improvement on placebo. However in the two longest studies both of reasonable size, benefits were maintained or increased over 12–16 weeks (Cohn & Wilcox 1984; Llorca et al., 2002). The size of the benefit appears clinically important with about a 20–30% higher response rate than placebo in studies without high placebo response rates.

The suggestion that benzodiazepines predominantly improve somatic rather than psychic anxiety symptoms in GAD (Rickels et al., 1993) is not strongly supported in the studies reviewed (equal effect in seven studies, more on somatic than psychic in three studies, more on psychic than somatic in one study). Two further studies found an early benefit for benzodiazepine on the somatic subscale which was not sustained (Castillo et al., 1987; Pourmotabbed et al., 1996), possibly suggesting an early effect on physical symptoms which does not necessarily go on to overall improvement. Studies allowing significant depression found that benzodiazepines improved depression scores more than placebo to a clinically significant degree (Boyer & Feighner, 1993; Goldberg & Finnerty, 1979; Zung, 1987). A recent meta-analysis (Mitte et al., 2005) found that the overall effect size for benzodiazepines against placebo was 0.32 for anxiety and 0.28 for depression (0.2 is considered a small, and 0.5 a moderate effect size). It has to be remembered that this is an effect size *over* that obtained by placebo as in most studies all patients generally improved greatly from baseline.

It is not possible to directly draw conclusions about the relative efficacy of different benzodiazepines from the available studies but there is a suggestion that lorazepam may have lower efficacy than some others. Mitte et al. (2005) found that the effect sizes of different benzodiazepines against placebo were alprazolam 0.33, diazepam 0.34, lorazepam 0.17.

The predominant side-effects of benzodiazepines in the studies were sedation and fatigue. Discontinuation of the benzodiazepine resulted in loss of efficacy in five studies reporting the effects, with discontinuation symptoms only occurring after 12 weeks treatment (Rickels et al., 2000b). However abrupt discontinuation, even after only short treatment, resulted in rebound anxiety in two of three studies (Fontaine et al., 1984; Power et al., 1985; Rickels et al., 1997). A further study in patients withdrawing from long-term benzodiazepines treatment for GAD (average duration 8.5 years) had a high failure rate for stopping the benzodiazepine when blindly randomised to placebo (62%) compared with only 17% for those who had been started on imipramine before the benzodiazepine taper. Patients randomised to buspirone had an intermediate, non-significant benefit (32% failure to stop the benzodiazepine) (Rickels et al., 2000b).

Antidepressants

Most antidepressant studies have been of eight weeks' duration with patients meeting criteria for DSM-IV GAD (see Tables 18.2 and 18.4). Three studies were of 24/26 weeks. There is a relapse prevention study with paroxetine. The antidepressants shown share the property of inhibiting the reuptake of 5-HT into the presynaptic neurone; some also inhibit the reuptake of noradrenaline (e.g. venlafaxine and imipramine). The effect of this is to increase synaptic concentrations of 5-HT ($+/-$ noradrenaline) which lead to secondary adaptive changes in neuronal function believed to be responsible for clinical efficacy (Feighner, 1999). The anxiolytic effects occur gradually over a few weeks and little benefit is experienced after acute dosing. Paradoxically some people can experience an increase in anxiety or agitation after starting antidepressants (Committee on Safety of Medicines, 2004) which has been described particularly with panic disorder (den Boer & Westenberg, 1988; Ramos et al., 1993) but is not reported as a problem in GAD studies.

Selective serotonin reuptake inhibitors

Paroxetine, sertraline and escitalopram are effective in GAD (Table 18.2). Gastrointestinal (especially nausea), stimulant (e.g. insomnia, anxiety and agitation), somnolence/asthenia and sexual dysfunction are recognised side-effects (Anderson, 2001).

The two paroxetine studies found significant improvement over placebo only on the psychic subscale of the HAMA, but not the somatic subscale. Sertraline was effective on both subscales with the larger study showing a 27% higher response rate for sertraline than placebo. Escitalopram was also effective on both subscales but with a larger effect on the psychic subscale with a drug-placebo difference in response rates of 20%. The paroxetine and escitalopram studies found significant drug-placebo differences on HAMA items 1 and 2, appearing as early as week 1 of treatment. The results raise the possibility that SSRIs may improve psychic more than somatic symptoms but caution is required because of potential confounds. These include the finding of Meoni et al. (2004) that placebo treatment improves somatic more than psychic symptoms and the possibility that some side-effects of SSRIs could act against the improvement in ratings of somatic symptoms.

Table 18.2 Placebo-controlled trials of antidepressants in Generalised Anxiety Disorder (excluding studies with active comparators)

Study	Diagnosis, entry severity, study duration	Drugs (N)	Outcome and response rate where reported (remission)	Comments
Allgulander et al., 2001	DSMIV. HAMA >19. 24 weeks	Placebo (130) Venlafaxine XR 37.5mg (138), 75mg (130), 150mg (131)	Venlafaxine 150mg, 75mg > Placebo at 8 weeks; all doses Venlafaxine > Placebo at 24 weeks	Efficacy on both HAMA subscales Lowest dose tended to lesser efficacy. Dose related discontinuation symptoms.
Allgulander et al., 2004	DSMIV. HAMA >17. 12 weeks	Placebo (189) Sertraline 50–150mg (184)	Sertraline > Placebo; 29% (18%) 56% (31%)	Efficacy on both HAMA subscales, depression, function and quality of life
Davidson et al., 2004	DSMIV. HAMA >17. 8 weeks	Placebo (157) Escitalopram 10–20mg (158)	Escitalopram > Placebo 38% 58%	Efficacy on both HAMA subscales (greater for psychic), depression and quality of life
Gelenberg et al., 2000	DSMIV. HAMA >17. 6 months	Placebo (123) Venlafaxine XR 75–225mg (115)	Venlafaxine > Placebo 42–46% weeks 6–28 69–73% weeks 6–28	Efficacy on both HAMA subscales
Lenox-Smith & Reynold, 2003	DSMIV. HAMA > 19. 24 weeks	Placebo (122) Venlafaxine XL 75–150mg (122)	Venlafaxine > Placebo 48% (19%) 53% (28%)	Efficacy on HAMA psychic subscale, function and quality of life

Study	Diagnosis	Treatment (n)	Results	Comments
Nimatoudis et al., 2004	DSMIV. HAMA >17. 8 weeks	Placebo (22) Venlafaxine XR 75–150mg (24)	Venlafaxine > Placebo 27% (9%) 92% (63%)	Efficacy on both HAMA subscales
Pollack et al., 2001	DSMIV. HAMA >19. 8 weeks	Placebo (163) Paroxetine 20–50mg (161)	Paroxetine > Placebo 47% (23%) 62% (36%)	Efficacy on HAMA psychic subscale only, and disability
Rickels et al., 2000a	DSMIV. HAMA >17. 8 weeks	Placebo (96) Venlafaxine XR 75mg (86), 150mg (81), 225mg (86)	Venlafaxine > Placebo	Highest dose most consistent. Efficacy on HAMA psychic subscale only
Rickels et al., 2003	DSMIV. HAMA >19. 8 weeks	Placebo (180) Paroxetine 20mg (189) 40mg (197)	Paroxetine > Placebo 46% (20%) 62% (30%) 68% (36%)	Efficacy on HAMA psychic subscale only, disability
Rynn et al., 2001	DSMIV. HAMA >15. 9 weeks	Placebo (11) Sertraline 25–50mg (11)	Sertraline > Placebo 9% (rem 0%) 91% (rem 18%)	Children/adolescents. Efficacy on both HAMA subscales
Stocchi et al., 2003	DSMIV. HAMA >19. 24 weeks	Placebo (288) Paroxetine 20–50mg (278)	Paroxetine > Placebo Relapse 40%, remission 34% Relapse 11%, remission 73%	Relapse prevention trial

HAMA: Hamilton Anxiety Rating Scale.

The only relapse prevention study that had been reported is that by Stocchi et al. (2003) (Table 18.2) with a clinically important 29% difference in relapse on paroxetine compared with placebo over 24 weeks providing the strongest evidence to date for the necessity of continuing antidepressant drug treatment beyond the short term in GAD.

Venlafaxine

Venlafaxine has been tested against placebo in six placebo-controlled studies, with efficacy found in five (Tables 18.2 and 18.4); in the sixth study diazepam also failed to separate from placebo (Hackett et al., 2003). Three studies were 24–26 weeks' duration and showed maintained efficacy with some continuing improvement on venlafaxine. Venlafaxine was more effective than placebo on HAMA items 1 and 2 considered separately. A pooled analysis found venlafaxine equally effective on both psychic and somatic subscales, but that relative to placebo it has a greater effect on psychic than somatic anxiety (Meoni et al., 2004). Doses from 37.5mg to 225mg daily have shown efficacy with some evidence for greater efficacy up to 150mg. The meta-analysis by Mitte et al. (2005) reported an effect size of 0.33 for venlafaxine against placebo.

Discontinuation symptoms were higher at 150mg compared with lower doses in one multiple, fixed dose, prolonged study. There was comparable efficacy above the lowest dose of 37.5mg/day (Allgulander et al. 2001) suggesting that 75–150 mg is the optimal dosing for most patients. Response rates are reported in four studies with differences from placebo ranging from 9–65%, the lowest in a study in general practice which had a high placebo response rate (Lenox-Smith & Reynolds, 2003).

Other antidepressants

The tricyclic antidepressant (TCA), imipramine, inhibits the reuptake of noradrenaline and 5-HT and antagonises other receptors, especially antimuscarinic and α_1-noradrenergic receptors to give characteristic side-effects including dry mouth, constipation and postural hypotension (Feighner et al., 1999). Imipramine was significantly better than placebo in one study and effective for both HAMA subscales (Rickels et al., 1993), but a second, underpowered, study failed to show a difference (McLeod et al., 1992).

The Rickels et al. (1993) study also included a group on the sedative antidepressant trazodone which performed similarly to imipramine. Trazodone is a $5\text{-}HT_2$ and α_1-noradrenergic antagonist with weak 5-HT reuptake inhibition. Of interest other $5\text{-}HT_2$ antagonists have been studied in GAD and some appear to have efficacy (e.g. Katz et al., 1993; Pangalila-Ratu Langi & Jansen, 1988).

Buspirone

Buspirone is a 5-HT$_{1A}$ partial agonist licensed for the treatment of GAD. There are other drugs with a similar mechanism of action such as ipsapirone, gepirone and lesopitron that appear to have similar efficacy (Table 18.4). Side-effects include dizziness, headache and some drowsiness (Gammans et al., 1992). Five placebo-controlled studies of buspirone showed efficacy with improvement on both psychic anxiety and somatic subscales of the HAMA in four studies (Tables 18.3, 18.4). Three studies had equivocal results. A meta-analysis of eight studies against placebo found improvement against placebo on all HAMA items as well as efficacy against depressive symptoms in patients with coexisting moderate depression (Gammans et al., 1992). Mitte et al. (2005) found an effect size of 0.30 comparing buspirone with placebo, the same as for benzodiazepines and venlafaxine. A longer-term RCT showed continuing efficacy to six months (Rickels et al., 1988) as did a 12-month open study (Feighner, 1987). The tolerability and efficacy of buspirone appears reduced if there has been benzodiazepine use within the previous month but not if more remote than this (DeMartinis et al., 2000). Possible explanations include a pharmacological interaction between benzodiazepine withdrawal and buspirone's therapeutic effects or patients missing the direct sedative and anxiolytic effects of benzodiazepines. Retention rates in trials are lower for buspirone than benzodiazepines (31% v 21%, p < 0.05) and similar to placebo (30%) (Mitte et al., 2005).

Buspirone lacks discernible discontinuation reactions or rebound anxiety even after 6 months' continuous use (Rickels et al., 1988).

Other Drugs

Hydroxyzine, a sedative antihistamine, has been shown to have acute efficacy in GAD in three studies (Tables 18.3, 18.4) without apparent withdrawal effects on abrupt discontinuation (Darcis et al., 1995). Other drugs with actions on the GABA$_A$-benzodiazepine receptor complex, suriclone and abecarnil, may also have anxiolytic effects in GAD, but the results for abecarnil have been inconsistent (Aufdembrinke, 1998). Two studies with low-dose typical antipsychotics suggest possible efficacy (Tables 18.3, 18.4). A drug marketed for neuropathic pain, pregabalin (a calcium channel antagonist) has also been shown to have short-term efficacy in GAD (Table 18.4, Pohl et al., 2005). Finally, results with an experimental beta-blocker did not suggest efficacy (Table 18.4).

There has been interest in the efficacy of Kava-kava (piper methysticum), a complementary therapy which has been withdrawn in the UK because of concerns about hepatotoxicity. Studies suggesting efficacy have included

Table 18.3 Placebo-controlled trials of non-benzodiazepine/non-antidepressant drugs in Generalised Anxiety Disorder (excluding studies with active comparators)

Study	Diagnosis, entry severity, study duration	Drugs (N)	Outcome and response rate where reported	Comments
Darcis et al., 1995	DSMIIR. HAMA >19. 4 weeks (+1 week abrupt withdrawal)	Placebo (56) Hydroxyzine 50mg (54)	Hydroxyzine > Placebo; 22% 57%	No rebound anxiety
Mendels et al., 1986	DSMIII. HAMA >19. 4 weeks	Placebo (208) Trifluoperazine 2–6mg (207)	Trifluoperazine > Placebo	Efficacy on HAMA psychic anxiety subscale. Low extrapyramidal side-effects
Sramek et al., 1996	DSMIIIR. HAMA >18. 6 weeks	Placebo (82) Buspirone 30–45mg	Buspirone > Placebo; 35% 55%	Efficacy on HAMA psychic (not somatic) subscale and depression.

HAMA: Hamilton Anxiety Rating Scale.

Table 18.4 Placebo-controlled trials in Generalised Anxiety Disorder with active comparators

Study	Diagnosis, entry severity, study duration	Drugs (N)	Outcome and response rate where reported (remission)	Comments
Benzodiazepines v antidepressants				
Hackett et al., 2003	DSMIV. HAMA >19. 8 weeks	Placebo (97) Venlafaxine XR 75mg (191) 150mg (179) Diazepam 15mg (89)	No significant differences 45% 59% 54% 56%	Numerically imipramine > alprazolam > placebo
McLeod et al., 1992	DSMIIIR. No minimum HAMA. 6 weeks	Placebo (14) Imipramine 25–300mg (14) Alprazolam 0.5–6mg (14)	No significant differences	Numerically imipramine > alprazolam > placebo
Rickels et al., 1993	DSMIII. HAMA >17. 8 weeks	Placebo (55) Imipramine 75–200mg (58) Trazodone 150–400mg (61) Diazepam 15–40mg (56)	Active drugs > placebo 33% 62% 60% 59%	Early onset with diazepam. Antidepressants efficacy on both HAMA subscales, diazepam somatic subscale only
Benzodiazepines v buspirone and buspirone-like drugs				
Boyer & Feighner, 1993	DSMIII. No minimum HAMA. 4 weeks	Placebo (52) Diazepam 15mg (55) Ipsapirone 15mg (48), 30mg (47)	Diazepam = Ipsapirone15 ≥ Ipsapirone30 > Placebo	Diazepam effective on both HAMA subscales, ipsapirone psychic subscale only. Effective on depression ratings

Continued

Table 18.4 Placebo-controlled trials in Generalised Anxiety Disorder with active comparators (*Continued*)

Study	Diagnosis, entry severity, study duration	Drugs (N)	Outcome and response rate where reported (remission)	Comments
Cutler et al., 1993	DSMIII. HAMA >17. 4 weeks	Placebo (85) Lorazepam 2–6mg (84) Ipsapirone 10–30mg (85)	Lorazepam = Ipsapirone > Placebo 33% 50% 55%	Ipsapirone, not lorazepam effective on both HAMA subscales individually
Enkelmann, 1991	DSMIII. HAMA >17. 6 weeks	Placebo (31) Alprazolam 1.5–4mg (32) Buspirone 15–40mg (31)	Active drugs > Placebo	Alprazolam earlier onset. Drugs effective on both HAMA subscales. Greater dropout on buspirone
Fresquet et al., 2000	DSMIV. HAMA >17. 6 weeks	Placebo (20) Lorazepam 2–4mg (30) Lesotripon 40–80mg (18)	Lorazepam ≥ Lesotripon > Placebo 5% 26% 21%	Subgroup with past history of anxiety; No significant efficacy in whole study (N = 161)
Goldberg & Finnerty, 1979	DSMII. HAMA >19. 4 weeks	Placebo (18) Diazepam 10–30mg (18) Buspirone 10–30mg (18)	Active drugs > Placebo 17% 61% 83%	Efficacy on both HAMA subscales and depression
Laakmann et al., 1998	DSMIII. HAMA>19. 4 weeks + withdrawal	Placebo (10) Lorazepam 9mg (75) Buspirone 45mg (58)	Active drugs > Placebo 20% 68% 58%	Efficacy on both HAMA subscales. Withdrawal worsening on lorazepam only.

Study	Criteria	Treatment groups (n)	Results	Comments
Pecknold et al., 1989	DSMIII. HAMA >17. 4 weeks	Placebo (40) Diazepam 10–40mg (43) Buspirone 10–40mg (42)	Active drugs > Placebo 43% 67% 67%	Buspirone > Placebo on HAMA psychic and somatic subscales. Diazepam > Placebo on psychic subscale only.
Rickels et al., 1997	DSMIII. HAMA > 19. 8 weeks (+ abrupt withdrawal)	Placebo (65) Diazepam 10–45mg (67) Gepirone 5–45mg (66)	Diazepam ≥ Gepirone > Placebo 33% 71% 45%	Diazepam faster onset. Withdrawal worsening on diazepam only
Benzodiazepines v other drugs and CBT				
Ansseau et al., 1991	DSMIIIR. HAMA >19. 4 weeks	Placebo (57) Diazepam 15mg (54) Suriclone 0.3mg (57), 0.6mg (56), 0.9mg (58), 1.2mg (59)	Active drugs > Placebo 33% 65% 50%–58%	Suriclone: benzodiazepine-like (cyclopyrrolone)
Feltner et al., 2003	DSMIV. HAMA>19. 4 weeks (+ 1 week taper).	Placebo (67) Lorazepam 6mg (68) Pregabalin 150mg (70) Pregabalin 600mg (66)	Lorazepam = Pregabalin600 > Placebo = Pregabalin150 44% (17%) 55% (27%) 52% (not stated) 59% (31%)	Pregabalin600 effective on both HAMA subscales, lorazepam somatic only. All drugs some discontinuation symptoms. Pregabalin: calcium channel antagonist

Continued

Table 18.4 Placebo-controlled trials in Generalised Anxiety Disorder with active comparators (*Continued*)

Study	Diagnosis, entry severity, study duration	Drugs (N)	Outcome and response rate where reported (remission)	Comments
Llorca et al., 2002	DSMIV. HAMA >19. 12 weeks.	Placebo (113) Bromazepam 6mg (116) Hydroxyzine 50mg (105)	Active drugs > Placebo 32% 57% 60%	Effective on HAMA psychic anxiety subscale
Lydiard et al., 1997	DSMIIIR. HAMA >17. 4 weeks (+ 1 week taper)	Placebo (62) Alprazolam 1–4.5mg (63) Abecarnil 2–9mg (67)	Active drugs > Placebo 42% 62% 53%	Alprazolam had faster onset. Withdrawal worsening on alprazolam only.
Moller et al., 2001	ICD10. HAMA >16. 4 weeks	Placebo (105) Alprazolam 2mg (102) Opipramol 200mg (100)	Active drugs > Placebo 47% 64% 63%	Opipramol: sigma-opioid drug
Power et al., 1990	DSMIII/RDC. HAMA >14. 6 weeks (+ 3 weeks taper)	Placebo (19) Diazepam 15mg (22) Diazepam 15mg + CBT (21) CBT (21) CBT + Placebo (18)	CBT groups > Diazepam = Placebo at end of withdrawal 36% 45% 87% 86% 72%	No assessment at end of active treatment. Non-CBT groups more psychiatric referrals in following 6 months
Rickels et al., 2000b	DSMIIIR. HAMA >19. 6 weeks (+ staggered withdrawal over 24 weeks)	Placebo (104) Diazepam 15–35mg (104) Abecarnil 7.5–17.5mg (102)	Diazepam ≥ Abecarnil > Placebo 45% 65% 54%	Discontinuation symptoms on diazepam only after ≥ 12 weeks treatment

Buspirone v non-benzodiazepine drugs

Study	Criteria	Drug (n)	Results	Notes
Davidson et al., 1999	DSMIV. HAMA >17. 8 weeks	Placebo (98) Venlafaxine XR 75mg (87) 150mg (87) Buspirone (93)	Active drugs ≥ PLA 39% 62% 49% 55%	Only venlafaxine effective on HAMA psychic subscale.
Lader & Scotto, 1998	DSMIV. HAMA >19. 4 weeks	Placebo (81) Buspirone 20mg (82) Hydroxyzine 50mg (81)	Hydroxyzine > Placebo ≤ Buspirone 29% 36% 42%	Drugs effective on depression ratings
Pollack et al., 1997	DSMIIIR. HAMA >19. 6 weeks	Placebo (112) Buspirone (15–45mg (115)) Abecarnil 3–9mg (116) 7.5–22.5mg (115)	Buspirone > Placebo = Abecarnil 52% 53% 53% 54%	
Other				
Bjerrum et al., 1992	DSMIII. HAMA>15. 4 weeks	Placebo (16) Flupentixol 2mg (15) CGP361A 2mg (19)	No significant differences 50% 67% 47%	CGP361A: β-blocker

HAMA: Hamilton Anxiety Rating Scale.

mixed anxiety groups (Stevinson et al., 2002; Volz & Kieser, 1997); the only small placebo-controlled study in GAD did not show efficacy (Connor & Davidson, 2002) although a non-placebo controlled trial suggested equal efficacy to buspirone and opipramol (Boerner et al., 2003).

Comparative Efficacy and Tolerability of Drug Treatments

In spite of a number of comparative drug trials it is difficult to identify consistent differences in overall efficacy between drugs, in particular between the three main groups, benzodiazepines, antidepressants and buspirone. Most of the non-placebo-controlled comparative studies have involved benzodiazepines and buspirone and, consistent with studies shown in Table 18.4, there appear no differences in efficacy. Earlier onset of action for benzodiazepines has been reported by a minority of studies (Ansseau et al., 1990; Enkelmann, 1991; Jacobson et al., 1985) with no studies finding buspirone had an earlier onset. In a meta-analysis of placebo-controlled studies, Mitte et al. (2005) found that more patients dropped out of treatment with buspirone than benzodiazepines suggesting poorer tolerability of the former. The few benzodiazepine-antidepressant comparisons also suggest equal efficacy with one study finding earlier onset for diazepam compared with imipramine (Rickels et al., 1993). Greater improvement for somatic compared with psychic symptoms on benzodiazepines and vice versa for buspirone and imipramine was reported in two studies (Hoehn-Saric et al., 1988; Rickels et al., 1982) but not in most studies.

One study has compared SSRIs without any difference being found between sertaline and paroxetine (Ball et al., 2005).

Hydroxyzine has only been compared with other drugs in two studies and appears at least as acutely effective as benzodiazepines and buspirone (Table 18.4).

It appears therefore that there is little to choose between available drugs in terms of short-term efficacy. Benzodiazepines may have a faster onset of action but this is offset by sedative side-effects and concerns about dependence in longer-term use. Buspirone is associated with more dropouts than benzodiazepines.

Choice of Drug and Practicalities of Treatment

Antidepressants, in particular SSRIs, have become the drug treatment of choice for GAD, based on their short and medium-term efficacy, preliminary relapse-prevention data, lack of potential for dependence and their efficacy against major depression and other anxiety disorders which are frequently co-morbid. Although there is only RCT evidence for three SSRIs it is likely that all are effective given their similar primary pharmacology and their comparable efficacy in trials in other conditions. Venlafaxine has the greatest amount of evidence for a single antidepressant and also the most data for longer-term efficacy. Recent concerns about its safety in overdose, cautions in cardiac disease with recommendations for cardiac monitoring and a limitation of its prescription to mental health specialists (National Institute for Clinical Excellence, 2004b) make it a second line drug at present.

In spite of trial evidence, buspirone has not been perceived as having good efficacy and tolerability in clinical practice and there are some suggestions of poorer tolerability in the trial data. If used, a gap of at least a month after stopping benzodiazepines is advisable because efficacy and tolerability may be reduced if started earlier (DeMartinis et al., 2000).

Although benzodiazepines are effective in GAD there are concerns about dependence, cognitive and psychomotor side-effects, interactions with sedative drugs and difficulty in stopping them after longer-term use. They have the advantage of probable earlier onset of action and in severe cases may be a useful short-term adjunct to antidepressants but guidelines recommend limiting their use to four weeks (National Institute for Clinical Excellence, 2004b).

From the study evidence, treatment trials of at least 8–12 weeks are indicated before stopping or changing drugs, especially with antidepressants and buspirone, and some patients will continue to improve after this. When to stop successful drug treatment is not known. It is clear that short courses of benzodiazepines alone (i.e. 4–6 weeks) do not bring lasting benefit (Tables 18.1 and 18.4) and worsening to placebo levels or even rebound anxiety is likely to occur after stopping. The continuing improvement seen up to 6 months in a number of studies, together with the relapse prevention study by Stocchi et al. (2003), indicates that treatment should continue for a minimum of 6 months after remission or substantial improvement. Indication for even longer-term use needs to be considered on an individual basis and clinical experience suggests past history, lack of complete recovery, length of history and life stressors should be taken into account.

Patients on long-term benzodiazepines were successfully weaned off them in the short-term by treatment with imipramine in one study where buspirone was less successful (Rickels et al., 2000b). Whether switching to an antidepressant is successful in maintaining improvement in the longer-term is unclear but is a reasonable clinical strategy.

Evidence is lacking regarding next-step treatments for patients failing to respond to initial drug therapy. Switching class of drug is a reasonable approach, and in more severe and non-responsive cases, drugs such as pregabalin, hydroxyzine and antipsychotics should be considered bearing in mind their drawbacks and lack of longer-term data. Newer, atypical, antipsychotics (such as olanzapine) have side-effect benefits over older antipsychotics and could be considered by extrapolation of the data. In treatment resistant cases, combining drugs with proven efficacy individually can be considered provided care is taken over the safety of the combination and the patient is fully involved in the decision.

THE PLACE OF DRUG TREATMENT IN RELATION TO PSYCHOLOGICAL TREATMENT

Perhaps surprisingly, there are relatively few trials of psychological treatment in GAD (Borkovec & Ruscio, 2001; Durham et al., 2003) and no informative drug-psychological treatment comparisons. Cognitive behavioural therapy (CBT) appears to have persisting benefits and the reported effect sizes are larger than for pharmacological treatment and other psychological approaches (Borkovek & Ruscio 2001) but caution is required because of the lack of direct comparative studies. One study has compared diazepam, CBT and their combination but its limitations make interpretation impossible (Power et al., 1990). Potential sustained benefit from CBT is suggested by studies to date (Borkovec & Ruscio, 2001; Durham et al., 2003). The same is true of drug treatment, but only as long as the drug is continued (see above). There is no evidence as to whether combining drug treatment with CBT produces benefits over either treatment alone (Foa et al., 2002).

The initial choice of drug therapy or CBT therefore needs to be decided on an individual basis, considering the availability of CBT and patient preference. Treating with CBT following failed drug therapy and vice versa would seem sensible, but clinical trial evidence is lacking. Evidence that combining drug treatment and CBT offers extra benefit is lacking but a pragmatic approach would be to combine them when partial improvement has occurred on either treatment given singly.

DISCUSSION

Drugs are effective in treating GAD and the evidence supports efficacy against worry and anticipatory anxiety (especially with antidepressants). Direct experimental evidence for psychological/neuropsychological effects of treatment is limited. Mogg et al. (2004) found that four weeks' treatment with citalopram or paroxetine reduced interpretative bias in GAD patients using an ambiguous homophone task, correlating with improvement on Spielberger Trait anxiety scores but not other anxiety ratings. The PSWQ only improved slightly, and less than other anxiety ratings, suggesting that SSRIs may not directly act on worry, at least early in treatment. Hoehn-Saric et al. (2004), using functional magnetic resonance imaging (fMRI), investigated the effect of citalopram treatment in GAD patients on brain response to statements describing a personal worry, compared with neutral statements. Both types of statements caused activation in prefrontal and thalamo-striatal regions which was greater for worry-related statements. Citalopram reduced anxiety ratings and brain activation to worry-related statements, and to a lesser extent activation to neutral statements. This was interpreted as overreaction in GAD to both pathology-specific and non-specific cues, improved by reducing anxiety. Although these studies show that SSRI treatment affects some underlying psychological processes associated with GAD, it is difficult to know whether they are primary, or secondary to a general improvement in anxiety.

There are hints that benzodiazepines, buspirone and antidepressants may act in different ways to treat GAD. The targets for these drugs are widespread and therefore the brain aversion system could be modulated at any or all levels. The more rapid onset seen with benzodiazepines is thought to reflect their immediate action on the inhibitory GABA system. Consistent with benzodiazepines' muscle relaxant properties there may be an early direct effect on some of the physical symptoms of anxiety, as seen in two studies where no final benefit over placebo was found (Castillo et al., 1987; Pourmotabbed et al., 1996). However an acute reduction in subjective anxiety is also evident in patients immediately after taking a benzodiazepine (McCracken et al., 1990). Antidepressants and buspirone appear to have a more delayed onset of effect than benzodiazepines with a consistent effect against psychic anxiety symptoms, possibly stronger than against somatic anxiety, which cannot be explained by direct sedative effects.

What is more striking than the differences between drugs is the similarity in their effects, at least using the instruments that have been applied to date. It seems likely that the current anti-anxiety drugs act at multiple levels of the brain aversion system, the components of which are involved in an overlapping distributed way, rather than as 'modules', in the syndrome of GAD. This results in a pattern of global improvement being the most common picture.

In future treatment studies it would be useful to try and investigate effects on specific components of GAD, in particular the core feature of excessive and uncontrollable worry. Standardising measures for both psychological and drug treatment studies would help identify the pattern and the time course of improvement of different aspects of GAD, possibly giving insight into principle mechanisms of action. Further investigation of the neuropsychology/neurobiology of GAD is also needed to try and identify which processes are abnormal and how treatments modify them.

REFERENCES

Allgulander, C., Dahl, A.A., Austin, C., Morris, P.L., Sogaard, J.A., Fayyad, R., Kutcher, S.P. & Clary, C.M. (2004). Efficacy of sertraline in a 12-week trial for generalized anxiety disorder. *American Journal of Psychiatry*, **161**, 1642–1649.

Allgulander, C., Hackett, D. & Salinas, E. (2001). Venlafaxine extended release (ER) in the treatment of generalised anxiety disorder: twenty-four-week placebo-controlled dose-ranging study. *British Journal of Psychiatry*, **179**, 15–22.

Anderson, I.M. (2001). Meta-analytical studies on new antidepressants. *British Medical Bulletin*, **57**, 161–178.

Ansseau, M., Olie, J.P., von Frenckell, R., Jourdain, G., Stehle, B. & Guillet, P. (1991). Controlled comparison of the efficacy and safety of four doses of suriclone, diazepam and placebo in generalized anxiety disorder. *Psychopharmacology*, **104**, 439–443.

Ansseau, M., Papart, P., Gerard, M.A., von Frenckell, R. & Franck, G. (1990). Controlled comparison of buspirone and oxazepam in generalized anxiety. *Neuropsychobiology*, **24**, 74–78.

Aufdembrinke, B. (1998). Abecarnil, a new beta-carboline, in the treatment of anxiety disorders. *British Journal of Psychiatry*, **34**, 55–63.

Ball, S.G., Kuhn, A., Wall, D., Shekhar, A. & Goddard, A.W. (2005). Selective serotonin reuptake inhibitor treatment for generalized anxiety disorder: a double-blind, prospective comparison between paroxetine and sertraline. *Journal of Clinical Psychiatry*, **66**, 94–99.

Bandelow, B., Zohar, J., Hollander, E., Kasper, S. & Moller, H.J. (2002). World Federation of Societies of Biological Psychiatry (WFSBP) guidelines for the pharmacological treatment of anxiety, obsessive-compulsive and posttraumatic stress disorders. *World Journal of Biological Psychiatry*, **3**, 171–199.

Bjerrum, H., Allerup, P., Thunedborg, K., Jakobsen, K. & Bech P. (1992). Treatment of generalized anxiety disorder: comparison of a new beta-blocking drug (CGP 361 A), low-dose neuroleptic (flupenthixol) and placebo. *Pharmacopsychiatry*, **25**, 229–232.

Boerner, R.J., Sommer, H., Berger, W., Kuhn, U., Schmidt, U. & Mannel, M. (2003). Kava-Kava extract LI 150 is as effective as Opipramol and Buspirone in Generalised Anxiety Disorder—an 8-week randomized, double-blind multi-centre clinical trial in 129 out-patients. *Phytomedicine*, **10(4)**, 38–49.

Borkovec, T.D. & Ruscio. A.M. (2001). Psychotherapy for generalized anxiety disorder. *Journal of Clinical Psychiatry*, **62(Suppl. 11)**, 37–42.

Boyer, W.F. & Feighner, J.P. (1993). A placebo-controlled double-blind multicenter trial of two doses of ipsapirone versus diazepam in generalized anxiety disorder. *International Clinical Psychopharmacology*, **8**, 173–176.

Brown, T.A., Barlow, D.H. & Liebowitz, M.R. (1994). The empirical basis of generalized anxiety disorder. *American Journal of Psychiatry*, **151**, 1272–1280.

Brown, T.A., Di Nardo, P.A., Lehman, C.L. & Campbell, L.A. (2001). Reliability of DSM-IV anxiety and mood disorders: implications for the classification of emotional disorders. *Journal of Abnormal Psychology*, **110**, 49–58.

Castillo, A., Sotillo, C. & Mariategui, J. (1987). Alprazolam compared to clobazam and placebo in anxious outpatients. *Neuropsychobiology*, **18**, 189-194.

Chouinard, G., Annable, L., Fontaine, R. & Solyom, L. (1982). Alprazolam in the treatment of generalized anxiety and panic disorders: a double-blind placebo-controlled study. *Psychopharmacology*, **77**, 229–233.

Cohn, J.B. & Wilcox, C.S. (1984). Long-term comparison of alprazolam, lorazepam and placebo in patients with an anxiety disorder. *Pharmacotherapy*, **4**, 93–98.

Committee on Safety of Medicines (2004). Report of the CSM expert working group on the safety of selective serotonin reuptake inhibitor antidepressants. http://medicines.mhra.gov.uk/ourwork/monitorsafequalmed/safetymessages/SSRIfinal.pdf.

Connor, K.M. & Davidson, J.R. (2002). A placebo-controlled study of Kava kava in generalized anxiety disorder. *International Clinical Psychopharmacology*, **17**, 185–188.

Cutler, N.R., Sramek, J.J., Keppel Hesselink, J.M., Krol, A., Roeschen, J., Rickels, K. & Schweizer, E. (1993). A double-blind, placebo-controlled study comparing the efficacy and safety of ipsapirone versus lorazepam in patients with generalized anxiety disorder: a prospective multicenter trial. *Journal of Clinical Psychopharmacology*, **13**, 429–437.

Darcis, T., Ferrer, M., Natens, J., Burtin, B. & Deram, P., French GP Study Group for Hydroxyzine (1995). A multicentre double-blind placebo-controlled study investigating the anxiolytic efficacy of hydroxyzine in patients with generalized anxiety. *Human Psychopharmacology*, **10**, 181–187.

Davidson, J.R., Bose, A., Korotzer, A. & Zheng, H. (2004). Escitalopram in the treatment of generalized anxiety disorder: double-blind, placebo controlled, flexible-dose study. *Depression and Anxiety*, **19**, 234–240.

Davidson, J.R., DuPont, R.L., Hedges, D. & Haskins, J.T. (1999). Efficacy, safety and tolerability of venlafaxine extended release and buspirone in outpatients with generalized anxiety disorder. *Journal of Clinical Psychiatry*, **60**, 528–535.

Deakin, J.F. & Graeff, F.G. (1991). 5HT and mechanisms of defence. *Journal of Psychopharmacology*, **5**, 305–315.

DeMartinis, N., Rynn, M., Rickels, K. & Mandos, L. (2000). Prior benzodiazepine use and buspirone response in the treatment of generalized anxiety disorder. *Journal of Clinical Psychiatry*, **61**, 91–94.

den Boer, J.A. & Westenberg, H.G. (1988). Effect of ocrotonin and noradrenaline uptake inhibitor in panic disorder: a double-blind comparative study with fluvoxamine and maprotiline. *International Clinical Psychopharmacology*, **3**, 59–74.

Durham, R.C., Chambers, J.A., MacDonald, R.R., Power, K.G. & Major, K. (2003). Does cognitive-behavioural therapy influence the long-term outcome of generalized anxiety disorder? An 8–14 year follow-up of two clinical trials. *Psychological Medicine*, **33**, 499–509.

Enkelmann, R. (1991). Alprazolam versus buspirone in the treatment of outpatients with generalized anxiety disorder. *Psychopharmacology*, **105**, 428–432.

Feighner, J.P. (1987). Buspirone in the long-term treatment of generalized anxiety disorder. *Journal of Clinical Psychiatry*, **48(Suppl.)**, 3–6.

Feighner, J.P. (1999). Mechanism of action of antidepressant medications. *Journal of Clinical Psychiatry*, **60(4)**, 4–11.

Feltner, D.E., Crockatt, J.G., Dubovsky, S.J., Cohn, C.K., Shrivastava, R.K., Targum, S.D., Liu-Dumaw, M., Carter, C.M. & Pande, A.C. (2003). A randomized, double-blind, placebo-controlled, fixed-dose, multicenter study of pregabalin in patients with generalized anxiety disorder. *Journal of Clinical Psychopharmacology*, **23**, 240–249.

Foa, E.B., Franklin, M.E. & Moser, J. (2002). Context in the clinic: how well do cognitive-behavioral therapies and medications work in combination? *Biological Psychiatry*, **52**, 987–997.

Fontaine, R., Annable, L., Chouinard, G. & Ogilvie, R.I. (1983). Bromazepam and diazepam in generalized anxiety: a placebo-controlled study with measurement of drug plasma concentrations. *Journal of Clinical Psychopharmacology*, **3**, 80–87.

Fontaine, R., Chouinard, G. & Annable, L. (1984). Rebound anxiety in anxious patients after abrupt withdrawal of benzodiazepine treatment. *American Journal of Psychiatry*, **141**, 848–852.

Fresquet, A., Sust, M., Lloret, A., Murphy, M.F., Carter, F.J., Campbell, G.M. & Marion-Landais, G. (2000). Efficacy and safety of lesopitron in outpatients with generalized anxiety disorder. *The Annals of Pharmacotherapy*, **34**, 147–153.

Gammans, R.E., Stringfellow, J.C., Hvizdos, A.J., Seidehamel, R.J., Cohn, J.B., Wilcox, C.S., Fabre, L.F., Pecknold, J.C., Smith, W.T. & Rickels, K. (1992). Use of buspirone in patients with generalized anxiety disorder and coexisting depressive symptoms. A meta-analysis of eight randomized, controlled studies. *Neuropsychobiology*, **25**, 193–201.

Gelenberg, A.J., Lydiard, R.B., Rudolph, R.L., Aguiar, L., Haskins, J.T. & Salinas, E. (2000). Efficacy of venlafaxine extended-release capsules in nondepressed outpatients with generalized anxiety disorder: A 6-month randomized controlled trial. *Journal of the American Medical Association 283*, 3082–3088.

Goldberg, H.L. & Finnerty, R.J. (1979). The comparative efficacy of buspirone and diazepam in the treatment of anxiety. *American Journal of Psychiatry*, **136**, 1184–1187.

Gray, J.A. & McNaughton, N. (2003). *The neuropsychology of anxiety: An enquiry into the functions of the septohippocampal system*. 2nd Ed., Oxford: Oxford University Press.

Guess, H., Kleinman, A., Kusek, J. & Engel, L. (2002). *The science of the placebo: towards an interdisciplinary research agenda*. London: BMJ Books.

Guy, W. (1976). ECDEU assessment manual for psychopharmacology, revised. US Department of Health, Education and Welfare publication (ADM). National Institute of Mental Health, Rockville Md.

Hackett, D., Haudiquet, V. & Salinas, E. (2003). A method for controlling for a high placebo response rate in a comparison of venlafaxine XR and diazepam in the short-term treatment of patients with generalised anxiety disorder. *European Psychiatry*, **18**, 182–187.

Hamilton, M. (1959). The assessment of anxiety states by rating. *British Journal of Medical Psychology*, **32**, 50–55.

Hoehn-Saric, R., McLeod, D.R. & Zimmerli, W.D. (1988). Differential effects of alprazolam and imipramine in generalized anxiety disorder: somatic versus psychic symptoms. *Journal of Clinical Psychiatry*, **49**, 293–301.

Hoehn-Saric, R., Schlund, M.W. & Wong, S.H. (2004). Effects of citalopram on worry and brain activation in patients with generalized anxiety disorder. *Psychiatry Research*, **131**, 11–21.

Jacobson, A.F., Dominguez. R.A., Goldstein, B.J. & Steinbook, R.M. (1985). Comparison of buspirone and diazepam in generalized anxiety disorder. *Pharmacotherapy*, **5**, 290–296.

Katz, R.J., Landau, P.S., Lott, M., Bystritsky, A., Diamond, B., Hoehn-Saric, R., Rosenthal M. & Weise, C. (1993). Serotonergic (5-HT2) mediation of anxiety—therapeutic effects of serazepine in generalized anxiety disorder. *Biological Psychiatry*, **34**, 41–44.

Kessler, R.C., Keller, M.B. & Wittchen, H.U. (2001). The epidemiology of generalized anxiety disorder. *Psychiatric Clinics of North America*, **24**, 19–39.

Laakmann, G., Schule, C., Lorkowski, G., Baghai, T., Kuhn, K. & Ehrentraut, S. (1998). Buspirone and lorazepam in the treatment of generalized anxiety disorder in outpatients. *Psychopharmacology*, **136**, 357–366.

Lader, M. & Scotto, J.C. (1998). A multicentre double-blind comparison of hydroxyzine, buspirone and placebo in patients with generalized anxiety disorder. *Psychopharmacology*, **139**, 402–406.

LeDoux, J.E. (2000). Emotion circuits in the brain. *Annual Review of Neuroscience*, **23**, 155–184.

Lenox-Smith, A.J. & Reynolds, A. (2003). A double-blind, randomised, placebo controlled study of venlafaxine XL in patients with generalised anxiety disorder in primary care. *British Journal of General Practice*, **53**, 772–777.

Llorca, P.M., Spadone, C., Sol, O., Danniau, A., Bougerol, T., Corruble, E., Faruch, M., Macher, J.P., Sermet, E. & Servant, D. (2002). Efficacy and safety of hydroxyzine in the treatment of generalized anxiety disorder: a 3-month double-blind study. *Journal of Clinical Psychiatry*, **63**, 1020–1027.

Lydiard, R.B., Ballenger, J.C. & Rickels, K. (1997). A double-blind evaluation of the safety and efficacy of abecarnil, alprazolam, and placebo in outpatients with generalized anxiety disorder. Abecarnil Work Group. *Journal of Clinical Psychiatry*, **58(Suppl. 11)**, 11–18.

Maier, W., Buller, R., Philipp, M. & Heuser, I. (1988). The Hamilton Anxiety Scale: reliability. validity and sensitivity to change in anxiety and depressive disorders. *Journal of Affective Disorders*, **14**, 61–68.

McCracken, S.G., de Wit, H., Uhlenhuth, E.H. & Johanson, C.E. (1990). Preference for diazepam in anxious adults. *Journal of Clinical Psychopharmacology*, **10**, 190–196.

McLeod, D.R., Hoehn-Saric, R., Porges, S.W. & Zimmerli, W.D. (1992). Effects of alprazolam and imipramine on parasympathetic cardiac control in patients with generalized anxiety disorder. *Psychopharmacology*, **107**, 535–540.

McNaughton, N. & Corr, P.J. (2004). A two-dimensional neuropsychology of defense: fear/anxiety and defensive distance. *Neuroscience and Biobehavioral Review*, **28**, 285–305.

Mendels, J., Krajewski, T.F., Huffer, V., Taylor, R.J., Secunda, S., Schless, A., Sebastian, J.A., Semchyshyn, G., Durr, M.I. & Melmed, A.S. (1986). Effective short-term treatment of generalized anxiety disorder with trifluoperazine. *Journal of Clinical Psychiatry*, **47**, 170–174.

Meoni, P., Hackett, D. & Lader, M. (2004). Pooled analysis of venlafaxine XR efficacy on somatic and psychic symptoms of anxiety in patients with generalized anxiety disorder. *Depression and Anxiety*, **19**, 127–132.

Meyer, T.J., Miller, M.L., Metzger, R.L. & Borkovec, T.D. (1990). Development and validation of the Penn State Worry Questionnaire. *Behaviour Research and Therapy*, **28**, 487–495.

Mitte, K., Noack, P., Steil, R. & Hautzinger, M. (2005). A meta-analytic review of the efficacy of drug treatment in generalized anxiety disorder. *Journal of Clinical Psychopharmacology*, **25**, 141–150.

Mogg, K., Baldwin, D.S., Brodrick, P. & Bradley, B.P. (2004). Effect of short-term SSRI treatment on cognitive bias in generalised anxiety disorder. *Psychopharmacology*, **176**, 466–470.

Moller, H.J., Volz, H.P., Reimann, I.W. & Stoll, K.D. (2001). Opipramol for the treatment of generalized anxiety disorder: a placebo-controlled trial including an alprazolam-treated group. *Journal of Clinical Psychopharmacology*, **21**, 59–65.

National Institute for Clinical Excellence. (2004a). Clinical Guideline 23. Depression: the management of depression in primary and secondary care. http://www.nice.org.uk/pdf/CG023NICEguideline.pdf.

National Institute for Clinical Excellence. (2004b). Clinical Guideline 22. Anxiety: Management of anxiety (panic disorder, with or without agoraphobia, and generalised anxiety disorder) in adults in primary, secondary and community care. http://www.nice.org.uk/pdf/CG022NICEguideline.pdf.

Nimatoudis, I., Zissis, N.P., Kogeorgos, J., Theodoropoulou, S., Vidalis, A. & Kaprinis, G. (2004). Remission rates with venlafaxine extended release in Greek outpatients with generalized anxiety disorder. A double-blind, randomized., placebo controlled study. *International Clinical Psychopharmacology*, **19**, 331–336.

Nutt, D.J. (2001). Neurobiological mechanisms in generalized anxiety disorder. *Journal of Clinical Psychiatry*, **62(11)**, 22–27.

Pangalila-Ratu Langi, E. & Jansen, A.A. (1988) Ritanserin in the treatment of generalized anxiety disorders: a placebo-controlled trial. *Human Psychopharmacology*, **3**, 207–212.

Pecknold, J.C., Matas, M., Howarth, B.G., Ross, C., Swinson, R., Vezeau, C. & Ungar, W. (1989). Evaluation of buspirone as an antianxiety agent: buspirone and diazepam versus placebo. *Canadian Journal of Psychiatry*, **34**, 766–771.

Piercy, M.A., Sramek J.J., Kurtz, N.M. & Cutler, N.R. (1996). Placebo response in anxiety disorders. *Annals of Pharmacotherapy*, **30**, 1013–1019.

Pohl, R.B., Feltner, D.E., Fieve, R.R. & Pande, A.C. (2005). Efficacy of pregabalin in the treatment of generalized anxiety disorder: double-blind, placebo-controlled comparison of BID versus TID dosing. *Journal of Clinical Psychopharmacology*, **25**, 151–158.

Pollack, M.H., Worthington, J.J., Manfro, G.G., Otto, M.W. & Zucker, B.G. (1997). Abecarnil for the treatment of generalized anxiety disorder: a placebo-controlled comparison of two dosage ranges of abecarnil and buspirone. *Journal of Clinical Psychiatry*, **58(Suppl. 11)**, 19–23.

Pollack, M.H., Zaninelli, R., Goddard, A., McCafferty, J.P., Bellew, K.M., Burnham, D.B. & Iyengar, M.K. (2001). Paroxetine in the treatment of generalized anxiety disorder: results of a placebo-controlled, flexible-dosage trial. *Journal of Clinical Psychiatry*, **62**, 350–357.

Pourmotabbed, T., McLeod, D.R., Hoehn-Saric, R., Hipsley, P. & Greenblatt, D.J. (1996). Treatment, discontinuation and psychomotor effects of diazepam in women with generalized anxiety disorder. *Journal of Clinical Psychopharmacology*, **16**, 202–207.

Power, K.G., Jerrom, D.W., Simpson, R.J. & Mitchell, M. (1985). Controlled study of withdrawal symptoms and rebound anxiety after six week course of diazepam for generalised anxiety. *British Medical Journal (Clinical Research Edition)*, **290**, 1246–1248.

Power, K.G., Simpson, R.J., Swanson, V. & Wallace, L.A. (1990). Controlled comparison of pharmacological and psychological treatment of generalized anxiety disorder in primary care. *British Journal of General Practice*, **40**, 289–294

Ramos, R.T., Gentil, V. & Gorenstein, C. (1993). Clomipramine and initial worsening in panic disorder: beyond the 'jitteriness syndrome'. *Journal of Psychopharmacology*, **7**, 265–269.

Rickels, K., DeMartinis, N. & Aufdembrinke, B. (2000a). A double-blind, placebo-controlled trial of abecarnil and diazepam in the treatment of patients with generalized anxiety disorder. *Journal of Clinical Psychopharmacology*, **20**, 12–18.

Rickels, K., DeMartinis, N., Garcia-Espana, F., Greenblatt, D.J., Mandos, L.A. & Rynn, M. (2000b). Imipramine and buspirone in treatment of patients with generalized anxiety disorder who are discontinuing long-term benzodiazepine therapy. *American Journal of Psychiatry*, **157**, 1973–1979.

Rickels, K., Downing, R., Schweizer, E. & Hassman, H. (1993). Antidepressants for the treatment of generalized anxiety disorder. A placebo-controlled comparison of imipramine, trazodone and diazepam. *Archives of General Psychiatry*, **50**, 884–895.

Rickels, K., Pollack, M.H., Sheehan, D.V. & Haskins, J.T. (2000c). Efficacy of extended-release venlafaxine in nondepressed outpatients with generalized anxiety disorder. *American Journal of Psychiatry*, **157**, 968–974.

Rickels, K. & Rynn, M.A. (2001). What is generalized anxiety disorder? *Journal of Clinical Psychiatry*, **62(11)**, 4–12; discussion 13–14.

Rickels, K., Schweizer, E., Csanalosi, I., Case, W.G. & Chung, H. (1988). Long-term treatment of anxiety and risk of withdrawal. Prospective comparison of clorazepate and buspirone. *Archives of General Psychiatry*, **45**, 444–450.

Rickels, K., Schweizer, E., DeMartinis, N., Mandos, L. & Mercer, C. (1997). Gepirone and diazepam in generalized anxiety disorder: a placebo-controlled trial. *Journal of Clinical Psychopharmacology*, **17**, 272–277.

Rickels, K., Weisman, K., Norstad, N., Singer, M., Stoltz, D., Brown, A. & Danton, J. (1982). Buspirone and diazepam in anxiety: a controlled study. *Journal of Clinical Psychiatry*, **43**, 81–86.

Rickels, K., Zaninelli, R., McCafferty, J., Bellew, K., Iyengar, M. & Sheehan, D. (2003). Paroxetine treatment of generalized anxiety disorder: a double-blind, placebo-controlled study. *American Journal of Psychiatry*, **160**, 749–756.

Ruscio, A.M. & Borkovec, T.D. (2004). Experience and appraisal of worry among high worriers with and without generalized anxiety disorder. *Behaviour Research and Therapy*, **42**, 1469–1482.

Rynn, M.A., Siqueland, L. & Rickels, K. (2001). Placebo-controlled trial of sertraline in the treatment of children with generalized anxiety disorder. *American Journal of Psychiatry*, **158**, 2008–2014.

Scarpini, E., Baron, P.G., Bet, L., Bottini, G., Bresolin, N., Meola, G., Pezzoli, G., Vallar, G., Monza, G.C. & Scarlato, G. (1988). Low doses of ketazolam in anxiety. a double-blind, placebo-controlled study. *Neuropsychobiology*, **20**, 74–77.

Schweizer, E. & Rickels, K. (1997). Placebo response in generalized anxiety: its effect on the outcome of clinical trials. *Journal of Clinical Psychiatry*, **58(Suppl. 11)**, 30–38.

Sramek, J.J., Tansman, M., Suri, A., Hornig-Rohan, M., Amsterdam, J.D., Stahl, S.M., Weisler, R.H. & Cutler, N.R. (1996). Efficacy of buspirone in generalized anxiety disorder with coexisting mild depressive symptoms. *Journal of Clinical Psychiatry*, **57**, 287–291.

Stevinson, C., Huntley, A. & Ernst, E. (2002). A systematic review of the safety of kava extract in the treatment of anxiety. *Drug Safety*, **25**, 251–261.

Stocchi, F., Nordera, G., Jokinen, R.H., Lepola, U.M., Hewett, K., Bryson, H. & Iyengar, M.K. (2003). Efficacy and tolerability of paroxetine for the long-term treatment of generalized anxiety disorder. *Journal of Clinical Psychiatry*, **64**, 250–258.

Volz, H.P. & Kieser, M. (1997). Kava-kava extract WS 1490 versus placebo in anxiety disorders—a randomized placebo-controlled 25-week outpatient trial. *Pharmacopsychiatry*, **30**, 1–5.

Walsh, B.T., Seidman, S.N., Sysko, R. & Gould, M. (2002). Placebo response in studies of major depression: variable, substantial and growing. *Journal of the American Medical Association* **287**, 1840–1847.

Wells, A. (1994). A multi-dimensional measure of worry: Development and preliminary validation of the Anxious Thoughts Inventory. *Anxiety, Stress and Coping*, **6**, 280–299.

Wilcox, C.S., Ryan, P.J., Morrissey, J.L., Cohn, J.B., DeFrancisco, D.F., Linden, R.D. & Heiser, J.F. (1994). A fixed-dose study of adinazolam-SR tablets in generalized anxiety disorder. *Progress in Neuropsychopharmacology and Biological Psychiatry*, **18**, 979–993.

Zung, W.W. (1987). Effect of clorazepate on depressed mood in anxious patients. *Journal of Clinical Psychiatry*, **48**, 13–14.

Chapter 19

CASE HISTORIES: TREATING WORRY ACROSS DISORDERS

Paul King

CASE HISTORIES: TREATING WORRY ACROSS DISORDERS

Cognitive-behavioural treatment of emotional disorders principally aims to modify the factors involved in the maintenance of dysfunction. These factors have been variously conceptualised and the emphasis may be on disorder specific and/or common factors across disorders. Recently, the theoretical work of Wells and colleagues has focused on common mechanisms, namely the role of worry and attention and underlying metacognitive factors influencing them.

This chapter describes the treatment of three patients presenting with different anxiety disorders. In each case worry and worry-related processes were conceptualised as important in problem maintenance and were targeted in treatment. The disorders were Generalised Anxiety Disorder (GAD), Post Traumatic Stress Disorder (PTSD) and Social Phobia. The treatments described are based on the metacognitive theory of emotional disorder (Wells, 2000; Wells & Matthews, 1994), and their implementation was guided by two treatment manuals (Wells, 1997; Wells & Sembi, 2004).

GENERALISED ANXIETY DISORDER

Background to Case

I can worry about anything: what's in the mail, my finances, my hearing loss, death, how much of my life I've wasted. Worry has been a problem since I was a young man. It has stopped me from achieving things in my life. I've done nothing with my life. I've wasted it.

Worry and Its Psychological Disorders: Theory, Assessment and Treatment. Edited by G. C. L. Davey and A. Wells. © 2006 John Wiley & Sons, Ltd.

The above quote is from a 59 year old married man with three children. He had developed a depressed mood since retirement, due to a shoulder injury two years previously. His role as a youth instructor had also been terminated by his injury. His work had always kept him extremely busy, and this had acted to distract him from feelings of generalised anxiety that were invariably present.

Currently he described himself as 'wound-up' all the time, with his mind racing with repetitious worry and other ruminative thoughts about how he should have done things in his life. His everyday activities had become erratic, and he found himself making frequent mistakes when doing DIY tasks at home. He met all criteria for GAD, with excessive worry across a number of domains, and a feeling that the worry was out of control. He presented with a range of typical GAD symptoms such as feeling restless and on edge, with poor concentration and irritability. He also had symptoms of a churning stomach and increased urination. Protracted, more intense periods of worry had in the past resulted in panic type symptoms such as palpitations, breathlessness and a dry mouth. He felt that the worry was interfering significantly with his life, and that if this could be alleviated he would not be depressed.

Formulation and Socialisation

The assessment included gathering further information to develop the disorder specific formulation, by engaging in the following Socratic dialogue.

Therapist (T) Can you think of a worry episode you've had over the last week?

Patient (P) Yes, my daughter needed her car fixing urgently. I couldn't sleep that night, and kept on trying to work out what could be wrong with it and if I'd be able to fix it or find a garage. She had to attend a job interview and I couldn't stop thinking what would happen if her car broke down on the way.

(T) Do you think there might be advantages to worrying like this?

(P) I think it helps me avoid problems and get things done.

(T) As the worry episode went on, did you find yourself becoming stressed? What sort of reactions did you notice?

(P) I felt very stressed and noticed my stomach churning. At one point it got so bad I noticed my heart racing.

(T) As the worry and stress continued, did you have any concerns about how it was affecting you?

(P) Yes, I worry that one day the stress might cause me serious harm.

(T) How could it do that?

(P) A stroke or heart attack. Can too much stress cause cancer?

(T) Could it have any other bad effects?

(P) I remember when I've been depressed in the past, and my worrying has been worse, I really felt as if I were losing control. I think if it got too bad you could go crazy.

(T) Do you have these sorts of negative thoughts about your worry in the daytime?

(P) Yes, but I'm also concerned how it prevents me from getting things done, or that things could go wrong because I can't concentrate. It's just that I never seem to be free of it, it's always there.

(T) So when you find yourself worrying do you do anything to deal with it?

(P) I'll try and reason things out in my mind, but sometimes find myself going around in circles. If I'm uncertain about something I'll plan things well in advance.

(T) Anything else?

(P) If my wife's around she'll reassure me sometimes. I've got in the habit of reassuring myself. I read a book on positive self-talk, saying things like 'I'm healthy and I feel good'. Distraction is good, going for a walk or something.

(T) What would happen if you didn't try to control your worry like this?

(P) It would just get worse and worse, everything would go wrong.

As the interview proceeded the formulation was mapped out on a white board for the client to see (Figure 19.1).

In drawing out the formulation, first the triggering situations were noted, and agreement was sought that these were general and not specifically a problem in themselves. Therapist: 'If we could solve this particular problem, would the worry problem also be sorted? Patient: No, I would just think of something else to worry about. Therapist: In that case would you agree that the problem is the tendency to worry, rather than the different things that can trigger it off?'

Next positive beliefs about worry were noted, illustrating how worry is to a degree motivated by positive expectations that this will solve, or deal effectively with the worries. Next, the content of the worries, or Type 1 worries were noted. The worry process was illustrated by highlighting

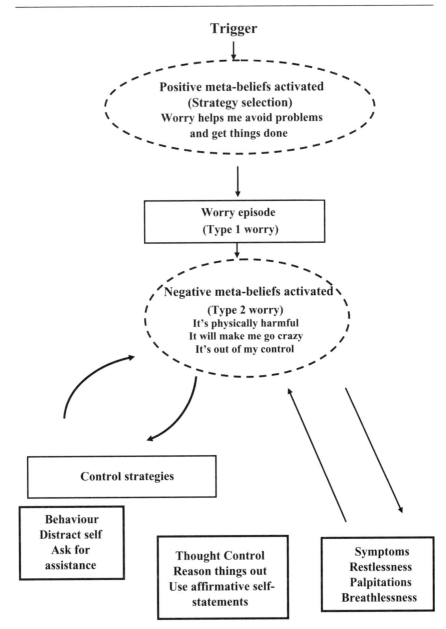

Figure 19.1   A formulation based on Wells' Metacognitive Model of GAD

how worry sets in chain a series of 'What if...?' questions that lead to simulations of more and more negative scenarios that often result in catastrophic ideas. The symptoms resulting from the worry process were added next. The therapist then explained how the combined effects of ongoing worry and anxiety symptoms act to trigger 'worry about worry', or Type 2 worries, essentially concerns about the uncontrollability of worry, and its potentially harmful effects on physical and mental health, and on ability to function. The attempts to control worry were then added as the final part of the formulation, separated into cognitive and behaviour control strategies.

Socialisation to the model involved a number of strategies. Feedback loops were added to illustrate how increasing anxiety levels act to fuel concerns about the harmful effects of worry. A thought suppression experiment was conducted to illustrate how thought suppression fails to eliminate the targeted thought, and how such a failure of control might increase beliefs about uncontrollability. The formulation was described so that negative beliefs about worry were seen as a central engine that drives the worry process. This was facilitated by Socratic questions such as, *'If you believed you had control over worrying how much of a problem would it be'*. and *'If you no longer believed that worry was harmful how much of a problem would it be'*. The formulation and socialisation process continued by illustrating how he tended to oscillate between engaging with his worries, e.g. by trying to reason them out, whilst at other times he would try to suppress them, through distraction for example.

Treatment

Following socialisation, the treatment proceeded to modify negative metacognitive beliefs, focusing initially on beliefs about the uncontrollability of worry. The first step in this process was the introduction of the idea of 'detached mindfulness' (Wells & Matthews, 1994), as a prerequisite for control experiments. The following dialogue ensued with this objective in mind:

(T) So, it seems that worrying thoughts are kept in consciousness because we tend to interact with them, either engaging with them, or trying to suppress them. What I would like you to try now is to treat them like any other thought, that is to do nothing with them, neither engaging nor suppressing. We call this 'detached mindfulness'. That is we are mindful of a thought in our consciousness, but we remain detached from it.

Disengaging From Maladaptive Control Strategies

Detached mindfulness was instructed and encouraged from the very first session, flowing from socialisation and the suppression experiment. The patient found this easy to do and described himself as just 'letting my worries roll through'. He practiced detached mindfulness, and used the controlled worry period, described below, on a regular basis throughout the treatment period. He had the belief that he could control his worries through positive self-talk. However, he acknowledged that this did not appear to work, and that it acted to engage him with the worries due to indirectly trying to suppress them. As such he agreed to drop this strategy and use detached mindfulness instead. Another maladaptive worry control strategy was using his wife to reassure him about his concerns. It was explained that although this behaviour might alleviate feelings of anxiety for a short time, it was indirectly an attempt to suppress worries. Focusing on worries in this way was likely to give validity to them, and also undermine his confidence in learning how to cope effectively with worrying thoughts. After this discussion he agreed to stop this behaviour.

Challenging Metacognitive Beliefs About Uncontrollability

He was instructed to combine detached mindfulness with a controlled worry period, during which he could worry as much as he liked, but for no longer than half an hour. Therapist: 'When you are aware of a worrying thought remind yourself that it doesn't mean anything, that you do not need to engage with it, but can return to it later during your controlled worry period if you need to.' This manoeuvre most often results in the patient finding the worries they had earlier in the day are no longer present or relevant when reviewed during the controlled worry period. He found this outcome very encouraging and also surprising. To facilitate reattribution of uncontrollability the therapist asked, 'If your thoughts are uncontrollable, how could you disengage from them? If they were uncontrollable, how could they just disappear, or not be relevant later on in the day?'

Challenging Metacognitive Beliefs About Harm

He had the belief that 'worry could make me go crazy'. To challenge the belief it was necessary to operationalise what 'going crazy' meant. He replied, 'I would totally lose control and be unable to do anything. This would be like a nervous breakdown and I would have to be hospitalised'. These catastrophic thoughts were challenged by asking him to recall the time when his worrying was at its worst. This had been thirty years previously when he described himself as worrying constantly about dying and suffering from a constant tension headache. Despite the intensity of his worrying at this time he was surprised to note that he had in fact coped with the demands of work and family, and had not required hospitalisation. He was then asked to identify someone he knew who had a 'nervous breakdown' due to worrying, which he was unable to do. He was finally asked to consider how many people in the population worry, compared with how many who have 'nervous breakdowns'. His estimates were 95% compared with 10%, indicating that there appeared to be little relationship between worrying and nervous breakdowns. The difference between psychotic and neurotic illness was also explained, and that only more severe mental disturbance resulted in hospitalisation. A paradoxical suggestion was made, that GAD could make a person more in 'control', as the person would tend to be more cautious and vigilant.

A second set of harm cognitions was related to the idea that worry could cause so much stress that it might result in a stroke or heart attack. This was challenged by asking him, with help from the therapist, to consider the various risk factors for heart attacks/stroke. He was then asked to weigh the contributions each of these risk factors made, expressed in a pie chart.

In addition he was given information about the nature of stress and its relationship to heart disease, through elevations in blood pressure over long periods of time, that is years rather than transitory changes that might occur during worry episodes. Once these pathological changes had occurred, little further contribution would be made by transitory stress responses caused by worry. His belief ratings before and after verbal reattribution were 80% and 10%. A similar exercise was conducted in relation to his fear that worry and stress might cause cancer.

Subsequent treatment sessions focused on his positive beliefs about worry by reviewing the evidence and counter-evidence for them. It turned out that little work was required in this domain as he had already discovered that he didn't appear to cope ineffectively when he had reduced his level of worrying and this appeared to have led to a revision of his positive beliefs.

Relapse Prevention

A therapy blueprint was prepared. This included a diagram of the formulation, information on the effect of thought suppression and a summary of the evidence that challenged his type 2 worry and beliefs about uncontrollability and harm. He was aware that at this point in time his lifestyle was somewhat restricted and we were concerned that this might be an avoidant strategy to prevent worry triggers. As such he agreed that he would seek

Table 19.1   Outcome data

Treatment	Pre-treatment	Post-treatment	Follow-up 1/3/6/12 month
GAD			
PSWQ	58	35	-/36/38/38
BAI	29	14	-/3/1/0
BDI	18	18	-/7/8/6
PTSD			
IES	54	25	18/ -/ -/-
BAI	10	5	8/ -/ -/-
BDI	13	8	9/ -/-/-
SOCIAL PHOBIA			
FNE	29	9	-/ 9/13/-
SAD	27	1	-/ 0/ 1/-
BAI	12	2	-/ 2/ 3/-
BDI	26	4	-/ 2/ 3/-

Note: Measures: PSWQ = Penn State Worry Questionnaire; BAI – Beck Anxiety Inventory; BDI = Beck Depression Inventory; IES = Impact of Event Scale; FNE = Fear of Negative Evaluation; SAD = Social Avoidance and Distress

out new challenges that might provoke worry in order that he could implement and practice the new cognitive strategies he had developed.

Outcome

In total this patient received six treatment sessions. His outcome data is shown in Table 19.1. As a participant in an open case series study he was followed up for a year post-treatment. At post-treatment he reported significant reduction in the time spent worrying and level of distress caused by worry. His anxiety and depression scores decreased substantially to within the normal range, and he no longer met criteria for GAD. The treatment gains were maintained over the 12-month follow up period.

POST TRAUMATIC STRESS DISORDER

Background to Case

I've lost all my confidence. I can't go out anymore. I can't stop thinking about why it happened to me. I'm always thinking about it. I just want to get back to how I used to be

The above quote was from a 64 year old man, who had been assaulted approximately 14 months prior to the interview. He had been knocked to the ground, sustaining concussion and a head injury requiring six stitches. He had developed depressive and anxiety symptoms with reduced appetite and weight loss, insomnia, fatigue, restlessness and sweating. He described a number of symptoms consistent with PTSD including: nightmares about being attacked, frequent intrusive thoughts, avoidance, hypervigilance, exaggerated startle and irritability. He had become avoidant of crowded places, especially where groups of youths might be encountered. If he was unable to avoid these locations he felt vulnerable and was hypervigilant. He had noted no improvement in these symptoms during the previous 14 months.

Theoretical Background

The treatment approach used in this case was metacognitive in nature. The metacognitive model and treatment of PTSD (Wells, 2000; Wells & Sembi, 2004), is based on the idea that worry/rumination and attentional coping strategies interfere with normal internal processes that automatically re-solve stress reactions. So if we formulate and remove these strategies and the factors contributing to them, then normal emotional processing should be facilitated.

Formulation

A Socratic dialogue drew out maladaptive cognitive coping in the form of worry and rumination. This in turn was driving avoidance and hypervig-ilant behavioural patterns.

Therapist (T) It sounds as if one of the problems is that you find yourself worrying about what happened a lot of the time.

Patient (P) Yes, I can't stop thinking about why it happened to me. It's really shaken my confidence, and I'm worried I won't get back to normal.

(T) What do you mean by back to normal?

(P) I've always felt confident I could deal with things. It seems to me that you're just not safe these days.

(T) How do you cope with these feelings?

(P) I seem to spend a lot of time reassuring myself everything will be alright.

(T) But despite this you have stopped going out.

(P) Yes I suppose I have, and when I do I can't relax, I'm forever looking over my shoulder.

Further questioning draws out maladaptive metacognitive beliefs about use of worry/ruminative coping strategies.

(T) Can I just check with you? Do you find worrying about what happened and reassuring yourself helpful?

(P) Well it's bound to make you feel better isn't it? Also, it keeps you on your guard, so you're wary. As long as I don't feel confident I won't go out.

As the interview proceeded the formulation model was mapped out on a whiteboard for the client to see. (Figure 19.2).

Socialisation

First, PTSD symptoms such as nightmares and exaggerated startle were reframed as normal reactions following traumatic events. Intrusive thoughts and preoccupations were seen as adaptive processing strategies in response to traumatic events that might signal threatening environmental conditions. It was explained that these would often resolve spontaneously. However, certain cognitive processing strategies could lead to persistence of traumatic thoughts and a sense of threat.

The socialisation process continued by asking him to consider whether there were any advantages or disadvantages to worrying about what had happened and the way it had affected him. This allowed the therapist to illustrate how worry/rumination served no purpose and contributed to locking him into a sense of threat.

(T) What happens to your anxiety when you worry?

(P) Well I guess it decreases my confidence, and when I'm feeling anxious I'll avoid going out.

(T) Does worrying help you feel better?

(P) The more I think about it the more angry I feel.

(T) Does worrying help you move on from the trauma?

(P) No, it just seems to keep the reaction going.

(T) Does worrying help you see the situation more clearly?

(P) No, it's not given me any answers as to why it happened to me.

(T) When you worry do you feel safer?

(P) No I just feel that danger lurks round every corner.

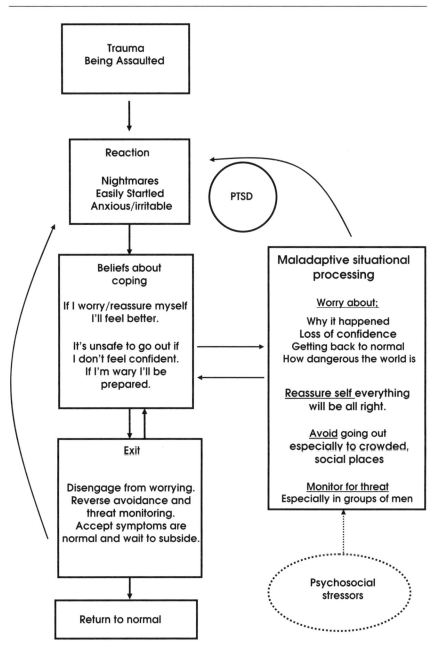

Figure 19.2   A formulation based on Wells' Metacognitive Model of PTSD

It was a surprise for him to realise that he really couldn't think of any advantages to worry/rumination.

As in the treatment of GAD, the next task was to illustrate how attempts at trying to suppress unwanted distressing thoughts would increase the likelihood of further intrusions and/or undermine confidence at being able to control these thoughts. This was done by use of the 'white bear' thought suppression experiment. It was also explained that his tendency to reassure himself was a form of thought suppression in that he was trying to 'cancel out' traumatic thoughts by doing this.

Socialisation continued to illustrate how worry about safety led to avoidance of going out, and hypervigilance if he did go out. In essence the hypervigilance was keeping him locked in a threat perception cycle. Again, an advantages/disadvantages analysis was used to illustrate the maladaptive effects of avoidance and hypervigilance. He came up with the following lists:

Advantages of avoiding going out

I can avoid the same situation.

Disadvantages of avoiding going out

Can't go out and enjoy myself/socialise.
I feel less confident socially now.
It's made me less confident about my safety.
I can't relearn that being in crowds is safe.

Advantages of being hypervigilant

If I'm wary I'll be prepared.

Disadvantages of being hypervigilant

I can't relax. I'm on edge, waiting for something to happen.
Being hypervigilant could make me look suspicious and attract attention.
I'm not paying attention to the people I'm with.
Being wary has not increased my confidence about going out.

Treatment

Treatment involved instructing him to disengage from worry/rumination activity in relation to traumatic thoughts and symptoms, preoccupations with negative consequences since and negative appraisals about not coping. This was achieved by teaching detached mindfulness accompanied by controlled worry period. Once he had achieved detached mindfulness and reduced worry/rumination he was instructed to reverse avoidance, whilst dropping hypervigilance in 'threatening' situations. By changing responses in this way it is possible to exit from the cycle shown in the formulation (Figure 19.2).

Training in Detached Mindfulness and Use of Controlled Worry Period

Following the socialisation process he was introduced to the idea of detached mindfulness through a series of illustrations. These included the 'clouds' and 'recalcitrant child' metaphor, free-association and green tiger tasks, and using naturally occurring intrusions in session to practice on (Wells & Sembi, 2004a, b). He was also instructed to remind himself with the phrase, 'It's only a thought, not a reality!'. Further instruction and in-session practice was continued as required, and adherence to these principles in everyday life was monitored closely.

To facilitate the disengagement process he was instructed to use a 'controlled worry period' for half an hour at a pre-set time each day, so that when worry/rumination occurred he could remind himself to disengage and postpone the activity until later. This strategy also helped to highlight how intrusions were transitory phenomena, as he frequently found that he was not predisposed to worry at the pre-set time. It was emphasised that rumination about symptoms must be treated in the same way, and that these symptoms were to be recognised as normal reactions following traumatic events, that would spontaneously subside.

He was able to use detached mindfulness after three 'coaching' sessions, and reported immediate benefits of reduced rumination about the assault and had spontaneously visited a pub after several months' avoidance. By the fourth treatment session he reported no trauma-related intrusions over the previous week, and had been on two further social outings without anxiety. He now felt that he would be able to return to his normal social routines without difficulty.

Dealing With Residual Symptoms

Following the three treatment sessions he was seen at one-month follow-up where he presented with some residual posttraumatic stress symptoms. Specifically, continuing nightmares, exaggerated startle, irritability and failure to return to his normal social routines out of the house. The nightmares were re-framed as normal ongoing processing of the traumatic event that would remit if allowed to take its course. Although it was acknowledged that it was not possible to use detached mindfulness at the time of a nightmare, it could, however, be applied when awake. When he became aware of intrusions relating to the nightmare, he was to remind himself this was normal, and that he need not worry about the nightmare, or engage with it in any other way. On the other hand he was to allow the nightmare theme to occupy its own space without trying to push it away or suppress it. In relation to his failure to return to normal routines, he was encouraged to go out as often as possible whilst dropping his hypervigilance. This included visiting the pub where he had been assaulted. If he experienced any arousal symptoms when out, such as exaggerated startle or irritability, he was to apply detached mindfulness, accepting the reaction had happened and was normal, whilst not engaging with any catastrophising thoughts about the symptoms, or trying to suppress them.

Outcome

At the follow-up session a week later, he reported that he had been able to visit the pub where he had been assaulted without any hypervigilance or anxiety reaction. He had only experienced one nightmare, and was no longer irritable. Outcome data are shown in Table 19.1.

SOCIAL PHOBIA

Background to Case

Everyone at work is outgoing, so that if I talk I've nothing interesting to say. I tend to just withdraw from conversations. I'm sure people think I'm inadequate. I worry that other people will see I'm anxious. I tend to look down and rub my hands a lot. I tend to isolate myself and avoid relationships. It's badly affected my job opportunities. My life feels restricted when I see others moving on.

The above quote is from a 35 year old single man who lived alone. He described himself as always having been quiet and withdrawn, but that this tendency was becoming worse. He currently found most social situations anxiety provoking including crowded pubs, any group with more than two people and meetings at work. His main diversion was typically a solitary one of going out running after work.

Formulation

The following Socratic dialogue drew out the disorder specific formulation.

Therapist (T) So when you're about to go into a social situation what sort of things go through your mind?

Patient (P) I can never think of what to say in social situations, and if I do say something it tends to be something stupid, or people take it the wrong way.

(T) And what sort of things go through your mind when you're in the situation?

(P) That people can see I'm anxious and about to lose control. They must think I'm stupid or inadequate in some way.

(T) And as you are having these thoughts, are you aware of how the anxiety is affecting you? Do you notice any specific reactions or symptoms caused by the anxiety?

(P) Well my face really flushes up. And I get twitchy, sort of fidgeting around.

(T) Anything else?

(P) My mind goes blank.

(T) And as you're feeling like this do you have an overall impression of how you look to other people?

(P) I imagine I'm looking very flushed, anxious, and twitchy. I must look very foolish.

(T) And what about how you sound?

(P) Just stupid, with a monotone voice.

(T) So as you're appraising the situation and predicting bad things might happen, do you do anything to try to control the situation?

(P) Well I'll rehearse what I'm going to say. And when I do say it, speak fast to get it over and done with. As I'm aware of how monotonous I sound I tend to be aware of this and modulate my voice to try and sound more interesting.

(T) Do you do anything else to cover up how you feel or look?

(P) I just try to divert attention away from myself by avoiding eye contact or asking other people questions.

As the interview proceeded the disorder specific formulation was mapped out on the whiteboard for the patient's consideration (Figure 19.3).

Treatment

The brief (metacognitive-focused) treatment for Social Phobia was used in this case. Wells has modified previous treatment (Clark & Wells, 1995,

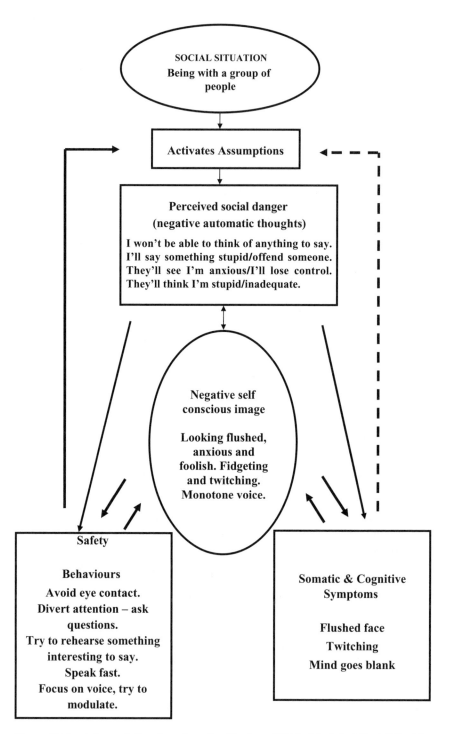

Figure 19.3   A formulation based on the Clark and Wells Model of Social Phobia

Wells, 1997) in line with his metacognitive theory and recent research findings (Wells & Papageorgiou, 1998, 2000) to emphasise attentional refocus and reduction of worry/rumination as more critical strategies. Crucial in the intervention is the instruction, early on in therapy, for the person to block worry and rumination about social events. This new processing plan for social situations leads to a decrease in self-consciousness and facilitates the person's ability to interrogate the social environment, thus gaining corrective feedback to counteract negative predictions and interpretations of social events. We have found that this treatment configuration is effective, without the use of verbal reattribution, and only minimal prompts to drop safety behaviours.

Socialisation of the patient at the outset of treatment proceeded through a series of Socratic questions to draw his attention to how his information processing tends to be based on internal information:

What is the evidence that people think you're stupid?

How do you know people think that about you?

Where does your information come from?

What thoughts went through your mind at the time?

In addition further questioning highlighted the effect of safety behaviours in reinforcing negative misinterpretations of the ongoing social encounter:

What is the effect of using your safety behaviour (e.g. saying little)?

What effect does it have on your self-consciousness?

What effect does it have on your performance?

What effect does it have on how friendly/conspicuous you appear?

What effect does it have on your symptoms?

The central role of self-consciousness in maintaining the problem was highlighted.

If you were no longer self-conscious, would you still have a problem?

If you stopped using safety behaviours would you feel more or less self-conscious?

Next a socialisation experiment was carried out. This involved asking him to give two five-minute presentations to a small group. During the first presentation he was asked to use his usual strategies involving self-monitoring and use of safety behaviours. In contrast the second presentation involved using an external focus of attention, and dropping of safety behaviours. The external attentional focus was emphasised as being of primary importance, and brief guidance was given on anchoring attention to external stimuli. The following analogy was used to facilitate this refocus.

Attention is like a big flashlight, so that wherever you focus it becomes highlighted or magnified. At the moment you are focusing the spotlight on yourself. What I want you to do is swing the light around to illuminate the people you are with.

With reference to each exposure condition the patient made the following ratings:

	Anxiety level predicted/actual	Self consciousness predicted/actual	Performance predicted/actual
Presentation with safety behaviour	90/90	90/90	10/10
Presentation without safety behaviour + external attention focus	90/70	90/70	10/30

This experiment allowed him to see experientially how dropping safety behaviours, and shifting to an external focus of attention during a social encounter, leads to a more positive interpretation of the social interaction.

Following this initial formulation and socialisation session his homework was to shift to an external focus of attention from then on, whilst dropping safety behaviours when he was aware of these occurring. External focus of attention was emphasised as the most important strategy, allowing him to effectively 'interrogate' his social environment. It was suggested that this external focus should be practised in most situations, and not just anxious situations, and consist of externally focusing on the environment whenever he was aware of being internally preoccupied.

Modification of Self-conscious Image Through Video Feedback and Observer Rating

At the very beginning of the first treatment session he was asked to engage in a ten-minute videotaped conversation with an unfamiliar person. His predicted 0–100 anxiety rating was 90, and maintained at 80 during the actual task. Post task he was asked to describe in detail how he looked. He predicted the following would be 80% noticeable: fidgeting with exaggerated movements, struggling to find things to say, avoiding eye contact by look-ing away, looking red and sweating. He was then asked to view the video, and re-rate how obvious these characteristics were. It was emphasised that he should rate himself as if he was seeing someone who he did not know, and without any insight into how they were feeling at the time. His re-rated value was 20, that is, he considered those characteristics as only mildly apparent. He found this feedback extremely surprising, and agreed to remind himself in future situations that 'I do not look how I feel even when extremely anxious'. At these times he was to bring to mind the video image of himself, as a way of correcting any distorted self image that might occur.

This feedback was supplemented by using a rating form of negative and positive social characteristics, to rate his performance during the social task. This was then compared with the ratings made by the person who had interacted with him. The patient rated himself more negatively than the rater did. This difference was used to emphasise how his internally gen-erated information about his social performance was distorted, and was used to reinforce the need to disengage self-focused processing. Following the video feedback during the second treatment session, he showed im-mediate benefits and later commented that he was surprised that he had noted improvement so quickly. 'It's as if someone has taken the magnifying glass away and "tweaked" everything down'.

Banning Worry and Rumination (Anticipatory Processing and the Post-mortem)

He reported that he habitually worried about social events in anticipation (anticipatory processing) and went over them in his mind afterwards (the post-mortem). An advantages/disadvantages analysis was carried out in relation to worrying in this way.

(T) Do you think there are any advantages to worrying in this way?

(P) Well, it helps me prepare myself, and if I go over things afterwards I can learn by my mistakes.

(T) If worrying helps you prepare yourself, why hasn't it been effective in eliminating your anxiety in social situations?

(P) Well I suppose that I tend to think about things going wrong which makes me feel anxious.

(T) Okay, are there any other disadvantages?

(P) Well I suppose it's a waste of energy because I can't change the past if things have gone wrong.

(T) Exactly, the worry tends to be about things you think have gone wrong. Let me ask you, when you're doing a post-mortem after the social event, what information are you using to work out how things went?

(P) Well, it's based on what I can remember of the event.

(T) And what sorts of things do you remember?

(P) How badly I'm coming across, looking like an idiot, and how anxious I'm feeling.

(T) In other words the information is based on thoughts about how you looked and came across to others, and on how anxious you felt. Is there a problem here?

(P) Well, on occasions someone's told me I looked relaxed in a situation when I'd felt anxious. So maybe I get it wrong sometimes.

(T) That fits with our formulation, that negative thoughts about our social performance are based on internal information, such as an ongoing negatively processed self-image, and anxiety symptoms occurring at the time. So in other words the conclusion you derive is based on erroneous internally generated information, rather than on information derived from being aware of the external social environment, and how people are actually responding to you. This information is then used to worry on prior to the next social event. Can you see how the tendency to engage in anticipatory processing and post-mortems will tend to strengthen negative appraisals and the internalised negative self-conscious image?

Following this analysis he agreed to ban worry and rumination whenever he caught himself doing it prior to or after social situations, reminding himself that the worries were based on inaccurate information, that made him feel anxious, and were not helpful in improving his social interactions.

Challenging Negative Appraisals Through Behavioural Experiments–Interrogating the Social Environment

The above dialogue leads into the rationale of beginning to interrogate the social environment in order to correct erroneous beliefs about others' perception of the social self.

(T) At this point you have reached the stage where you can check out what's really going on in social situations. This is dependent on you reversing your avoidance, and deliberately going into social situations that you may have been avoiding. From now on, when you are aware of having a worrying thought about some social catastrophe occurring, you can set up a situation to test out your negative prediction. By reminding yourself to drop any safety behaviours, you are not contaminating the situation, and can draw clear conclusions about what's going on. More importantly, now that you are keeping an external focus of attention, you can effectively interrogate the social environment to gather accurate information about how people are reacting towards you. Let's set a homework exercise up now using a method called PETS.

He had just joined a new gym and was concerned that he would not be able to maintain a conversation if he went to the bar afterwards.

(P)rediction: I won't be able to think of anything to say (Belief rating = 50).

(E)xposure: Three members of the department role play having a conversation in a bar at the gym. He is to enter and join the group for five minutes.

(T)est: Drop safety behaviours and keep an external focus of attention. Check whether any problems in maintaining conversation (e.g. do other people look bored or disinterested, are they staring?).

(S)ummary: No problems in maintaining conversation. (Re-rated belief = 10.)

During the above experiment, his anxiety rating pre-exposure was 70, but it dropped to 15 post-exposure. This observation was used as an example of the effect of anticipatory processing and he was reminded to ban worry before social encounters. He was encouraged to carry out such behavioural experiments as frequently as possible, with at least three of them conducted between sessions. In addition, at least two such behavioural experiments were conducted during each therapy session. In this way he was able to quickly disconfirm his ongoing negative appraisals of social situations that were being reinforced by worry and rumination, and maintained by unhelpful attentional strategies. Previously, he had been processing internally generated information, i.e. online negative appraisals, self-conscious image and anxiety symptoms. In contrast, he was now able to effectively interrogate his social environment to gather accurate information on which to base his appraisals.

Relapse Prevention

A therapy blueprint was produced to assist in relapse prevention. This included a Plan A versus Plan B table to contrast pre versus post therapy strategies:

Plan A	Plan B
Worry about what could go wrong (all day!).	Abandon worries.
Stay in the corner, say nothing. Count the minutes for the social encounter to end.	Engage in activity, e.g. club running. Externally focus attention, pay attention to what is being said.
Use safety behaviours, don't talk, avoid eye contact.	No safety behaviours, be spontaneous, no rehearsing.
Do a post-mortem afterwards, analyse every detail of what was said.	No post mortem.

Outcome

His outcome data is shown in Table 19.1. He was seen for six treatment sessions over a two-month period. After four treatment sessions his distress/avoidance ratings on the Social Phobia Rating Scale (Wells, 1997) were 1/0, dropping to 0/0, during the two final sessions. By session five he reported that he had joined a gym and a running club. He had been going to the pub after the running club and also enjoyed a day out to a running event in another part of the country. He was no longer concerned by being in large groups, and had been actively contributing during committee meetings at work, without any difficulty. Whereas previously he had struggled to get through social situations and would leave as soon as possible, he now enjoyed them and would take his time.

CONCLUSION

In this chapter treatment of three different cases with metacognitive focused therapy was described. There are clear similarities in the conceptualisation of worry and attentional processes across disorders. The treatments used focus on modifying worry/ruminative processes, attentional strategies, and other unhelpful coping strategies. These factors are non-specific and core features of disorder in the metacognitive theory of psychological disorder. Wells and Matthews (1994, 1997) have argued that a common treatment strategy may be developed that is applicable to a wide range of disorders with optional additional modules added to take care of specific issues.

REFERENCES

Clark, D.A. & Wells, A. (1995). A cognitive model of social phobia. In R. Heimberg, M. Liebowitz, D.A. Hope & F.R. Schneier (Eds), *Social Phobia: Diagnosis, Assessment and Treatment*. New York: Guilford Press.

Wells, A. (1997). *Cognitive Therapy of Anxiety Disorders: A Practice Manual and Conceptual Guide*. Chichester, UK: John Wiley & Sons, Ltd.

Wells, A. (2000). *Emotional Disorders and Metacognition: Innovative Cognitive Therapy*. Chichester, UK: John Wiley & Sons.

Wells, A. & Clark, D.A. (1997). Social phobia: a cognitive approach. In G.C.L. Davey (Ed.), *Phobias: A Handbook of Description, Treatment, and Theory*. Chichester, UK: John Wiley & Sons, Ltd.

Wells, A. & Matthews, G. (1994). *Attention and Emotion. A Clinical Perspective*. Hove, UK: Erlbaum.

Wells, A. & Matthews, G. (1997). Modelling cognition in emotional disorder: The S-REF model. *Behaviour Research and Therapy*, **32**, 867–870.

Wells, A. & Papageorgiou, C. (1998). Social phobia: Effects of external attention on anxiety, negative beliefs, and perspective taking. *Behaviour Therapy*, **29**, 357–370.

Wells, A. & Papageorgiou, C. (2000). Brief cognitive therapy for social phobia: a case series. *Behaviour Research and Therapy*, **39**, 713–720.

Wells, A. & Sembi, S. (2004a). Metacognitive Therapy for PTSD: A preliminary investigation of a new brief treatment. *Journal of Behavioural Therapy and Experimental Psychiatry*, **35**, 307–318.

Wells, A. & Sembi, S. (2004b). Metacognitive Therapy for PTSD: A core treatment manual. *Cognitive and Behavioural Practice*, **11**, 365–377.

Chapter 20

THE EFFICACY OF PSYCHOLOGICAL TREATMENTS FOR GENERALISED ANXIETY DISORDER?

Peter L. Fisher

INTRODUCTION

Traditional narrative reviews and meta-analyses on the efficacy of psychological treatments for Generalised Anxiety Disorder (GAD) consistently find that cognitive therapy (CT), cognitive-behaviour therapy (CBT) and applied relaxation (AR) are the most effective treatments for this disorder (e.g. Borkovec & Ruscio, 2001; Gale & Oakley-Browne, 2000). However, the overall effectiveness of these treatments remains rather limited. A review of the clinical significance of psychological treatments for GAD (Fisher & Durham, 1999) indicated that only 50% of patients achieve recovery following treatment. This study applied clinical significance methodology proposed by Jacobson and colleagues (e.g. Jacobson & Truax, 1991) to randomised controlled trials conducted on GAD since the advent of the DSM-III-R. All six outcome studies used the trait version of State Trait Anxiety Inventory (STAI-T; Speilberger et al., 1983) to index outcome. By applying standardised clinical significance criteria to the STAI-T across outcome studies, the review provided an overview of the absolute and relative merits of treatment efficacy. In summary, the two most effective psychological treatments for GAD were individual CBT and AR, with overall recovery rates at 6-month follow-up of 50–60%.

This chapter has three main aims. First, it will provide an up to date review of the clinical significance of psychological treatments for GAD by applying standardised clinical significance criteria to the raw outcome data from 11 randomised controlled trials conducted since 1990.

The second aim of this chapter is to overcome one of the limitations of the Fisher and Durham (1999) study, specifically the exclusive reliance on the

Worry and Its Psychological Disorders: Theory, Assessment and Treatment. Edited by G. C. L. Davey and A. Wells. © 2006 John Wiley & Sons, Ltd.

STAI-T to index outcome. Although, the STAI-T is widely used in clinical trials on GAD and captures some of the essence of GAD, it does not directly assess the cardinal feature of GAD, namely excessive worry that the individual experiences as difficult to control. Therefore, the current review applies Jacobson's clinical significance methodology to the Penn State Worry Questionnaire (PSWQ; Meyer et al., 1990), a measure designed to specifically assess the extent to which an individual experiences worry as excessive and uncontrollable. This will provide an estimate of the proportion of patients that achieve 'normal' levels of worry following a course of psychological treatment for GAD.

Third, substantial effort has been directed over the last two decades at improving the efficacy of cognitive and behavioural approaches for GAD. However, the outcome literature is replete with studies attempting to augment efficacy by either increasing treatment duration or by the amalgamation of existing treatment approaches. There is increasing recognition that we need to look beyond existing approaches if the psychological treatment of GAD is to develop. Two recent innovations in this area are the metacognitive model of GAD (Wells, 1995, 1999) and the intolerance of uncertainty model (Dugas et al., 1995, 2004). The efficacy of metacognitive and the intolerance of uncertainty treatments have both recently been evaluated in the context of randomised controlled trials (Dugas et al., 2003; Wells et al., manuscript in preparation). Applying standardised clinical significance criteria to these studies offers the first opportunity to compare the absolute and relative efficacy of these treatments against the psychological approaches which have predominated over the last 20 years.

This review begins with an overview of Jacobson's clinical significance methodology. Next, the basic characteristics of the studies included in this review are presented, followed by a brief description of the main psychological approaches used in the treatment of GAD. Next, the raw data on the STAI-T and PSWQ from these studies are reanalysed using standardised Jacobson methodology. This provides an estimate of the proportion of patients who recover for each treatment condition within each study and also across treatment types. The clinical implications of these results are then discussed.

THE JACOBSON APPROACH TO CLINICAL SIGNIFICANCE

Jacobson, Revernstorf and Follette (1984) proposed a two-fold definition of clinical significance designed to assess whether a person has 'recovered' following therapy. It is based on the premise that following a course of therapy, people will be indistinguishable from their well functioning peers. Patients need to meet a two-fold criterion in order to be classified as recovered or having made clinically significant change. First, a cut-off point is calculated on a measure with good construct validity for the disorder being treated. This determines whether an individual's post-treatment score has a greater probability of belonging to either a normal or a dysfunctional population. Second, the magnitude of change made needs to be statistically reliable and for this the Reliable Change Index (RCI) is computed. A patient is defined as recovered if they both cross the cutoff point differentiating the dysfunctional and functional populatious and they make statistically reliable change.

OVERVIEW OF PSYCHOLOGICAL TREATMENTS FOR GAD

The basic characteristics of the outcome studies included in this review are presented in Table 20.1. As can be seen the most frequently evaluated treatments are: behaviour therapy, cognitive therapy and cognitive behaviour therapy; each of these are now briefly described.

Behavioural Approaches

In the treatment of GAD, behavioural interventions are synonymous with relaxation procedures. Jacobson (1938) developed progressive muscle relaxation (PMR) to directly target the physiological arousal associated with anxiety and to enable clients to generally adopt a more relaxed response to life stresses. Versions of PMR are used in the two most frequently used relaxation therapies, namely Applied Relaxation (AR) and Self-Control Desensitisation (SCD). Clients are taught shortened forms of PMR in both therapies and once proficient at PMR, they are encouraged to use the relaxation skills in response to anxiety cues. In AR, practice of the relaxation response is conducted in vivo whereas imaginal exposure is predominantly utilised in SCD.

Cognitive Therapy

CT as practiced in the treatment studies included in this review is based on the approach of Beck, Emery and Greenberg (1985). The main treatment components include providing a formulation based on the cognitive model which places negative thinking patterns at the heart of GAD. Subsequently,

Table 20.1 Basic characteristics of the outcome studies

Study	Treatment conditions	n	STAI-T Pre-treatment mean	PSWQ Pre-treatment mean	Number, duration & frequency of treatment sessions
Butler et al. (1991)	CBT	19	58.6	–	12 × 1 hour (weekly) plus 3 boosters post-test
	BT	19	57.2	–	
Barlow et al. (1992)	AMT	10	55.2	–	15 × 1 hour (weekly)
	CT	14	46.6	–	
	CT + AMT	12	54.8	–	
White et al. (1992)	Group CBT	26	54.8	–	6 × 2 hours (weekly)
	Group BT	31	59.6	–	
	Group CT	29	57.6	–	
	Placebo	10	59.3	–	
Borkovec & Costello (1993)	ND	19	57.9	65.6	4 × 1.5 hours, then 8 × 1 hour (Twice weekly sessions)
	AR	18	56.5	68.3	
	CBT	19	54.7	65.5	
Durham et al. (1994)	AP *High contact*	14	60.6	–	16–20 × 1 hour (weekly)
	AP *Low contact*	15	60.7	–	8–10 × 1 hour (fortnightly)
	CT *High contact*	15	61.1	–	16–20 × 1 hour (weekly)
	CT *Low contact*	20	55.4	–	8–10 × 1 hour (fortnightly)
	AMT	16	56.9	–	8–10 × 1 hour (fortnightly)

Ost & Breitholtz (2000)	CT	18	57.9	56.6	12 × 1 hour (weekly)
	AR	15	53.7	60.8	
Borkovec et al. (2002)	AR/SCD	23	58.4	67.4	4 × 2 hours, then
	CT	23	57.5	69.1	10 × 1.5 hours (weekly)
	CT + AR/SCD	23	57.3	67.1	
Arntz (2003)	CT	14	57.0	–	12 × 1 hour (weekly)
	AR	10	54.2	–	
Dugas et al. (2003)	Group CT (IOU)	23	–	62.6	14 × 2 hours (weekly)
	Waitlist	24	–	62.2	
Durham et al. (2004)	Brief CT	19	55.1	–	5 × 1 hour (monthly)
	Standard CT	18	64.4	–	10 × 1 hour (fortnightly)
	Intensive CT	18	60.2	–	20 × 1 hour (weekly)
Wells (2005)	AR	8	62.2	70.7	8–12 × 1 hour weekly
	MCT	10	56.8	64.5	

Note: AMT = anxiety management training; AP = analytic psychotherapy; AR = applied relaxation; AR/SCD = applied relaxation plus self control desensitisation; BT = behaviour therapy; CBT = cognitive behaviour therapy; CT = cognitive therapy; Group CT (IOU) cognitive therapy based on intolerance of uncertainty model: MCT, metacognitive therapy; ND = nondirective therapy.

patients are helped to identify anxiogenic or danger related beliefs about the future, themselves and the world. Verbal and behavioural reattribution strategies are then used to modify these dysfunctional anxiety cognitions. CT also aims to modify behaviours such as avoidance or reassurance seeking as these behaviours prevent disconfirmation of the anxiety related beliefs.

Cognitive Behaviour Therapy (CBT)

CBT is based on the premise that each component of GAD needs to be targeted separately. So for example, CT techniques are used to address the anxiogenic cognitions and relaxation strategies are used to modify the somatic components of GAD. Other techniques are frequently included in a CBT package such as activity monitoring and scheduling pleasurable activities, which can be used to provide the client with counter evidence which has been supporting their anxious beliefs.

Intolerance of Uncertainty (IOU)

This cognitive model of GAD comprises four components: intolerance of uncertainty, erroneous positive beliefs about worry, poor problem solving and cognitive avoidance (Dugas et al., 2004). Intolerance of uncertainty is the predisposition to react negatively in ambiguous situations and within this model is thought to be central to the maintenance of GAD. This model differentiates between worries that can be effectively solved and worries that cannot be resolved or that may never happen. Cognitive exposure is thought to be appropriate to this second type of worry but not the first type of worrying. The treatment aims to address each of the four components and tries to help people to deal with future uncertainty in a non-worry based manner. This model and treatment are described fully in Chapters 12 and 17.

Metacognitive Therapy (MCT)

The metacognitive model of GAD (Wells, 1995, 1999) suggests that worry is not simply a symptom of anxiety, but is a motivated coping strategy fuelled by metacognitive beliefs. These metacognitive beliefs are considered pivotal in the maintenance of GAD. The model distinguishes between two types of worry. Type 1 worry refers to typical everyday worries and is associated with positive beliefs about the usefulness of worry as a coping strategy. Type 2 worry refers to worry people have about their worrying or 'metaworry' and is principally concerned with negative beliefs about the uncontrollability and dangerousness of worry. Treatment based on this model aims to modify an individual's positive and negative metacognitive beliefs about worry, through verbal attribution and behavioural experiments. It is noteworthy that this model does not focus on the content of everyday worries; instead the goal of treatment is to modify the positive and negative metacognitive beliefs and associated behaviours that maintain the worry process. See Chapters 11 and 15 for a detailed account of the model and treatment.

METHOD

Studies

The sample comprises randomised controlled trials examining the efficacy of psychological treatments for working age adults with GAD. Studies were located from searches of Medline, Psycinfo and the Cochrane Controlled Trials Register. Each database was searched using the following search terms, alone and in combination: generaliz(s)ed anxiety disorder treatment outcome, psychological trials, efficacy study, comparative study and clinical trial. Searches were also made of secondary sources (e.g. references in obtained articles) and by contacting researchers in the field. The search period covered 1990 through to December 2004. To be included, studies had to meet the following inclusion criteria:

(1) Structured diagnostic interviews (e.g. ADIS, Brown et al., 1994) used to assign a principal diagnosis of GAD according to DSM III-R (APA, 1987) or DSM IV (APA, 1994) criteria.
(2) Random assignment of patients to two or more psychological treatments or control conditions.
(3) 18–65 years of age.
(4) STAI-T and/or the PSWQ included as a main outcome measure.

As of December 2004, 12 studies met the inclusion criteria, but data was unavailable for the Ladouceur et al. (2000) study. This study compared individual cognitive therapy based on the intolerance of uncertainty model against a wait list control condition. Thus, the sample comprises 11 studies which used the STAI-T and/or the PSWQ as a main outcome measure. Raw data on the STAI-T and the PSWQ at pre-treatment, post-treatment and follow-up was requested and obtained from the authors of the studies included in the analysis. The final data set is comprised only of treatment completers. For the STAI-T, 10 controlled studies are included (n = 495) and the reanalysis on the PSWQ is based on five studies (n = 223).

OUTCOME MEASURES

State-Trait Anxiety Inventory—Trait Version (STAI-T; Spielberger et al., 1983)

The STAI-T is a 20-item self report inventory that assesses excessive worry, tension, and low self esteem. Respondents are asked to rate how much they agree with each of the 20 statements reflecting the above dimensions on a 0–3 Likert scale. Scores range from 20 to a maximum of 80. The STAI-T has good construct validity in respect of GAD and has sound psychometric properties. A more detailed discussion of the appropriateness of the STAI-T as an outcome measure in GAD can be found in Fisher & Durham (1999).

Penn State Worry Questionnaire (PSWQ; Meyer, Miller, Metzger, & Borkovec, 1990)

The PSWQ is a 16-item self report inventory designed to measure the pervasiveness, excessiveness and uncontrollable nature of worry. In essence, it is designed to assess the nature of worry as defined in diagnostic criteria. It has been shown to be a psychometrically sound measure and sensitive to treatment effects. (See Chapter 7 for a detailed account of the PSWQ.)

CLINICAL SIGNIFICANCE CRITERIA FOR THE STAI-T AND PSWQ

Jacobson and colleagues (Jacobson et al., 1984; Jacobson & Truax, 1991) provide three methods for determining a cut-off point. The least arbitrary, termed criterion (c) requires representative normative data on both clinical and non-clinical samples. Appropriate normative data is available for both the STAI-T and the PSWQ permitting criterion (c) to be used in this reanalysis.

STAI-T Outcome Criteria

Fisher and Durham's (1999) standardised criteria for recovery on the STAI-T (criterion (c), reliable change index = 8, cut-off point ≤45) is applied here to all treatment conditions by treatment study. It should be noted that there are some differences in recovery rates reported in the current review and those reported in the original article. The reason is patients with pre-treatment scores below the cut-off point were excluded in the original

Table 20.2   Data used to determine cut off point (c) and the RCI on the PSWQ

Symbol	Definition	Value
M_1	Pre-treatment mean of the PSWQ for GAD sample[*]	64.98
S_1	Standard deviation for GAD sample at pre-treatment	8.91
M_2	Mean of well functioning sample on PSWQ[§]	30.98
S_2	Standard deviation for the well functioning sample	8.13
X_1	Pre-treatment PSWQ score of an individual	
X_2	Post-treatment PSWQ score of an individual	
r_{xx}	Reliability of the PSWQ[†]	0.92
S_E	Standard error of measurement for the PSWQ	2.52
S_{diff}	Standard error of difference between the two test scores	3.56

[*] Comprises all available pre-treatment scores (n = 226) from the five outcome studies.
[§] Based on a non-anxious ADIS-R screened sample (n = 74) (Molina, S. & Borkovec, T. D. (1994). The Penn State Worry Questionnaire: Psychometric properties and associated characteristics. In G.C.L. Davey & F. Tallis (Eds), *Worrying: Perspectives on theory, assessment and treatment* (pp. 265–284). New York: John Wiley & Sons, Inc.
[†] Test-retest reliability over a 8–10 week period (Meyer, T.J., Miller, M.L., Metzger, R.L., & Borkovec, T.D. (1990). Development and validation of the Penn State Worry Questionnaire. *Behaviour Research and Therapy*, **28**, 487–495).

analysis and in this analysis all treatment completers are included regardless of their pre-treatment score.

PSWQ Outcome Criteria

The same approach has not been applied to the PSWQ and this necessitated the development of a cut-off point and reliable change index for the PSWQ. The data used to calculate cut off point c and the RCI in the present review are summarised in Table 20.2.

Cut-off point c on the PSWQ was calculated according to the following formula:

$$c = \frac{S_1 M_2 + S_2 M_1}{S_1 + S_2} = \frac{8.13(64.98) + 8.91(30.98)}{8.13 + 8.91} = 47.2$$

The cut-off point was taken as 47 so that post-treatment or follow-up scores of 46 or below were deemed to be within the functional distribution. The RCI was calculated using the following formulae:

$$RCI = (X_2 - X_1)/S_{diff}$$
$$S_E = s_1\sqrt{1 - r_{xx}} = 8.91\sqrt{1 - .92} = 2.52$$
$$S_{diff} = \sqrt{2(S_E)^2} = \sqrt{2}(2.53)^2 = 3.56$$

An RCI greater than ± 1.96 is required for reliable change ($p < .05$) so that a 7-point change on the PSWQ was required to ensure that reliable change had taken place (i.e. $\pm 1.96 \times 3.56$).

OVERVIEW OF DATA ANALYSIS

Two analyses were conducted using the above methodology. First, recovery rates for each treatment condition by study were derived for the STAI-T and PSWQ. Recovery rates are reported at post-treatment and at the six and 12-month follow-up points for the STAI-T and at post-treatment and 12 months follow-up for the PSWQ for treatment completers. In the Arntz (2003) study only those patients who underwent a clinician rated structured diagnostic interview are included in this analysis. It is also important to note that only those patients in the Dugas et al. (2003) study who were initially assigned to the active treatment condition are included.

Next, the same analysis is applied to different treatment approaches aggregated across treatment studies. The analysis is restricted to cognitive therapy, cognitive behaviour therapy, applied relaxation and the two disorder specific models of GAD, namely the intolerance of uncertainty and metacognitive models. In this analysis, cognitive therapy is an amalgamation of those studies which used the approach of Beck and Emery (1985), applied relaxation comprises treatment conditions which utilised either AR or SCD, whereas the cognitive behaviour therapy condition includes treatment conditions that utilised a combination of CT and AR. The treatment categories chosen, together with the treatment conditions comprising each category are listed below.

Individual Cognitive Therapy

Butler et al. (1991)—CBT
Durham et al. (1994)—CT
Ost & Breitholtz (2000)—CT
Borkovec et al. (2002)—CT
Arntz, (2003)—CT

Individual Cognitive Behaviour Therapy

Borkovec et al. (2002)—CBT
Borkovec & Costello (1993)—CBT
Durham et al. (2004)—CT

Individual Applied Relaxation

Butler et al. (1991)—BT
Ost & Breitholtz (2000)—AR
Borkovec et al. (2002)—SCD

Group CT (intolerance of uncertainty model)

Dugas et al. (2003)—CBT

Individual Metacognitive Therapy

Wells et al. (manuscript in preparation)—MCT

RESULTS

Recovery Rates by Outcome Study

Table 20.3 shows the percentage of patients defined as recovered for each treatment condition by outcome study at post-treatment and at six months and 12 months follow-up on the STAI-T. It appears that overall, psychological treatments produce relatively poor recovery rates in GAD with only 31% of patients recovered at post-treatment. A slight improvement in overall recovery rates across treatment approaches can be seen at the follow-up points (37% recovered at six months follow-up and 39% at 12 months follow-up). However, follow-up results must be interpreted with caution as a number of the participants across the studies received either additional psychological or pharmacological treatment during the follow-up period. However, these overall recovery rates mask marked differences between treatment conditions. Recovery rates for CT range from 0% in the Barlow et al. (1992) study to 61% in Borkovec & Costello (1993) study. A similar range of recovery rates are found for AR, ranging from 7% to 56% at post-treatment and 13% to 77% at six months follow-up. On an individual basis, metacognitive therapy achieves the highest percentage of recovered patients at post-treatment (80%), although the percentage drops to 70% at six months and 12 months follow-up.

Table 20.4 shows the percentage of patients who achieved recovery status on the PSWQ for each treatment condition by study. At post-treatment, of the ten active treatments (wait list and nondirective therapy excluded) only three achieve a recovery rate of at least 50%. Metacognitive therapy achieves a recovery rate at post-treatment of 80%, almost 30% higher than the next most efficacious treatment condition. At 12 months follow-up, the recovery rates for most treatments remain broadly equivalent to those obtained at post-treatment, with little evidence of deterioration. Indeed for

Table 20.3 Percentage of recovered patients at post-treatment and at six and 12 months follow-up based on Jacobson criterion c for STAI-T scores

Study	Treatment	Post-treatment		6 months follow-up		One year follow-up	
		n	Recovered	n	Recovered	n	Recovered
Butler et al. (1991)	CT	19	53	18	56	–	–
	BT	18	11	15	13	–	–
Barlow et al. (1992)	AR	6	17	–	–	–	–
	CT	9	0	–	–	–	–
	CT + AR	9	11	–	–	–	–
White et al. (1992)	Group CBT	24	21	20	20	–	–
	Group BT	30	17	27	30	–	–
	Group CT	27	30	24	29	–	–
	Group placebo	10	20	9	33	–	–
Borkovec & Costello (1993)	ND	18	17	16	38	13	39
	AR	18	56	17	77	15	53
	CBT	19	63	18	61	17	77
Durham et al. (1994)	AP low contact	15	7	15	7	15	0
	AP high contact	14	7	14	0	14	14
	CT low contact	20	30	20	35	20	30
	CT high contact	15	27	15	40	15	53
	AMT	16	19	16	6	16	6
Ost & Breitholtz (2000)	CT	18	17	–	–	18	22
	AR	15	7	–	–	15	13
Borkovec et al. (2002)	AR/SCD	23	48	22	46	21	67
	CT	23	61	21	48	21	43
	CT AR/SCD	23	57	23	52	23	52
Arntz (2003)	CT	14	36	14	50	–	–
	AR	10	36	10	40	–	–
Durham et al. (2004)	Brief CT	19	42	18	56	–	–
	Standard CT	18	39	16	38	–	–
	Intensive CT	18	28	16	31	–	–
Wells et al. (in prep.)	AR	10	10	9	29	6	33
	MCT	10	80	10	70	10	70
Total Percentages			31		37		39

three treatments, nondirective therapy, group CT and the AR condition of Ost & Breitholtz (2000) recovery rates are approximately 15% higher than at post-treatment.

Recovery Rates Between Treatment Conditions

Recovery rates by treatment approach on the STAI-T and PSWQ are shown in Figures 20.1 and 20.2, respectively. The recovery rates on the STAI-T for

Table 20.4 Percentage of recovered patients at post-treatment and 12 months follow-up based on Jacobson criterion c for PSWQ scores

Study	Treatment	Post-treatment		6 months follow-up	
		n	%Recovered	n	%Recovered
Borkovec &	ND	18	22	13	39
Costello (1993)	AR	17	47	14	50
	CBT	19	53	17	47
Ost & Breitholtz	CT	18	28	18	22
(2000)	AR	15	13	15	27
Borkovec et al.	AR/SCD	23	56	21	43
(2002)	CT	23	44	21	43
	CT AR/SCD	23	44	21	47
Dugas et al. (2003)	Group CT	23	48	22	64
	Wait list	24	4	–	–
Wells et al. (in prep.)	AR	10	10	6	17s
	MCT	10	80	10	80
Total Percentages			41		46

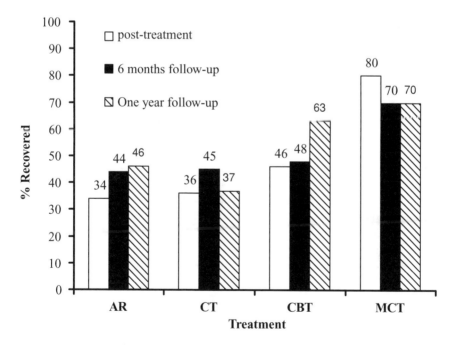

Figure 20.1 Percentage of recovered patients on the STAI-T by treatment approach at post-treatment, and at 6 & 12 month follow-up

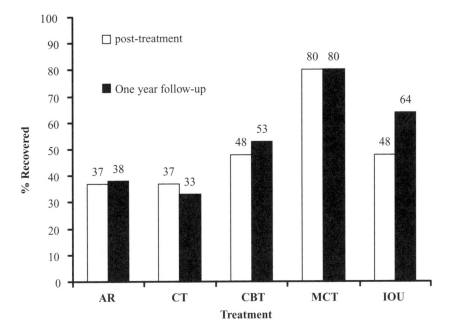

Figure 20.2   Percentage of recovered patients on the PSWQ by treatment approach at post-treatment, and at 6 & 12 month follow-up

the four treatment conditions indicate that at post-treatment, the least efficacious treatments are AR (34% recovered) and CT (36% recovered). CBT achieves a slightly higher recovery rate (46%) at post-treatment, with MCT appearing to be the most efficacious treatment with 80% of treated patients meeting recovery criteria. Over the follow-up period, the efficacy of AR and CBT appears to increase, CT does not improve through to the 12 month follow-up point and MCT shows a slight decrease, but remains the most effective treatment. The results at follow-up need to be interpreted cautiously as there may be differential rates of additional treatment between conditions over the follow-up period. In addition, not all of the studies had data available through to the 12 month follow-up point. For example, CBT at post-treatment and six months was based on three studies, whereas at 12 months, only data from two studies was available.

The recovery rates on the PSWQ by treatment approach (Figure 20.2) show that AR and CT have overall recovery rates of 37% at post-treatment and these rates of recovery are largely maintained through to 12 months follow-up. CBT appears to have a slightly higher rate than either treatment alone, with 48% recovered at post-treatment and 53% at 12 months follow-up. A central question asked in this review is how well do the two newer forms of cognitive therapy perform. Group IOU achieves comparable recovery rates to CBT at post-treatment, with both treatments achieving recovery rates of approximately 50%. However, IOU shows a marked increase in recovery rates from the end of treatment through to 12 months follow-up, increasing by 16% to 64%. Metacognitive therapy clearly achieves the highest recovery rates with 80% of patients recovered on the PSWQ at post-treatment and this rate of recovery is maintained through to the 12 months follow-up.

A comparison of rates of recovery on the STAI-T versus the PSWQ shows that AR, CT, CBT and MCT produce similar rates. The largest discrepancy between these measures is seen in AR where 34% of treated patients achieve recovery on the STAI-T and 37% on the PSWQ, a discrepancy of only 3%. At the 12 month follow-up, recovery rates remain broadly comparable between the two measures. Interestingly, AR, CT and CBT have slightly higher recovery rates on the STAI-T compared to the PSWQ. The reverse is true for MCT, a treatment which focuses much more specifically on modifying positive and negative beliefs about worry.

CONCLUSIONS

The first aim of this chapter was to provide an up to date review of the absolute and relative efficacy of psychological treatments for GAD. This aim has been achieved by including all available randomised controlled trials conducted on GAD since 1990 that used the STAI-T and/or the PSWQ to index outcome. The application of standardised Jacobson criteria to these two measures across outcome studies overcomes the limitation of researchers using idiosyncratic criteria to index clinically significant change and it facilitates a balanced and objective assessment of treatment efficacy.

Overall, the results from this reanalysis concur with previous reviews that the efficacy of AR, CT and CBT for GAD remains rather limited. In essence, the percentage of recovered patients in treatment trials has not altered significantly since GAD achieved independent status 18 years ago, with the advent of DSM-III-R (APA, 1987). For example, the CT condition evaluated in Butler et al. (1991) achieved a recovery rate of 56% at six months follow-up, which is 8% higher than the aggregated recovery rates for CT reported in the current review. It is noteworthy that there is considerable variability between the same treatment approach across studies. For example, the recovery rates in the applied relaxation conditions at post-treatment on the PSWQ range from 10% to 56%, and at 12 months follow-up, the discrepancy is slightly smaller, ranging from 7% to 43% at one-year follow-up. Similar variability is seen for recovery rates defined according to the STAI-T.

Such variability is not unique to applied relaxation, broadly comparable variability is seen for CBT and CT. Reasons for these highly disparate recovery rates across the same treatment conditions could include different sample composition resulting from the method of recruitment, differences in rates of comorbidity with regard to the overall level and nature of comorbidity, and socioeconomic factors. Other important differences may relate to levels of therapist competency or researcher allegiance effects. It was not possible to examine the role of these factors in the present study, and it therefore remains an intriguing research question.

The second aim of this review was to address a recommendation made by Fisher and Durham (1999) with respect to extending the clinical significance analysis to incorporate outcome measures that tap cardinal features of GAD. This has been achieved by applying the Jacobson methodology to the PSWQ, thereby increasing the generalisability of the results. With regard to the recovery rates aggregated by treatment approach across studies, the STAI-T and the PSWQ produce broadly equivalent results. However, when the results for individual treatment conditions within studies are examined, there are some marked differences between the PSWQ and the STAI-T. The greatest discrepancy is found in the CBT condition of Borkovec & Costello's study; 77% of patients achieved recovery on the STAI-T at one year follow-up compared to 47% on the PSWQ. A number of possible reasons may explain this discrepancy. CBT as conducted in Borkovec and Costello (1993) aimed to modify anxiogenic cognitions and the physiological component of GAD, rather than specifically trying to modify excessive and uncontrollable worry. This hypothesis would fit with studies demonstrating that the STAI-T not only assesses anxiety but is a measure of general negative affect (Bieling et al., 1998).

The final aim of this review was to enable a benchmark comparison between the more traditional psychological therapies for GAD and recent innovative cognitive approaches. A commonality between the intolerance of uncertainty and metacognitive approaches is that both seek to specifically modify excessive and uncontrollable worry, but they aim to target different underlying psychological mechanisms. Do either or both of these treatments hold promise for increasing the effectiveness of psychological treatments for GAD?

First, group cognitive therapy based on the intolerance uncertainty model of GAD was equivalent to traditional CBT at post-treatment, with both treatment approaches achieving a 48% recovery rate on the PSWQ. However, at 12 months follow-up, the recovery rates for IOU had substantially increased to 64%, which outperforms the aggregated recovery rates for AR, CT and CBT. These results may also have cost benefit implications for the treatment of GAD as this approach treated 4–6 patients in a small group format over a total of 28 hours. This equates to between 4.5 and 7 hours of therapist time per patient, which is considerably less time than is typically given in individual treatment approaches. It appears that group IOU treatment is a promising development in the treatment of GAD and warrants further controlled trials.

Second, the results from the first comparative trial involving MCT for GAD produced recovery rates of 80% at post-treatment on both the STAI-T and the PSWQ. These gains were largely maintained, with a slight reduction on the STAI-T to 70% whereas the gains were maintained on the PSWQ. These are extremely high recovery rates and are in fact the highest recovery rates achieved by any treatment condition across all studies on both the STAI-T and the PSWQ. These rates suggest that metacognitive therapy may be a very promising treatment for GAD. Furthermore, it appears to be relatively brief and therefore probably cost efficient. However, it must be borne in mind that only ten patients were treated. Larger scale comparative trials conducted by independent researchers are required to further establish the efficacy of metacognitive therapy for GAD.

In summary, the aggregated rates of recovery by treatment approach suggests that CBT, a combination of AR and CT techniques may be more effective than either AR or CT alone. This conclusion is supported by the obtained recovery rates on both the STAI-T and PSWQ. On the PSWQ, approximately 50% of patients treated with CBT recover; a recovery rate that is 15% higher than AR or CT. A very similar picture is seen for the STAI-T, although the overall recovery rates are slightly higher, approximately 60% for CBT. This level of efficacy shows that there is considerable scope for further improvement and it has been argued that there is a need to look beyond existing treatment strategies if the psychological treatment of GAD is to improve. The recovery rates obtained for metacognitive therapy (70–80%) at one year follow-up clearly indicate that improved efficacy for GAD is possible.

REFERENCES

American Psychiatric Association (1987). *Diagnostic and Statistical Manual of Mental Disorders* (3rd (Revised) ed.). Washington, DC.

American Psychiatric Association (1994). *Diagnostic and Statistical Manual of Mental Disorders* (4th ed.). Washington DC.

Arntz, A. (2003). Cognitive therapy versus applied relaxation as treatment of generalized anxiety disorder. *Behaviour Research and Therapy*, **41(6)**, 633–646.

Barlow, D.H., Rapee, R.M. & Brown, T.A. (1992). Behavioural treatment of generalised anxiety disorder. *Behaviour Therapy*, **23**, 551–570.

Beck, A.T., Emery, G. & Greenberg, R. (1985). *Anxiety Disorder and Phobias: A Cognitive Perspective*. New York: Basic Books.

Bieling, P.J., Antony, M.M. & Swinson, R.P. (1998). The State-Trait Anxiety Inventory, Trait Version: structure and content re-examined. *Behaviour Research & Therapy*, **36**, 777–788.

Borkovec, T.D. & Costello, E. (1993). Efficacy of applied relaxation and cognitive-behavioural therapy in the treatment of generalised anxiety disorder. *Journal of Consulting and Clinical Psychology*, **61(4)**, 611–619.

Borkovec, T.D., Newman, M., Pincus, A. & Lytle, R. (2002). A component analysis of cognitive behavioural therapy for generalized anxiety disorder and the role of interpersonal problems. *Journal of Consulting and Clinical Psychology*, **70(2)**, 288–298.

Borkovec, T.D. & Ruscio, A. (2001). Psychotherapy for generalized anxiety disorder. *Journal of Clinical Psychiatry*, **62(11)**, 37–42.

Brown, T.A., DiNardo, P.A. & Barlow, D.H. (1994). *Anxiety Disorders Interview Schedule for DSM-IV*. Albany, NY: Graywood Publications.

Butler, G., Fennell, M., Robson, P. & Gelder, M. (1991). Comparison of behaviour therapy and cognitive-behaviour therapy in the treatment of generalised anxiety disorder. *Journal of Consulting and Clinical Psychology*, **59**, 167–175.

Dugas, M.J., Buhr, K. & Ladouceur, R. (2004). The role of intolerance of uncertainty in etiology and maintenance. In R.G. Heimberg, C.L. Turk & D.S. Mennin (Eds), *Generalized Anxiety Disorder: Advances in Research and Practice*. New York: Guilford Press.

Dugas, M.J., Gagnon, F., Ladouceur, R. & Freeston, M.H. (1998). Generalized anxiety disorder: a preliminary test of a conceptual model. *Behaviour Research and Therapy*, **36(2)**, 215–226.

Dugas, M.J., Ladouceur, R., Leger, E., Freeston, M.H., Langlois, F., Provencher, M., et al. (2003). Group cognitive-behavioural therapy for generalized anxiety disorder: treatment outcome and long-term follow-up. *Journal of Consulting and Clinical Psychology*, **71(4)**, 821–825.

Durham, R.C., Fisher, P.L., Dow, M.G.T., Sharp, D., Power, K.G., Swan, J.S., et al. (2004). Cognitive behaviour therapy for generalised anxiety disorder: A clinical effectiveness study. *Clinical Psychology and Psychotherapy*, **11**, 145–157.

Durham, R.C., Murphy, T.J., Allan, T., Richard, K., Treliving, L. & Fenton, G.W. (1994). A comparison of cognitive therapy, analytic psychotherapy and anxiety management training in the treatment of generalised anxiety disorder. *British Journal of Psychiatry*, **165**, 315–323.

Fisher, P.L. & Durham, R.C. (1999). Recovery rates in generalised anxiety disorder following psychological therapy: An analysis of clinically significant change in STAI-T across outcome studies since 1990. *Psychological Medicine*, **29**, 1425–1434.

Gale, C. & Oakley-Browne, M. (2000). Generalized anxiety disorder. In *Clinical Evidence*. London: BMJ Publishing.

Jacobson, E. (1938). *Progressive relaxation*. Chicago, IL: University of Chicago Press.

Jacobson, N.S., Follette, W.C. & Revenstorf, D. (1984). Psychotherapy outcome research: Methods for reporting variability and evaluating clinical significance. *Behaviour Therapy*, **15**, 336–352.

Jacobson, N.S. & Truax, P. (1991). Clinical significance: A statistical approach to defining meaningful change in psychotherapy research. *Journal of Consulting and Clinical Psychology*, **59(1)**, 12–19.

Ladouceur, R., Dugas, M., Freeston, M., Leger, E., Gagnon, F. & Thibodeau, N. (2000). Efficacy of a cognitive-behavioural treatment for generalized anxiety disorder: Evaluation in a controlled clinical trial. *Journal of Consulting and Clinical Psychology*, **68**, 957–964.

Meyer, T.J., Miller, M.L., Metzger, R.L. & Borkovec, T.D. (1990). Development and validation of the Penn State Worry Questionnaire. *Behaviour Research and Therapy*, **28**, 487–495.

Molina, S. & Borkovec, T.D. (1994). The Penn State Worry Questionnaire: Psychometric properties and associated characteristics. In G.C.L. Davey & F. Tallis (Eds), *Worrying: Perspectives on theory, assessment and treatment* (pp. 265–284). New York: John Wiley & Sons, Inc.

Ost, L.-G. & Breitholtz, E. (2000). Applied relaxation versus cognitive therapy in the treatment of generalized anxiety disorder. *Behaviour Research and Therapy*, **38**, 777–790.

Spielberger, C.D., Gorsuch, R.L., Lushene, R., Vagg, P.R. & Jacobs, G.A. (1983). *Manual for the State-Trait Anxiety Inventory (Form Y Self-evaluation Questionnaire)*. Palo Alto, CA: Consulting Psychologists Press.

Wells, A. (1995). Meta-cognition and worry: A cognitive model of generalised anxiety disorder. *Behavioural and Cognitive Psychotherapy*, **23**, 301–320.

Wells, A. (1999). A metacognitive model and therapy for generalised anxiety disorder. *Clinical Psychology and Psychotherapy*, **6**, 86–96.

Wells, A., Welford, M., King, P., Wisely., J. & Mendel, E. (in preparation). A randomized trial of metacognitive therapy versus applied relaxation in the treatment of GAD.

White, J., Keenan, M. & Brooks, N. (1992). Stress control: A controlled investigation of large group therapy for generalised anxiety disorder. *Behavioural Psychotherapy*, **20**, 97–113.

Chapter 21

PREDICTORS OF TREATMENT OUTCOME

Robert C. Durham

INTRODUCTION

If cognitive behaviour therapy (CBT) was always precisely and skillfully targeted on the key factors maintaining anxious worry, and if outcome and follow-up assessments always indicated sustained recovery, then it might be expected that the right treatment would be the best predictor of outcome. In practice, of course, even our most effective treatments are influenced by a variety of social, psychological and biological factors that interact in complex and subtle ways to determine short- and long-term outcome. The field of outcome prediction in psychotherapy is important and fascinating just because it provides a testing ground for developing and improving the application of treatment technology in the light of theoretical models of vulnerability to psychopathology. Reliable knowledge in this area, however, has been slow to emerge. This is partly because of the complexity of the research methodologies involved, partly because relevant research with adequate sample sizes has only infrequently been reported and partly because an adequate conceptual framework in which to conduct research has been missing or only partially in place.

This chapter begins with a discussion of methodological issues, an essential starting point for understanding some of the inconsistencies and apparent absence of progress in the field. There follows an overview of the empirical evidence on treatment outcome prediction from two sources. The first comes from studies based on randomised controlled trials of CBT for generalised anxiety disorder (GAD) which, in so far as excessive worry can be regarded as a central defining feature of GAD, are of most direct relevance. The second comes from studies based on naturalistic follow-up investigations of the outcome of cohorts of patients with anxiety and depressive disorders. To the extent that worry is a central dimension of psychopathology,

Worry and Its Psychological Disorders: Theory, Assessment and Treatment. Edited by G. C. L. Davey and A. Wells. © 2006 John Wiley & Sons, Ltd.

common across all psychological disorders, and the evidence certainly suggests that this is so (Harvey et al., 2004; Wells & Matthews, 1994), these studies are also of importance. The next section provides a summary of the various influences on treatment outcome that have a reasonable degree of empirical support and this is then followed by a broad conceptual framework for prediction research that links these various influences together. Finally, a concluding section suggests strategies for future research and summarises some of the main themes of the chapter.

CONCEPTUAL AND METHODOLOGICAL ISSUES

This section provides a brief overview of some of the key methodological issues in research on outcome prediction. More detailed discussions of these and other considerations, particularly questions of data analysis, can be found elsewhere (Baron & Kenny, 1986; Offord & Kraemar, 2000; Shoham & Rohrbaugh, 1995; Whisman, 1993).

Predictors

Most prediction studies are confined to post-hoc analyses of those demographic variables and symptom severity measures collected at the start of a clinical trial. A few studies also assess personality, cognitive processes, the quality of the therapeutic alliance, the competency of the therapists delivering treatment, the expectations and preferences of clients regarding the treatment received and the response to therapy both in the early stages of treatment and at the end of a course of treatment. The inevitable result of a limited and variable range of predictors across studies is an inconsistency in findings. If some of the key variables are not in the regression equations their influence cannot be determined. To illustrate this point in the case of demographic variables, a perusal of 13 clinical trials concerning the efficacy of cognitive behaviour therapy for GAD, reviewed by Borkovec and Ruscio (2001), reveals that information on socioeconomic status, social adjustment and marital status is provided in only one, two and four studies respectively. It would be quite erroneous to assume that these variables have no influence on outcome if they are not included in the dataset.

Statistical Power

Unfortunately for researchers, as the number of predictors increases so must the sample size. Recommendations vary but ratios of predictors to sample size of less than 1:20 are unlikely to lead to reliable results. Regression analyses with total sample sizes of 50–80 that are typically found in clinical trials of CBT for GAD are, therefore, seriously underpowered if more than three or four predictors are included. This may explain problems of cross-validation of findings even when the clinical populations and selection criteria are broadly comparable. A prediction study by Butler (1993), for example, failed to replicate the findings of a previous prediction study (Butler & Anastasiades, 1988) even though both were based on clinical trials of CBT for GAD conducted in the same clinical setting with very similar patient samples and comparable measures. The logic of these considerations, given the relatively large number of possible predictors, is that researchers wishing to understand the overall influences on treatment outcome need to conduct studies with sample sizes of 500 and over.

Restricted Variability Within Predictors

Some inconsistencies in the findings of prediction studies may be purely a function of different sample characteristics (Steketee & Chambless, 1992). Socioeconomic status, for example, was found to be a significant outcome predictor in a clinical trial that selected patients from a wide range of socioeconomic backgrounds (Durham et al., 1997). In studies where the range of socioeconomic conditions is restricted, for example, in samples that are relatively affluent or generally poor, the same predictor will have too little variability to have predictive value. Context will amplify the importance of some predictors and minimise the importance of others.

Short- and Long-term Follow-up

GAD is a chronic condition which fluctuates in severity over time (Ballenger et al., 2001). Both cognitive therapy and applied relaxation result in clinically significant improvements in symptom severity in about 50–60% of cases with the balance of evidence suggesting that treatment effects are maintained for at least a year following the end of therapy. Sustained recovery, however, is less likely than symptomatic improvement and a minority of patients (30–40%) tend to do poorly. A recently completed follow-up, over 3–14 years, of two clinical trials of CBT for GAD found that treatment effects are significantly eroded over the very long-term (Durham et al., 2003). These facts suggest that outcome prediction needs to take a long-term perspective and that different sets of outcome predictors may be significant over different time periods as found in a recent clinical trial (Durham et al., 2004).

Moderators and Mediators

Research that is limited to an atheoretical 'fishing expedition' for outcome predictors is unlikely, in the long-term at least, to shed much light on the nature of individual vulnerability to excessive worry and the mechanisms by which specific therapeutic interventions reduce this vulnerability. Outcome prediction research should aim to test theoretical models regarding the underlying mechanisms of change and the factors that influence these mechanisms. This is the distinction between mediators and moderators of the change process discussed by Baron and Kenny in their influential article (1986). What psychological or biological processes change as a direct result of targeting worry with psychological therapy? How are these changes linked to subsequent reductions in the severity of worry and anxiety? Evidence for the mediating role of a specific variable requires evidence that it changes as a direct result of the treatment intervention and this change in turn is associated with changes in the outcome variable of interest. If changes in meta-cognitive beliefs about worry, for example, are thought to mediate changes in the severity of worry following cognitive therapy it is not enough to demonstrate that changes in metacognition are correlated with changes in worry; it is also necessary to demonstrate that these changes directly follow the appropriate therapeutic interventions. This is a stringent requirement that has not yet been adopted in the prediction studies of psychological therapy for GAD reviewed in the next section.

SUMMARY OF RELEVANT PREDICTION STUDIES

Controlled Trials of CBT for GAD

Table 21.1 summarises the results of studies of outcome predictors based on clinical trials of CBT for GAD. Studies were located from searches of Medline, PsycLIT and the Cochrane Controlled Trials Register over the 15-year period between 1990 and 2004. Search terms included: worry, generalised anxiety disorder, generalized anxiety disorder, treatment outcome, clinical trials, prognosis, prediction, follow-up. Searches were also made of secondary sources and by contacting researchers in the field. To be included, studies had to meet the following inclusion criteria: structured diagnostic interviews used to assign a principal diagnosis of GAD according to DSM III-R (APA, 1987) or DSM IV criteria (APA, 1994); random assignment of patients to two or more psychological treatments or control conditions; identification of predictors using regression analyses on outcome variables at post-treatment or follow-up.

Table 21.1 Prediction studies based on clinical trials of psychological therapy for generalised anxiety disorder since 1990

Author/Date	Sample size	Outcome variable(s)	Follow-up period Post-treatment (mths)	Predictors of worse outcome
Barlow et al., 1992	44	Rx Responder (20% imp. 3 of 4 outcome measures)	none	Higher pre-treatment severity of depression. Lower treatment credibility ratings.
Bond et al., 2002 (full version)	60	Composite measure of anxiety severity	12	Lower educational level (anxiety management group only). Higher age (non-directive therapy only). Use of problem-focussed coping (worse for non-directive therapy, better for anxiety management group).
Borkovec & Costello, 1993	54	Various measures of symptom severity	6, 12, 24	Lower expectations of improvement at initial session.
Borkovec et al., 2002	69	Composite measure of endstate functioning on 0–6 scale	6, 12, 24	Interpersonal difficulties still present by the end of therapy. Vindictive, intrusive and domineering relationships of particular predictive value.
Butler, 1993	57	Single measure of severity of anxiety symptoms	6	Higher pre-treatment severity of anxiety in behaviour therapy condition only. Higher pre-treatment tendency to interpret ambiguous stimuli as threatening in cognitive therapy condition only.

(*Continued*)

Table 21.1 Prediction studies based on clinical trials of psychological therapy for generalised anxiety disorder since 1990 (*Continued*)

Author/Date	Sample size	Outcome variable(s)	Follow-up period Post-treatment (mths)	Predictors of worse outcome
Durham, Allan & Hackett, 1997	80	Composite measure of endstate functioning used to indicate sustained improvement and relapse over follow-up period	6,12	Low socioeconomic status, single, widowed. Relationship difficulties. Axis one comorbidity. Previous psychiatric treatment. Low expectations of improvement.
Durham et al., 2004	55	Clinical Global Severity (CGS) rated by independent assessor	6	Quality of therapeutic relationship at post-treatment but not follow-up. Higher scores on a prognostic index measuring complexity and severity of problems, especially at follow-up.
Wetherell et al., 2005	65	Average reliable change indices (RCI) based on three outcome measures	6	Lower likelihood of completing homework assignments, lower initial severity of GAD symptoms and lower likelihood of psychiatric comorbidity, especially at follow-up.

Eight studies met the above criteria. The modal follow-up period post-treatment is six months with a range from 0 to 24 months. Perhaps the most striking pattern is the diversity of outcome predictors. Demographic variables (educational level, age, socioeconomic status, marital status), clinical status measures (symptom severity, axis one comorbidity, previous treatment), attitude to treatment ratings (treatment credibility, expectations of improvement), social adjustment measures, quality of therapeutic alliance, coping style and cognitive variables were all found to be of some predictive value.

Studies of the Course of Neurotic Disorder

Table 21.2 summarises the results of prediction studies based on long-term follow-up of cohorts of people with anxiety and depressive disorders treated in various clinical settings. These studies were also located from searches of Medline, PsycLIT and the Cochrane Controlled Trials Register over the same time period as the clinical trials, that is, between 1990 and 2004, but search terms were broader to include anxiety and depressive disorders as a whole. Searches were also made of secondary sources but no attempt was made to contact researchers in the field. To be included studies had to have followed up participants with one or more defined anxiety disorders with predictors identified using regression analyses on outcome variables at post-treatment or follow-up. The resulting six studies should be regarded as representative of recent investigations of reasonable methodological quality.

It can be seen that sample sizes are generally much larger than in the previous group with much longer follow-up periods and there is a greater degree of consistency in the overall findings. Poorer outcome is associated with demographic variables, clinical status measures, poor initial response to treatment, poor social adjustment and higher levels of treatment over the follow-up period. In the following section the significance of these various factors for chronic worry is explored in more detail.

THE VARIABLE INFLUENCES ON TREATMENT OUTCOME

General Prognostic Indicators

Demographic variables

The National Psychiatric Morbidity Survey of the UK (Jenkins et al., 2003) found higher rates of neurotic disorder in unmarried and post-married

Table 21.2 Prediction studies based on naturalistic follow-up of anxiety and depressive disorder since 1990

Author/Date	Sample size	Nature of study	Follow-up period	Predictors of worse outcome
Durham et al., 2005	342	Follow-up of participants in clinical trials of CBT for GAD, panic disorder and PTSD	3–14 years	Unemployed or unable to work. Higher level of social deprivation. Poorer quality of social adjustment. Higher symptom severity. Higher levels of treatment over follow-up period.
Ronalds et al., 1997	148	Study of outcome predictors of a cohort of primary care patients with depressive, anxiety or panic disorder	6 mths	Higher levels of initial depression. Lower levels of education. Unemployment. Persistent social difficulties.
Szadoczky et al., 2004	117	Study of outcome predictors in depression accompanied by high levels of anxiety	2 years	Lower levels of social support. Higher initial levels of trait anxiety (STAI-T > 61). Lower levels of education. Poor response to initial treatment.

Seivewright et al., 1998	182	Follow-up of psychiatric outpatients with GAD, panic disorder or dysthymic disorder using hospital and primary care records	5 years	Older age, recurrent episodes. Comorbid personality disorder. General neurotic syndrome (comorbid anxiety and depression, dependent and obsessional personality features, positive family history). Poor response to initial treatment.
Woodman et al., 1999	132	Follow-up of 64 patients with GAD and 68 patients with panic disorder who had participated in drug treatment studies	5 years	Higher severity of anxiety. Longer duration of disorder (for GAD only). Earlier age of onset. Previous episodes of treatment.
Yonkers et al., 2000	167	Follow-up, every 6–12 months, of participants with GAD in the Harvard-Brown Anxiety Research Program.	5 years	Comorbid personality disorder (cluster C). Poor overall life satisfaction. Poor relationships with spouse and relatives.

groups, in single parents and people living on their own, in the unem-
ployed, in urban rather than rural areas and in women rather than men.
Similarly, lower social class, no access to cars, home renting and low educational attainment were all associated with higher prevalence of neurotic
disorder (Lewis, Bebbington, Brugha, Farrell, Gill, Jenkins & Meltzer, 2003).
While the increased risk associated with any one of these factors may be
small, treatment outcomes in people with several risk factors are likely to be
adversely affected. The exact mechanisms by which these variables influence mental and physical health are uncertain but the role of negative emotions such as excessive worry are increasingly taking centre stage (Gallo &
Matthews, 2003). Any factor that is associated with more and less controllable stressors, lower social status and relatively fewer coping resources,
will tend to increase vulnerability to negative emotions and cognitions.
The effect of these factors on psychological treatment may be analogous
to the role that poor nutrition, infrequent exercise and excessive smoking
have on the power of medical interventions to treat physical disease.

Clinical presentation

The association between higher initial severity of symptoms and poorer
overall outcome is probably the most robust finding from the studies reviewed in the previous section. This is entirely consistent with the general
findings of psychotherapy outcome prediction research as a whole (Clarkin
& Levy, 2004; Luborsky, Crits-Christoph, Mintz & Auerbach, 1988). Other
things being equal, a higher frequency, intensity and duration of anxious
worry at the start of therapy is likely to have a negative impact on the
probability of remission at the close of therapy, and higher levels of residual symptoms will in turn have a negative impact on the overall course
of the disorder. Closely related to symptom severity is the degree of comorbidity with other clinical disorders and this is also associated with
poorer long-term outcome. Of interest in this connection is the close relationship between co-morbidity and the severity of positive and negative
affect (Chambers, Power & Durham, 2004). With each additional diagnosis there is a step-like increase in negative affect scores. This is similar to
the increases in mean neuroticism scores found with increasing numbers
of co-morbid lifetime diagnoses (Andrews et al., 1990). Such findings are
consistent with general predisposing personality factors as one of the de-
terminants of symptom severity.

Personality

Since vulnerability to psychopathology is generally assumed to be a function of biological and temperamental dispositions in conjunction with psychosocial stressors (Charney, 2004; Zuckerman, 1999), it would be surprising if the strength of anxious personality traits was not a significant

outcome predictor. Two relatively large-scale longitudinal studies of the relationship between temperament and psychological disorder in the general population do suggest that anxious personality traits are important. A study of causal relationships over a three-year period between neuroticism, chronic somatic conditions and psychiatric syndromes, found that neuroticism raises the risk for psychiatric and somatic morbidity, irrespective of treatment, but also results from them (Neeleman et al., 2004). A study of causal relationships between neuroticism, long-term difficulties (endogenous and exogenous) and psychological distress over a seven-year period, found that neuroticism and, to a lesser extent long-term difficulties, are powerful predictors of high levels of personal distress over protracted periods of time (Ormel & Wohlfarth, 1991). Duncan-Jones and colleagues (1990), suggest that any individual has a stable characteristic level of symptoms that fluctuates as a function of everyday stressors with strong, positive correlations (.79 to .93) between measures of symptoms and neuroticism. What is called 'neuroticism' may be better conceptualised as an individual's characteristic level of psychiatric symptoms.

Social adjustment

Relationship difficulties were found to be a significant outcome predictor in seven of the studies reviewed in the previous section. These difficulties are described in various ways as generally poor social adjustment (Durham et al., 2005; Ronalds et al., 1997), particular tensions in marital and family relationships (Durham et al., 1997; Yonkers et al., 2000), lower levels of social support (Szadoczky et al., 2004), dependent personality difficulties (Seivewright et al., 1998) and interpersonal difficulties present by the end of therapy (Borkovec et al., 2002). The manner in which these difficulties impact on the outcome of treatment is unclear but several possibilities suggest themselves. Social concerns are a significant focus of everyday worries and the existence of persistent interpersonal difficulties are likely to increase both the frequency and magnitude of threatening events, resulting in more to worry about, and at the same time a reduction in the degree of support available for keeping these worries in perspective. The dominating, vindictive and intrusive interpersonal styles identified by Borkovec and colleagues (2002) may be particularly problematic in this regard. More deep-rooted relationship difficulties stemming from childhood adversity and insecure early attachments are likely to be a more potent source of long-term vulnerability.

Cognitive processes

Despite the growth of sophisticated cognitive models of GAD only one prediction study (Butler, 1993) has reported evidence that a cognitive process was related to treatment outcome. In this particular study a higher pre-treatment tendency to interpret ambiguous stimuli as threatening was a significant predictor but only for the cognitive therapy condition. There is also evidence that preconscious biases in the processing of threat information co-vary with reductions in the severity of anxious thoughts and worries following cognitive behaviour therapy (Mogg et al., 1995). This may point to an important cognitive mediator of changes in chronic worry brought about by cognitive therapy although other candidates would include meta-cognitive beliefs (Wells, 1999), intolerance of uncertainty (Dugas et al., 1998) and automatic thoughts and underlying assumptions (Borkovec & Roemer, 1995). To date there has been no convincing demonstration that changes in specific cognitive processes, targeted by cognitive therapy, precede changes in worry *to the degree that would be expected from specific therapeutic interventions at particular stages of therapy* and that these changes are predictive of sustained improvement. Evidence of this kind is essential to support the claim that cognitive therapy has specific therapeutic ingredients for the treatment of chronic worry that go beyond the common factors model of the efficacy of psychotherapy. The fact that both applied relaxation and cognitive therapy appear to have broadly equivalent results in the treatment of GAD (Fisher & Durham, 1999) suggests that common factors between the therapies may be of most importance (Wampold, 2001) or at least that multiple pathways exist to the same endpoint.

Treatment Response Indicators

Therapeutic process

A positive therapeutic alliance as a predictor of better treatment outcomes is one of the few well-established findings in the psychotherapy literature (Martin et al., 2000) and this relationship receives some support from the clinical trials that included a direct or indirect measure of this variable (e.g. Barlow et al., 1992; Borkovec & Costello, 1993; Durham et al., 1997; Durham et al., 2004). Most clinical trials, however, have paid relatively little attention to process variables such as patient expectations, the strength of the alliance and the degree of adherence to treatment manuals. The strongest evidence for the quality of the therapeutic alliance as an outcome predictor (Durham et al., 2004) suggests that it has a significant relationship to treatment outcome at the end of therapy but is not a reliable guide to longer-term outcome. None of the clinical trials have investigated whether or not the degree of therapist adherence to the core therapeutic interventions believed to change vulnerability to worry is related to treatment outcome. Positive evidence on this point, of course, is absolutely fundamental to any claim that a particular therapy has specifically efficacious ingredients for treating worry.

Post-treatment clinical status

There is evidence from several studies that a failure to recover following therapy is related to a poorer long-term outcome (Durham et al., 2005). This is consistent with the general finding that recovery is protective against future relapse and that residual symptoms increase the likelihood of a poor long-term outcome. In short, chronicity breeds chronicity. Relevant to this issue is the increasing realisation that intractable or untreated GAD is associated with relatively high levels of physical morbidity. A significant minority of people with GAD (20–30%) suffer from poor health as well as chronic worry and anxiety. The best predictor of poor long-term outcome in the long-term follow-up study of CBT clinical trials in central Scotland was the amount of healthcare usage over the follow-up period (Durham et al., 2005). The people who received the most healthcare, for psychological and physical problems, had the worst outcomes. One mechanism which may help to explain this relationship is the concept of allostatic load (Charney, 2004). In brief, this refers to the deleterious effects on psychological and physiological functioning when full recovery from an episode of acute stress fails to occur. When the acute response persists, as it does in chronic worry and anxiety, and the normal homeostatic mechanisms that return biological stress mediators to their normal set point fail to work, the eventual result may be increased vulnerability to disease (McEwen & Steller, 1993). The promise of this work for predicting treatment outcomes in the future is in linking psychological indicators of poor outcome with neurobiological and psychophysiological markers of increased allostatic load and in linking both to development pathways (Luecken & Lemery, 2004).

A MODEL FOR OUTCOME PREDICTION IN GAD

The strongest theme that emerges from the evidence base is that the influences on treatment outcome are multifaceted. With the possible exception of symptom severity there is no 'prime mover' and it is likely that the cumulative effects of a number of vulnerability factors are of most prognostic significance. Complex interactions between biopsychosocial factors determine the outcome of therapy as well as the onset and persistence of psychopathology (Kendler, 2005). This type of consideration underlines the potential importance of a prognostic index comprising an additive scale of above average scores on a range of diverse factors (cf. Durham et al., 2004). A second theme that emerges is the importance of distinguishing between general prognostic indicators of the likely course of GAD, irrespective of treatment delivered, and more specific treatment response indicators that are related to the power of a particular treatment, as delivered by a particular therapist, to change the course of the disorder. The factors that influence the persistence of anxious worry are conceptually and clinically distinct from the treatment opportunities that exist in a particular clinical context.

A model of outcome prediction in GAD that draws together the various influences identified in the preceding sections is illustrated in Figure 21.1. The model assumes that worry is a fundamental component of negative emotional states and that the most parsimonious explanation for the pattern of outcome predictors found is that chronic worry is maintained by a dynamic interaction between the overall severity of the presenting disorder, the level of chronic stressors, anxious cognitive appraisal processes and the biological consequences of chronic tension and hypervigilance. Any factor which increases the likelihood of a negative emotional response to everyday events will tend to increase the frequency and/or severity of worry and thereby reduce the likelihood of an adaptive coping response. Those individuals with a number of negative prognostic factors will tend to experience the highest levels of worry and be most resistant to change over the long-term. Psychological therapy will be most effective in changing chronic patterns of anxious worry, at least over the short-term, in individuals who have fewer negative prognostic factors, and who come to therapy with positive expectations and an ability to establish a positive therapeutic alliance with a competent therapist. The degree to which good treatment outcomes are sustained over the long-term will depend on the degree to which therapy results in fundamental changes in vulnerability in respect of the level of chronic stressors, the tendency to anxious appraisal of such stressors or both. This will in turn depend on the degree to which the therapist delivers an effective therapeutic strategy and on the occurrence of life stressors – serious illness, for example – that are independent of behaviour.

CONCLUSION

Reliable knowledge will only emerge with investigations that address issues in outcome prediction from the start. As noted by Steketee and Chambless (1992), '... planned strategies for investigating hypotheses about predictors of treatment outcome are far preferable to unplanned ones in which investigators conduct a few analyses using variables they happened to collect during an outcome study'. There is an important place for two broad types of research. One strategy, exemplified by the research programme pursued by Borkovec and his colleagues, involves relatively small scale experimental tests of specific hypotheses regarding cause-and-effect relationships in the treatment of GAD. This programme has illuminated a number of psychological and physiological variables – dominant and hostile interpersonal styles, and deficiencies in parasympathetic tone, for example – that are important targets for experimental intervention to

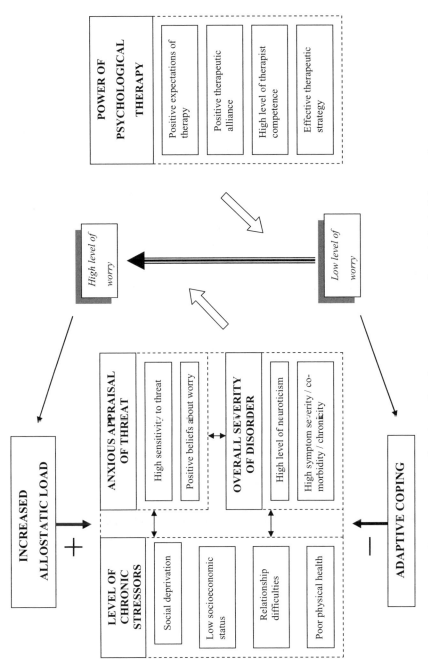

Figure 21.1 Summary of factors associated with good and poor outcomes of psychological therapy for worry

test whether or not changes in these variables are associated with short- and long-term outcome.

To obtain a broader perspective on the key influences on treatment outcome in routine clinical practice a complementary approach to the controlled experimental investigation is the large-scale, longitudinal study. Robust findings will require large sample sizes (500+ participants), long follow-up periods (5+ years), and careful assessment of both general prognostic indicators and the quality of therapy delivered. One product of this approach would be the development and refinement of a set of prognostic indices that reflect the main influences on treatment outcome, over the short and long term, as depicted in Figure 21.1. In time this may enable a more precise quantification of the characteristics of people who present with anxious worry and the level of therapist competence required for a sustained improvement. Both of these factors moderate the effects of what can be achieved with specific therapies and typically account for substantial intra-therapy 'error' variance in clinical trials (cf. Shoham & Rohrbaugh, 1995). Sustained reductions in vulnerability to excessive worry, in cases of high complexity and severity, may be strongly associated with therapist expertise in delivering specific treatment protocols. This is likely to be one of the key areas for future research.

Finally, although we can expect some real progress to be made in outcome prediction over the next decade or so it is important to bear in mind the following general caveats and methodological points regarding the science of prediction and prognostication (cf. Offord & Kraemar, 2000).

(1) Our ability to predict treatment outcome in a particular individual will always be limited by the complexity of interaction between variables of known importance and the dynamic nature of individual adaptation to changing environments and chance events.
(2) The strength of predictors in a particular clinical context will be significantly influenced by the natural variability of each predictor in that context, by the nature and timing of outcome assessments and by the power of individual therapies and therapists. It will be attenuated by unreliable measurement.
(3) It follows that of the variables that are known to influence outcomes no single set will prove to be equally useful, or of equal strength, across all clinical settings.

REFERENCES

American Psychiatric Association (1987). *Diagnostic and statistical manual of mental disorders* (3rd (Revised) ed.). Washington, DC.

American Psychiatric Association (1994). *Diagnostic and statistical manual of mental disorders* (4th ed.). Washington DC.

Andrews, G., Stewart, G., Morris-Yates, A., Holt, P. & Henderson, S. (1990). Evidence for a General Neurotic Syndrome. *British Journal of Psychiatry*, **157**, 6–12.

Ballenger, J., Davidson, J., Lecrubier, Y., Nutt, D., Borkovec, T., Rickels, K., Stein, D. & Wittchen, H.-U. (2001). Consensus statement on generalised anxiety disorder from the international consensus group on depression and anxiety. *Journal of Clinical Psychiatry*, **62 (Suppl. 11)**, 53–58.

Barlow, D.H., Rapee, R.M. & Brown, T. A. (1992). Behavioural treatment of generalised anxiety disorder. *Behavior Therapy*, **23**, 551–570.

Baron, R.M. & Kenny, D.A. (1986). The moderator-mediator variable distinction in social psychological research: Conceptual, strategic, and statistical considerations. *Journal of Personality and Social Psychology*, **51**, 1173–1182.

Blazer, D.G., Hughes, D. & George, L.K. (1987). Stressful life events and the onset of a generalised anxiety syndrome. *American Journal of Psychiatry*, **144**, 1178–1183.

Bond, A., Wingrove, J., Curran, H. & Lader, M. (2002). Treatment of generalised anxiety disorder with a short course of psychological therapy, combined with buspirone or placebo. *Journal of Affective Disorders*, **7**, 267–271.

Borkovec, T.D. & Costello, E. (1993). Efficacy of applied relaxation and cognitive-behavioural therapy in the treatment of generalised anxiety disorder. *Journal of Consulting and Clinical Psychology*, **61(4)**, 611–619.

Borkovec, T.D., Newman, M., Pincus, A. & Lytle, R. (2002). A component analysis of cognitive behavioural therapy for generalized anxiety disorder and the role of interpersonal problems. *Journal of Consulting and Clinical Psychology*, **70(2)**, 288–298.

Borkovec, T.D. & Roemer, L. (1995). Perceived functions of worry among generalised anxiety disorder subjects: Distraction from more emotional topics? *Journal of Behaviour Therapy and Experimental Psychiatry*, **21**, 9–16.

Borkovec, T.D. & Ruscio, A. (2001). Psychotherapy for generalized anxiety disorder. *Journal of Clinical Psychiatry*, **62(11)**, 37–42.

Butler, G. (1993). Predicting outcome after treatment for generalised anxiety disorder. *Behaviour Research and Therapy*, **31**, 211–213.

Butler, G. & Anastasiades, P. (1988). Predicting response to anxiety management in patients with generalised anxiety disorders. *Behavior Research and Therapy*, **26**, 531–534.

Chambers, J., Power, K. & Durham, R. (2004). The relationship between trait vulnerability and anxiety and depressive diagnoses at long-term follow-up of Generalised Anxiety Disorder. *Journal of Anxiety Disorders*, **18**, 587–607.

Charney, D. (2004). Psychobiological mechanisms of resilience and vulnerability: implications for successful adaptation to extreme stress. *American Journal of Psychiatry*, **161**, 195–216.

Clarkin, J. & Levy, K. (2004). The influence of client variables on psychotherapy. In M. Lambert (Ed.), *Bergin and Garfield's Handbook of Psychotherapy and Behaviour Change* (5th ed., pp. 194–226). New York: John Wiley & Sons, Inc.

Dugas, M.J., Gagnon, F., Ladouceur, R. & Freeston, M.H. (1998). Generalised anxiety disorder: A preliminary test of a conceptual model. *Behaviour Research and Therapy*, **36**, 215–226.

Duncan-Jones, P., Fergusson, D., Orel, J. & Horwood, L. (1990). *A model of stability and change in minor psychiatric symptoms: results from three longitudinal studies* (Psychological Medicine Monograph Supplements No.18). Cambridge: Cambridge University Press.

Durham, R.C., Allan, T. & Hackett, C. (1997). On predicting improvement and relapse in generalised anxiety disorder following psychotherapy. *British Journal of Clinical Psychology*, **36**, 101–119.

Durham, R., Chambers, J., Macdonald, R., Power, K. & Major, K. (2003). Does cognitive behavioural therapy influence the course of generalised anxiety disorder? 10–14 year follow-up of two clinical trials. *Psychological Medicine*, **33**, 499–509.

Durham, R., Chambers, J., Power, K., Sharp, D., Macdonald, R., Major, K., Dow, M. & Gumley, A. (2005). Long-term outcome of clinical trials for CBT in central Scotland. *Health Technology Assessment*, **9**(42) www.ncchta.org.

Durham, R., Fisher, P., Dow, M., Sharp, D., Power, K., Swan, J. & Morton, R. (2004). Cognitive behaviour therapy for good and poor prognosis generalised anxiety disorder: a clinical effectiveness study. *Clinical Psychology and Psychotherapy*, **11**, 145–157.

Fisher, P.L. & Durham, R.C. (1999). Recovery rates in generalised anxiety disorder following psychological therapy: An analysis of clinically significant change in STAI-T across outcome studies since 1990. *Psychological Medicine*, **29**, 1425–1434.

Gallo, L. & Matthews, K. (2003). Understanding the association between socioeconomic status and physical health: do negative emotions play a role? *Psychological Bulletin*, **129(1)**, 10–51.

Harvey, A., Watkins, E., Mansell, W. & Shafran, R. (2004). *Cognitive behavioural processes across psychological disorders: A transdiagnostic approach to research and treatment*. Oxford: Oxford University Press.

Jenkins, R., Lewis, G., Bebbington, P., Brugha, T., Farrell, M., Gill, B. & Meltzer, H. (2003). The National Psychiatric Morbidity Surveys of Great Britain–initial findings from the Household Survey. *International Review of Psychiatry*, **15**, 29–42.

Kendler, K.S. (2005). Toward a philosophical structure for psychiatry. *American Journal of Psychiatry*, **162**, 433–440.

Lewis, G., Bebbington, P., Brugha, T., Farrell, M., Gill, B., Jenkins, R. & Meltzer, H. (2003). Socio-economic status, standard of living, and neurotic disorder. *International Review of Psychiatry*, **15**, 91–96.

Luborsky, L., Crits-Christoff, P., Mintz, J. & Auerbach, A. (1988). *Who will benefit from psychotherapy? Predicting therapeutic outcomes*. New York: Basic Books.

Luecken, L. & Lemery, K. (2004). Early caregiving and physiological stress responses. *Clinical Psychology Review*, **24**, 171–191.

Martin, D., Garske, J. & Davis, M. (2000). Relation of the therapeutic alliance with outcome and other variables: a meta-analytic review. *Journal of Consulting and Clinical Psychology*, **68**, 438–450.

McEwen, B. & Steller, E. (1993). Stress and the individual; mechanisms leading to disease. *Archives of Internal Medicine*, **153**, 2093–2101.

Neeleman, J., Bijl, R. & Ormel, J. (2004). Neuroticism, a central link between somatic and psychiatric morbidity: path analysis of prospective data. *Psychological Medicine*, **34**, 521–531.

Offord, D. & Kraemar, H. (2000). Risk factors and prevention (EBMH Notebook). *Evidence-Based Mental Health*, **3**, 70–71.

Ormel, J. & Wohlfarth, T. (1991). How neuroticism, long-term difficulties, and life situation change influence psychological distress: A longitudinal model. *Journal of Personality and Social Psychology*, **60**, 744–755.

Ronalds, C., Creed, F., Stone, K., Webb, S. & Tomenson, T. (1997). Outcome of anxiety and depressive disorders in primary care. *British Journal of Psychiatry*, **171**, 427–433.

Seivewright, H., Tyrer, P. & Johnson, T. (1998). Prediction of outcome in neurotic disorder: a 5 year prospective study. *Psychological Medicine*, **28**, 1149–1157.

Shoham, V. & Rohrbaugh, M. (1995). Aptitude times treatment interaction (ATI) research: Sharpening the focus, widening the lens. In M. Aveline & D. Shapiro (Eds), *Research Foundations for Psychotherapy Practice* (pp. 73–95). Chichester, UK: John Wiley & Sons, Ltd.

Steketee, G. & Chambless, D. (1992). Methodological issues in prediction of treatment outcome. *Clinical Psychology Review*, **12**, 387–400.

Szadoczky, E., Rozsa, S., Zambori, J. & Furedi, J. (2004). Predictors for 2-year outcome of major depressive episode. *Journal of Affective Disorders*, **83**, 49–57.

Tyrer, P., Seivewright, N., Ferguson, B., Murphy, S. & Johnson, A.L. (1993). The Nottingham study of neurotic disorder: Effect of personality status on response to drug treatment, cognitive therapy and self-help over two years. *British Journal of Psychiatry*, **162**, 219–226.

Wampold, B. (2001). *The great psychotherapy debate. Models, methods, and findings.* London: Lawrence Erlbaum Associates.

Wells, A. (1999). A metacognitive model and therapy for generalised anxiety disorder. *Clinical Psychology and Psychotherapy*, **6**, 86–95.

Wells, A. & Matthews, G. (1994). *Attention and emotion: A clinical perspective.* Hove, UK: Erlbaum.

Wetherell, J., Hopko, D., Diefenbach, G., Averill, P., Beck, J., Craske, M., Gatz, M., Novy, D. & Stanley, M. (in press). Cognitive-behavioural therapy for late-life generalized anxiety disorder: Who gets better? *Behaviour Therapy*.

Whisman, M. (1993). Mediators and moderators of change in cognitive therapy of depression. *Psychological Bulletin*, **114**, 248–265.

Woodman, C.L., Noyes, R., Black, D. W., Schlosser, S. & Yagla, S.J. (1999). A 5-year follow-up study of generalised anxiety disorder and panic disorder. *Journal of Nervous and Mental Disease*, **187**, 3–9.

Yonkers, K., Dyck, I., Warshaw, M. & Keller, M. (2000). Factors predicting the clinical course of generalised anxiety disorder. *British Journal of Psychiatry*, **176**, 544–549.

Zuckerman, M. (1999). *Vulnerability to psychopathology.* Washington, DC: American Psychological Association.

INDEX

Note: Abbreviations used in the index are: AnTI = Anxious Thoughts Inventory; CBT = cognitive-behavioral therapy; GAD = generalized anxiety disorder; MCQ = Meta-Cognitions Questionnaire; MCT = metacognitive therapy; PSWQ = Penn State Worry Questionnaire; S-REF model = Self-Regulatory Executive Function model; TCQ = Thought Control Questionnaire.

The Wiley Series in

CLINICAL PSYCHOLOGY